Books are to be returned

A BAHIAN COUNTERPOINT

B. J. BARICKMAN

A Bahian
Counterpoint

SUGAR, TOBACCO, CASSAVA, AND SLAVERY
IN THE RECÔNCAVO, 1780–1860

STANFORD UNIVERSITY PRESS
STANFORD, CALIFORNIA
1998

Stanford University Press
Stanford, California

© 1998 by the Board of Trustees of the
Leland Stanford Junior University
Printed in the United States of America

CIP data are at the end of the book

The Press gratefully acknowledges the support of
the Oliver M. Dickerson Fund of the Department of
History of the University of Illinois at Urbana–Champaign
and the Provost's Author's Support Fund of the University
of Arizona in the publication of this book.

For my parents

Acknowledgments

Every book has its own history. In the especially long history of this particular book, I have accumulated an enormous number of debts. Only a lack of space and time, not gratitude, prevents me from mentioning here all those who have, in one way or another, given me much-needed help and encouragement during the past fourteen years.

I should perhaps begin by acknowledging the financial support of the Tinker Foundation (through the Center for Latin American and Caribbean Studies of the University of Illinois at Urbana-Champaign), the Social Science Research Council, the Fulbright-Hays Program, the Graduate College of the University of Illinois at Urbana-Champaign (through the Department of History), the Department of History at the same university, and the Social Science Research Board of the University of Arizona. The funds provided by these institutions allowed me to carry out my research and write the book. No less important was the cheerful assistance I received in the Brazilian archives and libraries where I did most of my research: the Arquivo Público do Estado da Bahia, the Arquivo Regional da Cachoeira, the Seção de Manuscritos of the Biblioteca Nacional, the Arquivo Nacional, and the Instituto Histórico e Geográfico Brasileiro. My research also benefited from the competent assistance I received in Salvador from Epifania Firmo de Assis Neta, who never failed to take a keen and informed interest in the project.

In Brazil, I came to rely on the generous hospitality of Frank and Sandra Falkenhein, Amilcar and Cláudia Martins, Carlos Alberto and Isabel Braga, Marcus Joaquim Maciel de Carvalho, and José and Tercina Vergolino. For close to two years, the late D. Eglantina da Silva Vieira and Ivone Lucinda dos Santos did more than merely tolerate my presence in their apartment; they befriended me and willingly answered my endless questions about *papa-jacas* and life in Curralinho. I am also grateful to the families of Sr. Celso Guilherme de Oliveira e Silva and D. Rosinha Barreto Vianna e Silva, of César Barreto Vianna e Silva and Cláudia Stockler Portugal Grangier e Silva, and of Sr. Alexandre Grangier, Jr., and D. Marina Stockler Portugal Grangier, who have opened their homes to me with exceptional generosity and hospitality on numerous occasions during the past two decades.

Several scholars in both Brazil and the United States graciously took the time to discuss my research, to read earlier versions of chapters, to offer valuable suggestions, or to point out potentially useful sources: Dain Borges, Ciro Cardoso, José Gabriel Costa Pinto, the late Peter Eisenberg, João Fragoso, Ricardo Gazel, Richard Graham, Donna Guy, Amilcar Martins Filho, Michael Meyer, Luiz Mott, Nancy Naro, João Reis, Rebecca Scott, Francisco Carlos Teixeira da Silva, Robert Slenes, and Margarida de Sousa Neves all showed friendly and learned interest in this project. To Stuart Schwartz and Katia M. de Queirós Mattoso, I am grateful for their willingness to share their ideas and their knowledge of the Bahian archives. Stuart Schwartz also provided valuable and timely suggestions for changes and revisions. Martha Few deserves to be mentioned here; during the past few years, she has provided me with trustworthy and competent assistance and at the same time has displayed real enthusiasm for the project. Needless to say, I alone am responsible for the conclusions reached in this book and any errors it may contain.

My gratitude also extends to Donald Crummey, Nils Jacobsen, Joseph L. Love, and Charles Stewart of the University of Illinois, who first read the dissertation on which this book is based and offered valuable comments. I owe a special debt to Joseph Love, who, beyond providing invaluable intellectual guidance, has, over the years, gone to great lengths in seeking ways to encourage and support my studies and research.

From more than two years of research in Brazil, I brought back not only notecards but also, I like to think, the friendship of Judith Allen. I shall always be grateful to Judith for the hours of conversations in the archives in Salvador and Cachoeira and at the Gruta, for her truly collegial spirit of collaboration, and for the Estrada de Belém.

I also wish to thank the many friends who gave me help and encouragement while I worked on this book: John Campbell, Marcus Carvalho, Phyllis Conn, Linda Darling, Kevin Gosner, Julia Greider, Lola Laborda, Jacira Mendes, Iolanda do Nascimento, Anne Reisner, Osvaldo and Teca Sarmento, Laura Tabili, Doug Weiner, José and Teca Vergolino, and Marta Zambrano. I am especially grateful to Suzanne Wilson, who, even while working on her own research, was always there to help; to listen; to discuss ploughs, *farinha*, and slaves; and then to listen to it all over again.

Finally, I thank my parents, who, over the many years of study, work, and research that lie behind this book, have never failed to offer me every possible type of support and encouragement. They have done far more than any son could reasonably expect. To them I dedicate this book.

B. J. B.

Contents

Tables, Figures, and Maps

Tables

Figures

Maps

Weights and Measures, Currency, Orthography, and Fiscal and Calendar Years

Weights and Measures

The following list shows the principal Brazilian weights and measures and their closest metric equivalents.

> 1 alqueire = 36.27 liters (roughly one English bushel)
> 1 arroba = 14.746 kilograms
> 1 braça = 2.2 meters
> 1 légua (league) = between 5,555 and 6,666 meters
> 1 tarefa – an area of 30 braças by 30 braças (4,356 square meters), or roughly one acre

Currency

Both before and after independence, the basic unit of currency in Brazil was the real (réis in the plural), which existed only as a money of account. The sum of 100 réis was commonly written Rs.$100. Larger sums were calculated in mil-réis (literally one thousand réis), with one mil-réis written as Rs.1$000. One thousand mil-réis equaled one conto de réis (or simply one conto), written Rs.1:000$000 or Rs.1:000$. Thus, a sum of Rs.4:563$000 should be read as 4 contos 563 mil-réis, and Rs.1$320 as 1,320 réis.

Orthography

Not until the early 1940s did a single, standardized orthography for the Portuguese language come into use in Brazil. This text follows the rules of the most recent standardization for spelling Portuguese words, the names of places and persons, and other proper nouns. It does, however, retain a few older spellings of proper nouns where these remain today in widespread use (for example, Góes, Souza, Maragogipe, and São Felipe for Góis, Sousa, Maragojipe, and São Filipe, respectively). In citing manuscript materials in the notes, the spellings of correspondents' names have been modernized; but the titles of documents have been transcribed as they appear in the documents. Similarly, following convention, author-title information for older published works is cited as it appears on the title page.

Fiscal and Calendar Years

At least from 1817 on, accounts for the export trade at Bahia were opened annually on 1 October and closed on 30 September of the following year. Sources, as a result, sometimes provide information on exports in fiscal years (for example, 1853–54). Wherever necessary in the tables and figures, fiscal years have been "converted" to calendar years, using, for example, 1854 rather than 1853–54. This conversion makes it easier to present data graphically in the figures and facilitates comparisons with series based on calendar years (for example, the exchange rate of the mil-réis).

Abbreviations

The following abbreviations are used in the Tables, Maps, Notes, and Bibliography.

AAPEB	*Anais do Arquivo Público do Estado da Bahia* (title varies)
ABN	*Anais da Biblioteca Nacional*
adm.	administrador
AMS	Arquivo Municipal do Salvador, Salvador, Bahia
APEB	Arquivo Público do Estado da Bahia, Salvador, Bahia
	RET Registros Eclesiásticos de Terras
	SH Seção Histórica
	SH, MNC Seção Histórica, material não classificado (1986–88)
	SJ, IT Seção Judiciária, Inventários e Testamentos
AN	Arquivo Nacional, Rio de Janeiro, Brazil
ARC	Arquivo Regional da Cachoeira, Cachoeira, Bahia
	IT Inventários e Testamentos
	PAE Papéis Avulsos e Encaixotados
Bahia, *CL*	Bahia, *Collecção das leis e resoluções da Assembléa Legislativa* . . .
BN	Biblioteca Nacional, Seção de Manuscritos, Rio de Janeiro, Brazil
Cach.	Cachoeira
Câm.	Câmara

cap.-mor   capitão-mor (captain-major)
CHLA   *Cambridge History of Latin America*
CP   Celeiro Público (Public Granary)
CPE   Centro de Planejamento e Pesquisas, Salvador
EL, [Bahia]   *Informações sobre o estado da lavoura,* "Trabalho da Commissão [da Bahia]."
Eng°   Engenho
Faz.   Fazenda(s)
Gov.   Governor (of the Captaincy of Bahia, unless otherwise specified)
HAHR   *Hispanic American Historical Review*
IBGE   Instituto Brasileiro de Geografia e Estatística, Rio de Janeiro
IHGB   Instituto Histórico e Geográfico Brasileiro, Rio de Janeiro
insp. de f.   inspetor de farinhas
int.   interino
inv. (invs.)   inventory (inventories)
Jag.   Jaguaripe
jz   juiz (judge, justice)
jz mun.   juiz municipal
jz ord.   juiz ordinário
Marag.   Maragogipe
Naz.   Nazaré
N.S.   Nossa Senhora
ouv.   ouvidor (royal judge)
PP   *Parliamentary Papers* (Commons), Great Britain
    A&P   Accounts and Papers
Pres.   President (of the Province of Bahia, unless otherwise specified)
pres.   president
RIGHBa   *Revista do Instituto Geográfico e Histórico da Bahia*
RIHGB   *Revista do Instituto Histórico e Geográfico Brasileiro*
S.   Santa, Santo, or São
SA   Santo Amaro
SFC   São Francisco do Conde
SEPLANTEC   Secretaria de Planejamento, Tecnologia, e Ciência, Bahia
ST   Great Britain. Parliament. *Slave Trade* (British Parliamentary Papers)
SUDENE   Superintendência do Desenvolvimento do Nordeste
vig.   vigário (vicar)

A BAHIAN COUNTERPOINT

CHAPTER I

Introduction

Monoculture, latifundia, and slavery—with those three elements Gilberto Freyre in the 1930s defined the society and economy that emerged, flourished, and then declined in the coastal regions of Northeastern Brazil between the mid-sixteenth and late nineteenth centuries.[1] Theoretical frameworks and interpretative schemes have gone in and out of fashion over the past six decades, but the consensus among scholars has, until recently, remained solid: monoculture, latifundia, and slavery did indeed define and shape Brazilian society throughout the colonial period (1500–1822) and during most of the nineteenth century. That consensus has produced what Maria Yedda Linhares aptly calls a "plantationist" perspective of Brazilian history.[2] Historians have devoted their attention almost exclusively to the plantation—the large estate that employed slave labor in the monocultural production of export crops—and, by extension, to the export economy.[3] In practice, this has often meant depicting Brazil as a vast plantation—as an economy limited to the extensive and large-scale production of a few tropical staples and the trade in those staples and as a society consisting of two classes: the masters who owned the plantations and the slaves who labored on them. Social groups and economic activities that do not fit easily into this picture have been dismissed as irrelevant to any understanding of Brazil's historical development.

Only in the past few years has the validity of the plantationist perspective come into question. Scholars who have looked beyond the boundaries of the plantation have demonstrated that export agriculture did not dominate the countryside everywhere in Brazil and that the largest Brazilian cities possessed a vigorous social and economic life. Extensive trade networks supplied those cities with essential provisions, cloth goods, and other manufactures, all produced in Brazil.[4] Yet for all its valuable contributions, this growing body of research on the internal economy has only indirectly challenged the plantationist perspective. Much of this scholarship has focused either on urban centers or on regions where export agriculture failed to take firm root, leaving intact the long-held view that the plantation completely defined and shaped social and economic life in Brazil's main regional centers of export production. By the same token, recent studies have, on the whole, also failed to explore in any depth questions about the possible diversity in slave-based export agriculture and about the evolving relationships between export agriculture, the development of an internal economy, and slavery in colonial and nineteenth-century Brazil.

This book also looks beyond the plantation to examine the use of slave labor in the Brazilian countryside in the late eighteenth and early nineteenth centuries. But unlike much recent research, it does not skirt questions about the relationships between export agriculture, slavery, and the internal economy, nor does it avoid the plantation. Instead, it explores the agrarian history of the region known as the Recôncavo in the Northeastern captaincy, later province, and now state of Bahia. One of the birthplaces of plantation agriculture in the New World, the Recôncavo belonged to the Northeast of Gilberto Freyre.[5] Throughout the period 1780–1860, the region produced large quantities of sugar and tobacco for the world market. Indeed, Bahia at the beginning of the nineteenth century exported more sugar than any other captaincy in Brazil. From Bahia also came nearly all the tobacco Brazil sold to Europe.

This study thus confronts the plantationist perspective on its home ground. Integrating research on the internal economy with a broader investigation of slave-based agriculture, it demonstrates that, even when applied to an archetypical plantation region, the plantationist perspective proves inadequate. The agrarian history of the Recôncavo in the early nineteenth century is not the story of the unbridled spread of large-scale monoculture. Rather, it is the story of how plantation and nonplantation forms of slave-based agriculture, together with a vigorous local market, allowed the growth and expansion of the Bahian export economy. It is also the story of how slaveowning agriculturalists, in adapting to local conditions, specific crop requirements, and both overseas and local markets, created and re-created in the rural Recôncavo a complex and varied social and economic landscape.

In attempting to uncover the diversity that characterized slave-based agriculture in the rural Recôncavo and in charting the region's agrarian history, this study follows two main strategies. First, it investigates the relationship between production for local needs and the dominant export economy by focusing on *farinha de mandioca*, or cassava flour, the single most important staple in the Bahian diet. That means more than simply calling into question, for Bahia, older and now largely discredited arguments that cities, because they were small both in size and number, failed to stimulate any significant demand for locally produced goods in colonial and nineteenth-century Brazil. It means reexamining broad generalizations that scholars have, even in recent years, continued to endorse. One of those assumptions is that virtually no rural market existed, because Brazilian planters produced on their properties most of the food needed to feed themselves, their families, and their slaves. Another is that the widespread use of slave labor in itself prevented or severely limited the emergence of a domestic market by maintaining a large segment of the Brazilian population at a level of mere subsistence and denying that population access to a monetary income.[6]

Taking it for granted that markets for essential provisions remained weak and small has, in turn, all too often led to the assumption that production for local needs must have been poorly and haphazardly organized. Indeed, the historiography has seldom challenged the assertion first made by Caio Prado Júnior in 1942 that the task of provisioning Brazil's internal markets fell to the "residual" elements in colonial society: "decadent" and "degenerate" farmers who rarely employed slave labor and who practiced a "paltry" form of agriculture.[7] Rather than accepting those generalizations and simply assuming that a significant internal economy failed to develop in Bahia, this study explores how slavery and export agriculture shaped the production and marketing of essential foodstuffs for local needs in the Recôncavo.

It shows that the widespread use of slave labor in export agriculture did not forestall the emergence in the Recôncavo of a well-developed urban and rural market for locally produced foodstuffs. On the contrary, the expansion of the export economy directly and indirectly fostered, and even required, the growth of a local market. The hundreds of small farmers who supplied that market regularly used slave labor to produce substantial surpluses of cassava flour. Outside the more familiar circuits of international trade, those farmers played a critical role in ensuring locally the day-to-day reproduction of highly specialized slave-based export agriculture on the sugar plantations and cane farms of the Recôncavo.[8] Already linked to a monetary economy and enjoying access to slave labor, the small farmers of the Recôncavo took advantage of the opportunities created by the growth of the Bahian export economy between 1780 and 1860. But instead of abandoning food crops and transforming themselves into planters, they diversified the output on their farms and thereby achieved increases in the production of both export crops and cassava for the local market. Increased supplies of cassava flour, in turn, made possible the further expansion of sugar production on the region's plantations.

The production and marketing of essential foodstuffs therefore cannot be regarded as merely subsidiary activities, simple appendages to the export economy, or even, in the language of developmental economics, "backward linkages." They were vitally necessary for the growth and expansion of a broader regional economy dominated by slave-based export agriculture. Yet the mutually dependent relationships that linked production for export and the internal market also set limits on the further development of that market. Restricted, for the most part, to the most essential provisions, Bahia's internal market underwent extensive growth between the late eighteenth and mid-nineteenth centuries; but that growth did not generate any dynamic transformation of the regional economy as a whole.

The second main strategy this study follows is to compare patterns of land tenure, the use of slave labor, and agricultural practices in the production of the Recôncavo's three main crops: sugar, tobacco, and cassava. The comparison reveals an agrarian economy where, relying on slave labor, great planters and small farmers adapted land use and agricultural practices not only to specific crop requirements but also to the pull of an emerging world economy, as well as to local conditions and local markets. The adaptations they made did not create a single, uniform pattern of extensive export monoculture based on large landholdings. Rather, those adaptations allowed them to achieve, in the early nineteenth century, increases in production both for export and for local markets. They also permitted the survival in the rural Recôncavo of a complex variety of social and economic structures.

That variety appears most strikingly in the marked contrasts that distinguished sugar and tobacco production in Bahia. Although both sugar and tobacco were export staples sold on the world market, the tobacco farms of the Recôncavo were not simply smaller versions of the region's sugar plantations. In patterns of land tenure and land use, in labor recruitment, in provisioning, and in field techniques, sugar and tobacco displayed significant and fundamental differences. Neither merely another example of export monoculture nor strictly a peasant activity, tobacco farming in Bahia demonstrates that within slave-based export agriculture, there were alternatives to the plantation.[9]

The arguments presented here in some ways parallel the conclusions reached by Fernando Ortiz in *Cuban Counterpoint*, a classic comparative study of Cuban export agriculture, first published in 1940. "Sugar and tobacco," Ortiz wrote, "are all contrast." Indeed, his work uses that contrast to weave a "counterpoint" between sugar and tobacco in Cuba. This book likewise stresses for Bahia the differences between sugar and tobacco. But it also goes further; it compares those two export crops with cassava and examines the interlocking relationships that linked the daily lives of Bahian sugar planters, urban consumers, cassava growers, rural slaves, and tobacco farmers to both overseas and local markets.[10]

Thus, looking both beyond and within the boundaries of the plantation, this study attempts to forge a necessary link between what have until now remained two largely separate strands of scholarship: the growing number of studies on the internal economy of colonial and nineteenth-century Brazil, and the older and better-established literature on slavery and export agriculture. In attempting to forge that link, this book joins ongoing efforts to replace the plantationist perspective with a better paradigm for interpreting Brazil's past, especially its agrarian history, and for understanding how, over more than three centuries, slavery and export agriculture shaped social and economic life in Brazil.

In broader terms, this book uses a study of sugar, tobacco, and cassava production in the Recôncavo to bring into clearer focus larger issues in the comparative history of slavery and export agriculture in the Americas. Over several centuries, a common pattern of slave-based production of export staples characterized vast areas of the Americas, from Maryland to coastal Venezuela, from Jamaica to Southeastern Brazil. Yet despite many shared features, the societies and economies that emerged in those areas differed significantly from one another, not only at any given moment in time but also in the ways they evolved and developed over time. Efforts to understand and explain those differences cannot stop at simple references to the supposedly all-powerful demands of a world economy or appeals to abstract definitions of the plantation. The search for a full explanation must, at the very least, include a close examination of the strategies that, in each area, ensured the reproduction of slave-based agriculture: the day-to-day reproduction of the slave work force, whether through local and even international markets for basic necessities or through various forms of internal production that largely bypassed market exchanges; the yearly reproduction of slave-based farms and estates as enterprises, which means assigning greater importance to annual work routines and land-use patterns; and the long-term reproduction of the enslaved workers, whose labor supplied the staples that fostered the growth of an emerging world economy.[11] Exactly how, in various political contexts, those strategies intersected with local conditions, with specific crop requirements, and with the broader demands of the world economy can go far in explaining the differences between and within slaveholding regions in the Americas.

In this regard, a study exploring the agrarian history of the Recôncavo in the late eighteenth and early nineteenth centuries represents an ideal point of departure. Not only was the Recôncavo, by the end of the eighteenth century, one of the oldest and best-established areas of slave-based export agriculture in the New World; but within its fairly compact boundaries, the Recôncavo displayed a remarkable degree of physical, social, and economic diversity—combining, as it were, Jamaica and Saint-Domingue with Tidewater Virginia and Maryland in a single slave-based regional economy.

Sources and Terms

To investigate the Recôncavo's agrarian economy in the early nineteenth century, this study draws on a wide variety of manuscript sources.* Among them are surveys of rural properties from the mid-nineteenth century (the so-called ecclesiastical registers of lands); notarial records, such as deeds and rental contracts; correspondence between local officials and the colonial, and later provincial, government in Salvador; and the records of Salvador's Public Granary (*Celeiro Público*).

Many of the conclusions presented here are based on work with more than five hundred postmortem inventories of estates left by sugar planters and by farmers who grew sugarcane, tobacco, and food crops. Probate records are, by their very nature, a biased source. Although Portuguese law (valid in Brazil until 1917) normally required that an inventory be carried out after every death, the surviving probate records make clear that the great majority of the free population did not receive such attention. Only when an estate included real property or slaves did heirs go to the expense of calling in court-appointed appraisers. Inventories from the eighteenth and nineteenth centuries for rural estates that list neither land nor slaves are extremely rare. Thus, as a source, postmortem inventories cast light on that segment of the rural population that owned either land or slaves.[12]

Yet, despite their built-in bias, inventories constitute an invaluable source for information about agricultural practices, the size and value of rural establishments, slavery, and working and living conditions in the countryside. Occasionally, these probate records contain running accounts of expenditures and receipts. When litigation or other complications delayed the division of property among heirs, the executor remained responsible for the estate's upkeep. Before the property was finally divided, the executor submitted more or less detailed accounts to justify the expenditures he had made. In Brazil, where plantation records have rarely survived, such accounts represent one of the very few sources of firsthand information about day-to-day operations on rural estates.

This study also makes extensive use of manuscript censuses from the last decades of the eighteenth century, as well as the years 1825–26 and 1835. Together, the censuses and the postmortem inventories yield information on more than twenty thousand slaves who worked on Bahian plantations and farms in the late eighteenth and early nineteenth centuries. That infor-

* The archival research for this study was carried out between 1986 and 1988 and in 1992 and 1993. Except for final revisions, I finished writing the main body of the text by late 1993. In making those revisions, I resisted, for the most part, the temptation to incorporate into the text or the notes works published after mid-1994. But at least one recent and important work on slavery and export agriculture in nineteenth-century Brazil should be cited here: the collection of essays edited by Hebe Maria Mattos de Castro and Eduardo Schnoor, *Resgate: Uma janela para o oitocentos* (1995).

mation makes it possible to explore in detail patterns of slaveholding and labor recruitment in the rural Recôncavo.

The task of presenting the results of historical research resembles in some ways the work of translation. After all, "the past is," David Lowenthal reminds us, "a foreign country."[13] The work of translation is twofold when not only time but language and culture separate historians from the past they try to make intelligible. Throughout, this study has tried to provide English equivalents for the terms and expressions that Bahian planters, farmers, and slaves used in describing their world and their daily lives. But in many cases, it proved more convenient to employ Portuguese words instead of attempting to translate them. Most of these are defined when they first occur in the text. Some, however, resist simple one- or two-word definitions and are therefore explained here at the outset.

Engenho. Although plantation agriculture has profoundly influenced the historical development of Brazilian society, the Portuguese language contains no exact equivalent for the English word *plantation*. Indeed, when Brazilian authors wish to refer broadly to a large estate producing tropical or semitropical staples for export, they often resort to writing *plantation* in English. But when they wish to refer specifically to a sugar plantation, they have at hand the word *engenho*, which originally meant a mill for crushing sugarcane and was, by extension, also applied to a plantation with a mill. One of the peculiarities of the Brazilian sugar industry was the distinction between sugar plantations with mills and those without mills. Only the former were known as engenhos. Owners of such plantations were, in turn, called *senhores de engenho* (literally, lords of the mill). Although *engenho* is occasionally used in the text in its more restricted sense of a mill for grinding cane, the word most often appears as a synonym for a sugar plantation with a mill. Likewise, the expressions *sugar plantation* and *sugar planter* are used only in referring to engenhos and to senhores de engenho.

Lavrador. This Portuguese word simply means farmer, grower, or agriculturalist. Thus, a *lavrador de fumo* (or *de tabaco*) was a tobacco farmer and a *lavrador de mandioca* a cassava grower. Similarly, the expression *lavrador de cana* can be translated as cane farmer. Indeed, when the word was not qualified, it was generally understood to refer to a cane farmer. Cane farmers were sugar planters who did not own their own milling equipment. They cultivated sugarcane on their own estates or on rented land. In either case, they turned over to the owner of an engenho a share (usually one-half) of their crop in exchange for having their cane milled and manufactured into sugar. When they cultivated cane on rented land, they surrendered an additional share of the crop as rent to the landowner, who was usually the proprietor of a mill. Throughout the text, these sugar planters without mills arc referred to as cane farmers, lavradores de cana, or, following common usage, simply lavradores.

Fazenda and *sítio* refer to rural properties. Both terms are translated as *farm*. Although today *sítio* often connotes a smaller property, that distinction does not appear with any uniformity in eighteenth- and nineteenth-century sources. Sometimes a single source that describes a property in one passage as a sítio will elsewhere refer to the same property as a fazenda.

Roça means a field cleared and planted with food crops, especially cassava. By extension, roça might sometimes designate a farm where such crops were grown. The farmers who cultivated roças were consequently known as roceiros. The word roça could also be applied to the small plots of land where, working in their "free" time, slaves were allowed to cultivate food crops for their own use.

Cova. In everyday usage, this word means pit, hollow, hole, or grave. In the Brazilian countryside, perhaps because they vaguely resemble freshly dug graves, covas can also be the small mounds in which certain crops—cassava, for example—are planted. By extension, the word can also mean the plant itself. Thus, in the colonial period, several royal decrees ordered sugar producers to plant a fixed number of covas of cassava. The text retains this word in order to avoid what would often be a cumbersome direct translation.

Bahian. Until recently, it was the rule, even in official documents, to refer to the city of Salvador as the city of Bahia. For that reason, Bahian (baiano) continues to serve a double purpose; it may refer either to a resident of Bahia (the captaincy, the province, the state) or, more narrowly, to a resident of Salvador. Although it might seem confusing to employ one noun (or adjective) with two meanings, the only real alternative would be to use Soteropolitan (soteropolitano) for residents of Salvador. Derived from the Greek word for city of the Saviour, Soteropolitan is much less common than Bahian and decidedly more pedantic. Context should make it clear whether Bahian in a particular passage refers to residents of Salvador or to residents of Bahia as a whole.

The study that follows is divided into six chapters and a conclusion. Chapter 2, which is based chiefly on series of trade statistics for major export staples compiled from various sources, examines the movement of the export economy in the eight decades after 1780.[14] Compiling those series was necessary because, to date, no study has attempted to chart in any detail the main trends in the Bahian export economy between 1780 and 1860.[15] By charting those trends, this chapter provides a point of departure for exploring changes in export agriculture, as well as the relationships in Bahia between a dominant export economy and production for local needs. It demonstrates that, overall, the Bahian export economy underwent real growth in the years 1780–1860 (increases in physical output and in real earnings). That growth contrasts with the decline experienced in the decades both before 1780 and after 1860. Thus, the 80 years that stretch from the last decades of the eighteenth century to the middle of the nineteenth constitute a distinct period in Bahia's economic history.

Chapter 3 begins by establishing that farinha de mandioca (cassava flour) was the chief breadstuff in the diet of both urban and rural Bahians. It then attempts to gauge the size of the local market for cassava flour. Momentary crises in the price and supply of cassava flour in that market are discussed in Chapter 4. That chapter also provides evidence that between 1780 and 1860, production of cassava in the Recôncavo increased despite the spread of export agriculture. The real price of cassava flour in Salvador's market during those same years failed to follow any consistent upward trend. With Chapters 5 to 7, the focus shifts from markets, whether overseas or local, to the rural Recôncavo. These chapters investigate the diversity *within* slave-based agriculture by examining land tenure, the structure of slaveholding, patterns of labor recruitment, and the agricultural practices that Bahian planters and farmers followed. The remainder of this introduction presents the geographic setting for this study.

The Recôncavo

Recôncavo. The word in Portuguese means simply back bay or the inland shore of a bay, any bay. But in Brazil, the word has become firmly attached to the region around one particular bay—the bay that early Portuguese explorers christened the Baía de Todos os Santos (Bay of All Saints).[16] At roughly 13 degrees south latitude, a rocky promontory signals the entrance to a spacious gulf that the sea has carved out of the smooth coastline of Northeastern Brazil (see Map 1). Measuring at its widest point some 50 kilometers across, this gulf encloses 750 square kilometers of generally calm water and holds within its confines nearly 100 islands. The smallest of these are mere specks of land lost amid the expanse of blue-and-green water, while Itaparica, the largest, claims an area of almost 250 square kilometers. Countless creeks, coves, and inlets along the bay's edges create an irregular shoreline, made all the more so by the mouths of numerous rivers and streams: the Sergi, the Acu, the Subaé, the São Paulo, the Guaí, the Jaguaripe, the Paramirim, and the Batatã, to name but a few. The most imposing of the rivers is the Paraguaçu, which flows over a course of several hundred kilometers from its headwaters in the interior before it empties into the western side of the bay.

Extending back from the shore of the bay is a gently undulating landscape of low, rounded hills that, here and there, give way to sizable stretches of strikingly flat terrain. Only in a few low *serras* (chains of hills) and along rivers where erosion has created steep bluffs does the landscape take on a truly rugged appearance. The hills, bluffs, and plains of the northern Recôncavo bear, for the most part, soils of cretaceous origin that consist of varied mixtures of clay and sand. Bahians called the lightest and sandiest of those soils *areias* (literally, sands). The heaviest, those with the greatest clay content, were known as *massapés*, while the name *salões* was used to designate an intermediate mixture of clay and sand. Elsewhere, on the western and southern sides of the bay, sandy loams predominate.

Portuguese settlers and their Brazilian-born descendants built around

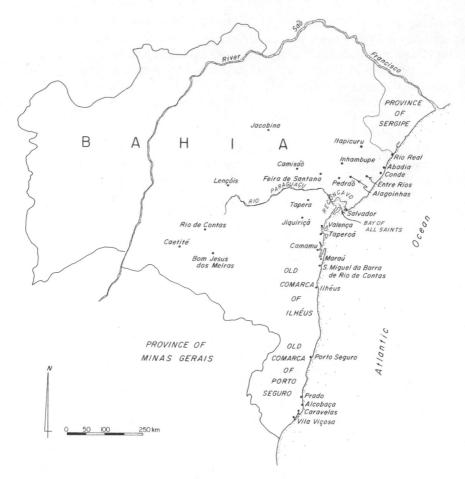

Map 1. The Province of Bahia in the Mid-Nineteenth Century

this bay one of the most enduring slave societies of the New World. For more than three hundred years, enslaved men and women brought by force from Africa and their sons and daughters born in Brazil worked in the Recôncavo in nearly every imaginable occupation. They served their masters as field hands, artisans, cooks, porters, maids, boatmen, clerks, sailors, fishermen, and overseers.

The contours of that society began to take shape in the mid-sixteenth century. In 1549, Tomé de Sousa established, on a high bluff overlooking the mouth of the bay, the settlement that would become the city of Salvador and that, from the start, was the seat of royal government for Portugal's American colonies. Venturing out into the countryside, the early settlers forced the Indians to clear fields from the tropical forest and to plant sugarcane. They built mills to transform the cane into sugar for sale in distant European markets. When, in a few decades, disease and warfare had greatly reduced the Indian population, the settlers replaced them with slaves imported from Africa. Gradually, the combination of export-based commerce and royal government transformed Tomé de Sousa's primitive settlement into a flourishing town, which, by the early eighteenth century, counted a population of some twenty thousand. Although the viceregal capital would be transferred in 1763 to Rio de Janeiro, Salvador still retained its position as the administrative center for the vast captaincy of Bahia, which, until 1820, included the present-day state of Sergipe. After independence (1822), the city would continue to serve as the capital of Bahia, now a province in the newly formed Empire of Brazil.

At the heart of that province was Salvador's immediate hinterland, the Recôncavo. Small in proportion to the more than 561,000 square kilometers that made up Bahia, the Recôncavo remained throughout the nineteenth century the most densely settled and economically important region in the province. Identifying with any precision the boundaries that circumscribed the Recôncavo has, however, always proved difficult. Geographers and other social scientists, using different criteria, have put forth different definitions of the region.[17] But on one point nearly all the definitions agree: ready access to the Bay of All Saints and hence close and constant contact with the city of Salvador have always shaped life in the Recôncavo. Those definitions also coincide in setting the Recôncavo apart from the other regions of Bahia— from the arid and semi-arid *sertões* (backlands) of the interior and from the southern coast, the old *comarcas* (judicial districts) of Ilhéus and Porto Seguro—where, by contrast, year-round heavy rainfall permitted the growth of especially dense tropical forests.[18]

For Luís dos Santos Vilhena, the chronicler who, in the last years of the eighteenth century, wrote one of the most complete descriptions of life in colonial Bahia, the Recôncavo encompassed the city of Salvador, its rural suburban parishes, and the five townships that surrounded the Bay of All Saints: São Francisco do Conde and Santo Amaro da Purificação on the northern shore, Cachoeira to the west, and Maragogipe and Jaguaripe on the south. By the mid-nineteenth century, those townships numbered nine. Districts lying north of Salvador, which Vilhena had classified among the city's suburban parishes, now formed the townships of Mata de São João and Abrantes. The provincial assembly made the island of Itaparica into an independent municipality, and from the inland parishes of Jaguaripe it created the township of Nazaré. Vilhena's Recôncavo falls within the limits that Manoel Aires de Casal and Ferdinand Denis traced around the region in the first half of the nineteenth century. Both these authors described the Recôncavo as extending 6 to 10 leagues (approximately 36 to 60 kilometers) in all directions from the edges of the bay.[19] Those limits come remarkably close to the definition of the Recôncavo used today by the state government of Bahia: a region of roughly 10,400 square kilometers encircling the Bay of All Saints. This is the initial working definition used in this study[20] (see Map 2).[21]

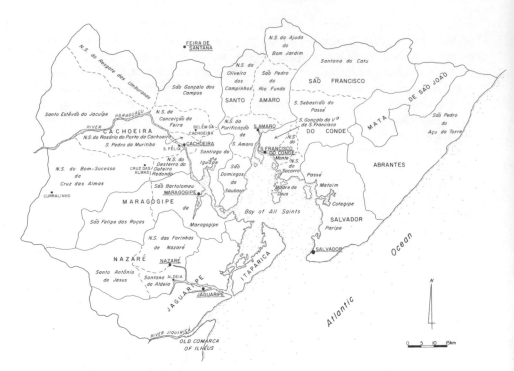

Map 2. Townships and Parishes in the Recôncavo in the Mid-Nineteenth
Century
SOURCES. Brazil, IBGE, *Enciclopédia dos municípios*; Bahia, SEPLAN-
TEC, . . . , *Informações básicas*, vols. 4, 5; *Mappa estatistico . . . da Provincia
da Bahia.* See n. 21.
NOTE. Boundaries are approximate. Names in large capitals indicate townships. Italicized names are parishes. Solid lines designate township boundaries;
dotted lines are boundaries between parishes within townships. Underlined
names in small capitals are towns and cities that served as township seats.
Names of villages and hamlets (not all of which are shown) are also in small
capitals, but are not underlined.

In the late eighteenth century, this region sheltered three distinct crop
zones. Early on, Portuguese settlers in Bahia had discovered that the heavy
massapé soils of the northern Recôncavo were ideally suited for the cultivation of sugarcane. They had also learned that cane would grow nearly as
well—and actually better in wet years—in the lighter salões. To a large extent, the distribution of massapés and salões had, in fact, determined the
geography of the sugar industry in the Recôncavo. Wherever Bahians found
land bearing these clayish soils near the bayshore or close to a navigable
stream flowing into the bay, they planted cane and built engenhos. The cultivation of cane thus came to dominate the landscape in a wide arc that extended along the edge of the bay from the parishes of Cotegipe and Pirajá on

the outskirts of Salvador as far west as the parish of Santiago do Iguape at the mouth of the Paraguaçu. In the townships of São Francisco do Conde and Santo Amaro, sugar also expanded inland into the parishes of São Sebastião do Passé and São Pedro do Rio Fundo. Together, the suburban parishes of Salvador, the two townships of São Francisco do Conde and Santo Amaro, and the parish of Iguape constituted the chief centers of sugar production in the Recôncavo. Approximately 90 percent of the 221 engenhos that milled cane in Bahia in the mid-1790s were located in those districts.[22]

Many of the oldest and largest engenhos in Bahia were situated in parishes along or near the northern shore of the bay, where easy access to water transportation made shipping sugar to Salvador less costly than overland methods. At least half of those bayshore estates belonged to the twenty or so families that made up Bahia's planter "aristocracy," the families that enjoyed great social prestige and exercised equally great influence in local and, later, national politics. These wealthy and well-respected planters built for themselves impressive country houses with thick masonry walls, wide verandas, and often ornate chapels. There they spent the better part of the year supervising their slaves and imposing their authority on tenants and less well-to-do neighbors. They lost few opportunities to point out their ties, in some cases spurious, to noble lineages in Europe; and at all times they insisted on being known as senhores de engenho (lords of the mill). They had to share that title, however, with many less wealthy planters. In truth, despite all its pretensions, Bahia's planter "aristocracy" never formed a closed group. Sugar was a business; a "noble business," but nonetheless a business. Just as declining fortunes in that business could drive some aristocratic families into debt, loss of property, and ultimately obscurity, planters who prospered could rise to the ranks of the "aristocracy." Through marriage, moreover, the great planter families brought into their fold wealthy immigrant merchants from Portugal and high-ranking bureaucrats from the colonial government.[23]

To the west of the sugar zone lay the large township of Cachoeira, where, in most parishes, sandy loams rather than clayish soils covered the land. In those sandy loams, farmers on several thousand fazendas and sítios cultivated tobacco for export to both Europe and West Africa. Bahian farmers specialized in producing twist tobacco, tobacco tightly woven into ropelike cords and then wound into heavy rolls (rolos) that might weigh as much as 25 arrobas (367.5 kilograms). Most of that tobacco came from the "fields of Cachoeira," an area of open land with little forest cover that extended north and west from the River Paraguaçu, through the parish of São Gonçalo dos Campos, and beyond into the interior. Farmers also cultivated tobacco in the less densely settled parishes south of the Paraguaçu, where they produced much of the leaf tobacco that the Portuguese state monopoly shipped from Bahia to Goa in India.[24]

The sandy soils of Cachoeira extended south into the townships of Maragogipe and Jaguaripe, where bitter cassava (*mandioca*), also called manioc or yucca, was the main crop. The roceiros of Maragogipe and Jaguaripe harvested the roots or tubers of the bitter cassava plant, which contain lethal amounts of prussic acid. Grating, pressing, and toasting, however, removed the deadly acid and transformed the roots into a coarse flour known as *farinha de mandioca* (cassava flour) or simply *farinha* (flour).* Cassava flour, although it contains few vitamins and only negligible amounts of protein, is nevertheless a substantial and filling foodstuff; consisting mainly of starch, it can serve as a rich source of calories. Parish names such as Nossa Senhora de Nazaré das Farinhas (Our Lady of Nazareth of the Flours) and São Felipe das Roças (Saint Philip of the Cassava Farms) attest to the importance cassava and cassava flour held on this side of the bay. The roceiros of the southern Recôncavo produced flour for home consumption and for sale at weekly market fairs in the ports of Nazaré and Maragogipe. There, merchants and dealers bought up stocks of farinha that they shipped by boat across the bay to Salvador.[25]

Only in part does this three-way pattern of specialization confirm the common assertion that in colonial Brazil, sugar planters monopolized the best lands, relegating the production of foodstuffs and other crops to areas with poorer soils.[26] True, Bahian senhores de engenho did attempt to control the fertile massapés of the northern Recôncavo. But massapés were the "best soils" for sugarcane alone. Neither tobacco nor cassava grew well in the heavy clays—which, during the rainy winter months, became an almost impassable mire of sticky mud and in summer developed a rock-hard crust. Tobacco and cassava both fared much better in lighter and sandier soils.[27]

Geographic specialization, moreover, was by no means absolute. Sugar production, for example, had scarcely begun to spread into the coastal districts north of Salvador that would later become the townships of Mata de São João and Abrantes. There, in *aldeias* (officially supervised villages), remnants of the original Indian population cultivated cassava and a small amount of cotton. The farms owned by Portuguese-speaking residents in those two townships produced farinha, cotton, and tobacco; some raised cattle as well. Farmers also grew tobacco and cassava in Santana do Catu, São Pedro do Rio Fundo, and Nossa Senhora da Oliveira dos Campinhos. Although these parishes belonged to the sugar-producing townships of São Francisco do Conde and Santo Amaro, they were all located inland at considerable distances from the northern shore of the bay.[28]

Even in parishes closer to the bay, where sugar production was well established, tenant farmers found room to cultivate cassava on patches of land between the engenhos and the cane farms. Cassava was, in all likelihood, the chief crop in the hilly parish of São Domingos da Saubara. Despite its location on the northern bayshore, Saubara would never become an impor-

---

* When, in the eighteenth and nineteenth centuries, Bahians needed to refer to wheat flour, they spoke, just as they do today, of *farinha-do-reino* (flour from the kingdom; i.e., from Portugal). Unqualified, *farinha* was and is universally taken to mean cassava flour.

tant center of sugar production; its soils were too sandy. Most residents of Saubara earned their livelihood by cutting firewood, raising cattle, fishing, and making lime.[29]

Similarly, canefields had already begun to expand into the tobacco- and cassava-growing districts of the western and southern Recôncavo. At scattered points in those districts, sugar planters had built more than a dozen engenhos. Even more numerous, no doubt, were *engenhocas*, small mills that manufactured *rapaduras* (cakes of unrefined brown sugar) for local consumption and that distilled *cachaça* (sugarcane brandy). Throughout Cachoeira, owners of fazendas and sítios grew not only tobacco but also food crops. Moreover, by the late eighteenth century, tobacco had already gained a foothold in Maragogipe. There and in the neighboring township of Jaguaripe, pottery works lined the riverbanks, producing tiles and earthenware china, which was sold in markets as far away as Rio de Janeiro. Jaguaripe also had a timber industry that supplied planks to Salvador's shipyards.[30]

Yet even after taking into account these varied activities, it is clear that a rough pattern of specialization did prevail in the Recôncavo. Sugar came mainly from São Francisco do Conde, Santo Amaro, and the parish of Santiago do Iguape; tobacco from Cachoeira; and farinha from the southern townships.

By the end of the eighteenth century, the Recôncavo—with an economy based on the production of both export and food crops, its plantations and farms, and its numerous towns, villages, and hamlets—stood out as one of the most densely settled regions in all of Brazil. It is, however, no easy task to determine the size of the population that lived in Salvador and its immediate hinterland. Although civil and ecclesiastical authorities did occasionally attempt to take population counts in colonial Bahia, they often found their efforts hindered by the indifference of local officials. They also, as Vilhena noted, had to overcome the widespread notion that censuses served only for assessing new taxes and for military recruitment. The decades following independence brought little improvement. James Wetherell, British vice consul in Salvador, noticed in the 1850s the same fear of censuses that had drawn Vilhena's attention half a century earlier. "The people," he wrote, "generally appear to have an inveterate dislike 'to be numbered.'" Time and time again, authorities failed in their attempts to carry out a complete and accurate census of the entire province.[31]

In the end, however, we have little choice but to rely on the census counts that have come down to us. Although seldom completely trustworthy, they alone provide usable information on the size of Bahia's population. Those counts indicate that around 1780, the Captaincy of Bahia had a population of almost 220,000. Of these, more than two-thirds, or approximately 150,000, lived in Salvador and its immediate hinterland.[32] That population would, over the next nine decades, undergo a threefold increase to reach a total of 451,678 by 1872, the year of Brazil's first national census.[33]

Throughout the eighteenth and nineteenth centuries, only a minority—

perhaps less than one-fifth—of the inhabitants of the Recôncavo were white.[34] Indians were likewise few. The great majority of the population consisted of African- and Brazilian-born blacks and of Bahians of mixed European and African descent—*pardos, mulatos,* and *cabras.** The black and mulatto population of the Recôncavo included freed slaves, freeborn descendants of slaves, and a large number of enslaved men and women. Perhaps as many as 89,000 slaves lived in the region in 1816–17.[35] Even in the early 1870s, a full twenty years after the end of the transatlantic slave trade, the number of slaves in Salvador and in the townships surrounding the Bay of All Saints would still stand at more than 70,000.[36]

When, in the sixteenth century, African slaves first began to work on the plantations and farms of the Recôncavo, Bahia was little more than a newly established outpost on the far edges of an expanding world economy. For the next three hundred years, the trade in sugar, tobacco, and other export staples would continue to tie Bahia to the world economy. The work that went into the production of those crops and, later, coffee would, in turn, consume the lives of thousands of slaves. The export trade is, then, an appropriate starting point for a study of slavery and agriculture in the townships around the Bay of All Saints.

* *Pardo* was the term most often used to describe anyone of mixed African and European descent. A *cabra* had, at least in principle, one black parent and one mulatto parent or was the child of two *cabras.*

CHAPTER 2

The Export Economy, 1780–1860

Around 1790, Luís Antônio de Oliveira Mendes prepared an "economic description" of Bahia with the goal of showing the progress recently achieved in the captaincy's export economy; or, as he put it, to draw "the parallel" between the agriculture, navigation, and trade of former times and their present state. Mendes found evidence of great progress. By his account, the mid-eighteenth century had been a "calamitous time" when Bahian export agriculture languished in "misery, ruin, and utter decadence." All that had now changed. Agriculture had vigorously reestablished itself in only a few years. The recovery, Mendes recognized, was incomplete and sometimes interrupted by alarming downturns. He even feared that it might already be ending. Nevertheless, the export economy had, it seemed, entered a new "happy epoch."[1]

A modern reader easily finds fault with Mendes's economic description: his language often sounds exaggerated and inappropriate for a treatise on trade and agriculture; he betrays a strong prejudice against merchants; and the trade figures he uses as evidence are sometimes little more than informed guesses. Nevertheless, Mendes succeeded in depicting with fair accuracy the general trends in the captaincy's export economy.

The mid-eighteenth century had indeed been a time of hardship and economic depression. For sugar producers, the troubles had started a hundred years earlier, when the Dutch invasions of Northeastern Brazil destroyed plantations and disrupted trade. Bahians rebuilt their plantations and reestablished commercial ties with Europe, but they found no adequate solution to the new and more serious problem of competition. The fighting with the Dutch and the resulting interruptions in trade had encouraged the development of sugar production elsewhere in the Americas. From the late seventeenth century on, the British and French colonies in the West Indies began to export an ever-increasing amount of sugar and to capture from Brazil a large share of the world's market. As more and more ships laden with Caribbean sugar arrived in European ports, the sugar trade at Bahia stagnated. Tobacco hardly held out more promise; the earlier growth in tobacco exports had by the 1750s given way to decline. To worsen matters, the depression spread beyond Bahia and the other sugar-producing regions of Northeastern Brazil. Gold production, centered in the Southeastern captaincy of Minas Gerais, also declined from the mid-eighteenth century on. Accompanying the drop in gold exports, Anglo-Portuguese trade on the other side of the Atlantic fell precipitously. In sum, a "prolonged economic malaise" took hold of both Brazil and Portugal in the 1760s and 1770s. The times were, as Mendes later wrote in his exaggerated style, "calamitous."[2]

The task of reversing this situation fell to Sebastião José de Carvalho e Melo, later made the marquess of Pombal, who ruled Portugal as a virtual dictator from 1750 to 1777. Pombal responded to the economic depression with a whole series of reforms, both at home and in the colonies, which he hoped would restore Portugal's position in Europe and reduce Portuguese economic dependency on England. In Brazil, his reforms included efforts to revitalize the traditional export trade in sugar and tobacco, as well as to diversify Brazilian export agriculture. After Pombal's fall from power, his successors abandoned some of his policies but continued to work for a revival of colonial trade. They promoted new export crops and encouraged improvements in the cultivation and processing of established crops. In these matters, their efforts were joined by those of a new generation of Brazilian intellectuals inspired by the Enlightenment, who, like the Bahian José da Silva Lisboa, believed that theirs was the "age of agriculture."[3]

Historians have so far failed to reach any firm consensus on what Portuguese colonial policy after 1750 achieved for Brazil. In particular, Pombal's reforms (and Pombal himself) remain subject to various interpretations. It is clear that the reforms brought no sustained recovery to export agriculture in the short run. An assessment of the longer-term effects is more difficult. With or without those measures, the Industrial Revolution would, in all likelihood, have led to an increased demand for the agricultural commodities exported by Brazil. Moreover, the wars and revolutions of the late eighteenth and early nineteenth centuries often resulted in higher prices for tropical products and opened new markets for Brazilian exports. Perhaps the most important of these was the revolution in the French colony of Saint-Domingue, modern Haiti. Saint-Domingue, before its collapse in the 1790s, had been the wealthiest of all the plantation colonies in the Americas and the world's largest supplier of both sugar and coffee. Whatever the true impact of the colonial policies of Pombal and his successors, these wars and revolutions undoubtedly did much to bring about a veritable "agricultural renaissance" in Bahia and throughout Brazil in the late colonial period.[4]

For Brazil as a whole, diversification characterized this resurgence. The growth registered by traditional exports such as sugar, tobacco, and hides was matched after 1780 by increases in relatively new products: cotton, coffee, rice, cocoa, and even wheat. At the same time, experiments with pepper, cinammon, tea, cloves, and a dozen other crops went ahead. An expanding and more diversified export trade put an end to the economic malaise that had afflicted Portugal and Brazil in the 1760s and 1770s. More than that, it brought changes in trading relationships between Portugal and other European nations and between Portugal and Brazil. In Europe, where the Portuguese had long suffered commercial deficits, trade balances from the 1790s on shifted in Portugal's favor. Yet the positive balances achieved in Europe only served to reveal an increasing dependency on Brazil. Brazilian products accounted for 60 percent of all Portuguese exports to other European markets between 1796 and 1811. Thus, commercial surpluses in Europe came at the cost of deficits in Portuguese trade with Brazil. The flow of specie now defied any mercantilist notions that may have guided policymakers in Lisbon; gold and silver flowed from England and France to Portugal and thence to Brazil. As Mendes observed, a "happy epoch" had indeed begun.[5]

This chapter takes the late colonial agricultural renaissance as its starting point and attempts to chart the broad trends in Bahia's export economy from the beginning of its recovery to the mid-nineteenth century, when the first signs of fundamental transformations appeared. This overview also provides the opportunity to trace some of the changes in the agricultural geography of the Recôncavo between 1780 and 1860.

Long-Term Growth

Perhaps the first questions of interest here are whether Bahia's export economy as a whole grew or declined between 1780 and 1860, and how that growth or decline compared with earlier trends. Detailed information on the total value of Bahian exports would immediately answer those questions, but unfortunately, almost no such information currently exists for years before 1796. Indirectly, however, tax receipts collected on imports give a rough idea of the state of the export trade in the 1770s and 1780s. Customs House receipts indicate a marked upturn in commercial activity after 1775 that peaked in the early 1780s and then again, after a slight fall, in the late 1790s. Contemporary testimony suggests that broadly similar fluctuations characterized the volume and value of exports of sugar, tobacco, and other staples in those years.[6]

Although the record improves after 1796, official trade statistics are lacking for most years until the late 1840s, when it becomes possible to construct an uninterrupted series for the total value of Bahian exports. The figures that make up that series are expressed in mil-réis, the purchasing power of which varied considerably between 1796 and 1860. This means that, before we can accurately interpret the series, we must first adjust it for inflation. Here, for want of any better deflator, the series has been adjusted with a price index for British exports. Since much of what Bahia imported both before and after independence consisted of British manufactures, the series deflated with this index tells whether, from year to year, Bahians could purchase more or less with their export earnings; it provides, in other words, an idea of real changes in the value of Bahian exports. An index, calculated from this adjusted series, is displayed graphically in Figure 1.[7]

Several observations are in order. First, Figure 1 makes it readily apparent that the value of export revenues sometimes fluctuated greatly from one year to the next. The reasons for these fluctuations remain in many cases unclear; in other instances, they are easily explained. For example, in 1807, Napoleon's armies invaded Portugal. The invasion disrupted shipping between Brazil and Lisbon—hence the sudden fall in export revenues at Bahia the following year. The invasion also forced Portugal's Prince-Regent, Dom João VI, to flee to Brazil, where he immediately declared Brazilian ports open to merchants from "friendly nations"; Bahians could for the first time ship their sugar and tobacco directly to England and other North Atlantic markets. The opening of Brazil's ports to direct trade contributed to the quick recovery of export revenues after 1808 and their growth between 1809 and 1816. In all likelihood, revenues suffered an equally sudden and perhaps more spectacular fall in 1823. The war for independence from Portugal, fought almost exclusively in Bahia, virtually paralyzed the export trade in that year. Such fluctuations, in any case, make very tentative any conclusions drawn about the performance of Bahia's export economy during the long stretch of years, from 1817 to 1847, for which information on the total value of exports is largely lacking.

We can be much more confident in describing the long-term trend in revenues from foreign trade between 1796 and 1860; it is clearly ascendant, indicating substantial growth in the export economy as a whole. That growth would, without doubt, appear even more impressive if the series shown in Figure 1 included export revenues from the depressed 1750s and 1760s. Likewise, the upward trend between the late eighteenth and mid-nineteenth centuries would also stand out if it were set against the dismal performance of the export economy after 1860.[8]

All of this adds up to only the roughest outline of changes in the export economy between 1780 and 1860. A much more detailed picture emerges from an examination of how trade in specific export staples fared from the late eighteenth century on.

Major Export Staples

Export revenues in Bahia came from the overseas sales of a wide variety of products. Lists of Bahian exports often included more than 50 items, rang-

Index

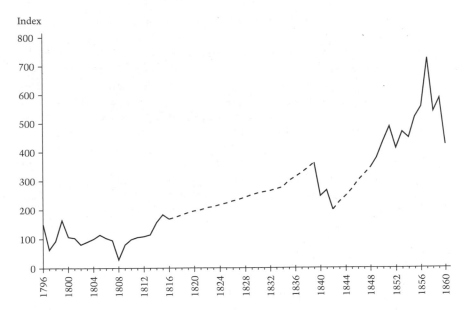

Figure 1. Bahia. Index of the Deflated Value of All Exports, 1796–1860 (1800=100).
SOURCES. Morton, "Conservative Revolution," p. 156; Simonsen, p. 364; Arruda, *O Brasil*, p. 204; "Mappa Geral da Exportação q. fez a Bahia ... 1798 a 1807" and "Mappa da Exportação da ... Bahia ... 1808," BN, I–17,12,4; "Mappa da Exportação da Bahia ... 1809," APEB, SH, 146, fol. 567; *Almanach*, p. 245; Lugar, "Merchant Community," p. 112; M. Calmon, *Memoria*, pp. 40–41; *ST*, 26: 338–40; Bahia, *Falla* (1841, P. J. de Mello Azevedo e Brito), p. 24; idem, *Falla* (1854, J. M. Wanderley), "Mappa ... da exportação ... 1851 ... 1853," n.p.; idem, *Falla* (1855, J. M. Wanderley), "Mappa ... da exportação," n.p.; idem, *Falla* (1857, J. L. V. Cansanção de Sinimbu), "Mappa ... dos generos nacionaes exportados ...," n.p.; idem, *Falla* (1861, A. da Costa Pinto), "Recapitulação das mercadorias nacionaes exportadas ...," n.p.; Simonsen, pp. 407–8, 431, 454 and Leff, 1: 246 (for exchange rates); Imlah, pp. 93–98 (for price index of British exports).
NOTE. The total nominal value of exports for 1796 and 1797 was estimated from the value of exports to Portugal for 1796 and 1797 on the assumption that their value represented 91.25 percent of all export revenues (their average between 1798 and 1807). For 1840, 1841, 1842, the British consul recorded the value of exports for nine commodites (sugar, cotton, coffee, cocoa, rice, "tapioca," tobacco, sugarcane brandy, and molasses). His figure for 1840 amounts to 91.06 percent of the value of all exports as reported by the provincial president. The total value of exports for 1841 and 1842 was estimated on the assumption that the same nine commodities also supplied 91.06 percent of all export revenues in those years. The value of the price index for British exports for 1813 was calculated as the midpoint between the values for 1812 and 1814. Also see n. 7.

ing from obscure medicinal plants and "objects of natural history" to empty sacks and earthenware pottery. The lists suggest that Bahia should not be equated with such West Indian plantation colonies as Barbados, St. Kitts, or even Trinidad, where as much as 98 percent of all export earnings might come from sugar and a few sugar byproducts.[9] Yet the same lists, because they include obscure and altogether unimportant items, give the false impression that the province possessed a highly diversified export economy. Table 1 shows the composition of Bahian exports by value for three periods: 1796–1807, 1840–1842, and 1851–1860. Nine or ten products supplied nearly all of what Bahia earned through its overseas trade; their share of total earnings seldom fell below 90 percent. Sugar and tobacco, the traditional mainstays of the province's export economy, usually accounted for at least two-thirds of all earnings; sugar's share was approximately 50 percent.

The late colonial efforts to find and develop new export commodities had yielded only meager results in Bahia. In many cases, production of new commodities scarcely went beyond the experimental stage. Cloves, cinnamon, quinine, hemp, tea, and pepper never became exports of any consequence. Other products, such as rice and cotton, that seemed to bear great promise in the 1790s failed to gain stable overseas markets in the following decades. Only two entirely new products, coffee and cocoa, grew steadily in importance, but neither could be described as major items in the province's export trade in the 1850s. Cocoa, destined to become Bahia's main export commodity after 1900, still accounted for less than 1 percent of total export earnings in the middle of the nineteenth century. Clearly, Bahia did not develop a significantly more diversified export economy in the 80 years following 1780.

Yet on closer inspection, Table 1 does suggest shifts and changes in the composition of Bahian exports. Between 1807 and the early 1840s, tobacco lost much of its former importance. Whereas between 1796 and 1807 it had contributed as much as a fourth of all export revenues, its average share from 1840 to 1842 stood at under 8 percent. Just as striking was the increased importance of sugar, which by itself accounted for two-thirds of the value of all exports between 1840 and 1842. Bahia in these years came closer than it had at any time since the early seventeenth century to having a monocultural export economy.[10]

That trend was reversed by the 1850s. Diamonds and coffee became significant sources of export earnings. More important, tobacco partly recovered its former importance; its average share of Bahia's export trade nearly doubled between the early 1840s and 1860. Sugar's share, by contrast, tended to decline, falling below 50 percent in 1856 and again two years later, then to less than 27 percent in 1860. Sugar would rebound from this low in the next few years, but never again would the most traditional of all Bahian export staples account for more than half of the province's overseas trade.

These changes, although significant in themselves, occurred within narrow limits; they in no way altered Bahia's overwhelming dependence on three or four agricultural export staples: sugar, tobacco, cotton until the 1840s, and coffee thereafter. The remainder of this chapter examines in greater detail the trade in these staples from the late eighteenth to the mid-nineteenth centuries.

COTTON

Cotton, although indigenous to Brazil, became a major export only after shipments from the Captaincy of Maranhão in the 1760s proved highly profitable. Cultivation expanded rapidly, and in a few years, the cotton trade became one of the few successes among late colonial efforts to diversify the Brazilian economy. Throughout large areas of Northeastern Brazil, cotton soon established itself as the main export crop. Senhores de engenho in Pernambuco and Paraíba sometimes grew both cane and cotton on their plantations.[11]

Although the crop never achieved in Bahia the importance it gained in other parts of the Northeast, cotton exports from Salvador did increase dramatically in the late eighteenth and early nineteenth centuries. Whereas shipments in the 1770s had amounted to less than 100 arrobas a year, by the late 1790s, they had grown to an average of nearly 40,000 arrobas a year. Exports continued to increase during the next three decades; thereafter, they declined sharply, falling from a total of nearly 300,000 arrobas in 1829 to an annual average below 45,000 arrobas in the 1850s.[12]

The reasons for this decline are clear enough. With the growth of exports from the southern United States and, to a lesser extent, Egypt, cotton's international price fell markedly after 1820. Brazilian cotton no longer found a ready market in Europe. Bahian exports revived during the worldwide cotton "famine" of the 1860s, caused by the Civil War in the United States; but that revival lasted no more than few years. By the late 1870s, the amount of cotton sent overseas from Bahia once again stood at insignificant levels.[13]

Beyond the general problem of North American and Egyptian competition, which was common to all regions of Brazil, another difficulty beset Bahian cotton: high transport costs. Heavy rainfall during the winter months prevented cotton from ever becoming an important crop in the Recôncavo, where its cultivation was largely confined to parishes around the region's western edges. It was more profitably grown in townships north of the Recôncavo, such as Inhambupe, Itapicuru, and Abadia, which had generally drier climates. Although all those districts were fairly close to the coast, the main cotton-growing areas in Bahia lay far in the interior, in the distant townships of Caetité, Rio de Contas, Jacobina, and Bom Jesus dos Meiras. As long as international prices remained high, transport costs were not a serious problem; but once prices began to fall, cotton from the interior had no chance of competing in the world market.[14]

Far less clear than the reasons for the decline in exports is whether most of the cotton shipped from Salvador ever came from Bahia. As early as the 1790s, the port of Salvador was exporting cotton not only from Bahia but also

TABLE I

Value of Major Export Staples as a Percentage of All Export Revenues, Bahia, Selected Years, 1796–1860

Year	Sugar	Tobacco[a]	Cotton	Coffee	Sugarcane brandy	Cocoa	Hides, etc.[b]	Gold	Timber[c]	Diamonds	Total
1796	68.2%	14.4%	8.7%	0.2%	*	*	6.1%	1.3%	0.2%	—	99.1%
1797	59.1	26.3	8.0	0.1	*	*	5.0	—	0.7	—	92.2
1798	67.0	18.6	7.4	0.6	*	*	5.9	—	0.3	—	99.8
1799	50.7	28.5	9.3	0.5	0.2%	*	5.0	1.5	0.3	—	96.0
1800	42.3	12.9	15.7	0.8	0.2	0.1%	13.0	9.9	0.3	—	95.2
1801	53.8	n.a.	15.1	0.6	—	0.1	9.9	6.4	0.3	—	86.2[d]
1802	20.1	19.0	22.4	0.5	—	—	9.0	4.4	0.3	—	75.7
1803	48.5	14.4	22.1	0.4	2.9	*	8.4	1.2	0.5	—	98.4
1804	50.6	15.6	15.0	0.7	0.5	—	14.5	0.3	0.4	—	97.6
1805	53.7	15.0	13.3	0.4	0.6	1.2	11.8	0.4	0.2	—	96.6
1806	44.4	11.8	12.2	0.7	0.3	*	17.4	1.4	0.3	—	88.5
1807	49.4	11.7	20.2	0.5	1.2	0.7	10.5	0.6	0.4	—	95.5
Ave., 1796–1807	50.7%	17.1%	14.1%	0.5%	0.5%	0.2%	9.7%	2.3%	0.4%	—	95.5%
Adj. ave., 1796–1807[e]	47.3%	24.9%	13.1%	0.5%	0.5%	0.2%	9.0%	1.9%	0.4%	—	97.8%
1840	63.6	7.7	11.7	3.4	4.1	0.2	n.a.	n.a.	n.a.	n.a.	90.7[g]
1841[f]	72.9	5.2	7.6	2.7	2.8	0.3	n.a.	n.a.	n.a.	n.a.	91.5[g]
1842[f]	64.4	10.6	8.2	4.0	3.4	0.3	n.a.	n.a.	n.a.	n.a.	90.9[g]
Ave., 1840–42	67.0%	7.8%	9.2%	3.4%	3.4%	0.3%	n.a.	n.a.	n.a.	n.a.	90.9%[g]

TABLE 1 (continued)

Year	Sugar	Tobacco[a]	Cotton	Coffee	Sugarcane brandy	Cocoa	Hides, etc.[b]	Gold	Timber[c]	Diamonds	Total
1851	69.5%	12.9%	3.3%	4.3%	1.8%	0.5%	2.1%	—	0.9%	3.4%	99.0%
1852	58.3	14.5	3.5	4.2	2.2	0.5	3.1	*	1.6	10.8	98.7
1853	66.5	8.2	3.6	3.3	2.7	0.3	2.4	*	1.0	11.5	99.5
1854	59.5	17.0	0.8	4.7	4.1	0.6	4.3	*	2.1	5.6	98.7
1855	53.6	14.1	1.1	8.6	6.1	0.5	5.6	*	1.2	8.1	98.9
1856	49.4	12.8	2.0	8.0	4.1	0.9	5.6	*	0.7	15.2	98.4
1857	50.3	16.7	2.1	6.8	3.0	0.8	5.5	—	0.9	13.0	99.1
1858	43.8	14.4	1.1	8.9	4.4	2.3	7.2	*	1.4	10.1	93.6
1859	56.8	15.9	0.4	6.0	2.7	0.8	3.7	0.2%	1.6	9.9	98.0
1860	26.6	21.9	0.6	9.3	1.2	1.6	6.7	0.3	3.6	14.5	86.3
Ave., 1851-60	53.5%	14.8%	1.9%	6.4%	3.2%	0.9%	4.6%	*	1.5%	10.2%	97.0%

SOURCES: Arruda, O Brasil, pp. 204, 360–61, 375–76, 381–82, 400–401, 407–8, 418–19; ST, 26: 338–40; Bahia, Falla (1854, J. M. Wanderley), "Mappa . . . da exportação . . . 1851 . . . 1853," n.p.; idem, Falla (1855, J. M. Wanderley), "Mappa . . . da exportação . . .," n.p.; idem, Falla (1857, J. L. V. Cansanção de Sinimbu), "Mappa . . . dos generos nacionaes exportados . . .," n.p.; idem, Falla (1861, A. da Costa Pinto, "Recapitulação das mercadorias nacionaes exportadas . . .," n.p.

NOTE: n.a. = no information available on the value of exports; * = less than 0.1 percent; — = no exports of this commodity reported for the year in question.

[a] Includes cigars, snuff, and other tobacco products.

[b] Includes raw and tanned hides, half soles, and other leather goods.

[c] Excludes firewood.

[d] Excludes the value of tobacco products.

[e] The percentages shown for the period 1796–1807 are based on the value of exports to Portugal. They do not therefore take into account trade with Africa and Portuguese India (Goa), for which detailed information on the composition and value of exports is not available. Only in the case of tobacco does this lack of information present a serious problem. Earlier in the eighteenth century, the volume of tobacco exported to West Africa was only slightly smaller than the amounts shipped to Portugal. (See Alden, "Late Colonial Brazil," pp. 622–23). There is every reason to believe that Bahia continued to export large amounts of tobacco to West Africa and smaller amounts to West Central Africa and to Goa. As a result, percentages based solely on trade with Portugal significantly understate the weight of tobacco exports within the Bahian economy. I have therefore estimated adjusted averages for the period 1796–1807. In calculating these estimates, I have assumed (1) that exports to Africa and Goa accounted for 47.6% of all tobacco shipped overseas (a conservative estimate because it is based on shipments to West Africa alone) and (2) that the unit value of the tobacco sent to Africa and India was, on average, half that of tobacco exported to Portugal.

[f] Calculated against estimates of the total value of Bahian exports. The British consul recorded the value of exports for nine commodities (sugar, cotton, coffee, cocoa, rice, "tapioca," tobacco, sugarcane brandy, and molasses) for 1840, 1841, and 1842. His figure for 1840 amounts to 91.06 percent of the value of all exports as reported by the provincial president. The total value of exports for 1841 and 1842 was estimated on the assumption that the same nine commodities also supplied 91.06% of all export revenues in those years.

[g] Does not include hides, gold, timber, or diamonds.

from other Northeastern captaincies. Cotton production in Bahia averaged only 51,000 arrobas a year in the 1830s, while annual exports from Salvador often surpassed 200,000 arrobas. By the early 1850s, Bahian-grown cotton accounted for only a small portion—perhaps less than 25 percent—of all the cotton the province exported.[15]

COFFEE

Coffee would ultimately prove the most successful of all the new export crops of Brazil's late colonial agricultural renaissance, but few observers in the 1780s or 1790s could have foreseen its future importance. Coffee cultivation in Brazil began in the 1720s. Over the next 80 years, exports increased, but coffee remained a minor item in Brazil's foreign trade; it ranked only eighth among all exports in the first years of the nineteenth century. After that, however, it assumed enormous importance in the Brazilian economy. In the 1830s, coffee, produced mainly in Southeastern Brazil, took sugar's place as the country's chief export staple and came to account for more than half of all Brazilian exports in the 1850s. The country had by then established itself as the largest supplier to the world's market.[16]

Unlike Rio de Janeiro or São Paulo, Bahia never became a major center of coffee production. Nevertheless, the crop made considerable progress in the province. Details about the beginnings of cultivation in Bahia remain obscure. The earliest recorded shipment from Salvador to Lisbon took place in 1777 and consisted of a mere 33 arrobas. By the late 1790s, annual exports had reached an average of 2,500 arrobas (see Figure 2). That average doubled in the first five years of the next century.[17]

Much of the coffee exported from Salvador at this time came from the comarca of Ilhéus, just south of the Recôncavo. There, farmers in the township of Camamu had begun to plant coffee at least by the early 1780s; from Camamu, the new crop spread to neighboring townships. Some coffee may have also come from the comarca of Porto Seguro in far southern Bahia. Two wandering Italian missionaries reportedly introduced the beverage to residents of Porto Seguro around 1788. Soon afterward, farmers in the area began to plant coffee groves with the seeds the missionaries had left.[18]

After 1810, information on total coffee exports virtually disappears. Nevertheless, it is clear that exports generally increased between 1810 and 1830. Coffee cultivation was expanding in those years; output surely grew as well. By the second decade of the nineteenth century, the crop was no longer restricted to coastal areas to the south of the Recôncavo; it was also being grown in the parish of Muritiba in the township of Cachoeira and had, in all likelihood, already begun to spread into the cassava-growing districts of the southern Recôncavo.[19]

By midcentury, three main centers of coffee production had emerged in Bahia. The first was located near Porto Seguro and Caravelas along the province's extreme southern coast. Growers in this region exported much of their output through Rio de Janeiro rather than through Salvador. A large

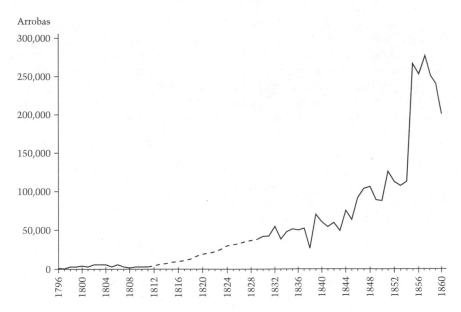

Figure 2. Bahia. Coffee Exports, 1796–1860 (in arrobas).
SOURCES. Arruda, *O Brasil*, pp. 418–19; "Mappa da Exportação . . . em 1808,"
BN, I-17,12,4; "Mappa da Exportação . . . em 1809," APEB, SH, 146, fol., 567;
Almanach, p. 246; Spix and Martius, 2: 661; Soares, *Notas*, p. 241; *ST*, 26: 338–
40; Bahia, *Falla* (1854, J. M. Wanderley), "Mappa . . . da exportação . . . 1851 . . .
1853," n.p.; idem, *Falla* (1855, J. M. Wanderley), "Mappa . . . da exportação," n.p.;
idem, *Falla* (1857, J. L. V. Cansanção de Sinimbu), "Mappa . . . dos generos nacionaes exportados . . . ," n.p.; idem, *Falla* (1861, A. da Costa Pinto), "Recapitulação
das mercadorias nacionaes exportadas . . . ," n.p.

part of that output came from the Colônia Leopoldina, a settlement of
mostly German and Swiss immigrants founded in 1818. Much farther north,
coffee had become the principal export crop in the townships of Camamu,
Ilhéus, and Valença. The third main area lay in the Recôncavo, stretching
from Nazaré north into the township of Cachoeira as far as the River Paraguaçu.[20] There, higher elevations and heavier rainfall favored coffee and allowed farmers to develop a superior variety known as Maragogipe, distinguished by its large berries and aromatic flavor.[21]

The results of expanding production were already evident in the early
1830s, when Bahia was exporting, on average, 46,000 arrobas a year. That
amounted to nearly an eightfold increase over the previous twenty years.
The next two decades saw even greater growth, so that by the late 1850s,
annual exports reached an average of more than 243,000 arrobas.[22]

Nevertheless, Bahia supplied in the 1850s only about 2 percent of the
coffee exported from Brazil. Although the coffee trade continued to grow
after 1860, Bahia's share did not increase substantially. Moreover, large-
scale monocultural production of coffee failed to develop in Bahia; the crop

rarely gave rise to great estates like those in Southeastern Brazil, where coffee plantations sometimes had well over a hundred slaves and several hundred thousand trees.[23] The 55 coffee "plantations" (*fazendas*) at the Colônia Leopoldina in far southern Bahia were perhaps the only exceptions to this rule, but even they tended to be modest in size. A few of these "plantations" had no slaves at all. Elsewhere in Bahia, farmers generally planted coffee as a secondary rather than a main crop. Their groves seldom contained more than a few thousand trees and were often much smaller.[24]

TOBACCO

Tobacco stood apart from such novelties as cotton, coffee, or cocoa; it had long ranked as one of the chief staples of Bahia's export trade, second in importance only to sugar. Commercial cultivation of the crop commonly and appropriately known in Brazil as *fumo* (smoke) began before 1640, and by the early eighteenth century, Bahian tobacco had well-established markets in Europe, Asia, and North America. Bahia, moreover, virtually monopolized the Brazilian tobacco trade. The "fields of Cachoeira" and farms in the townships beyond the Recôncavo's edges supplied almost all the tobacco sent to Portugal—perhaps nine-tenths in the seventeenth and eighteenth centuries and an even higher share (over 99 percent) in the years 1796–1811.[25]

The importance of Bahian tobacco did not escape the attention of colonial and metropolitan authorities, who surrounded the tobacco trade with an unwieldy mass of controls and restrictions. They sought, on the one hand, to prevent smuggling and fraud, and on the other, to provide Portugal with a regular supply of high-quality tobacco for reexport to other European markets. The restrictions included the requirement that all tobacco brought to Salvador be stored in a single warehouse (the *casa de arrecadação*), where officials from the Board of Inspection (*Mesa de Inspeção*) examined it and judged its quality. They selected the rolls of first- and second-grade twist tobacco for export to Portugal and reserved the best leaf tobacco for annual shipments to Portuguese India (Goa) by a crown monopoly. Despite fraud, sometimes less than half the total harvest met the board's standards for approval; the rest was rejected as *refugado* (refuse).[26]

This refuse tobacco had a large market in Brazil; but far more important than local sales were exports to West Africa, where Bahian merchants exchanged low-grade tobacco for the slaves so necessary to the colony's entire economy.[27] Trade became freer after 1808 and much more so after independence in 1822, but at least some of the colonial restrictions apparently remained in effect until 1828, when the provincial government of Bahia abolished the Board of Inspection.[28]

Those restrictions and controls had never prevented marked fluctuations in the tobacco trade. By the 1670s, for example, the tobacco industry, like sugar production in Bahia, was facing a depression. For tobacco, however, the slump did not last long; it gave way to a new period of growth and expansion in the first half of the next century. Gold production in Southeastern Brazil in those decades required ever larger numbers of African slaves, obtained by Bahian merchants in exchange for tobacco. Thus, while yearly tobacco exports to Portugal remained constant at about 170,000 arrobas, those bound for West Africa grew from less than 30,000 arrobas to more than 200,000 between 1700 and 1750. But when gold production began to diminish after 1750 and the demand for African slaves in the mining districts fell off, tobacco exports likewise tended to stagnate. Between 1750 and 1766, exports to both Portugal and West Africa averaged only 320,000 arrobas a year.[29]

Tobacco growers and merchants found new opportunities to expand production and trade at the end of the eighteenth century, when the resurgence of export agriculture in Bahia and throughout Brazil stimulated the demand for slave labor. Wars and revolutions during the same period often brought higher prices and opened new markets. Already in the 1780s annual exports had nearly doubled to reach an average of 615,000 arrobas (see Figure 3). Later peaks, in the 1790s and in the years 1810–1815, confirmed tobacco's recovery. In the 1830s, Miguel Calmon du Pin e Almeida, the future marquess of Abrantes, recalled the first decade-and-a-half of the nineteenth century as a moment of great prosperity for the Bahian tobacco industry. Prices were high and credit easy. The brisk trade with both European and African markets encouraged "vast speculations," while the tobacco fields of Cachoeira expanded to form a seemingly endless "sea of green."[30]

Not even the "most somber spirit," Calmon went on to remark, would have then predicted the depression that shortly thereafter overtook the tobacco trade. In effect, exports began to decline from 1816 on. They recovered in 1821, but that one-year surge did not alter the general downward trend. Exports had reached their nadir by the early 1830s, when they averaged only 169,500 arrobas a year, roughly a quarter of the annual average for 1810–14. Although trade occasionally revived in the following years, no upward trend in exports would become visible until the late 1840s.

Poor growing conditions had played a part in bringing about the decline. A severe drought in 1817–19 left crops "burned" in the fields. Indeed, lack of rainfall in those years probably explains much of the sudden decline in exports between 1816 and 1820. Drought would strike again in 1831 and 1832, only to be followed by 30 months of heavy rainfall and then by another drought. At the same time, an epizootic plague reduced the herds of cattle needed to fertilize tobacco fields.[31]

The vagaries of weather explain the diminished harvests of specific years, but they could hardly have caused the prolonged depression in tobacco exports after 1815. Instead, the depression's main cause was the contraction of overseas markets for Bahian tobacco, both in Africa and in Europe, as a result of Brazil's independence from Portugal and British attempts to suppress the slave trade.

The British parliament had prohibited the importation of African slaves

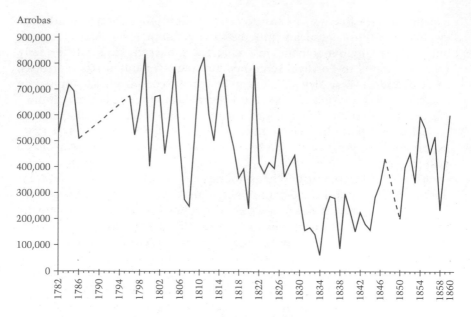

Figure 3. Bahia. Tobacco Exports, 1782–1860 (in arrobas).
SOURCES. Alden, "Late colonial Brazil," pp. 632–33; Arruda, *O Brasil*, pp. 381–
82; Lugar, "Merchant Community," p. 117 and "Portuguese Tobacco Trade," p.
54; "Mappa da Exportação . . . da Bahia . . . 1800," APEB, SH, 141, fol. 89; "Mappa
da Exportação . . . da Bahia . . . 1806," APEB, SH, 144, fol. 129; M. Calmon, *Memoria*, p. 39; Soares, *Notas*, p. 237; *ST*, 26: 338–40; Bahia, *Falla* (1854, J. M. Wanderley), "Mappa . . . da exportação," n.p.; idem, *Falla* (1855, J. M. Wanderley),
"Mappa . . . da exportação," n.p.; idem, *Falla* (1857, J. L. V. Cansanção de Sinimbu), "Mappa . . . dos generos nacionaes exportados . . . ," n.p.; idem, *Falla*
(1861, A. da Costa Pinto), "Recapitulação das mercadorias nacionaes exportadas . . . ," n.p.
NOTE. Total exports for 1782–86, 1796–1799, 1801–5, and 1807 were estimated
from the volume of tobacco shipped to Portugal. Alden ("Late colonial Brazil,"
pp. 632–33) has calculated for the eighteenth century that, on average, 52.4 percent of Bahian tobacco went to Portugal and the rest (47.6 percent) went to the
Mina Coast in West Africa and then used those percentages to estimate the "total" volume of tobacco exports for several years between 1750 and 1801. His
estimates for the years 1782–1786 are included in the series. Using the same
assumptions, I have calculated my own estimates for the years 1796–99, 1801–
1805, and 1807 with figures from the General Trade Accounts as reported by
Arruda (*O Brasil*, pp. 381–82) and Lugar ("Merchant Community," p. 117). These
estimates only approximate the true volume of Bahian tobacco exports since
they do not take into account the smaller amounts of tobacco shipped to Central
Africa and Goa.

into British colonies after 1 January 1808. Seven years later, at the Congress of Vienna, Britain sponsored a declaration, to be signed by all the major European powers, that committed them to eventually ending the transatlantic slave trade. Portugal, under British pressure, agreed to sign the declaration and even ratified a treaty with Britain that forbade the slave trade between the African coast north of the Equator and Brazil. Other countries moved effectively in the next decades to end their participation in the trade. Portugal did not; nor did the government of independent Brazil after 1822. Both Portugal before 1822 and Brazil after that date made only halfhearted efforts to abide by the 1815 treaty and to abolish slaving north of the Equator. Similarly, Brazilian authorities largely ignored an 1826 treaty that made the importation of slaves from any part of Africa illegal after March 1830. The slave trade to Brazil flourished between 1830 and 1850 as never before; despite the treaties, well over one-half million slaves were imported from Africa. Only after 1850 did the slave trade finally end when, again under British coercion, the Brazilian parliament passed another law prohibiting the importation of African slaves.[32]

Although it was ineffective in curbing the slave trade, the 1815 treaty apparently did have an impact on the Bahian tobacco trade. News of the treaty depressed the price of tobacco and put an end to the "vast speculations" in refugado tobacco in Salvador's market. Of course, as long as Bahian merchants continued to sail for the coast of Africa to procure slaves, growers still had an outlet for their low-grade tobacco. Increasingly limited, however, were the opportunities to sell that tobacco to slave traders of other nations. The Dutch at the fortress of El-Mina (in modern Ghana) had long acquired rolls of Bahian tobacco for their own slave trade by levying a toll on slave ships from Bahia. British slavers on the coast had regularly exchanged manufactures for Bahian tobacco. Together with the French, they had also bought tobacco at Lisbon before sailing for Africa. In 1790, the director of the Portuguese fortress of Ajudá (Ouida or Whydah in present-day Benin) complained that the English and the French were ruining the slave trade on that stretch of the coast by flooding local markets with Bahian tobacco purchased at Lisbon.[33]

More important for tobacco, perhaps, was that while the slave trade to Brazil as a whole thrived, the slave trade specifically to Bahia seems to have suffered a substantial decline after 1830. Bahian merchants had in the previous five years imported record numbers of slaves, partly out of fear that the impending ban might indeed be effective. With Salvador's market abundantly stocked with African captives, the volume of imports fell to much lower levels and would not revive again until the late 1840s.[34] This decline in the slave trade surely diminished the demand for tobacco.

By that time, Bahian tobacco had already lost some of its traditional European markets. The war for independence in 1822–23 had temporarily paralyzed the tobacco trade. During the first six months of 1823, not a single ship laden with tobacco sailed from Cachoeira, seat of the provisional government, for Salvador, still held by Portuguese troops. Shipments resumed in late 1823 with the end of the war, but many of the Portuguese merchants involved in the export trade now began to abandon Bahia. Their evacuation severed commercial links. As a result, importers in Portugal had to look elsewhere for supplies, as did their clients in Spain and Italy who had depended on Portuguese reexports of Bahian tobacco. Moreover, tobacco from Brazil no longer received automatic preference in the purchases made by the Portuguese state monopoly. Gone, too, were the monopoly's annual shipments from Bahia to India.[35]

The loss of these markets occurred at a time when the forms of tobacco consumption in Europe were undergoing fundamental changes. Quid chewing, for which the twist tobacco produced in Bahia was well suited, had already gone out of fashion, and preferences were once again changing. European consumers increasingly were switching from snuff and pipe tobacco to cigars. Cigars, in turn, required cured leaf tobacco such as that supplied by Cuban growers. Thus, to regain European markets, growers in Bahia needed to adapt to the change by producing leaf tobacco rather than tobacco prepared as twists, in which they had traditionally specialized. Yet Bahian growers seem to have responded slowly to the changing patterns of European tobacco consumption. Shipments of leaf tobacco declined from 15 percent of all exports in 1820 to less than 4 percent by 1829. Even in the mid-1840s, when its share had grown, leaf tobacco still represented less than one-fifth of all the tobacco shipped from Bahia. The continuing importance of twist tobacco in the transatlantic slave trade quite possibly discouraged a more rapid shift to leaf tobacco.[36]

The slow reaction of Bahian growers did not result from unfamiliarity with leaf tobacco or its preparation. The first experiments with a Cuban variety of leaf tobacco and with North American curing methods took place in 1757. Although the Cuban variety apparently failed to gain acceptance among Bahian farmers, they did begin to produce some leaf tobacco. From the mid-1770s on, a regular supply of cured leaf tobacco, pressed into bales, reached Salvador for export to Goa. Cuban and Virginian varieties were reintroduced in the 1780s and then again in 1810; after independence, provincial authorities continued to promote their cultivation and improvements in the curing and pressing of leaf tobacco. The record of a shipment of seven "bales" (fardos) of cigars from Cachoeira to Salvador in 1829 further indicates that by that date, Bahians had mastered the art of cigarmaking. Yet the few existing tobacco "factories" in the province in the first half of the nineteenth century produced mainly snuff rather than cigars.[37]

Bahian growers did finally shift on a large scale from twist to leaf tobacco in the late 1840s. Throughout the next decade, leaf tobacco accounted for the bulk of all tobacco exports (over 75 percent on average). That change and increasing international prices for tobacco laid the foundation for a revival of the tobacco trade.[38] The upward trend in exports that began about 1846 continued into the next decade. Bahia was exporting by the late 1850s an average of nearly 475,000 arrobas a year—almost a threefold increase over the average for 1830–34.

Although still partial, the recovery was solid. It had brought about the geographic expansion in the cultivation of tobacco, which became a major export crop in the cassava-growing districts of the southern Recôncavo. At the same time, a domestic cigarmaking industry had developed in and around the towns of Cachoeira, São Félix, Maragogipe, and Nazaré, providing full- or part-time employment for a large number of free workers and slaves. Together with recently founded factories, the cottage industry manufactured for export alone more than 1.5 million cigars and cigarettes a year in the 1850s. Output for local consumption must have also been considerable. The shift to leaf tobacco, the spread of cultivation, and a growing cigar industry would allow a full recovery of tobacco exports to their former levels in the years after 1860.[39]

SUGAR

In any survey of Bahia's export economy, the sugar trade necessarily commands a special place. Sugar was the province's oldest agricultural export; the Portuguese colonists who settled the Recôncavo in the mid-sixteenth century had crossed the Atlantic with plans to cultivate cane and establish mills. In the following centuries, other products entered the roll of Bahian exports; but none, before the late nineteenth century, ever rivaled sugar. This staple rarely accounted for less than 45 percent of all export revenues in the period 1780–1860, and its share was often greater. The Bahian export economy as result could know no true prosperity when depressed conditions prevailed in the sugar trade.

For a hundred years, from the 1680s to the 1780s, depression and stagnation did characterize the sugar trade. A sustained recovery began only in the last decades of the eighteenth century. This late colonial resurgence certainly owed much to the great slave rebellions that forced the collapse of Saint-Domingue in the 1790s. Those rebellions, as they became a revolutionary struggle for independence and against slavery, opened up vast new opportunities for the growth of sugar production in Brazil and elsewhere. Yet in Bahia, sugar's recovery began more than a decade earlier. The war for independence in British North America disrupted trade between the Caribbean and Europe in the late 1770s and left planters in the English colonies of the West Indies cut off from supplies of essential provisions. The result was a surge in sugar prices both in London and in Salvador.[40]

Although Bahian planters must have welcomed the surge, they no doubt remained cautious. In the past, they had seen sugar prices soar during wars and then fall again to very low levels as soon as peace was restored. Prices in Salvador dropped sharply after 1782, to the alarm of observers such as Luís Antônio de Oliveira Mendes; but by the end of the decade, they rose again. As prices increased in the 1790s, planters gained confidence in the recovery and translated their confidence into expanded production. Whereas sugar exports before 1770 had generally stood at about 400,000 arrobas a year, Mendes estimated that in the 1780s they averaged 480,000 arrobas. Even so, they still fell short of the 507,000 arrobas that João André Antonil had reckoned for the captaincy's total output of sugar in 1710.[41]

Shipments of sugar from Salvador (which also included exports from Sergipe) would pass that mark in the late 1790s, when they rose to an annual average of nearly 760,000 arrobas (see Figure 4). The long decades of stagnation and decline had definitely ended; exports would, despite occasional downturns, remain strong for the next 30 years. Already in 1798, the governor of Bahia, Dom Fernando José de Portugal, could report to his superiors in Lisbon that sugar production had "grown extraordinarily" during his term in office and that an "infinite number of engenhos" had been built.[42] Table 2 shows that the number of engenhos had in fact increased, from 126 in the mid-1750s to 260 by the end of the eighteenth century.

Records for annual output at Bahian engenhos supply further evidence of sugar's late colonial recovery. Those records become available from 1807 on, as a result of a reform in the royal tithe charged on sugar.[43] Until 1800, the Royal Treasury Board (Junta da Real Fazenda) in Salvador had farmed out the right to collect the tithe to a "contractor," usually a merchant, at regular public auctions. The system had worked well enough during the many years of stagnation in the sugar trade, but with sugar fetching "prices never before imagined," its efficiency came under official scrutiny. As merchants clamored for the right to collect the tithe and offered enormous sums for the contract, the governor of Bahia and the local Treasury Board became convinced that the tithe would yield greater revenues if the government assumed direct responsibility for its collection. The crown accepted the suggestion and in 1800 abolished the practice of farming out the tithe. In turn, after some initial experimentation, the Treasury Board devised a new system for assessing the tithe, which resembled the one already used for tobacco and which would remain in effect until 1842.[44]

Not least among the innovations introduced was an end to payment of the tithe in kind. The tithe contractor, under the old system, had collected one-tenth of all sugar produced. In their accounts, planters accordingly set aside one-tenth of each year's harvest as "belonging to God" (Cabe a Deus), to be delivered to the contractor.[45] After 1800, the Treasury Board assessed the tithe as 10 percent of the sugar's market value in Salvador, to be paid in cash.

This reform made it possible for the Treasury Board to keep close track of annual sugar production in the captaincy. (By "production," officials meant sugar brought to warehouses in Salvador from Bahia and Sergipe for local sale or export.) The production figures, compiled by the board after 1807, show the same upward trend as exports (see Figure 4). The average sugar harvest almost doubled in size between 1807 and 1820.

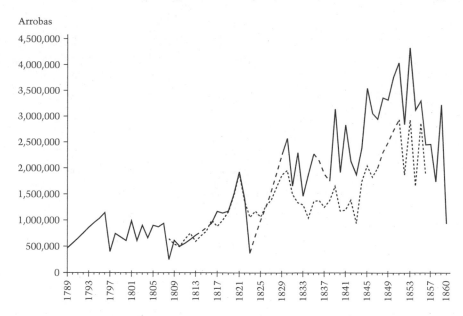

Arrobas

Figure 4. Bahia. Sugar Exports, 1789–1860; Sugar Production, 1808–56 (in arrobas).
SOURCES. For exports: [Mendes], p. 315; Arruda, *O Brasil*, pp. 360–61, 375–76; "Mappa da Exportação . . . Bahia . . . 1808," BN, I-17,12,4; "Mappa da Exportação . . . Bahia . . . 1809," APEB, SH, 146, fol. 567; *Almanach*, p. 246; Spix and Martius, 2: 661–62; Walsh, 2: 535; Sturz, p. 102; Fairbanks, p. xii; Soares, *Notas*, p. 230; Bahia, *Falla* (1854, J. M. Wanderley), "Mappa . . . da exportaçao . . . 1851 . . . 1853," n.p.; idem, *Falla* (1855, J. M. Wanderley), "Mappa . . . da exportação," n.p.; idem, *Falla* (1857, J. L. V. Cansanção de Sinimbu), "Mappa . . . dos generos nacionaes exportados . . . ," n.p.; and idem, *Falla* (1861, A. da Costa Pinto), "Recapitulação das mercadorias nacionaes exportadas . . . ," n.p.; Bahia, . . . , CPE, *A inserção*, 2: 20 and 4: 103, 106. For production: Soares, *Notas*, p. 238; M. Calmon, *Ensaio*, pp. 188–89; Fairbanks, p. xiii; tables for annual "*safras* [harvests]" of sugar and other commodities on unnumbered pages in Bahia, *Falla* (1853, J. M. Wanderley); idem, *Falla* (1854, J. M. Wanderley); idem, *Falla* (1855, J. M. Wanderley); idem, *Falla* (1856, A. T. de Moncorvo e Lima); and idem, *Falla* (1857, J. L. V. Cansanção de Sinimbu).
NOTE. Solid line = exports of sugar (in arrobas); dotted line = production of sugar (in arrobas).

Under the new system, the Treasury Board also attempted to make allowances for the higher transport costs that producers farther away from Salvador had to pay. Each engenho now received a "discount" in the tithe based on its distance from Salvador. The board therefore began to keep a register of sugar plantations. As newly built engenhos started to send sugar to Salvador, their names were added to the register. This practice provides yet another measure by which to gauge sugar's continued resurgence in

TABLE 2

Engenhos in Bahia, Selected Years, 1710–1925

Year	Bahia and Sergipe	Bahia	Year	Bahia
1710	146	n.a.	1837	540+
1755	172	126	1852	800[a]
ca. 1790–95	353	221	1855	1,274[b]
ca. 1799	400	260	1873	892
1818	469	315	1925	705[c]

SOURCES: Antonil, p. 274; J. Caldas, pp. 222–27; "Quadro dos engenhos," [ca. 1790–95], BN, 7,3,27; Vilhena, 1: 57; "Matrícula dos Engenhos da Capitania da Bahia pelos Dízimos Reais administrados pela Junta da Real Fazenda" [1807–1874], APEB, SH, 642; Sturz, p. 102; Soares, *Notas*, p. 227; Bahia, *Falla* (1855, J. M. Wanderley), p. 38; *EL*, [Bahia], table "B," n.p.; Grangier, p. 54.

[a] "800 big mills" and perhaps more than 400 engenhocas.

[b] Includes engenhocas.

[c] Does not include the 5,866 engenhocas in Bahia in 1925 and probably excludes the 17 *usinas* (plantations that also served as central sugar factories) then operating in the state.

these years. Between 1807 and 1818, the board registered 315 engenhos in Bahia proper and 154 more in Sergipe, many of which had recently been built (see Table 3).[46] Just before independence, the total for Bahia had grown to 341, fully 80 more engenhos than had existed in the late 1790s.

Historians have sometimes assumed that independence brought an abrupt end to sugar's late colonial revival. On this matter, they have agreed with the assessment made by Francisco Marques de Góes Calmon in 1925. For Góes Calmon, the brief war for independence (1822–23) dealt the prov-

TABLE 3

Engenhos Registered with the Tithe Authorities, Bahia, 1807–74

Years	Average number of new engenhos registered per year	Total number of new engenhos registered	Cumulative total
1807–18[a]	—	—	315
1818–20[b]	8.7	26	341
1821–29	12.2	110	451
1830–34	26.4	132	583
1835–39	11.6	58	641
1840–44[c]	3.2	16	657
1845–49	10.8	54	711
1850–54	13.2	66	777
1855–59	6.2	31	808
1860–64	3.6	18	826
1865–69	1.8	9	835
1870–74	1.0	5	840

SOURCE: "Matrícula dos Engenhos . . . ," APEB, SH, 642.

NOTE: The numbers shown refer only to engenhos located in Bahia proper (excluding Sergipe). Obvious duplicate registrations have also been excluded.

[a] 30 Sept. 1807 to 24 July 1818. Engenhos registered during this period include plantations established before 1807.

[b] 25 July 1818 to 18 Dec. 1820.

[c] After 1842, planters were no longer required to register new engenhos.

ince's economy a "terrible blow" and unleashed an "endless series of misfortunes" that would "pursue" Bahia throughout the rest of the nineteenth century. Plantations were razed, lives and capital lost.[47]

On balance, however, the evidence hardly bears out the view that independence provoked a sudden depression in Bahia's sugar industry. Both exports and production, it is true, fell after 1822. At the same time, the prices paid for sugar in London had begun a steady fall. But a similar decline in the exchange rate of the mil-réis largely offset the fall in prices.[48] Lower prices, in any event, do not seem to have discouraged planters, who worked quickly to restore output to its former levels. Sugar production, as a result of their efforts, fully recovered by the late 1820s from whatever damage the war had caused. By that time, moreover, Sergipe had become an autonomous province, no longer administratively subordinated to Bahia. The tithe authorities in Salvador accordingly stopped including sugar from Sergipe in their production records. Thus, the greater harvests registered after 1825 reflect the output of Bahian mills alone. Those harvests allowed Bahia to export in 1829 and 1830 more sugar than in any year before independence.

A surge in investments in new plantations provides further proof of sugar's continuing strength. Bahians began in the 1820s to build engenhos in unprecedented numbers. They registered, on average, twelve new engenhos a year, to give Bahia a total of perhaps 450 plantations with mills by 1830, and many more were still being built. The construction of more than one hundred new engenhos in itself represented a vast flow of capital and energy into sugar—an investment on a scale that would be scarcely imaginable if the sugar industry had been depressed.

Conditions did indeed favor the establishment of new plantations. Prospects for tobacco, Bahia's other main export staple, worsened from one year to the next. In credit transactions, inflation may have shifted the balance between merchant lenders and landowning debtors to favor the latter. A plentiful supply of recently imported African slaves was on hand to form the work forces new plantations needed. A final stimulus came from the provincial government, which in 1827 abolished the requirement that planters obtain a license before building a new mill.[49]

Construction of an engenho still took usually between seven and eight years; seldom less than four.[50] As a result, many of the new engenhos planned in the late 1820s began to manufacture sugar only in the early 1830s. Between 1830 and 1834, the tithe authorities listed in their register an average of 26 new engenhos a year.

As those new engenhos started operations, many planters must have regretted the decisions made a few years earlier to invest in milling equipment. They found that the first harvests fell below their expectations when, in the early 1830s, Bahia suffered several years of drought, interspersed with excessively wet winters. Even before the weather turned against the planters, British merchants with experience in Salvador had come to believe that the province's sugar industry was no longer profitable. They knew that the restoration of peace in Europe and expanding production elsewhere in the Americas (especially in Cuba) had brought a slow but steady decline in the price of sugar. Prices in London fell from their all-time high of 97s a hundredweight in 1814 to under 40s in the mid-1830s. As the mil-réis gained strength against sterling, the exchange rate no longer offset the fall in prices. The merchants also knew that tariff barriers effectively barred Brazilian sugar from the British market. Whereas a hundredweight of sugar from British colonies in the East and West Indies was subject to a tariff of only 30s, the same quantity of foreign sugar paid duties in Britain of 63s.[51]

Falling prices and exclusion from the British market doubtless did much to bring a new period of stagnation to Bahia's sugar industry. Both production and exports failed to grow significantly after 1830; some years even saw slight declines. Sugar no longer attracted the interest of those with capital to invest; not a single new engenho was registered in either 1841 or 1842.

To overcome the slump, Bahian planters needed, at the very least, to find larger overseas markets for their sugar. Those markets appeared after 1845 in Germany and Great Britain. In 1845–46, the viscount (later marquess) of Abrantes, acting on behalf of the Brazilian government and in the interest of his own family (which owned several large engenhos in Bahia), negotiated a trade agreement with the German Customs Union that allowed Brazil to export sugar more freely to the Union's member states. Meanwhile, in Britain, advocates of free trade finally defeated the representatives of the West Indian sugar planters in Parliament. They succeeded in passing legislation in 1846 to lower duties on foreign sugar. Later legislation gradually eliminated the double tariff schedule that discriminated against sugar produced outside the British Empire.[52] The sugar trade at Bahia immediately revived. Exports increased rapidly from 1845 on, heading toward peaks of over four million arrobas in the early 1850s. Production likewise grew. Their confidence in sugar restored, Bahian planters once again built new engenhos.

The planters were perhaps too confident, for, although sugar's recovery impressed some observers, it was neither solid nor long-lasting. To be sure, Bahian sugars now entered Britain and Germany more freely, but prices there continued to fall—to below 25s a hundredweight in some years in London. Moreover, gaining access to larger European markets had come at a considerable cost; it had required a major change in the quality of the sugar produced by Bahian planters. The reductions in British and German tariffs applied above all to lower-grade sugars, the raw material for Great Britain's and Germany's own sugar-refining industries.

Thus, planters in Bahia could no longer turn out the superior clayed white sugars in which they had specialized since colonial times. Clayed whites, although unrefined, were suitable for immediate sale in overseas markets; they needed no further refining. Even though it meant forgoing the higher prices paid for clayed whites, Bahian planters lost little time in adapting production at their mills to European tariff schedules. Whereas clayed whites had made up two-fifths of all the sugar exported in the early

1850s, dark brown muscovado sugars, which required further refining, accounted for 80 percent of all exports by the end of that decade. The balance would continue to shift in the following years so that, by the mid-1860s, few planters in Bahia bothered to clay any sugar at all.[53] Once suppliers of a finished product to the world market, they had become, in the 1850s, producers of cheap raw materials for a foreign industry.

By the mid-nineteenth century, the fluctuating world demand for Bahian sugar not only had led to changes in the quality of sugar exported from Salvador; it had also brought about a great expansion in the cultivation of cane in Bahia. Although neither tobacco nor cassava ever disappeared from the Recôncavo, the successive upturns in sugar exports from the late eighteenth century on spread cane throughout the region and beyond.

Thanks to the register of engenhos kept by the Treasury Board after 1807, we can accurately trace the geographic expansion of sugar production until 1842. The register records the name of every engenho, its owner, its location (township and often parish as well), and its distance from the nearest local port—information the board needed to implement its reformed system of assessing the tithe on sugar. After 1842, when a simple export tax replaced the tithe, planters were no longer required to register new engenhos; some did, others did not.[54] The authorities, moreover, made no attempt to remove from the register engenhos that had ceased production. Consequently, for information about the geography of the sugar industry after 1842, we must depend on an official survey carried out in 1873–74. Since relatively few new plantations seem to have been established after 1860, the survey may be taken as a fairly reliable guide to the location of Bahian engenhos at midcentury. Finally, it is worth noting that neither source contains information on engenhocas—the smaller mills that made rapaduras (cakes of dark brown sugar) for local consumption and distilled cachaça (cane brandy) for sale both in Brazil and abroad. Often the construction of engenhocas in an area represented the first step toward the development of larger mills, true plantations that would produce sugar for foreign markets.

As a result, Tables 4 and 5 show only the expansion of *export-oriented* sugar production. Although engenhos seemingly sprang up everywhere, that expansion occurred along four main fronts. The first of these extended north from Salvador into the townships of Abrantes and Mata de São João, and on into the coastal and inland areas beyond the Recôncavo. These areas included districts where, until the early nineteenth century, tobacco and cotton had been the chief export crops. Although the climate there was generally drier than in districts near the bay, planters found, along the river valleys, well-watered bottomlands that were suitable for the cultivation of cane.

The second route of sugar expansion was into the townships of the southern Recôncavo, which had specialized in the production of farinha in the late eighteenth century. Here, large stands of forests, numerous free-flowing streams and rivers all favored the establishment of sugar planta-

TABLE 4

Geographic Distribution of Engenhos in
Bahia, 1818, 1829, 1842, and 1873

Location	1818		1829		1842		1873	
	No.	Pct.	No.	Pct.	No.	Pct.	No.	Pct.
Recôncavo	292	92.7%	385	85.4%	505	78.2%	635	71.2%
Coastal townships north of the Recôncavo[a]	13	4.1	27	6.0	52	8.0	70	7.8
Inland townships north of the Recôncavo[b]	3	1.0	22	4.9	54	8.4	54	6.1
Townships west of the Recôncavo[c]	5	1.6	7	1.6	12	1.9	9	1.0
Townships southwest of the Recôncavo[d]	0	0.0	0	0.0	0	0.0	82	9.2
Coastal townships south of the Recôncavo[e]	2	0.6	9	2.0	17	2.6	42	4.7
TOTAL	315		451[f]		646[f]		892	

SOURCES: "Matrícula dos Engenhos . . . ," APEB, SH, 642; EL, [Bahia], table "B," n.p.
[a] Conde, Abadia, and Entre Rios.
[b] Inhambupe, Alagoinhas, and Itapicuru.
[c] Purificação and Feira de Santana.
[d] Tapera and Jiquiriçá.
[e] Valença, Taperoá, Camamu, Barra do Rio de Contas, Maraú, Ilhéus, and Porto Seguro.
[f] Includes engenhos located in unspecified townships (1 in 1829 and 6 in 1842).

tions—so much so that, by the mid-nineteenth century, Nazaré and Marago-gipe had nearly as many engenhos as the traditional cane-growing townships of Santo Amaro and São Francisco do Conde on the other side of the bay. From the southern Recôncavo, sugar production spread further inland; it also expanded south along the coast into areas that, like Nazaré and Marago-gipe, had once been devoted almost exclusively to cassava cultivation.

The third front was the tobacco-growing parishes of Cachoeira. Tobac-co's severe decline after 1820 no doubt encouraged wealthier farmers in these parishes to switch to cane and to invest in milling equipment. Once the tobacco trade began to recover in the middle of the nineteenth century, cane's expansion halted and the number of engenhos in the tobacco dis-tricts fell.[55]

Fourth, sugar expanded on the northern side of the bay in the traditional cane-growing districts. The construction of some 80 new engenhos here guaranteed that despite the spread of cane into other areas, these districts would always remain the center of Bahia's sugar industry. Most of the expan-sion in the northern Recôncavo took place in such inland parishes as Rio Fundo and Bom Jardim in Santo Amaro, and São Sebastião do Passé and Catu in São Francisco do Conde. Yet there was also room for some expansion nearer the bay. To build an engenho in a bayshore parish, a planter might need to subdivide an existing estate; nevertheless, new engenhos close to the bay were not necessarily small. On the contrary, they included large plantations.[56]

In sum, the spread of cane considerably transformed the Recôncavo.

Whereas in the late eighteenth century, sugar production had been concentrated in a relatively small area along the northern shore of the bay, eight decades later, engenhos could be found in parishes throughout the Recôncavo.

Tendencies and Fluctuations

This chapter might conclude with a few summary observations. Bahian exports of sugar and coffee underwent long-term growth between 1780 and 1860; trade in cotton and tobacco suffered a long-term decline. In the case of cotton, the decline would continue throughout the rest of the nineteenth century; for tobacco, the downward trend in exports was reversed by the 1850s. Knowledge of these trends is certainly valuable, but even a brief sur-

TABLE 5

Geographic Distribution of Engenhos
in the Recôncavo, 1818, 1829, 1842, and 1873

	1818		1829		1842		1873	
Location	No.	Pct.	No.	Pct.	No.	Pct.	No.	Pct.
Traditional sugar districts of the northern Recôncavo								
Bayshore parishes[a]	128	43.9%	141	36.6%	157	31.1%	166[b]	26.1%
Other parishes[c]	90	30.8	115	29.9	136	26.9	154	24.3
SUBTOTAL[d]	239	81.8	284	73.8	322	63.8	320	50.4
Tobacco-growing parishes of Cachoeira[e]	19	6.5	27	7.0	48	9.5	20	3.1
Cassava-growing townships of the southern Recôncavo[f]	19	6.5	35	9.1	69	13.7	214	33.7
Northeastern Recôncavo[g]	14	4.8	38	9.9	61	12.1	81	12.8
Itaparica	1	0.3	1	0.3	5	1.0	0	0.0
TOTAL	292		385		505		635	

SOURCES: "Matrícula dos Engenhos . . . ," APEB, SH, 642; EL, [Bahia], table "B," n.p. The location of engenhos, where information on the matter was incomplete or ambiguous in the "Matrícula," was determined with the following sources: B. da S. Lisboa, "Memoria sobre a Provincia da Bahia . . ."; "Divizão dos Districtos das Freguezias da Villa de S. Franco, e seu termo" (1833), APEB, SH, 1433; parish surveys of engenhos (1854) in APEB, SH, 4597; the "Registros eclesiásticos de terras" in APEB, SH; Sampaio, Carta; Brazil . . . , IBGE, . . . , Carta do Brasil—escala 1:100 000, folha SD-24-J-I: Jaguaripe; idem, Carta do Brasil—escala 1:100 000, folha SD-24-X-A-IV: Baía de Todos os Santos; Brazil, . . . , SUDENE, Região Nordeste do Brasil—1:100.000, folha SD-24-V-B-III: Santo Estêvão; idem, Região Nordeste do Brasil—1:100.000, folha SD-24-V-B-IV: Santo Antônio de Jesus; idem, Região Nordeste do Brasil—1:100.000, folha SD-V-D-III: Valença; SEPLANTEC, Informações básicas, vols. 4 and 5 (municipal maps); and postmortem estate inventories, APEB, SJ, IT and ARC, IT.

[a] Pirajá, Cotegipe, Paripe, Matoim, Santana da Ilha de Maré, and Passé in the City of Salvador; S. Gonçalo da Vila de S. Francisco, Monte, and Socorro in the township of S. Francisco do Conde; N.S. do Rosário and N.S. da Purificação in the township of S. Amaro; and Iguape in the township of Cachoeira.

[b] Includes a few engenhos located in the parish of N.S. do Rosário do Porto da Cachoeira.

[c] All other parishes in the city of Salvador and in the townships of S. Amaro and S. Francisco do Conde.

[d] Includes engenhos located in unspecified parishes in the city of Salvador and in the townships of S. Amaro and S. Francisco do Conde.

[e] All parishes of Cachoeira except Santiago do Iguape.

[f] Maragogipe, Nazaré, and Jaguaripe.

[g] Abrantes and Mata de S. João.

vey of Bahia's export economy should not stop there. By definition, long-term trends reveal nothing about the equally significant short-term fluctuations that accompanied growth and decline. Although those fluctuations have been outlined in the preceding pages, there remains the task of showing how they sometimes coincided to form broader tendencies in the export economy as a whole. Indeed, narrowly focusing on the trends, long- or short-term, for specific products brings the risk of losing sight of Bahia's export economy as a whole. Its history would then become fragmented into the separate histories of sugar, tobacco, coffee, and cotton.

To avoid that risk, it is necessary to draw on all the evidence presented in this chapter. This in turn makes it possible to establish, for the export economy as a whole, the following rough periodization.[57]

1776–86: Recovery marked by an upturn in commercial activity at Salvador and probably also by exports that peaked in the early 1780s.

1787–1821: Prosperity based on substantial growth in the trade in major export staples, with high points in the late 1790s and the 1810s.

1822–29: Possibly slower growth as a result of, first, the disruption in trade during the war for independence and immediately thereafter; second, the persistent decline in tobacco exports; and third, increasing political and social unrest.[58]

1830–45: Depression characterized by decline or stagnation in exports of sugar, tobacco, and cotton; only trade in coffee, still a minor export staple, experienced growth.

1845–60: Recovery founded on the renewed growth in exports of sugar and tobacco and the continuing strength of coffee exports, and further stimulated by the trade in diamonds.

The recovery that began in the mid-1840s did not lead to another period of great prosperity comparable to the late colonial resurgence of export agriculture. It gave way, instead, to long decades of stagnation and decline. Total export revenues failed to grow in the years after 1860; for a growing population, that amounted to a decline in income from overseas trade. Accompanying this long-term stagnation were profound changes in Bahia's export economy, the first signs of which were already manifest in the late 1850s. The growth registered in exports of tobacco and coffee in those years continued apace after 1860. These two commodities came to account for an ever-larger share of the province's foreign trade; indeed, in some years, tobacco surpassed sugar as an earner of export revenues. Sugar's share of those revenues, by contrast, fell from about 50 percent at midcentury to below 30 percent by the 1870s.[59]

These changes were not merely relative; they reflected a long-lasting decline in the Bahian sugar industry. Sugar exports from Bahia stagnated from the mid-1850s on, even as other provinces in Northeastern Brazil produced more and more sugar for sale abroad. Then, in the late 1880s, the Bahian sugar trade nearly collapsed. In 1889, Bahia shipped overseas only 114,268 arrobas of sugar, an absolutely insignificant quantity that amounted to less than 3 percent of the sugar the province had exported in an average year in the mid-nineteenth century. The Bahian sugar industry would never fully recover from the collapse it suffered in 1889. As late as the decade 1900–1910, exports averaged only 8,600 metric tons a year, or about 600,000 arrobas—less than one-fifth than of their peak levels in the early 1850s.[60]

The changes went still further; they struck at the very foundations of Bahian export agriculture. For all practical purposes, Brazil ended its participation in the transatlantic slave trade by 1852. No longer would ships reach Bahian beaches, their holds filled with enslaved Africans to replenish the work forces on the province's plantations and farms. Slaves were still plentiful in the 1850s, but their number declined steadily in the following decades. The end of the slave trade, moreover, proved to be only the first in a series of measures that led to the complete abolition of slavery in Brazil in 1888. As the slave population dwindled and new laws restricted slavery as an institution, Bahian planters and farmers were forced to find alternatives to the system of labor on which they had depended since the first years of Portuguese settlement in the Recôncavo.

Stuart Schwartz, in his study of Bahian sugar plantations in the colonial period, writes that "to say 'Bahia' was to say the 'Recôncavo,' and the Recôncavo was always engenhos, sugar, and slaves."[61] Although much changed, Schwartz's definition might still be loosely applied to the Recôncavo of the mid-nineteenth century; after 1860, it quickly became an anachronism.

CHAPTER 3

Farinha de Mandioca — "The Bread of the Land" — and Its Market

E xports of sugar, tobacco, and coffee might in good times yield fine profits for merchants in Salvador and for planters and farmers in the surrounding countryside, but the produce of Bahian export agriculture could not by itself sustain them. Sugar and coffee supplied at most a small part of their dietary needs; tobacco satisfied none. Nevertheless, the slaves who planted cane, tobacco, and coffee, the planters and farmers who were their masters, and the citizens of Salvador whose livelihoods in one way or another depended on a steady flow of commodities overseas—all had to eat. Somewhere and somehow, Bahians in both the city and the countryside had to obtain sustenance of some sort.

Their demand for what eighteenth- and nineteenth-century observers called "goods of first necessity," like the fluctuations in the export trade, helped shape the social and economic landscape of the rural Recôncavo. Local production to meet that demand, in turn, shared both conflicting and complementary relationships with Bahia's dominant export economy. This chapter takes a first step toward exploring those relationships by examining the regional market for farinha de mandioca (flour made from the root of the bitter cassava plant). For no other foodstuff, except perhaps fresh meat, is the documentary record so extensive. But the relative abundance of sources about farinha, its marketing, and its production only reflects its capital importance in Bahia. Cassava, for making flour, was by far the most widely cultivated food crop in the Recôncavo, and farinha was an indispensable staple in the Bahian diet. Therefore the purposes of this chapter are first to establish farinha's importance as a staple breadstuff, and second, to gauge the demand for marketed cassava flour.

Farinha in the Common Diet

The residents of eighteenth- and nineteenth-century Salvador, of course, ate a great deal more than just farinha. Bahians today take pride in the cuisine they have developed by combining Portuguese, West African, and American Indian ingredients and cooking techniques. Many of the dishes for which Bahian cuisine is now famous had come into use by the end of the eighteenth century. On the streets, slave women hawked *carurus, vatapás, acarajés, feijão de leite, abarás,* and "sweetmeats of an infinite variety." Climate and location, moreover, allowed Bahians to consume a broad range of foodstuffs. A year-round growing season kept the city's markets stocked with plentiful supplies of fresh vegetables and tropical fruits. The seaside location made shellfish and whale meat readily available; fresh fish, however, was often expensive. Living in a port city, Bahians could also include in their diet imported *carne de charque* or *carne seca* (jerked beef) from the River Plate and Southern Brazil; palm oil from West Africa; olive oil, wine, garlic, cheese, wheat flour, and salted codfish from Europe. But the humid coast had a disadvantage: it did not favor cattle ranching in Salvador's immediate hinterland. For fresh meat, the city relied on the herds raised in the distant but drier interior. Ranchers in the backlands of Bahia, Piauí, and Goiás sent their herds to the coast on long drives that provided an adequate, if irregular, supply of cattle for the city's stockyards. Although often of poor quality, fresh beef was widely consumed. By contrast, Bahians apparently ate little pork, mutton, or veal.[1]

Yet no matter how varied or even rich it may have been, the common diet rested on a few staples. Chief among these was farinha de mandioca. In this regard, the diet of most Bahians resembled that consumed until recently in many agricultural societies. Such a diet typically centers on complex carbohydrates, supplied by one or two main cereals or root crops eaten alone or combined with legumes, such as beans. Other foods—vegetables, fruits, oils, fats, meat, fish, and spices—may furnish vital nutrients, but their role as a source of calories is secondary.[2] Calories come overwhelmingly from a major staple starch; in Bahia, that staple starch was undoubtedly cassava flour.

Bahians, to be sure, ate other locally grown cereals and root crops; *aipim* (sweet cassava), yams, white sweet potatoes, maize, and rice all had a place in their diet. They also ate imported wheat. From the mid-1600s on, large amounts of bread made from imported wheat flour appeared on the tables of wealthier Bahians. But in the population as a whole, bread consumption remained limited, even at the end of the eighteenth century. Luís dos Santos Vilhena, the late colonial chronicler, remarked that only rich Portuguese

immigrants insisted on eating only bread made from wheat flour. For everyone else, farinha usually took its place. Indeed, native Brazilians and Africans living in Bahia regarded bread not "as sustenance, but rather as a treat."
"Experience," Vilhena went on to note, "has shown that when out of necessity they are given bread, they ask for farinha to eat with it; and such force
has this custom that even dogs, if given bread, smell it, but will not touch
it."[3]

Rice, maize, and beans were, without doubt, more widely consumed, but
none of them played more than a secondary role in the common diet. Of this
there is no better evidence than the records of Salvador's Public Granary
(Celeiro Público). Between 1785 and 1851, rice, maize, and beans together
represented only 12 percent of all the grains and cereals that entered the granary. Farinha alone accounted for the other 88 percent.[4]

Bahians, if they could afford to do so, ate every day at least one-tenth of
a quarter-alqueire of cassava flour (0.907 liters or approximately 567 grams).
This was the standard ration issued to the soldiers garrisoned in Salvador
and to the slaves employed by the Public Granary. Poor prisoners held in
Salvador's jails in the late 1860s received the same.[5]

Farinha was certainly no less basic in the countryside. It probably made
up an even larger share of the rural slave's diet. Given the harsh conditions
under which slaves labored, diet could make a great difference in their
chances of reaching middle age. Diet thus indirectly serves as one indicator
of slaves' physical treatment. More than that, food, its quantity, and its quality were part of the complex mixture of coercion and rewards that marked
relationships between masters and slaves in Brazil. Thus, writers from Jorge
Benci and André João Antonil in the 1700s to Miguel Calmon and Francisco
de Lacerda Werneck in the following century gave special attention to matters of food and diet in their recommendations to masters on the "government" of slaves. Yet most scholars today would agree that despite such recommendations, Brazilian slaves were often poorly or even wretchedly fed.[6]

To describe the slaves' diet as poor, however, tells nothing about what
slaves actually ate. Here we confront a major difficulty with the available
sources: they refer almost exclusively to a few basic and usually nonperish-
able or purchased staples. These certainly did not represent the full range of
foodstuffs slaves consumed; they ate anything edible that came within their
grasp.[7] Nevertheless, those sources do indicate that the two main staples of
the slave diet were jerked beef and farinha de mandioca.[8]

The jerked beef, which was the slaves' main source of protein, came in
the form of either imported carne seca or its local equivalent, *carne do sertão*, from the backlands of the Northeast. Slaves occasionally received
smaller amounts of fresh beef as well. During Lent, some planters issued
salted codfish instead. Poultry rarely entered the diet of most slaves unless
they raised their own fowl. Only the sick received chickens from their masters, and even then they did not always have the chance to eat them. The
administrator of three engenhos in the parish of Matoim, for example,

bought several chickens in 1822 and 1823 for sick slaves, but he used them to prepare homemade *vomitórios* (emetic remedies).[9]

Bacon (*toucinho*) was likewise a great rarity. After the death of Francisco de Oliveira Guedes in 1858, an executor took over the management of his two engenhos near Maragogipe until the final settlement of his estate in 1864. The executor's purchases of not only carne seca and fresh meat but also butter and bacon led to a dispute with one of Guedes's heirs. These items, the heir complained, did not belong in the slave diet. The executor responded that he had bought them not for the slaves but for the overseers, craters (*caixeiros*), and craftsmen he had hired to work on the engenhos. These free employees could not "be treated like slaves" and be expected to "eat only boiled or jerked beef with no bacon."[10] Shellfish, however, did serve as a supplementary source of protein in the diet of rural slaves. Engenhos and larger cane farms located near the bay sometimes had slaves specially trained in catching crabs, oysters, shrimp, and crawfish (*mariscadores* and *mariscadeiras*).

For carbohydrates and calories, rural slaves depended on the same staple starch that weighed so heavily in the diet of urban Bahians: farinha de mandioca. Rural slaves, no doubt, also consumed maize and beans, perhaps even in large amounts on tobacco farms; but only occasionally do the existing records mention these staples as part of the slave diet on sugar plantations. Just as in the city, moreover, the standard ration in the rural Recôncavo was a quarter-alqueire of cassava flour every ten days. Some planters issued a smaller ration: half of a quarter-alqueire per week (0.647 liters or 405 grams per day).

In both cases, this ration may seem implausibly large. It greatly surpasses the consumption of farinha even among the poorest residents of Salvador today. In the early 1960s, members of households with the lowest incomes in the city consumed, on average, 130 grams of cassava flour a day. The rations issued in eighteenth- and nineteenth-century Bahia stand out not only for their size but also for their monotony. This diet, moreover, based squarely on carne seca and large amounts of farinha, contrasts with the much more varied rations issued to slaves on coffee plantations in Southeastern Brazil during the same period. Slaves there regularly received *fubá* (coarsly ground maize), beans, rice, coffee, and bacon, as well as jerked beef and cassava flour.[11]

But despite these contrasts, the sources on this matter are consistent: for both free and slave in the Bahian countryside, they indicate, almost without exception, a daily ration of 0.907 or 0.647 liters of farinha. The few conflicting sources report even larger rations. For example, in the 1870s, Julius Naeher, who visited the Engenho Subaé near Santo Amaro, observed that the daily issue to slaves consisted of a piece of jerked beef and 1.5 or 2 liters of farinha. The slaves received nothing more to sustain them through a day's work.[12]

The two items that filled the slaves' hollowed-out calabashes at the Engenho Subaé would remain staples for laborers in the Bahian countryside long after the abolition of slavery. Information on the common diet in *rural* Bahia in more recent times bears this out. Surveys of plantation workers and poor tobacco farmers from the 1940s and the 1970s found a diet generally lacking in sufficient calories and consisting mainly of jerked beef, salted fish, whale meat, and cassava flour. Homegrown *aipim*, beans, and sweet potatoes added variety for part of the year, but once the harvests of those crops had ended, day laborers and small farmers returned to a diet based on cassava flour. Meat and fish served mainly as condiments (*temperos*) rather than as dishes in themselves; they made it easier to swallow large amounts of farinha.[13] The daily fare of those who work in the cane and tobacco fields of the Recôncavo seems to have changed little in the past one hundred years. Like their enslaved forefathers, the rural poor continue to depend vitally on farinha.

The same cannot be said of the urban poor in Salvador, where, over the last two hundred years, new patterns of consumption have emerged and have significantly changed the common diet. Even poorer residents of the city today regularly eat beans, rice, and bread as well as cassava flour. Bread made from wheat flour holds a major place in their diet. The trend toward greater consumption of bread probably dates back to the first decades of the nineteenth century. In 1808, Henry Hill, the U.S. consul stationed at Salvador, remarked that as long as sugar prices remained "brisk," imports of wheat flour could be expected to increase "vastly . . . in a few years." Although the price of sugar sometimes flagged after 1808, imported wheat flour did become a major item in the province's overseas trade. By 1847, a commission studying Salvador's Public Granary could report that bread consumption in the city had grown greatly in the previous 30 years. The number of bakeries had also increased: by 1855, the city had 33, as well as 21 establishments specializing in pasta (*massas*). Bakeries by the late nineteenth century had also become common in the towns around Salvador. Clearly, bread was no longer restricted to the tables of a few wealthy immigrants. Even poor prisoners in Salvador's jails in the late 1860s ate a daily breakfast of coffee, sugar, and a six-ounce loaf of bread.[14]

More important, however, is that those same prisoners received for their second and last meal of the day a tenth of a quarter-alqueire of cassava flour. A small loaf of bread for breakfast did not diminish their daily ration. Although even poor Bahians might have a roll with their morning coffee, they relied on farinha, accompanied or, for the less fortunate, merely seasoned by meat or salted fish, to fill their stomachs at midday. James Wetherell, who served for many years as British vice consul at Salvador, perceived this clearly. Wetherell took a keen interest in Bahian cookery and its variety; he even went to the trouble of collecting recipes. But when he sought to sum up the daily fare of most Bahians in the mid-1850s, he mentioned only three staples: "skinny beef dried in the sun, farinha, which is a description of sawdust, and bacalhào [sic], dried codfish, a kind of salted piece of board."[15]

Farinha's continuing importance in the common diet throughout the first half of the nineteenth century always become painfully evident when shortages drove up its price in the city's market. At those moments, poor Bahians did not, as crowds in European cities did, take to the streets in bread riots; instead, they demanded farinha, the staple that continued to be the basis of their subsistence. Bread probably gained very little ground against farinha in the diet of slaves who lived in the city; for them, it continued to be, as in Vilhena's time, a "treat," a special nourishment given to them when they fell ill.[16]

Thus, there is no reason to doubt the sources on this matter. Bahians in both the countryside and the city ate great amounts of farinha. They served it dry and uncooked; they made it into small cakes for frying or baking; they fried it lightly in oil or butter (*farofa*); or, most common of all, they mixed it with water or with fish or meat stock to make a heavy porridge (*pirão*). However Bahians prepared it, farinha was truly "the bread of the land."[17]

The Local Market for Cassava Flour

The importance of cassava flour is thus beyond dispute. Found on the tables of rich and poor alike and in the calabashes used by slaves for want of proper dishes, it formed the basis of the common diet. Here, then, was a product with a potentially large local market. But was that market actually large and, more to the point, large enough to have any real impact on the social and economic landscape of the Recôncavo? Had a significant trade in farinha developed by the late eighteenth century? The first step in answering these questions is to determine, however roughly, the demand for *marketed* farinha.[18] We must, in other words, ask what portion of the Bahian population regularly bought farinha rather than planting cassava to meet its own immediate needs.

THE URBAN DEMAND

Bahians who made their homes in the towns of the Recôncavo, and especially those who lived in Salvador, must have purchased much of the farinha sold in the local market. Their numbers were not insignificant: in Brazil, where the vast majority of the population still lived in the countryside, the Recôncavo stood out as a region of exceptional urbanization, and Salvador as one of the leading cities.

Efforts to estimate the size of the farinha market should therefore start with figures for Salvador's population. This should be done, however, with certain qualifications. To begin with, not everyone in the urban population necessarily bought farinha. Wealthier residents sometimes owned roças planted with kitchen gardens, orchards, and cassava on the city's outskirts. The flour made from that cassava allowed them to escape dependence on the market. Likewise, large landowners who spent part of the year in the city might have provisions sent to them from their estates in the country.

Even poorer Bahians might receive farinha from friends and kin who lived in the countryside. Research elsewhere has revealed a whole range of non-monetary exchanges between cities and their rural hinterlands in preindustrial societies.[19] Similar exchanges surely took place in eighteenth- and nineteenth-century Salvador; but precisely because those exchanges bypassed the market, their volume and frequency went undocumented. All of this means that figures for the city's population can give only a rough idea of the size of the urban demand for flour.

Locating such figures presents further problems. After independence, no reasonably reliable count of the city's population took place until 1872, the date of the first national census. Some 60 years separate that count from the last of the colonial censuses. The city of Salvador together with its suburbs (a cidade e seu termo), moreover, encompassed far more than the built-up area with its truly urban population. It also included thoroughly rural suburban parishes. Fortunately, contemporaries distinguished the nine, later eleven, "urban" parishes that made up the city proper from the surrounding rural suburbs. But the distinction can be misleading, for in several "urban" parishes lay a good deal of open countryside. The built-up area, as the city grew, expanded into these parishes in the nineteenth century, making them increasingly urbanized. Nevertheless, farms, country retreats, and even a few sugar plantations could still be found in the outlying "urban" parishes of Vitória, Brotas, and Santo Antônio além do Carmo in the 1850s.[20] As a result, census figures for the city proper exaggerate the strictly urban population to some extent, more so in the eighteenth century than in the nineteenth; that is, they tend to overstate the number of inhabitants who generally would have had no recourse but to buy farinha.

Censuses, despite all their shortcomings, remain the best source of information about the size and growth of Salvador's urban market and thus about the demand for farinha in the city. Therefore, Table 6 brings together figures from various eighteenth- and nineteenth-century censuses. They suggest that the city's population stood at just under 40,000 in 1780 and may have reached 50,000 by 1807. Salvador ranked during this late colonial period as the most populous city in Portuguese America. Although it lost that position to Rio de Janeiro after 1808, it remained Brazil's second-largest city for at least the next eight decades. The Bahian capital thus constituted one of the most important urban markets in eighteenth- and nineteenth-century Brazil. Furthermore, Salvador, with its busy harbor and bustling, crowded Lower Town (Cidade Baixa), gave the impression of being even larger. Foreign visitors and Brazilians alike frequently placed the city's population at between 70,000 and 185,000.[21]

For much of the nineteenth century, these estimates are the only source of information about the city's population, but their usefulness is limited. As the 1870 and 1872 censuses proved, Salvador's appearance could be deceiving. The results of the 1870 census, carried out by the police, certainly

TABLE 6

Population of Salvador, Selected Years, 1706–1872

Year	Population	Year	Population
1706	21,601	1775	33,635
1755	37,453	1780	39,209
1757[a]	34,442	1805	45,600
1757[a]	37,323	1807	51,112
1759	40,263	1870	77,686[b]
1768	40,922	1872	108,138

SOURCES: Th. de Azevedo, pp. 185, 188–89; J. Caldas, p. 38; Martinho de Mello e Castro, "Instrucção para o Marquez de Valença" (1779), *ABN*, 32 (1910): 437; "Mappa de todas as Freguezias que pertencem ao Arcebispado da Bahia" (1775), *ABN*, 32 (1910): 296–97; A.J. da Costa, estampa 3; "Mappa da enumeração da gente e povo desta Capitania" (1780), *ABN*, 32 (1910): 480; Mattoso, *Bahia: A cidade*, p. 129; Gov. to the Visconde de Anadia (16/6/1807), *ABN*, 36 (1914): 460; Repartição da Polícia, "Quadro da população livre e escrava da Provincia da Bahia" (1870), APEB, SH, 1600; Brasil, . . . , *Recenseamento* (1872).
[a] The results of two separate counts, both dated 1757.
[b] The results of a police census; an obvious undercount.

represent an undercount, but the generally more reliable national census two years later registered far fewer than the 185,000 inhabitants estimated by Sebastião Ferreira Soares in 1865. Yet the same national census also revealed that in the previous seven decades, the city had more than doubled in size. We can therefore cautiously conclude that Salvador's population grew from 40,000 around 1780 to perhaps 90,000 by 1860 and more than 110,000 in the early 1870s.[22]

Alongside the city's permanent residents moved a substantial floating population. The hundreds of boats that arrived from various points in the Recôncavo and the larger ships of the coastwise and transatlantic trades could, on any given day, put ashore as many as 2,200 sailors. The ships reaching the city from Africa brought not only sailors but also enslaved men, women, and children. As a major transatlantic slave port, Bahia housed arriving slaves until they were sold to plantations in the interior or re-exported to other parts of Brazil. The number of slaves imported varied greatly from year to year, but some decades saw annual averages of more than 7,000.[23] While in the city, both sailors and slaves in transit had to eat; thus they, too, made their presence felt in Salvador's urban market.

That market also handled purchases of farinha for consumption outside the city. Departing ships took on provisions. Similarly, slave traders loaded their vessels with farinha to feed slaves on the return trip from Africa. These purchases resembled exports of a sort, but the cassava flour that passed through Salvador's market also entered the conventional export trade. Usually in small amounts, it often appeared on the lists of products sent overseas from Bahia.[24]

In summary, the urban demand for farinha consisted of two broad segments, one relatively stable and the other more variable. The first was the permanent residents of Salvador. Although their number increased from

1780 to 1860, they required a generally fixed amount of farinha from one year to the next. By contrast, the second, smaller segment, comprising slaves in transit, sailors, outbound ships, and exports, could fluctuate considerably each year. These two segments together formed an undeniably large urban market for farinha that would more than double in size between the last decades of the eighteenth century and the middle of the nineteenth.

Still, this summary furnishes a less-than-complete picture of the urban demand. Census figures and estimates of the floating population tell us how many people had to be fed in a given year; they refer to the overall volume of the demand for cassava flour. The elasticity of that demand, however, also shaped the workings of the urban market. Consequently, we need to ask whether, when prices rose, Bahians bought less cassava flour and demand fell. Although the sources required to answer that question with any precision are not at hand, information on the composition of Salvador's population and the distribution of wealth among the city's inhabitants allows for meaningful speculation.

In Salvador, a white minority lived side by side with a majority of blacks and mulattos, which always provoked comments from foreign visitors. Robert Avé-Lallemant's remarks, made in 1859, are typical: "One might," he wrote, "with a little imagination take the city for an African capital, the residence of a powerful black prince, in which a population of foreign whites passes entirely unnoticed." He added, "everything seems black: blacks on the beach, blacks in the city, blacks down below, blacks up above. Everything that runs, shouts, works, everything that carries and fetches is black."[25]

Avé-Lallemant and other travelers tended to exaggerate their descriptions of the city's population. Either they failed to notice the whites (who often stayed indoors and off the streets), or they were striving for greater dramatic effect. Still others may have exaggerated because, as one Portuguese visitor wrote in 1788, such a population "at once strikes the eye of those unaccustomed to seeing colonies." At any rate, they did not greatly overstate the proportion of blacks and mulattos. According to an 1807 census, whites represented 28 percent of the city's population. The proportion of whites registered by the 1872 national census was nearly the same (31 percent). Blacks and mulattos made up the rest of the population.[26]

Salvador owed its large black and mulatto population to the widespread use of slave labor in its economy. So common was slaveholding in the city that, in José da Silva Lisboa's opinion, it was "proof of great indigence not to have at least one slave; a slave will be had no matter what the domestic inconvenience." Slaves worked not only as household servants but in every type of manual labor, in many skilled occupations, and in petty commerce. Slaveholding in Salvador was not the privilege of a small and wealthy minority; on the contrary, it penetrated deep into the city's social structure. Widows, spinsters, and other Bahians with very modest means often subsisted on what their single slave earned as a day laborer or street vendor. Freed slaves themselves acquired slaves when they could afford to do so. As a result, slaves made up somewhere between one-third and two-fifths of the city's population in the late eighteenth and early nineteenth centuries.[27]

Another major segment of the population consisted of freed slaves and poor free men and women, whose material living conditions often differed little from those suffered by slaves. The extreme poverty that characterized most of the city's residents appalled Louis-François de Tollenare, who lived in Salvador in 1817 and 1818. The French traveler noted in his journal that "in walking through the more removed neighborhoods and suburbs, one is struck to see there the swarming of an immense population of free Brazilians, piled up in small houses. They all live off nothing and are clothed in the same." In the insurrections and riots of the 1820s and 1830s, these poor free men and women, often unemployed, would take to the streets and sack shops and stores.[28]

Whether slave or free, most Bahians, even in prosperous times, lived on the margins of subsistence. They survived from one day to the next on the cheapest foodstuffs: jerked beef, salted codfish, and above all, farinha. When the price of farinha rose, they could not turn to cheaper substitutes; bread made from imported wheat flour must generally, if not always, have been more expensive. Nor could rice, maize, or beans serve; they never reached the city's market in large enough quantities. Therefore, when faced with higher prices for farinha, most Bahians had no choice; they had to pay. They might buy less meat; they might go into debt; but they bought less farinha only as a last resort. To do so would have meant hunger. As a result, the demand for farinha must have been relatively inelastic in Salvador's market.

All of this does not yet exhaust a discussion of the demand for marketed farinha. Salvador did not stand in isolation, cut off from the surrounding countryside; the city was part of a region. Likewise, the city's market formed part of a larger regional demand for farinha and other basic foodstuffs. The Recôncavo was one of the most densely settled areas in Brazil. Within its boundaries lay half a dozen towns and many more villages and hamlets that, together with Salvador, made up one of Brazil's oldest urban networks. These towns, most of them small, served mainly as centers of administration and commerce for nearby rural areas. Even at the beginning of the nineteenth century, they often consisted of little more than a town hall and a parish church around which clustered a handful of houses, shops, and warehouses for sugar or tobacco.[29]

Not all the towns, however, were such modest settlements. For example, Cachoeira, the Recôncavo's largest town, had become a major entrepôt of interregional trade by the mid-eighteenth century. Herds of cattle from the backlands passed through the town's outskirts on the way to Salvador. Ships and boats moored in the River Paraguaçu took on heavy cargoes of tobacco and sugar from the township's rural parishes and, from more distant inland areas, cotton, hides, and gold. They set ashore cloth goods, hardware, and other European manufactures that the town's merchants, in turn, sent on the backs of mules and packhorses to settlements throughout Bahia's vast interior. Thanks to this rich and varied trade, Cachoeira grew and prospered. The town, together with São Félix, its suburb on the opposite bank of the Paraguaçu, had 1,096 households in 1804 and a population of perhaps 7,000. To European travelers, it presented a thoroughly urban appearance. Cachoeira and São Félix continued to flourish in the first half of the nineteenth century with the development of the cigarmaking industry. Other towns in the region also grew: by the 1880s, Santo Amaro and Nazaré had come to rival Cachoeira in size and wealth.[30]

Small or large, the region's towns all constituted markets in their own right. Their inhabitants, like the residents of Salvador, depended on local trade for a regular supply of essential provisions. They thus contributed to a broad regional demand for marketed cassava flour.

THE RURAL DEMAND

Outside the towns, slaves on plantations and farms grew sugarcane, tobacco, and coffee for export. Did these slaves, on their own or on their masters' orders, plant cassava and other food crops as well? The commonly held view that they did, and thereby ensured their own subsistence, often rests on little more than conjecture. Rather than trusting simple conjecture, it is better to examine closely the question of self-sufficiency, on Bahian farms and plantations.*

On tobacco farms, self-sufficiency was indeed the rule. Constant cultivation of tobacco very quickly destroys soil fertility. To combat soil exhaustion, Bahian farmers not only manured their fields but also rotated tobacco with cassava and often beans and maize as well. They were, as a result, able to harvest generally enough cassava to feed themselves, their families, and their slaves. Often they even produced a surplus of farinha.[31]

The questions of self-sufficiency and provisioning become more complex in the case of Bahia's sugar plantations and cane farms. This complexity appears in one of the first sources to deal with these questions, the "economic description" of Bahia written by Luís Antônio de Oliveira Mendes about 1790. Mendes attempts to estimate the costs of operating a typical engenho, but does not include in his calculations any expenditures for foodstuffs because, as he explains, a senhor de engenho could produce on his property all he needed for the sustenance of his family and his slaves. In the same text, however, Mendes calls on the senhores de engenho to stop purchasing farinha. He argues that if they took the trouble to plant cassava and other food crops, they could reduce their costs and increase their profits.[32]

Mendes may have written his "economic description" hastily and failed

---

* In the following discussion, self-sufficiency refers only to self-sufficiency in terms of necessary supplies of farinha.

to notice that he had contradicted himself. But it is quite possible that the contradiction in his work reflects an awareness of the diversity of practices found on Bahian engenhos and cane farms. Although it is still difficult to sort out clear patterns in that diversity, a first step in that direction is to consider specifically how senhores de engenho and lavradores de cana could obtain farinha for their families and slaves.

Three different strategies were open to them.[33] First, planters could use their slaves to cultivate cassava, just as the tobacco farmers did, then use estate-grown cassava to distribute rations of farinha. Second, planters could provide their slaves enough land and "free" time to grow all the cassava they needed. Both these strategies would make their estates self-sufficient in normal times. The third strategy, in contrast, involved reliance on the market. Planters could purchase farinha and distribute it in regular rations. As Mendes's contradictory remarks suggest, all three strategies could be found in use in the Recôncavo at any given time. Moreover, they were not mutually exclusive; planters could and did combine them. Still, in trying to determine which provisioning strategy prevailed, it is best to examine each of them separately. Not only can that examination help answer questions about the size of the local market for farinha; it can also reveal a great deal about the way Bahian planters ran their estates and the lives their slaves led.

Estate-grown Cassava

For both senhores de engenho and cane farmers, using their slaves to cultivate subsistence crops was more than one possible provisioning strategy; it was a legal obligation. Concerned with the social and political problems that scarcity could bring, the crown and local authorities more than once tried to guarantee an adequate supply of foodstuffs through legislation. Royal decrees in 1642, 1680, and 1690 required planters to grow cassava. Later laws renewed that obligation and specified that planters should cultivate at least five hundred covas for every slave in their service.[34]

The repetition of such laws is in itself suggestive; had they been obeyed, there would have been no need to reenact them every time shortages threatened. The chronicler Vilhena, writing in the late 1790s, had no doubts about the matter; he knew of no planter who cultivated the required number of covas. A decade-and-a-half later, the *juiz de fora* (crown-appointed judge) of Santo Amaro and São Francisco do Conde confirmed Vilhena's remarks when, in 1817, he informed the governor that in his jurisdiction—the very heart of sugar production in Bahia—the laws about planting cassava were no longer enforced.[35]

Those laws were resisted largely because they were burdensome. Five hundred covas of cassava would have yielded far more farinha than one slave could consume in a year. Legislators in Portugal and the colony issued these laws not merely, or even primarily, out of concern for the sustenance of rural slaves; rather, they sought to ensure an abundant supply of farinha for local markets. They hoped that, harvesting one-third of the cassava, the planter could sustain his family and his slaves. The remaining two-thirds would then be available for sale to the people (povo).[36] Understandably, planters resisted such efforts to transform their plantations into cassava farms.

Smaller plots of cassava, sufficient for the plantation's internal consumption, would, of course, save the planter the expense of buying farinha. As on tobacco farms, moreover, agricultural practices encouraged planters to make their own farinha. They sometimes grew cassava on newly cleared land to "soften" the soil before planting cane for the first time. They occasionally planted subsistence crops, including cassava, between rows of cane. In other cases, land no longer considered fertile enough to produce good-quality sugar was turned over to cassava for a few years. Perhaps as a result of such practices, cassava production became common on plantations in the newer, outlying sugar districts, such as São Pedro do Açu da Torre, and also, it seems, in the parishes of Cachoeira (except Iguape) and in the southern Recôncavo.[37]

None of those areas, however, was at all representative of Bahia's traditional sugar-producing districts. They possessed lighter and sandier soils than the heavy, clayish massapés that planters on the northern side of the bay considered ideally suited for cane. It was therefore easier for senhores de engenho in Açu da Torre, Cachoeira, and the southern Recôncavo to plant both cane and cassava on their properties. Still, soil quality was nowhere an absolute obstacle to the cultivation of cassava. Although harvesting might be more difficult and yields might fall below average, cassava would grow in massapé soils. Moreover, even in the massapé districts, most planters could find on their properties some stretch of light, sandy soil suitable for growing cassava. If not, they surely had a few fields where cane no longer grew well. Failing all else, planters could, as Miguel Calmon suggested, acquire or rent farms in districts with sandy soils for growing cassava.[38]

Nevertheless, many planters displayed an open hostility toward subsistence agriculture. In their view, cassava cultivation only sped up deforestation and thereby deprived their mills of the firewood needed in making sugar. Planting food crops also meant diverting resources—land and, more important, labor—from the more profitable production of sugarcane. It is not surprising, then, that senhores de engenho in Santo Amaro went so far as to prohibit their tenants from planting cassava in the 1810s. They no doubt agreed with High Magistrate João Rodrigues de Brito, who in 1807 stated that it was nonsense "to occupy the rare and precious massapé soils with the wretched cassava." On the same occasion, Manoel Ferreira da Câmara, a wealthy and enlightened senhor de engenho, declared with evident pride and in defiance of the laws, "I do not cultivate a single plant of cassava in order not to fall into the absurdity of renouncing the best crop in this country for the worst and in order not to hinder and complicate the cultivation of one crop with work of a different nature." A quarter century later, Miguel Calmon, whose family owned several large engenhos, observed that food crops of any sort were seldom found on Bahian sugar plantations.[39]

Finally, we have the evidence from a sample of more than 150 postmortem inventories from the principal sugar districts of the Recôncavo. They indicate that only 36 percent of the lavradores de cana possessed any equipment for preparing cassava flour and that on only one-fifth of the engenhos was such equipment present. Clearly, many sugar planters and cane farmers grew no cassava at all.

Provision Grounds

The sugar plantations and cane farms of the Recôncavo may have still been largely self-sufficient. Taking advantage of their "free" time to work in roças (provision grounds or garden plots) granted to them by their masters, slaves may have grown enough cassava to feed themselves. In that case, even though planters and cane farmers themselves grew little or no cassava, they would have avoided the cost of purchasing farinha in the market.[40]

Allowing slaves to cultivate provision grounds or garden plots for their own use was a common practice in many areas of slave-based agriculture in the Americas. Scholars studying the West Indies and the southern United States have shown that slaves often had, by custom, the "right" to such plots and to the time needed to work in them. Those scholars have also shown that by cultivating food crops on their own, slaves achieved a limited but real measure of autonomy in their daily lives. More than that, in some areas, provision grounds allowed slaves to develop extensive independent production and marketing activities. Similarly, recent research has uncovered evidence that slaves in other areas of Brazil also kept roças.[41]

Although provision grounds were found in many areas of plantation agriculture, their role in the subsistence of slaves varied greatly from one region to another and over time. At one extreme, slaves in Jamaica, French Guyana, Martinique, and Grenada drew most of their sustenance from what they grew in their plots. Many even managed to harvest sizable surpluses for sale in local markets. At the other extreme, slaves in Barbados, Antigua, and the southern United States depended chiefly on rations distributed by planters.[42]

Such diversity makes it necessary to proceed cautiously in evaluating the use of provision grounds in Bahia. In particular, Jacob Gorender has argued that provision grounds were seldom found on Northeastern sugar plantations, where the agricultural calendar included almost no slack time and where work on the main staple crop kept slaves occupied for nearly the entire year.[43] The first task, then, is simply to establish whether Bahian slaves often had access to provision grounds.

On this question, there is no lack of evidence. The length of the agricultural calendar did not, by itself, preclude the possibility of allowing slaves time and land to grow food crops in a roça. Bahian chroniclers from the late eighteenth century, such as José da Silva Lisboa, Luís Antônio de Oliveira Mendes, and Luís dos Santos Vilhena, all referred to the practice. Manoel Ferreira da Câmara, the owner of a large engenho in the Recôncavo, also mentioned it in the 1830s.[44] Writing at the same time, Miguel Calmon proclaimed the advantages that accrued to planters when they granted their slaves provision grounds.

> A master should give his slave some property or make it easier for him to acquire some on his own and should encourage his industry. This is a power-ful means of distracting him from the ideas that go hand in hand with his sad condition and of inspiring in him a desire to work and even of inviting him to form a family. The practice of encouraging him to plant a roça, espe-cially with food crops, of allowing him to have some livestock or to exercise some trade—this without doubt will lead to his happiness because it can modify the unruly tendencies that slavery generates and fosters.[45]

Significantly, Calmon spoke of giving *property* to slaves. He acknowledged that slaves had "rights," if not by law then by custom, over the plots they cul-tivated.[46]

While Calmon and Câmara were writing about provision grounds, the administrator of the Fazenda da Capela de Santa Maria, a large cane farm in the parish of Iguape, was paying slaves to work on Sundays and holy days, time they could have spent at work in their roças. Miguel de Teive e Argolo, the owner of the Engenho Santo Estêvão, did the same twenty years later. At about the same time, two English Quakers visiting the Engenho Vitória in Iguape learned that adult slaves there cultivated "provision-grounds for their own benefit."[47]

Further evidence comes from an 1854 survey of plantations in the parish of Matoim (Salvador), a few miles from Santo Estêvão, that describes the Engenhos Novo Caboto and Matoim as "occupied by canefields, pastures, and the slaves' cassava plants [*as mandiocas dos escravos*]." This survey, in mentioning the slaves' roças, stands out from other contemporary descrip-tions of Bahian plantations, which rarely refer to the existence of roças, let alone their location, their size, or the crops planted in them. This also holds true for sources such as postmortem estate inventories, which might be ex-pected to supply this information. Estate appraisers often recorded in great detail the plantation's boundaries, the size and location of canefields, the state of repair of fences, the quality of soils found on the property, and the tools, including broken hoes and axes, that plantation slaves used in their daily work. The appraisers sometimes even took the trouble to list and as-sess individual *dendezeiros* (oil palms), fruit trees, coconut palms, and *touceiras de bananeiras* (clumps of banana trees). Yet they almost never took notice of the provision grounds cultivated by slaves. The lack of ex-plicit references to provision grounds obviously makes the historian's work more difficult. But, as João Fragoso and Manolo Florentino rightly argue, in not recording and evaluating provision grounds, estate appraisers implicitly acknowledged that the crops slaves planted in roças did not belong to the late property owner. In effect, both appraisers and heirs followed widespread custom and conceded that in practice, slaves had "rights" to the crops they cultivated for their own use.[48]

Thus it is not surprising that a European visitor has left the most detailed description of provision grounds on any Bahian engenho. The French diplomat Baron Forth-Rouen took advantage of a stopover in 1847 to visit several engenhos in the Recôncavo. At a plantation belonging to the viscount of Pedra Branca, he found,

> each [slave] possesses a lot [*une portion de terre*] that he chooses where he likes and cultivates when and how he pleases. They [the slaves] all have a horse; some have several horses that they hire out to their master. They also have cattle, sheep, etc.[49]

Forth-Rouen added that in this matter, the viscount allowed his slaves exceptional freedoms and that he was constantly worried about their well-being. Most other planters surely had a say in where slaves could grow food crops and when slaves could work in their provision grounds. It is also unlikely that many slaves in the Recôncavo owned horses. What was not exceptional, however, was their freedom to plant their roças as they pleased.[50]

The question now becomes whether provision grounds furnished slaves with the bulk of their subsistence. According to José da Silva Lisboa, writing in 1781, they did: "the sustenance of slaves is not usually a burden to their masters because, by an almost universal custom, [the slaves] are granted the days of Saturday and Sunday to plant whatever they need and a plot of land." Lisboa may have exaggerated; the church in colonial Bahia at times complained that planters allowed their slaves to work in their roças only on Sundays when they should, like other Christians, be resting. Nearly twenty years later, in the late 1790s, Luís dos Santos Vilhena likewise observed that only some planters refused to give their slaves rations and forced them to subsist solely on the produce of their garden plots. These planters, in Vilhena's view, were the cruelest and most inhumane in the treatment of their bondsmen. Like Vilhena, Manoel Ferreira da Câmara, in the 1830s, also denounced as inhumane those slaveowners who failed to distribute rations. Because slaves could not survive on their provision grounds alone, he argued, denying them rations amounted to telling them, "Go out and steal to sustain yourselves." Câmara offered the example of some of his neighbors who did not give out rations. Their slaves had, he claimed, "stolen from me even leftover bits of yams, and not a single bunch of bananas escapes their grasp."[51]

Miguel Calmon, writing at the same time, could find all sorts of advantages for the planter in the custom of assigning provision grounds, but among them he significantly did not list the possibility of turning over to the slaves full responsibility for their own subsistence. On the contrary, he followed Vilhena and Câmara in condemning those masters who gave their bondsmen "a *day* instead of a *ration*." Those slaveowners, according to Calmon, acted not so much out of "cruelty" as out of "stolid indifference" to the well-being of their slaves, but the result was hardly humane; he described the slaves belonging to those masters as the very picture of "*misery*, *vice*, and *death*."[52]

All in all, the comments of Vilhena, Câmara, and Calmon do not take us very far. They merely establish that on *some* plantations, slaves obtained most of their subsistence from their roças. At no point do these authors even hint that this occurred on a majority of Bahian plantations. Moreover, in denouncing those planters who did not give out rations, all three authors do little more than resurrect moralistic arguments that reformist writers, such as the Jesuits André João Antonil and Jorge Benci, had first put forth in the early eighteenth century.[53] At most, we might very tentatively conclude that, with the revival of the sugar trade, the number of plantations where slaves did not receive rations diminished between the early 1780s, when Lisboa referred to the matter, and later decades, when Vilhena, Câmara, and Calmon took up the same question.

To go beyond those limited remarks, we need to approach the question from a different direction and with different sources. We can, for example, look for evidence of slaves selling produce from their roças. Almost everywhere slaves sold some of the produce they harvested, but the volume and frequency of those sales varied considerably. In those regions of the Americas where provision grounds supplied most of the food slaves ate, they often yielded marketable surpluses as well. Slaves in Jamaica, Saint-Domingue, Grenada, St. Vincent, Martinique, and French Guyana not only grew much of their own food but also produced considerable amounts of vegetables and other foodstuffs (including cassava flour) for sale in local markets.

Did Bahian slaves do the same? The well-known example of the 1789–91 slave rebellion at the Engenho Santana has been cited as evidence that they did. In the peace treaty they negotiated with the plantation owner setting forth the terms under which they would return to work, Santana's slaves demanded more time to work in their roças, greater freedom to choose where they could clear ground to plant food crops, and even, in another clause, a boat large enough to accommodate their "cargoes" when it went to Salvador. Santana, however, is not a reliable example from which to generalize. The engenho was not typical either of sugar plantations in the Recôncavo or of engenhos in the main sugar regions of Northeastern Brazil; it was located outside the Recôncavo, some two hundred miles south of Salvador at an isolated point near Ilhéus, a sparsely settled township that suffered a chronic shortage of foodstuffs.[54]

The Recôncavo, by contrast, had more than two hundred engenhos, comparatively thick settlement, and well-stocked local markets. If slaves on the sugar plantations of the Recôncavo drew most of their sustenance from what they grew in their roças, they may have regularly sold produce to their masters and eventually, like some of their Caribbean counterparts, may have played a major role in provisioning local markets with basic foodstuffs.

Evidence for slave marketing activities should then appear in postmortem inventories from the Recôncavo's sugar districts. These probate records, for example, almost always contain declarations of unpaid debts, including debts owed to slaves. Such debts might easily arise when slaves sold their masters produce they had harvested from their provision grounds. In addition to lists of debts, inventories sometimes contain running accounts of expenditures made by the executors; not only major expenditures, such as the acquisition of new equipment or the salaries paid to overseers, but also small sums spent in purchasing vegetables, poultry, maize, beans, farinha, and other foodstuffs—products that slaves could have furnished from their provision grounds. Researchers working with comparable probate records in other areas of Brazil have demonstrated that rural slaves in those areas did sell surplus produce from their roças and even, in some cases, livestock as well.[55]

Bahian inventories also yield examples of rural slaves selling produce on their own behalf. These examples go far in suggesting that slaves in the sugar districts of Bahia could indeed achieve a restricted, but still real, measure of autonomy by cultivating roças and by exploiting in other ways their "free" time. Numbering no more than a handful, however, the examples fall short of demonstrating the widespread and regular sale of surplus produce by those slaves.

The first example is the debt for the sum of Rs.37$680, owed by José Manoel to Teodósio da Silva, a pardo slave. When José Manoel, a poor resident of Iguape and sometimes cane farmer, died in 1824, Teódosio received permission from his mistress, José Manoel's daughter, to submit the following bill:[56]

> Account of how much Senhor Manoel owes to Teodósio da Silva the following items, to wit:

The first time in money when he planted cane with the deceased Gabriel	Rs. 8$000
2nd ditto. Idem in money—11 *patacas* [*pataca*, a coin worth Rs.$320]	Rs. 3$520
3rd ditto. In cloth that I sold him, to wit: 11 *côvados* of *xita* [1 *côvado* = 0.66m; *xita*, a type of cotton cloth] and one blade—13 patacas	Rs. 4$160
4th time. For payment of the debt your son Florêncio owed me and you assumed the debt	Rs.13$000
5th time. Value of two *capados* [gelded goats or pigs or possibly rams] that belonged to me and you received them from Senhor Pedro, your acquaintance in the city	Rs. 9$000
Sum—Save Error or Omission	Rs.37$680

Teodósio's bill, although written by the local vicar, is not altogether clear. How, for example, had Florêncio, José Manoel's son, come to owe Teodósio Rs.13$000? The first item in the bill is frustratingly ambiguous: who planted cane with the late Gabriel—José Manoel or Teodósio? If it was José Manoel, had Teodósio then somehow financed the planting of cane by his mistress's late father? If, as would seem more likely, it was Teodósio, his bill shows that Bahian slaves could use their "free" time to cultivate garden plots and also to earn money as hired field hands. Not only did Teodósio work as a field hand, but he also raised livestock and was something of a part-time peddler. That meant that he had connections with local merchants who could furnish him with wares. All in all, Teodósio's bill shows that he was involved in a remarkable and unusually wide range of activities. The amount of money José Manoel owed his daughter's slave was, moreover, substantial. With Rs.37$680, Teodósio could have bought one or two horses or the freedom of an infant slave. He could have also kept himself, a wife, and three children supplied with all the farinha they needed for a full year.[57]

In the same parish of Iguape where, three-and-a-half decades later, Teodósio would submit his bill, Dona Ana Joaquina de São José, as executrix of her late husband's estate, assumed full responsibility for administering the Engenho Maroim between May and December 1790. During those months, she hired carpenters to carry out repairs on the plantation's sugar mill. The accounts Dona Ana Joaquina prepared and then had attached to her husband's inventory record, among other expenses, the wages she paid the carpenters and the food she purchased for their meals. On at least one occasion, she bought palm oil and beans from her slave Benta. Although the accounts unfortunately do not record how much oil and beans Dona Ana Joaquina purchased, the sum she paid Benta, Rs.4$000, indicates that she had purchased a fair amount of both. Rs.4$000 would have bought one-third of an alqueire, or approximately eleven kilograms of beans in Salvador; and Benta, in all likelihood, did not receive the current price.[58]

A third example comes from the inventory of José Francisco das Neves, owner of the Engenho Genipapo in the township of São Francisco do Conde. As administrator of the engenho, the executor made the following entry in his accounts:

1842. 8 February. A portion of cassava bought from the slave Bento Rs.6$000

Bento had sold a respectable amount of cassava. His "portion" may have occupied a full tarefa of land (4,356 square meters), planted with more than 4,000 covas of cassava. That number of covas would have easily yielded enough farinha to feed Bento and four other slaves for a year.[59]

Clearly, Bahian slaves did cultivate roças, and, at least occasionally, they harvested enough from them to sell a surplus. Slaves in Bahia, like slaves in many parts of the Americas, found in their garden plots and their "free" time a restricted, but nonetheless significant "economy" of their own. Their roças may often have been mere scraps of land, the hours to work in them few, and the harvests pitifully small, but there the slaves, not their masters, made the decisions. Within the limits imposed by slavery, they were slaves who, to use Eduardo Silva's expression, "negotiated."[60] They "negotiated" with their masters and even with slavery itself.

Yet the evidence also suggests that the slaves' economy was far less developed than in some Caribbean sugar colonies. Bahia had nothing to compare with the markets and fairs of Jamaica, Saint-Domingue, Antigua, Grenada, Martinique, and Barbados, which were frequented by hundreds and even thousands of rural slaves. The purchases of beans and palm oil at the Engenho Maroim and the "portion" of cassava at the Engenho Genipapo, furthermore, appear paltry when set against examples found by João Fragoso in probate records of coffee planters in the province of Rio de Janeiro. At the Fazenda Caxambu, the administrator acquired from that plantation's slaves 39 percent of all the foodstuffs he purchased between 1880 and 1882. The slaves supplied, in one six-month period alone, 391 alqueires of maize, almost 29 alqueires of beans, and 60 sacks of rice. The slaves' share at another coffee plantation in the 1850s reached 60 percent of all the foodstuffs purchased.[61] It becomes clear, then, that in the period 1780–1860, slaves on Bahian plantations usually did not grow most of their own food. The produce of provision grounds served mainly to supplement rations in the slaves' diet.

Reliance on the Local Market

To summarize: planters in Bahia generally did not plant cassava in sufficient amounts; nor did their slaves usually grow enough food in their provision grounds to sustain themselves. How, then, did Bahian planters feed their slaves? By resorting to the third strategy open to them: they bought farinha; that is, they relied on the local market.

Evidence of purchases of farinha by planters is abundant. Both Luís Antônio de Oliveira Mendes and Luís dos Santos Vilhena, writing at the end of the eighteenth century, mentioned such purchases. In the 1830s, Manoel Ferreira da Câmara and Miguel Calmon publicly urged planters to grow food crops because they believed that it was *no longer* economical to buy farinha. The time had come, they argued, for planters to change their habits and to stop buying farinha. Both Câmara and Calmon, however, were reacting to the extraordinarily high prices of farinha in the early 1830s, and both recognized that they were opposing a well-established habit among planters.[62] Even Câmara's own heirs did not follow his advice; after his death, they purchased farinha for the more than one hundred slaves at his Engenho da Ponta in Iguape. His heirs, like many other planters, continued to calculate that on average, it was cheaper to buy farinha than to plant cassava.[63] Vilhena noted that senhores de engenho had long reckoned that with an arroba of sugar, they could profitably buy four alqueires of farinha. By Câmara's time, the ratio had changed, but the reasoning remained the same. "All say with a single voice," he wrote

> that it costs less to make an arroba of sugar than an alqueire of farinha; that, in an ordinary year, two alqueires of farinha can be bought with the earnings from one arroba of sugar; and that, therefore, the planter who stopped growing [cane] . . . and grew cassava would be buying farinha at double the price.[64]

Planters quite simply considered buying farinha more profitable than making their own.

Local officials in the cassava-growing districts and in Salvador routinely reported on shipments of farinha to the sugar-producing areas of the Recôncavo. Some of the reports even specify that the flour being shipped was intended to supply engenhos. Occasionally, planters even sent their own boats to ports in the cassava-growing districts to buy stocks of farinha. Without going so far, they could also buy farinha from neighboring roceiros. Other planters relied on Salvador's market to provision their estates. Farinha was sold both in the city's Public Granary and on boats at anchor in the harbor. While the farinha brought ashore was reserved for urban consumers, the stocks that remained aboard ship were available for sale to plantation owners.[65] The existence of such an arrangement attests to the regularity with which planters bought farinha to feed their slaves.

Even more direct evidence comes from postmortem inventories. Table 7 lists 30 inventories of senhores de engenhos and lavradores de cana in which unpaid debts or accounts prepared by executors indicate farinha purchases. Drawn from the main sugar-producing areas of the Recôncavo and covering almost the entire period from 1780 to 1860, these examples reinforce the evidence already presented and further support the conclusion that many planters normally bought farinha to feed their slaves.

Among the examples in the table are a small number of properties with equipment to make cassava flour and even a few with cassava fields. These examples show that even when planters had the wherewithal to make their own flour, they sometimes preferred to purchase it. Buying farinha, then, was a strategy that planters chose to follow, not a strategy imposed on them.

This raises an important point: precisely because engenhos and cane farms were slave-based agricultural enterprises, planters had a full range of options. At one extreme was self-sufficiency: planters such as those in Açu da Torre grew enough cassava or granted their slaves sufficient land and time to grow much of their own food. At the other extreme, planters relied entirely on the market to provision their estates. Inventory accounts often record purchases of farinha large enough to provide every slave on the property a full ration of farinha. Between the two extremes were planters who mixed strategies, exemplified in Table 7 by the Engenho Genipapo. There, the slaves grew cassava in their own provision grounds as well as in their master's fields. The engenho also bought farinha. Soil quality, distances from market towns, and the relative prices of sugar and farinha no doubt determined which strategy a planter chose to follow. The options of home production and purchasing, however, were always open to all planters.

This potentially gave planters and cane farmers great leeway in managing their plantations and farms. They could switch from one strategy to another as the relative prices of farinha and sugar changed over time. When shortages raised the price of farinha, or the income from sugar fell, they could turn to home production to reduce their out-of-pocket expenses. Inversely, when sugar prices were high or farinha was cheap, they could again rely on the market to provision their estates. The relatively long upward trend in sugar prices that began in the late eighteenth century no doubt encouraged many planters to switch from home production to purchasing flour.

In principle at least, planters could also change their provisioning strategies from year to year as the price of farinha rose and fell. Those short-term adjustments would have resulted in a highly elastic rural demand for marketed farinha. Yet in all likelihood, few planters attempted to adjust to short-term price changes by switching back and forth between provisioning strategies. Table 7 includes examples from years when farinha sold for high prices. Planters knew from experience that the price of farinha fluctuated greatly from to year to year. They also knew that a planter who tried to adjust to all these fluctuations might easily find himself, as Manoel Ferreira da Câmara put it, "buying farinha at double the price." Cassava, moreover, takes at least a full half-year to mature; most varieties require twelve to eighteen months. By the time a planter had harvested any cassava, the price of farinha might again have fallen. Adjustments also meant upsetting established work patterns on the plantation. Planters either reassigned some slaves to cultivate cassava and prepare flour or granted all the slaves more "free" time to work in their roças. In both cases, work on the main crop, sugarcane, suffered.[66]

All the evidence, therefore, points to the same conclusion: to a varying degree, many and perhaps even most Bahian sugar plantations and cane farms were not self-sufficient. Planters and cane farmers bought farinha to feed their slaves. The result was a surprisingly large rural market. By a rough but conservative estimate, in 1818 that market comprised at least 9,300 slaves.[67] This figure hardly exaggerates the rural demand for marketed farinha; indeed, an estimate of 13,000 might be more realistic. At any rate, to feed 9,300 slaves would have required annual purchases of almost 85,000 alqueires of farinha, or one-fifth of all the flour handled yearly at the time by Salvador's Public Granary.[68] As sugarcane cultivation continued to expand throughout the Recôncavo after 1818 and as the number of engenhos multiplied, even greater quantities of farinha would be needed to supply this rural market.

Plantation Agriculture, Slavery, and the Internal Market

The demand for marketed cassava flour thus extended far beyond the city and into the countryside. Salvador, the towns of the Recôncavo, and the region's sugar plantations and cane farms combined to form an impressively large and growing market. Some fifty thousand consumers may have depended on that market for their daily sustenance at the end of the eighteenth century; by 1860, their number had surely surpassed one hundred thousand. These figures, given the problems with the available census materials, are no more than rough estimates. But whatever the true number of consumers,

TABLE 7

Purchases of Farinha by Sugar Planters and Cane Farmers, 1788–1864

Years[a]	Estate of	Type of property (owned or rented) and location: parish (where known) and township	Type of evidence
1788–89	Manoel Dias Rocha	Cane farm, Iguape, Cach.	Accounts
1789–90	João Pereira de Magalhães	Cane farm, Iguape, Cach.	Accounts
1790	Félix Alves de Andrade	Eng° Maroim, Iguape, Cach.	Accounts
1797	André Gonçalves da Costa	Eng° Cruz das Almas, Santana do Catu, SFC	Debt
1800–1801	Sebastião Vieira Tosta	Eng° Esconso, Outeiro Redondo, Cach.	Accounts
1804	Luís da Costa Ribeiro Correia	Cane farm, S. Gonçalo, SFC	Debt
1810–12	Diogo António de Sá Barreto	(1) Eng° Laranjeiras, S. Sebastião do Passé, SFC; (2) Eng° Cabaxi, Monte, SFC	Accounts
1822–23	[João Teixeira Barbosa?[b]	Eng° Passagem, Eng° S. Inês, and Eng° Cachoeirinha, all three: Matoim, Salvador	Accounts
1823–24	Diogo José Ferreira	Cane farm, Iguape, Cach.	Accounts
1826–27	Serafim dos Santos Araújo	Cane farm, S. Sebastião do Passé, SFC	Accounts
1833–34	António Lopes Ferreira e Souza	Eng° Preguiça, [?], SA	Accounts
1836–39	Luísa Rosa de Gouveia Portugal	Eng° S. Gonçalo, Socorro, SFC	Accounts
1836–40	José Francisco da Costa Lobo	Cane farm, S. Sebastião do Passé, SFC	Accounts
1837–41	Manoel Estanislau de Almeida	Cane farm, Iguape, Cach.	Accounts
1838–41	Maria Bernardina da Conceição e Vasconcelos	Cane farm, Iguape, Cach.	Accounts

TABLE 7 (continued)

Years[a]	Estate of	Type of property (owned or rented) and location: parish (where known) and township	Type of evidence
1839	Domingos Américo da Silva	Eng⁰ S. Domingos and Eng⁰ S. Catarina, both: Iguape, Cach.	Accounts
1839–40	Ponciano da Costa Araújo	Cane farm, S. Sebastião do Passé, SFC	Accounts
1839–42	Antônio Joaquim de Meneses Dória and Ana Egídia de Araújo Góes	Cane farm, S. Sebastião do Passé, SFC	Accounts
1842	João Francisco das Neves	Erg⁰ Genipapo, S. Sebastião do Passé, SFC	Accounts
1842–43	Joaquim Ferreira Bandeira	Eng⁰ Macaco and Eng⁰ Buranhém, both: S. Gonçalo, SFC	Accounts
1842–45	Maria Rosa de Matos	Eng⁰ Marapé, S. Gonçalo, SFC	Accounts
1846	Joana Maria de Vasconcelos	Cane farm, Monte, SFC	Accounts
1849–50	Baron of Maragogipe (Bento de Araújo Lopes Vilas Boas)	(1) Eng⁰ S. Antônio das Varas, Cotegipe, Salvador; (2) Eng⁰ Pimentel and (3) Eng⁰ Bom-gosto, both: S. Sebastião do Passé, SFC	Accounts
1849–50	Guilhermina Galo Gomes	Cane farm, Socorro, SFC	Accounts
1854–59	[Miguel de Teive e Argolo][c]	Eng⁰ S. Estévão, Socorro, SFC	Accounts
1854–57	Viscount and Viscountess of Pirajá	(1) Eng⁰ Nazaré, Rio Fundo, SA; and (2) Eng⁰ S. Miguel, N.S. da Purificação, SA	Accounts
1855–56	Antônio Pedreira de Cerqueira	Eng⁰ da Pedra, N.S. da Purificação, SA	Accounts
1857–60	Hilária Maria de Jesus	Eng⁰ do Mocambo, (?), Maragogipe	Accounts
1858–63	Francisco de Oliveira Guedes	Eng⁰ Vira-saia and Eng⁰ Sururu, both: (?), Maragogipe	Accounts
1860–65	Matilde Flora da Câmara Bittencourt e Chaby	Eng⁰ da Ponta, Iguape, Cach.	Accounts

sources: Postmortem inventories, APEB, SJ, IT and ARC, IT; APEB, SH, 247.

[a] Years covered by accounts or date of debt.

[b] This set of accounts, catalogued together with correspondence received by the colonial government, is very probably a misplaced fragment of an inventory. The "Matrícula dos Engenhos" lists João Teixeira Barbosa as the owner of the Engenhos Passagem, Santa Inês, and Cachoeirinha.

[c] Miguel de Teive e Argolo had accounts from his engenho attached to the inventory of Maria de Assunção Freire de Carvalho to help settle a dispute among Carvalho's heirs.

the very existence of this urban and rural market had far-reaching implications.

To begin with, its existence introduced competition into the otherwise complementary relationship between Salvador and the sugar districts in its immediate hinterland. Merchants based in the city furnished planters with the slaves and many of the services and inputs they needed to maintain operations on their estates. The planters, in turn, paid the merchants with consignments of sugar. On the overseas sales of that sugar, accounting generally for at least half of Bahia's export trade, the well-being of Salvador's entire urban economy ultimately depended. But this complementary exchange gave way to competition when the urban consumer met the planter at the Public Granary or in other local marketplaces. Both then bargained for the same farinha. Their competition for the most important of all staples in the common diet could easily become intense whenever supplies temporarily fell short.

That any such competition should take place seemed, to urban consumers and royal officials alike, a complete anomaly; it violated what ought to have been the proper relationship between a town and its agricultural hinterland. The countryside should, they believed, not only feed itself but also produce a sizable surplus to provision nearby urban markets. Authorities in both Bahia and Lisbon repeatedly tried through legislation to wrest just such a surplus of flour from the Recôncavo's engenhos and cane farms. All their attempts failed because, in the end, neither the crown nor the merchants who sat on Salvador's city council were willing to forgo the revenues and income to be earned from greater exports of sugar.

The existence of a rural market for farinha also points to the high degree of specialization the Bahian sugar industry had already achieved by the beginning of the nineteenth century. Closely tied to an emerging world economy, planters in the Recôncavo tended to concentrate all their resources in the production of a small number of commodities: sugar, cane brandy, and molasses. Specialization, it should be stressed, represented only a tendency, frequently offset by the broader range of productive activities found on individual engenhos.

Still, as farinha purchases suggest, the tendency could be strong. In the nineteenth century, the Bahian sugar industry certainly did not form a "semi-closed economy," in which planters purchased "only indispensable tools and a few European products for their own consumption" and slaves lived off subsistence crops grown on the plantation.[69] On the contrary, the rationality that governed daily operations on Bahian engenhos and cane farms created multiple and varied links between the sugar industry and other sectors of the regional economy. For example, the many planters who did not maintain kilns on their estates had to buy roof tiles, bricks, and clay molds for purging sugar from the potteries of the southern Recôncavo. By 1766, more than twenty olarias and casas de louça (pottery works) already lined the riverbanks in the townships of Maragogipe and Jaguaripe. Near them lay the farms where, by 1780, more than seven hundred roceiros planted cassava and made flour for sale.[70]

Income from the plantations also flowed into the pockets of the hundreds of free artisans who lived in the sugar districts. Plantation accounts attached to postmortem inventories are filled with entries for wages paid to blacksmiths, carpenters, caulkers, masons, boatmen, sawyers, joiners, wainmen, and barber-surgeons. The accounts also register the purchases of numerous locally produced goods: rope, whale and castor oil (both for lighting), hides, tallow, firewood, timber, and lime, to name but a few. When they did not have their own stillhouses, planters even purchased cane brandy. Thus, specialization in the sugar industry made possible specialization in other areas of the economy. It would follow, then, that the expansion of sugar production between 1780 and 1860 should have fostered economic growth elsewhere. The commercial production of cassava flour, in particular, should have increased over the same period. Larger supplies of farinha in local markets would have encouraged more planters to abandon the cultivation of cassava. At the same time, slaves would have had fewer opportunities to market produce harvested from their roças.[71]

Planter purchases of farinha also throw into question the argument that the reliance on slavery, rather than some form of free labor, prevented or greatly hindered the emergence of any internal market. Slavery on Bahian sugar plantations quite evidently did not represent an unsurmountable obstacle to the development of a significant rural market. Planters routinely bought for their slaves not only cassava flour but also jerked beef, salt cod, and fresh meat, as well as cloth goods. Precisely because a high degree of specialization characterized the sugar industry, the day-to-day reproduction of its slave labor force depended heavily on that market. The most fundamental components of the diet slaves ate and the cotton goods that clothed them reached the plantations by passing through that market.

Here it would be tempting to fall into rash revisionism and assert that slavery did not at all hinder the development of the internal market. The demand for basic foodstuffs in the Recôncavo's sugar districts would no doubt compare favorably with the rural market found in a region where a free and largely self-sufficient peasantry made up most of the population in the countryside. By definition, such peasants would not purchase basic foodstuffs; they might even manufacture at home other articles of everyday use.[72] But if the point of reference were a modern industrial society, we should necessarily conclude that, at least partly as a result of the widespread use of slave labor in agriculture, the rural market of the Recôncavo was both poorly developed and precariously established. The commodities planters purchased for their slaves—a few basic foodstuffs and cheap cotton fabrics— can by no means match the volume and variety of goods that circulate in a mature capitalist economy.

The possibilities for further development, moreover, were limited. The market certainly grew, as the number of engenhos multiplied after 1780 and as the slave labor force employed in the sugar industry increased; but it did not undergo significant qualitative changes. Planters wanted bondsmen who, at every morning's roll call, would be healthy and ready to march into the canefields and take their posts in the millhouse. Their purchases of food-stuffs and cotton goods aimed at ensuring that minimum. Beyond that, they would have gained nothing if their slaves consumed greater quantities of an ever wider variety of goods; on the contrary, purchasing those goods would have only raised their expenses and cut into their income.

Engenho accounts from the last three decades before abolition (1888) show that Bahian planters in those years continued to buy for their slaves the very same items their grandfathers had purchased in the late eighteenth century. The few additions—such as LeRoy's patent purgative and lauda-num alongside chickens, leeches, and port wine, or the services of a physi-cian rather than those of a barber-surgeon—hardly amount to substantial changes. The "luxuries" that North American slaves bought for themselves as soon as they could after emancipation—brightly colored clothes, house-hold wares, cheeses, hams, sardines, boots, brass jewelry—never appear among the articles Bahian planters purchased *para o sustento da fábrica* (for the sustenance of their bondsmen). Restricted to the most essential food-stuffs and the cheapest cotton goods, the rural market in the Recôncavo could scarcely stimulate fundamental changes elsewhere in the regional economy.[73] In principle, moreover, that market could contract at any given moment. Planters always had the option of cultivating cassava; likewise, nothing prevented them from employing some of their slaves in spinning and weaving.

Still another obstacle stood in the way of the growth and development of the rural market: the essential foodstuffs and cheap cotton goods sold there ensured only the day-to-day reproduction of the work force employed in the Bahian sugar industry. To increase and even simply to maintain the size of that work force, planters and cane farmers relied on a different market: they imported slaves from Africa. Farinha produced and marketed in Bahia did not sustain the young men and women whom slave merchants acquired on the coast of Africa. Foodstuffs produced in Africa, not Bahia, sustained those young men and women until they reached the age where they could be profitably shipped across the Atlantic and sold to planters and cane farmers in the Recôncavo.

In sum, directly and indirectly, the slave-based export economy fostered and even required the development in the Recôncavo of a large and signifi-cant urban and rural market for farinha and other essential provisions. The complementary relationships that linked production for local needs with the export economy permitted extensive growth in the internal market. But those same relationships severely limited the possibility that an expanding internal market would bring about dynamic qualitative changes in the econ-omy as a whole.

CHAPTER 4

Crises and Trends in the Regional Farinha Market

By the late colonial period, a lively trade in cassava flour and other "goods of first necessity" had made Salvador the focal point of a network of exchanges linking the city with its immediate hinterland and with regions all along Brazil's Atlantic coast. So vigorous was the Bahian market for farinha alone that the normally level-headed José da Silva Lisboa slipped into wild exaggeration when he estimated in the early 1780s that more than a million alqueires of flour were sold in the city every year.[1]

The volume and variety of goods handled by Bahia's internal trade could impress even Thomas Lindley, an experienced English merchant. With an eye toward future commercial ventures, Lindley wrote in 1805 that "the trade carried on in the immediate confines of the bay, of which a great part is inland, is astonishing. There are full eight hundred launches and sumacks [smacks] of different sizes, daily bringing their tribute of commerce to the capital." The goods they transported included, according to Lindley, tobacco, sugar, cotton, and timber for export as well as maize, firewood, whale oil, vegetables, "the greatest assortment of common earthenware from Iaguaripe [sic]," salt fish, and, of course, farinha for local consumption. He added that with this constant waterborne traffic, "a degree of wealth, unknown in Europe, is thus put into circulation." Lindley was no less impressed by the "abundant display" of "tropical produce" and "culinary stores" he found in Salvador's "green-market."[2]

In later years, other European travelers left vivid descriptions of the city's bustling wharfside market. There, amid heaps of vegetables, sacks of farinha, and piles of tropical fruit, consumers bargained with black market-women while half-naked slave porters jostled with young children, live chickens, squawking parrots, dogs, and even small monkeys. A "miniature fleet" of ships and boats, "laden with produce for the consumption of the city," filled the harbor. Some of the *barcos vivandeiros* (provision boats) would now and then draw near the quay to unload crates of live fowl, sacks of farinha, and conical palm-leaf baskets containing tropical fruit and fresh vegetables of every description. Meanwhile, many more boats, "forming a floating shop," stood at anchor in the harbor, waiting for customers to sail out in small canoes and make their purchases on board.[3]

The smacks, launches, brigantines, and sloops that made up that "floating shop" had often come great distances. In the late colonial period, stocks of flour reached Salvador from four main supply areas: Sergipe, where boats and ships took on cargoes not only of farinha and maize but also of sugar made at more than one hundred engenhos; settlements in the sparsely populated comarca of Porto Seguro in far southern Bahia; the coastal townships of the comarca of Ilhéus, just south of the Recôncavo; and the townships of the southern Recôncavo, Maragogipe and Jaguaripe (including the parish of Nazaré das Farinhas), which, given their proximity to Salvador, were the single most important supply area for the Bahian market.[4]

Thus, by the late eighteenth century, Salvador and the sugar districts of the Recôncavo drew on the production from a long stretch of coast, extending more than 250 kilometers to the north and nearly 700 kilometers to the south. Along this coast, the pull of the Bahian market penetrated to the very edges of Portuguese settlement, where farmers cleared forests and, in places, risked Indian attacks to plant cassava and prepare farinha for the daily meals of urban consumers and rural slaves. Yet their production sometimes failed to meet the demand, and Bahia often had to import farinha from Rio de Janeiro, São Paulo, and Santa Catarina in southern Brazil.[5]

The constant flow of farinha from these far-flung supply areas helped create the quayside market that seemed so colorful and exotic to European travelers; it reminded them of the bazaars of Cairo and Constantinople or the marketplaces in trading towns on the West Coast of Africa. But, for residents of Salvador, the noisy crowds of consumers and marketeers were everyday scenes, hardly worth the lavish prose of nineteenth-century travelers. Bahians instead took notice when no "miniature fleet" of barcos vivandeiros filled the harbor, when slave porters waited idly on the quays with no sacks of cassava flour to haul. Those were sure signs of a coming crisis in the city's market; as supplies fell short, prices would soar. The poor then went hungry, and their hunger laid bare the tensions and conflicts in Bahian society.

Salvador, like other preindustrial cities, suffered numerous food crises, moments of scarcity that alternated with times of plenty. Some of the crises were relatively short and mild, others prolonged and acute. Every crisis, no matter how severe or long-lasting, at the very least raised the prospect of hunger and hardship for Bahians, and especially for poor Bahians. Rising farinha prices often also revealed the contradictions built into Salvador's urban economy. Although their livelihoods ultimately depended on a constant and growing trade in sugar, tobacco, and coffee, residents of Salvador frequently found that increased production for export left them unable to afford farinha for their daily meals. Prosperity in the export economy only worsened the problem of high prices in a market where poor growing conditions resulted in periodic shortfalls in supplies. Yet in the long run, the contradiction between an expanding export economy and production for local needs disappeared. The advance of export agriculture in the early nineteenth century brought neither falling supplies of farinha nor consistently higher real prices. This chapter demonstrates that relationship by examining both short-term fluctuations and long-term trends in the Bahian market.

A study of those fluctuations and trends has become feasible in recent years largely as a result of pioneering research by Katia M. de Queirós Mattoso. Working with the account books of Salvador's main charity hospital, the Santa Casa de Misericórdia, Mattoso has compiled series of annual average prices for farinha and seventeen other foodstuffs, including sugar.[6] Unfortunately, Mattoso could not locate the hospital's account books for several years in the 1830s and the 1840s; her series consequently contain a ten-year gap between 1833 and 1843. Farinha prices taken from the records of Salvador's Public Granary (*Celeiro Público*) partly fill this gap.[7] The granary's records further complement Mattoso's series with detailed information on the amounts of farinha, rice, maize, and beans entering the city between 1786 and 1851. The records thus make it possible to construct annual series for the supplies of locally produced grains on hand in Salvador.[8]

The Public Granary

Yet without some understanding of how the granary worked, the meaning of these series for grain supplies may not be clear.[9] The very name "Public Granary" encourages misinterpretation insofar as it suggests false analogies with the muncipally controlled storehouses found in Europe and some parts of Spanish-speaking Latin America in the eighteenth century.[10] Those storehouses were true public granaries: they held reserves of wheat, maize, or some other breadstuff that municipal authorities used to regulate the price and supply of grains in local markets. When shortages threatened and prices began to rise, the authorities sold the reserves to prevent even sharper price increases, which might provoke public disorder.

Governor Dom Rodrigo José de Meneses may have hoped that the granary he founded in late 1785 would function similarly. But in practice, Salvador's Public Granary—the only institution of its kind in colonial and early nineteenth-century Brazil—was not a storehouse at all. Probably modeled in part on the *terreiros do trigo* (municipal grain markets) of Lisbon and other Portuguese cities, it would be more accurately described as an officially supervised market for farinha and other locally produced grains that reached the city by boat. Its employees did not, as a rule, intervene directly in the grain trade by buying stocks of farinha to build up reserves or by selling reserves in times of dearth. Instead, they oversaw grain sales in the city to guard against monopolies and merchant attempts at forestalling, engrossing, and regrating—that is, buying stocks before they reached the market, hoarding them, and purchasing them speculatively for later resale in the same market. They were also responsible for ensuring that merchants did not charge consumers more than the legal maximum price of Rs.$640 for an alqueire of flour; at least until that price was abolished in 1795. Because Salvador depended overwhelmingly on waterborne trade for essential foodstuffs, the sales overseen by the granary's authorities accounted for much and perhaps even most of the farinha marketed in the city.[11]

Those sales took place inside the granary and its adjoining forecourt as well as "in the sea" (*no mar*), on the ships at anchor in the harbor. The market inside the granary primarily handled farinha for retail sale to urban consumers, while the market "in the sea" specialized in bulk sales of flour from supply areas outside the Recôncavo (*barra fora*) to planters, ships' pursers, slave traders, export merchants, and probably some retailers. Every alqueire of grain, whether destined for sale inside the granary or "in the sea," paid a "contribution" of Rs.$20, which defrayed the granary's operating costs and supported a hospital for lepers, founded the same year.[12]

Collecting the contribution in Salvador's two marketplaces required the services of two overseers (*feitores*). One checked the sacks of flour put ashore by merchants and dealers, while the other, sometimes accompanied in later years by a police corporal, made daily rounds of the harbor in a small sailing canoe. Boarding newly arrived provision boats, the second overseer compared their cargoes with their manifests, then instructed the master of each vessel to present himself at the granary and pay his Rs.$20 per alqueire.

The obligation to pay this tax extended to merchants and masters of barcos vivandeiros even if they had no intention of selling their farinha in Salvador. The master of a vessel could not, for example, legally take a cargo of flour from Nazaré straight to Santo Amaro or São Francisco do Conde on the other side of the bay. He first had to sail to Salvador, present his papers to the granary, and pay the "contribution." He would then receive permission to go on to Santo Amaro or São Francisco do Conde, but only if no shortage of flour threatened the city. On returning to his home port, he needed to show a signed receipt from the granary before local authorities would grant him new sailing papers. Although these restrictions lapsed for trade in the Bay of All Saints in the 1830s, they continued to apply to farinha from areas outside the Recôncavo at least until 1851.[13] Merchants always had to obtain a license from either the granary's administrator or the provincial president before shipping farinha from Salvador to other parts of Brazil.[14]

The granary, then, was much more than a simple public market. It exercised broad authority over all waterborne trade in farinha in the province. All farinha not consumed near its point of production went, at least in principle, to Salvador, where a centralized administration determined its further distribution according to the city's needs. Series for farinha handled by the granary therefore refer to most of the farinha marketed and consumed in the city, as well as to farinha legally exported from Bahia to other parts of Brazil, stocks sold to outward bound ships, and some of the farinha purchased by planters to feed their slaves.

Had the granary exercised absolutely effective control, it would have left nearly complete records of all the waterborne trade in farinha in the province of Bahia. But, not surprisingly, the granary's control, although it improved somewhat over time, was never absolutely effective. Merchants and boat masters resorted to innumerable subterfuges, both ingenious and obvious, to bypass the restrictions on their trade and to manipulate for their own benefit the price and supply of farinha. They sometimes relied on the collaboration of corrupt officials in local ports or in the granary itself. Even when officials refused bribes, their enforcement of controls was often lax or sporadic. They found it impossible to monitor all the isolated coves and inlets of Bahia's long coastline, for example; there, unobserved, a vessel could take on a cargo of farinha and sail for any destination. Of course, if caught, the master of the vessel faced penalties. He might spend a few days in jail, or he might have the sails and rudder temporarily removed from his craft. After 1806, he also had to pay a "double contribution" (*duplo*) of Rs.$40 on every alqueire of flour in his cargo. Likewise, suspected "monopolists" could be expelled from the granary.

Facing such penalties, traders might think twice before "smuggling" farinha or attempting to evade the granary's controls. But when scarcities forced up the price of farinha, they willingly accepted the risks. To the despair of officials, such as one crown judge in Ilhéus, they would then wage a "terrible war" against the restrictions. "The ambition of these men," the judge wrote, "stops at nothing now that they have convinced themselves that the penalty for this type of contraband amounts to no more than a few days in jail, after which the profit and the gain remain in their pockets. . . . Such is [their] insolence and disobedience."[15]

As a result, a substantial share of the waterborne trade in farinha escaped the control and supervision of the Public Granary. Smacks and launches always, even before the 1830s, carried on a more or less intense trade between the ports in the cassava-growing townships of the southern Recôncavo and the sugar districts on the other side of the bay. Similarly, farinha from extreme southern Bahia often found its way to markets in Rio de Janeiro and Pernambuco.[16] Nevertheless, comparisons with the other available evidence suggest that the series drawn from the granary's records are a reasonably reliable source; they allow us to trace fluctuations in the amounts of farinha reaching Salvador's market.

Short-term Crises

Prices and supplies did fluctuate greatly, even over very short timespans. Luís dos Santos Vilhena recalled an instance in the late 1790s where the price of an alqueire of farinha had risen from Rs.$960 at nine o'clock one morning to Rs.1$280 by eleven o'clock the same morning—more than 30 percent in only two hours' time. Violent fluctuations also appear in the weekly records of the Public Granary available for a few months in 1835 and 1836. Any number of causes could produce sharp increases and abrupt declines such as those shown in Figure 5. Unexpectedly large purchases by outgoing ships—that is, a sudden and brief surge in demand—could easily drive up prices. News that military press gangs had arrived in the cassava-

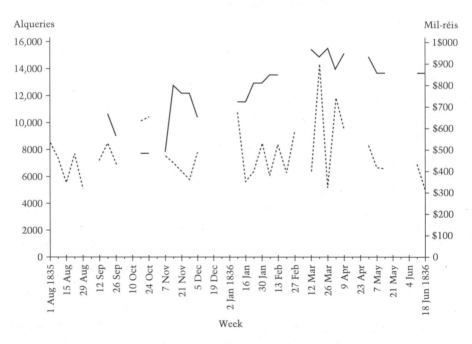

Figure 5. Salvador. Volume of Farinha Entering the Public Granary (in alqueires) and Price of One Alqueire of Farinha (in current mil-réis), Weeks of 1 August 1835–18 June 1836.
SOURCES. "Mappa semanario da farᵃ entrada, consumida e existᵉ nos meses de agtº a dezbrº, 1835" and the weekly "Relação do nº de alqueires de farinha na presente semana . . . " (9/1/1835–18/6/1836, with interruptions), all in APEB, SH, 1609.
NOTE. Dotted line=volume of farinha (in alqueires); solid line=price of one alqueire of farinha (in current mil-réis).

growing districts might lead to a temporary fall in supplies, first in local ports and then in Salvador. Rather than going into town where they and their sons risked forced recruitment, frightened roceiros preferred to stay home and forgo income from the sale of their flour.[17] A spell of stormy weather could disrupt trade and bring about a shortfall in supplies.

Far more serious than these weekly fluctuations were the often brusque increases in the average price of farinha from one year to the next. They marked more or less prolonged periods of acute scarcity. Even though Bahians apparently never experienced true famine, such periods were all too familiar.[18]

The hardship caused by such crises made the price and supply of farinha a matter of constant concern for colonial governors in the 1780s and 1790s. Issuing numerous decrees and orders every year, successive governors attempted to legislate into existence bountiful supplies of farinha at moderate prices. "Farinha inspectors" took up posts in the parishes of the southern Recôncavo, where they kept a close watch on the farinha trade, regularly reported on growing conditions, and prepared weekly or monthly reports on farinha shipments to Salvador. From time to time, they also carried out surveys to determine how much cassava farmers had planted. Elsewhere in Bahia, those responsibilities fell to judges, local militia officers, and town councils. The Public Granary, created during these years, served not only as Salvador's first grain market hall but also as the centerpiece of legislative efforts to ensure abundant supplies and low prices.[19]

Repeated crises in the supply of farinha also helped to fuel social and political unrest from the late 1790s through the 1830s. In those years, few Brazilian provinces could rival Bahia's turbulent record: rebellions, conspiracies, assassinations, a spectacular series of slave revolts, anti-Portuguese riots, military insurrections, uprisings by settled Indians, an officially sanctioned war against unconquered Indians, and the only major land battles of Brazil's brief war for independence from Portugal. The unrest was not a simple "spasmodic" response to high food prices; to explain it as such would ignore the whole pattern of political and social instability that characterized Brazil in the early nineteenth century. But even when national and regional factors are taken into account, scarcities of farinha and other basic foodstuffs remain an important part of any overall explanation for Bahia's turbulent history during this period.[20]

Rendering the lives of both merchants and roceiros insecure, the unrest became, in turn, part of the problem. Soldiers released from their batallions after the war for independence roamed the countryside of the Recôncavo, attacking small towns. In 1832, they threatened to invade Nazaré and halt all trade in foodstuffs. Three years later, the danger came at sea: armed bandits in sailing canoes robbed provision boats of their cargoes in the straits between the mainland and the island of Itaparica. At the same time, the entire free population of the Recôncavo lived in almost constant fear of slave revolts.[21]

Although no record survives of any revolt on a cassava farm, roceiros could not afford to ignore the possibility that their slaves might also turn on them. They probably recalled the two hundred to three hundred escaped slaves who unsuccessfully tried to seize the village of Nazaré das Farinhas in 1809. They had also undoubtedly heard reports about the marauding bands of runaway slaves who attacked isolated farmsteads in the cassava-growing township of Camamu, just south of the Recôncavo, between 1825 and 1837.[22] The insecurity of rural life in these years scarcely encouraged a smooth and regular flow of farinha from the countryside to local ports and to Salvador. To make matters worse, in the 1820s and 1830s, counterfeiters flooded the Bahian market with "false copper money." The counterfeit currency, popularly known as xenxém, complicated sales of farinha and other "goods of first necessity" and, on more than one occasion, completely disrupted trade in Salvador and the markets of the Recôncavo.[23]

High farinha prices again exposed barely hidden social and political tensions in the late 1850s. Hoping to stop a particulary steep rise in prices, the municipal council of Salvador in 1857 passed an emergency ordinance that imposed strict controls on all sales of farinha in the city. When, nearly a year later, the council still had not gained approval for its ordinance from Provincial President João Lins Vieira Cansanção de Sinimbu, it went ahead anyway and implemented the controls. Sinimbu promptly suspended members of the council, only to find that he had provoked the anger of Salvador's lower classes. Crowds chanting "farinha sem caroço, carne sem osso" (roughly, farinha without stones, meat without bones) gathered in the center of the upper city and demanded official measures to reduce prices. When the cavalry arrived and began to disperse the crowds violently, many fled in such haste that they left their shoes and sandals behind to litter the city streets.[24]

The crisis that led to the so-called Revolt of the Sandals (Revolta dos Chinelos), like other crises before it, struck a society in which much of rural life revolved around production for export rather than for local markets. That fact stands at the center of what has become "the best-known model" for explaining such crises in colonial and nineteenth-century Brazil. The model, which has gained widespread acceptance precisely because it fits so well into a plantationist perspective of Brazil's past, links those moments of scarcity to prosperity and growth in the export economy. Although few studies have ever attempted a systematic test of the argument—indeed, most authors mention it only in passing—the mechanisms supposedly at work are clear enough.[25]

The model starts from the premise that export agriculture in Brazil spread generally at the expense of production for local needs. As the cultivation of sugarcane, tobacco, or coffee expanded, farmers who grew food crops withdrew into marginal areas of poor soils located farther and farther from urban markets on the coast. When international prices rose for the commodities Brazil sent overseas, this process accelerated.

Export agriculture then expanded along three main fronts. First, planters tended to cut back on any subsistence production on their estates and to employ all their slaves and all their arable land in the cultivation of export crops. Demand for farinha and other marketed foodstuffs consequently rose as more and more planters purchased provisions to feed their slaves. Second, senhores de engenho and other planters acquired, by one means or another, lands until then used for growing food crops to enlarge their estates and to plant still more cane, coffee, or tobacco. Third, those cassava growers who succeeded in holding on to their land and who owned enough slaves abandoned production for the internal market and began to cultivate export crops. Only the poorest roceiros continued to plant cassava, but they were the growers least capable of meeting the greater demand for farinha. Sooner or later, the combination of increasing demand and declining production inevitably led to a crisis characterized by severe shortages and high prices.

The relevance of this model to a study of food crises in Bahia between 1780 and 1860 should be obvious. Several periods of particularly rapid expansion carried forward the long-term growth of the province's export economy in those eight decades. That growth spread export crops into areas both in the Recôncavo and elsewhere in Bahia that had, in the late eighteenth century, specialized in the production of farinha for Salvador's market. Contemporary testimony, moreover, seems to bear out the model. Observers in the 1780s and 1790s and again in the 1850s often drew a connection between higher farinha prices and the increased cultivation of export crops. Vilhena at the end of the eighteenth century, for example, outlined a rough version of the model when, commenting on the high price of farinha sold in Salvador, he explained,

> The price of sugar has now risen to such heights . . . that . . . there is no one who does not want to be a lavrador de canas. And this is the reason why farmers who have always grown cassava are now ceasing to grow that crop in order to produce sugar, one arroba of which buys them four alqueires of farinha.[26]

Likewise, referring specifically to the Bahian market, Stuart Schwartz has presented what is perhaps the most recent version of the model. He writes that as the "export surge intensified" in late colonial Bahia, "the problem of food supply in the captaincy worsened. . . . Attracted by high prices for sugar and tobacco," cassava growers "abandoned food production" for the local market to take advantage of the recovery in the export economy.[27]

In Bahia, the growth of the export economy did indeed strain the price and supply of farinha in Salvador's market. The close general relationship between sugar and farinha prices is clearly visible in Figure 6, which charts price movements for the two staples between 1770 and 1865. Just as the model implies, increases in the price of sugar tended to provoke a corresponding upward adjustment in farinha prices.[28]

Mil-réis

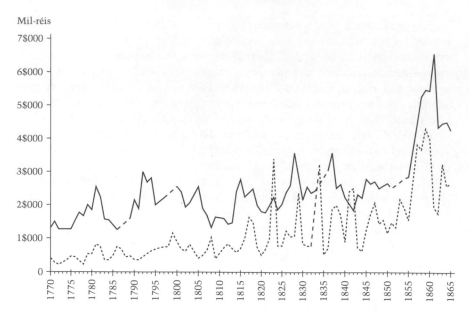

Figure 6. Salvador. Price of One Alqueire of Farinha and Price of One Arroba of White Sugar, 1770–1865 (annual averages in current mil-réis).
SOURCES. Mattoso, "Au Nouveau Monde," Annexes, pp. 445–61; "Conta corrente da despeza e receita que houve no Celleiro Publico . . . " (1834–43, with interruptions), APEB, SH, 1609 and 1610; bills of sale for white sugar attached to postmortem inventories, APEB, SJ, IT and ARC, IT. See n. 7.
NOTE. Solid line=price of sugar; dotted line=price of farinha.

Yet, taking into account only fluctuations in the export economy, the model yields an incomplete and ultimately distorted picture of crises in the local market. The model's weaknesses appear when the focus shifts from price movements in general to those specific moments when the price of farinha peaked and when, presumably, shortages were most severe. Those peaks sometimes did follow in the wake of increasing sugar prices; at other times, the price of farinha rose sharply and peaked even though sugar prices had held steady or fallen in previous years.

Some of the worst crises Bahia suffered actually took place in the two decades after independence, when growth slowed to stagnation and then briefly to decline in the export economy. One measure of their severity comes from the writings of Manoel Ferreira da Câmara. Influenced by the works of classical political economy, this wealthy and well-read senhor de engenho had, in 1807, proclaimed his belief in the principle of the division of labor. That principle, he argued, dictated that sugar planters should cultivate only cane and should willingly buy farinha at whatever price the market set. Although at times, purchasing provisions might prove expensive, planters would, over the years, gain more than they lost from specialization.

The crises of the late 1820s and early 1830s shook Câmara's faith in political economy. He wrote in 1834, "What is certain is that sugar has never sold for the price at which farinha is currently bought; and that net income [from sugar] has not sufficed for anyone to sustain himself and his slaves." As a result, he now proposed that planters no longer trust the market to supply them with reasonably priced rations for their slaves and that they instead grow cassava and other food crops.[29]

If the wealthy surrendered their principles, the poor gave up much more. As in all crises, they suffered hunger, but now, for the first and only time, the documentary record explicitly mentions deaths. The town council of Cachoeira reported in 1834 that several residents of that township had already died for want of provisions. George Gardner, an English botanist who visited Bahia shortly thereafter, learned that some slaves had been forced to subsist on nothing but jackfruit.[30] Similar crises overtook the Bahian market in the late 1830s and early 1840s.

It becomes clear that the movement of the export economy alone cannot fully account for the timing of crises. Countless factors, many altogether unrelated to changes in the price of sugar, combined to determine the price Bahians paid in any given year for an alqueire of flour. One factor that stands out for its recurring and especially marked influence is the weather. Crisis years, with only a few exceptions, coincided with droughts or exceptionally wet winters, both in the Recôncavo and elsewhere (see Table 8).[31] That is, prices peaked when poor growing conditions provoked temporary shortfalls in production. Thus, even though export agriculture dominated much of Salvador's hinterland, scarcities of farinha in Bahia resembled the subsistence crises that, in the eighteenth and early nineteenth centuries, struck cities in Europe and in other areas of Latin America.[32]

Given cassava's well-deserved reputation as a particularly hardy cultigen, it may seem surprising that weather should have had any influence on the price and supply of farinha. Cassava does stand out among other food crops for its exceptional resistance to drought. Cassava plants rarely perish in times of scarce rainfall; instead, they lose their leaves and become "essentially inert." Once the rains return, the plants quickly revive. Droughts do, nevertheless, adversely affect the cultivation of cassava. Without rainfall, newly sown cuttings will not germinate; planting then becomes futile. Soils hardened by drought also make harvesting difficult or, in extreme cases, virtually impossible. Similarly, heavy rainfall also hinders field work and, unlike droughts, can quickly destroy a crop. When waterlogged even for brief periods, the all-valuable root of the cassava plant rots.[33] Thus, when the summer was long and dry or when the winter brought torrential rains, either crops were lost altogether or, at the very least, planting and harvesting were delayed.

The delayed or failed harvests caused by the vagaries of weather threw into the market Bahians who normally did not purchase farinha: the owners of the suburban roças that surrounded Salvador; those planters who, in good

TABLE 8

Peaks in the Price of Farinha, Salvador, 1780–1860

Year	Price[a]	Observations
1781	$831	1779: A "great shortage" foreseen because drought has delayed planting and a plague of caterpillars has attacked the already planted crops at Nazaré. Outbreak of smallpox in Bahia.
1786	$751	1783–84: Drought in Northeastern Brazil. 1785: In Sergipe, the "rigorous winter . . . has destroyed everything." Shortages foreseen. Exports of farinha from Salvador to Pernambuco. 1786: Widespread hunger as a result of crop failures are reported in Sergipe.
1796	$740	1791–93: The "great drought" of the eighteenth century in Northeastern Brazil. 1792: Urgent appeals for farinha from Natal (Rio Grande do Norte), where backlanders fleeing to the coast have died along the roadside. The drought prevents planting in Sergipe, where the interior experiences a "total lack" of flour. 1793: Drought continues to prevent planting in Sergipe; crops and cuttings for future plantings are lost. 1793–95: Exports of farinha from Salvador, townships in Ilhéus, and Sergipe to Pernambuco. 1794: A plague of caterpillars reduces harvests at Nazaré.
1799	1$147	1799: Heavy rains cause "formidable damage" to cassava crops in Nazaré. Cumulative impact of droughts in previous years?
1803	$847	1802: Lack of rainfall prevents planting in Sergipe. In Rio de Janeiro, excessive rains spoil crops of cassava. 1803: Drought in Northeastern Brazil. In Sergipe, "the monstrous drought . . . has reduced everything to nothing."
1808	1$052	1807: Drought in Bahia. Arrival from Portugal of the royal family, accompanied by several thousand refugees and a squadron of the British fleet, all en route to Rio de Janeiro.
1812	$867	1809–10: Drought in Bahia and throughout Northeastern Brazil. 1812: Crops ruined by caterpillars in Rio de Janeiro.
1817	1$632	1814: Drought in Rio de Janeiro leads to shortages of farinha in 1816. 1815–17: Severe drought in Bahia (including the Recôncavo) and throughout Northeastern Brazil. 1817: Reserves of farinha exhausted in the cassava-growing township of Estância (Sergipe).
1823	3$417	1822–23: War for independence. City besieged.
1826	1$280	1824–26: Drought in Northeastern Brazil. 1825: Drought in Bahia. 1825–26: Exports to Pernambuco

years, grew enough cassava to feed their slaves; and normally self-sufficient tobacco farmers like the widow Maria Francisca das Virgens. Maria Francisca saw the tobacco and cassava crops planted on her farm in São Gonçalo dos Campos wither and burn during the drought year 1817–18. For nine months, as a result, she was forced to buy an alqueire of flour a week for a total expense of Rs.45$980, more than two-thirds of all the income she earned from her meager tobacco crop that season (Rs.64$550). Once the rains returned, Maria Francisca lost no time in ensuring that she and her family would enjoy an abundant surplus of flour during the following year; she had her three slaves plant 14,000 covas of cassava. The crises of the calamitous 1830s affected even impoverished cassava growers. Thus, around 1834, after several years of drought broken only by one unusually wet winter, Manoel Anselmo de Souza, a roceiro who worked a rented farm in Maragogipe, had

TABLE 8 *(continued)*

Year	Price[a]	Observations
1829	2$390	1827: Drought in Bahia. 1828–29: Drought in Northeastern Brazil.
1834	3$209	1830–32: Drought in Bahia. 1832: Drought in Northeastern Brazil. 1833: Heavy winter rains, which ruin cassava crops in Bahia and prevent new plantings, are followed by another year of drought (1834).
1838	1$958	1835–37: Drought in Bahia and Northeastern Brazil. 1836: Exports to Alagoas. Nov. 1837–May 1838: Siege of the city during the Sabinada revolt. 1838: Exports to northern provinces.
1842	2$504	1839: Drought in the Recôncavo. 1841: "Terrible drought" in the Recôncavo diminishes harvests.
1847	2$057	1844–45: Severe drought in the interior of Bahia provokes large-scale migrations. 1845: Exports to northern provinces.
1851	1$476	1850–51: Drought in the Recôncavo.
1853	2$183	1852: Heavy rains in Bahia followed by a year of drought (1853).
1857	3$866	1857–61: Catastrophic drought in Bahia.
1859	4$360	

SOURCES: José Moniz Nunes to the Gov. (7/2/1779), BN, I-31,29,62; Gov. to Martinho de Mello e Castro (19/1/1779), *ABN*, 32 (1910): 421; Alden and Miller, p. 83; Câm. de Sergipe to the Gov. (11/3/1782), APEB, SH, 201-7; jz ord. (S. Luzia) to the Gov. (14/9/1785), APEB, SH, 201-9; [José da Silva Ribeiro (tesoureiro, CP)], "Discurso" [1807 or 1808], BN, II-33,24,40; Câm. de Natal to the Gov. of Bahia (7/12/1792) and Gov. (Rio Grande do Norte) to the Gov. of Bahia (11/12/1792), both in APEB, SH, MNC; Câm. de S. Luzia to the Gov. (7/12/1792), APEB, SH, 201-8; idem to the Gov. (10/7/1802) and Câm. de Sergipe to the Gov. (10/11/1802), both in APEB, SH, 216; idem to the Gov. (1/4/1803), APEB, SH, 205; João Gomes da Cruz to the Gov. (1/6/1793 and 17/6/1793), APEB, SH, 201-40; ouv. (Ilhéus) to the Gov. (28/5/1793), APEB, SH, 184; insp. de f. (Naz.) to the Gov. (31/3/1794), APEB, SH, 201-31; idem to Gov. (3/12/1799), BN, II-33,18,14; Cunniff, pp. 34–35, 51 n. 66; Brown, "Internal Commerce," p. 113; M. Calmon, *Ensaio*, p. 70; E.A. de C. Britto, p. 83; ouv. (Sergipe) to the Gov. (31/3/1817), APEB, SH, 235; Henderson, p. 341; jz de fora (SA e SFC) to the Gov. (8/6/1817), APEB, SH, 241; Câm. de Camamu to the Pres. (22/7/1826), APEB, SH, 1282; Camara, *Memoria* (1834), p. 5; adm. (CP) to the Pres. (27/7/1836 and 7/6/1838), APEB, SH, 1609; idem to the Pres. (28/3/1845 and 6/6/1845), APEB, SH, 1610; Bahia, *Falla* (1840, T. X. Garcia de Almeida), p. 17; idem, *Falla* (1851, F. Gonçalves Martins), pp. 16, 35; idem, *Falla* (1853, J.M. Wanderley), p. 15; inv. of Antônio Joaquim de Menezes Dória and Ana Egídia de Araújo Góes (1841), APEB, SJ, IT; Góes Calmon, pp. 63–64, 72; Mansfield, pp. 426–27; the correspondence on droughts in APEB, SH, 1607; R. H. Brooks, p. 41; and Mattoso, *Bahia: A cidade*, p. 343.

[a] Of one alqueire of cassava flour in current mil-réis.

to sell his only cow and two calves to provide himself and his three young children with farinha.[34]

The combination of insufficient harvests and greater demand made Salvador and the Recôncavo all the more dependent on farinha produced outside the region. Town councils sent urgent appeals for shipments of farinha to authorities in the capital, where they believed supplies were more plentiful. Bahian merchants would seek out supplies wherever they could find them in coastal Brazil, while local authorities in cassava-growing districts to the north and the south of the Recôncavo received strict orders to dispatch as much farinha as possible to Salvador. The provincial government intervened even more directly in 1853, when it arranged for the importation of some six thousand alqueires of flour from Camamu at its own expense.[35]

Greater imports explain a paradox in the records of the Public Granary: in years when prices rose and commentators complained of scarcities, the volume of farinha handled by the granary did not always fall. On the contrary, it sometimes increased.[36] Although Salvador in those years successfully imported farinha in larger-than-normal amounts, the shortages that provoked complaints were nonetheless real. Reduced harvests in the Recôncavo had temporarily created a regional demand greater than increased imports could satisfy.

Even when fair growing conditions prevailed in the Recôncavo, lack of rainfall elsewhere could influence prices and supplies in Salvador. The arid interior of Northeastern Brazil, the sertão, periodically suffers severe and prolonged droughts. When droughts struck, backlanders (sertanejos), just as they do today, would migrate to the more humid coastal areas in search of refuge and food. Backlanders who chose to remain in the interior also looked to the coast for provisions. In the early 1790s, farmers in the cassava-growing districts of Sergipe, rather than shipping their flour to Salvador, preferred to sell it for an extraordinarily high price to the convoys (comboios) of packhorses that backlanders sent to the coast. The convoys returned in the drought year of 1817, but this time the backlanders did not trouble themselves with the formalities of purchasing flour; they simply took whatever reserves farmers had by force.[37] Whether backlanders fled droughts by migrating or not, their demand for farinha could make itself felt in Salvador's market.

More serious, perhaps, were the problems caused by drought in other provinces, especially those north of Bahia. The same easy water transport that allowed Salvador to import farinha, and thereby to avoid true famine when local supplies of cassava fell short, exposed the city's market to fluctuations in harvests and prices elsewhere in Brazil and even across the Atlantic.[38] Merchants from Pernambuco and Alagoas, eager to buy large quantities of flour, repeatedly descended on Salvador whenever droughts provoked scarcities in their home markets. Colonial and, later, provincial authorities did attempt to limit and sometimes even prohibit purchases by those merchants, but export controls seldom proved effective. If barred from making purchases in Salvador, merchants from drought-stricken provinces either smuggled farinha out of the city or sailed on to one of the cassava-growing districts of Bahia's long and poorly monitored coast. There they easily obtained the farinha they could not legally purchase in Salvador.[39]

As Vilhena put it, in times of scarcity, Northeastern Brazil turned to Bahia just as ancient Rome had relied on Sicily. But Bahia could hardly afford to serve as the Northeast's granary; unlike Sicily, it was not rich in reserves of surplus grains. Exports of farinha quickly produced shortages and high prices in Salvador. The crisis that followed was no less severe than if drought had struck the Recôncavo.[40]

Altogether, the evidence from Bahia, while broadly endorsing the model the historiography has proposed as an explanation for subsistence crises, also suggests refinements in that model. In the short run, changes in sugar prices did significantly influence the price of cassava flour in Salvador's market; an increase in sugar prices tended to provoke a corresponding but gradual rise in flour prices. Yet crises—the sudden leaps in the price of flour that Bahian consumers dreaded and that colonial and provinicial governments vainly sought to prevent through legislation—obeyed a chronology that cannot be deduced directly from the movement of sugar prices alone. Those moments of extreme scarcity most often began in the cassava fields—not so much because established roceiros had suddenly planted sugarcane in those fields, but rather because drought had made planting cassava impossible or heavy rains had diminished the harvest. In the end, the price Bahians paid for an alqueire of cassava flour in Salvador linked their daily lives both to the fluctuating demand for sugar in distant overseas markets and to the rhythms of planting and harvesting on the engenhos and cassava farms of the nearby Recôncavo.

Long-term Trends

The crises that punctuated life in Bahia between 1780 and 1860 coincided with a period of long-term growth in the province's export economy. On first consideration, it might seem that such growth could have only worsened the perennial problems of short supplies and high prices in Salvador's market. The spread of export agriculture into all parts of the Recôncavo could quite conceivably have brought about a long-term decline in cassava production in the region. Increasingly, as sugar planters and tobacco farmers enlarged their estates, roceiros would have found themselves forced to withdraw into ever more distant inland districts. Cane, tobacco, and other export crops would eventually come to monopolize all the arable land around the Bay of All Saints. In Salvador's market, that monopoly would translate into a sustained and exceptionally sharp rise in the price of farinha. The arguments invoked here would amount, in other words, to a logical extension of the same model commonly used to explain subsistence crises in Brazil: over both the short and the long term, production for local markets lost ground to the advance of export agriculture.

Although plausible, those arguments do not, on the whole, fit the evidence for Bahia. The growth of the province's export economy did not result in consistently higher real prices for farinha; nor, in the Recôncavo, did it lead to any discernible fall in the production of marketed farinha.

Certainly no sign of falling production appears in the records of the Public Granary. Between 1786 and 1851, the volume of farinha entering the granary grew at an annual rate of 0.8 percent—despite generally looser controls over trade in the Bay of All Saints after the 1830s and increased consumption of bread (see Figure 7).[41] But without evidence from other sources, that growth may not be particularly meaningful. Salvador's population also grew between 1786 and 1851, and growth in the urban population virtually presupposed larger supplies of foodstuffs. In truth, then, it would be altogether surprising if the amounts of farinha on hand in the city's market fell in the

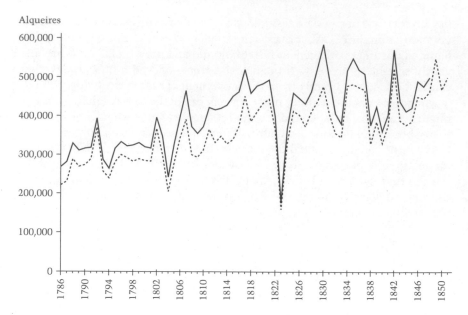

Figure 7. Salvador. Volume of Grains Registered at the Public Granary, 1786–
1851 (in alqueires).
SOURCES. "Mapa da farinha, arros, milho e feijão q. introu no Celeiro publico
da Bahia ... " (1813), AN, Códice 623; "Mappa demonstrativo do numero d'alqueires" (1849) and the annual summary statement for 1850, both in APEB, SH,
1611. For 1849 and 1851, total volume estimated from incomplete sets of
monthly accounts which show entries of 493,219.5 alqueires for Jan.–Nov. 1849
and of 157,217 alqueires for Jan.–Apr. 1851 (including farinha subject to the
duplo). For 1839, 1842–44, 1846, 1848, and 1850, complete sets of monthly accounts and annual summary statements (which furnish month-by-month information on entries, including again farinha assessed the *duplo*) in APEB, SH,
1610 and 1609. Also see n. 8.
NOTE. Solid line=volume of all grains (farinha, rice, maize, and beans) (in alqueires); dotted line=volume of farinha (in alqueires).

long run. The upward trend found in the granary's records might reflect
nothing more than a steady increase in imports of farinha from southern
Brazil and might mask a long-term decline in cassava production in Bahia.

An elderly sugar planter who anonymously published a treatise on agriculture in the province in the early 1870s believed that just such a decline
had taken place during the first half of the nineteenth century. In the previous 50 years, he declared, the cultivation of cassava had all but disappeared
from the Recôncavo. As a result, the region had become almost entirely dependent on farinha imported from other Brazilian provinces. This planter's
assertions roughly match the conclusions reached a few years earlier by a
commission from the Imperial Bahian Institute of Agriculture.[42] They are,
however, contradicted by other evidence. Throughout the mid- and late

nineteenth century, travelers and local officials continued to describe cassava as a crop widely cultivated in many areas of coastal Bahia. When, moreover, in 1844, the president of the province sought information on which areas regularly supplied Salvador with farinha, the administrator of the Public Granary listed Nazaré and Maragogipe, as well as townships all along Bahia's southern coast—the very same areas that had produced farinha for the city's market in the late eighteenth century.[43]

Fortunately, it is possible to weigh the conflicting and somewhat vague testimony of contemporary observers against evidence from other sources. Scattered throughout the documentary record are "statistical maps" of annual harvests, surveys of lavradores de mandioca, reports on trade in the traditional cassava-growing districts, and estimates of farinha production made by various local authorities. For a given year, some of these sources list the number of covas of cassava planted in a particular district; others refer to the amount of flour produced; and still others record the quantities of farinha marketed by growers. This lack of uniformity obviously complicates comparisons; it dictates caution in drawing conclusions about how cassava production changed over time in a specific area. We can, nevertheless, usually discern with reasonable certainty the direction of that change and, in some cases, estimate its magnitude.

In the cassava-growing districts in the old comarca of Porto Seguro in far southern Bahia, for example, the first half of the nineteenth century did witness a decline in production. At the beginning of that century, the townships of Caravelas, Vila Viçosa, Alcobaça, and Prado may have shipped nearly 130,000 alqueires of flour to Salvador and other markets. By the late 1840s, shipments from the same four townships barely surpassed 76,000 alqueires. The introduction and rapid dissemination of coffee in all likelihood accounts for much of the decline in shipments from Caravelas and Vila Viçosa. Coffee exports from the two townships around 1848 already stood at over 65,000 arrobas. Competition from export agriculture cannot, however, explain why farinha output failed to increase significantly in Alcobaça and Prado. In the mid-nineteenth century, farmers in the first township produced only trifling amounts of coffee; in the second township, they produced none at all.[44]

Thus, the evidence for far southern Bahia does not, in any clear-cut fashion, bear out the argument that greater cultivation of export crops resulted in falling production of farinha for the internal market. But perhaps the cassava-growing districts of Porto Seguro do not represent an appropriate test case for that argument. Far southern Bahia remained, throughout the nineteenth century, a poor and sparsely populated backwater with only weak links to Brazil's export economy.[45]

Less ambiguous evidence should come from the old comarca of Ilhéus, just south of the Recôncavo. There, in townships that had long supplied farinha for the Bahian market, export agriculture took firm root in the late eighteenth century. Farmers and planters in Camamu, Maraú, and São Miguel do Rio de Contas in 1799 produced at least 44,000 *canadas* (301,400 liters) of sugarcane brandy and 2,000 arrobas of coffee, as well as smaller amounts of cocoa and rice. All this alarmed authorities, such as the comarca's crown judges, who feared that increased cultivation of cane and rice would inevitably threaten local supplies of farinha.[46] Their occasional efforts to strengthen laws obligating all farmers to plant only cassava came to nought. During the next six decades, as the coffee and cocoa groves grew in both size and number, sugar planters established some 40 engenhos along this stretch of the Bahian coast. Far from declining in those decades, however, production of farinha increased (see Table 9).

At Camamu and Valença, output appears at least to have doubled; at Rio de Contas, the growth may have been even greater. It is no less noteworthy that the township of Ilhéus exported more than 2,600 alqueires of flour in 1864 and nearly 4,500 alqueires the following year. Those amounts were certainly modest—almost insignificant when compared with exports of sugar, cocoa, and coffee from the same township. But Ilhéus, unlike other townships in the region, had not produced farinha for Salvador's market in the late eighteenth century; on the contrary, its local market had been so poorly stocked that townsfolk and travelers had often found it difficult to purchase provisions there.[47] Now, despite vastly expanded cultivation of cane, cocoa, and coffee, the township sent a surplus of flour to Salvador. In the old comarca of Ilhéus, then, greater participation in Bahia's export economy did not prevent increases in production for the local market.

The same holds true for the Recôncavo, where, if nowhere else, competition from export agriculture should have brought about a pronounced and highly visible decline in the cultivation of cassava. From the late eighteenth century on, export crops transformed the cassava-growing townships of Maragogipe and Jaguaripe (including the parish, after 1831 the township, of Nazaré das Farinhas) in the southern Recôncavo. In parishes where, in the 1780s and 1790s, farinha production had dominated the rural economy and only a handful of engenhos had milled cane, several dozen plantations would, in the mid-nineteenth century, manufacture sugar for export.

The plantations established in the southern Recôncavo overlooked countless smaller fazendas and sítios, where, by the 1840s, farmers were employing their slaves in tobacco fields and coffee groves. But instead of abandoning cassava for export monoculture, those farmers continued to make farinha for sale in Salvador and other nearby markets. The evidence presented in Table 10 indicates, moreover, that they increased their production. For example, the entire cassava crop planted by roceiros in Maragogipe and Jaguaripe in 1780 would have yielded a marketable surplus of roughly 180,000 alqueires of flour. It is more than likely that a good deal of that marketable surplus never reached Salvador. After setting aside part of the surplus as reserves, farmers would have sold some of their flour to residents of nearby villages and towns and to the owners of neighboring pottery works. The rest they would have sold to merchants and farinha dealers, who, in-

TABLE 9

Estimates of Farinha Production in the Comarca of Ilhéus, 1785–1865

Township	Year	Alqueires of flour	Observations
S. Miguel do Rio de Contas	1799	30,000	Shipments to Salvador.
S. Miguel do Rio de Contas	1866	100,000–150,000[a]	Shipments to all parts.
Camamu	1799	40,000	Production.
Camamu	ca. 1860	30,000	Shipments to Salvador "in the years of greatest scarcity."
Camamu	ca. 1860	80,000	Shipments to Salvador "in favorable years." Estimates made by the town council.
Valença[b]	1785	20,550	Marketable surplus. Estimates based on the amount of cassava planted by 188 growers.[c]
Valença	1844	65,000–70,000	Shipments to all parts. Estimate made by municipal judge after questioning local merchants.
Valença	1875	208,000–390,000[d]	Shipments to all parts. Estimate made by local merchants.
Ilhéus	1864	2,656	Shipments to Salvador.
Ilhéus	1865	4,466	Shipments to Salvador.

SOURCES: B. da S. Lisboa, "Memoria sobre a Comarca dos Ilhéos" (1802), pp. 13, 15; Hartt, p. 261; "Relação da planta da mandioca, q. fez distribuir o Sen.do da Camr.a da V.a do Cayru . . ." (1786), BN, I-31,30,51; iz mun. e delegado (Valença) to the Pres. (22/10/1845), APEB, SH, 2629; Representação dos comerciantes da Cidade de Valença (1875), APEB, SH, 1456; tables of exports from Ilhéus for 1864 and 1865 in Bahia, Falla (1866, M. P. de Souza Dantas), n.p.

[a] Hartt, passing on information received at Rio de Contas, reports annual shipments of 50,000 sacks of flour. Records of shipments of flour from Nazaré in 1803 refer to sacks of two alqueires. "Relação das Lanxas de fr.a q. remette p.a B.a . . ." (11/5/1803), APEB, SH, 417. Such sacks would be roughly equal in size to those currently used in the farinha trade. But in the mid-nineteenth century, larger sacks were also used. A sample drawn from the records of the Public Granary in the early 1860s indicates an average volume of approximately three alqueires per sack. AMS, 55-1 and 55.2.

[b] The source for this estimate is a survey of farmers in districts that, in the 1780s, were still part of the township of Cairu. The place names listed in the survey (e.g., Sítio de Mapendipe, Rio da Una, Fonte da Prata) refer to districts that would later be dismembered from Cairu to create the township of Valença.

[c] Marketable surplus (for a yield of 40 alqueires per 1,000 covas) was estimated with the same assumptions used in Chap. 7 to estimate production and marketable surplus in the Recôncavo.

[d] The merchants placed weekly shipments at between 2,000 and 2,500 sacks of flour, which would amount to annual shipments of 104,000 to 130,000 sacks. Thus, depending on the size of the sacks used (2 or 3 alqueires; see note a above), the number of alqueires annually shipped would lie within the range given.

TABLE 10

Estimates of Farinha Production in the Recôncavo, 1780–1845

Location (parish, township, etc.)	Year	Alqueires of flour[a]	Observations
Jaguaripe (including Nazaré)	1780	100,126	Marketable surplus. Estimate based on the amount of cassava planted by 310 growers.[b]
Jaguaripe (including Nazaré)	1781	86,577	Marketable surplus. Estimate based on the amount of cassava planted by 218 growers.[b]
Jaguaripe (including Nazaré)	1789	156,411	Marketable surplus. Equivalent to 60.0% of all the flour handled by the granary.[c] Estimate based on the amount of flour made weekly by 299 growers.[b]
Jaguaripe (including Nazaré)	1825–26	235,571	Shipments to Salvador. Equivalent to 61.1% of all the flour handled by the granary.[c] Estimate based on the quantity of flour shipped in the twelve months from 1 Oct. 1825 through 31 Oct. 1826 (excluding June 1826, for which information is lacking).
Nazaré and Aldeia	1788	197,455	Shipments to Salvador. Equivalent to 76.8% of all the flour handled by the granary.[c] Estimate based on the quantity of flour shipped between 14 May 1788 and 9 June 1788.
Nazaré and Aldeia	1789	152,297	Marketable surplus. Equivalent to 56.2% of all the flour handled by the granary.[c] Estimate based on the amount of flour made weekly by 290 growers.[a]
Nazaré and Aldeia	1789	169,338	Marketable surplus. Equivalent to 62.5% of all the flour handled by the granary.[c] Estimate based on the amount of cassava planted by 305 growers.[a]
Nazaré and Aldeia	1803	209,248	Shipments to Salvador. Equivalent to 73.1% of all the flour handled by the granary.[c] Estimate based on the quantity of flour shipped during the week ending 11 May 1803.
Nazaré	1813	229,840	Quantity of flour entering Nazaré's weekly market fair. Estimate based on the amount of flour brought to the fair during the week of 15 Oct. 1803.
Nazaré	1823	320,736	Quantity of flour entering Nazaré's weekly market fair. Estimate based on the amount of flour brought to the fair during the week of 12 Jan. 1823.

TABLE 10 (*continued*)

Location (parish, township, etc.)	Year	Alqueires of flour[a]	Observations
Recôncavo (Jaguaripe and Maragogipe)	1780	179,964	Marketable surplus. Estimate based on the amount of cassava planted by 712 growers.[b]
Recôncavo	1835–36	252,161	Volume of farinha reaching the granary. Equivalent to 57.3% of all the flour handled by the granary. Estimate based on the quantity of farinha registered with the granary in thirty-six weeks between 1 Aug. 1835 and 18 June 1836.
Recôncavo	1836	246,841	Volume of farinha reaching the granary. Equivalent to 56.1% of all the flour handled by the granary. Estimate based on the quantity of farinha registered with granary in seventeen weeks between 16 May and 10 Sept. 1836.
Recôncavo	1845	260,000–312,000	Volume of farinha reaching the granary from the Recôncavo. Equivalent to 66.8–80.1% of the flour handled by the granary. Estimate made by the administrator of the Public Granary.

SOURCES: Lista dos lavradores de mandioca de Jaguaripe (1780), APEB, SH, 199; cap.-mor (Jag.) to the Gov. (30/11/1781), BN, I-31,30,52; "Lista dos lavradores de mandioca das rossas de Nazareth . . ." (1789) and insp. de f. (Naz.) to the Câm. de Jaguaripe (25/2/1789), both in BN, II-34,5,28; monthly "Rellação das farinhas que forão exportadas para o Celleiro Publico . . . deste termo de Jaguaripe" (1825–1826) in APEB, SH, 1609, 2440, and 2470; Câm. de Jaguaripe to the Gov. (2/8/1788), BN, II-33,21,64; cap.-mor (Jag.) to the Gov. (11/5/1803), APEB, SH, 417; "Mappa especulativo dos efeitos entrados pellas estradas territorios da Povoaçao de Nazrᵉ . . . na Semnᵃ de 15 a 22 d8brᵒ [*sic*] de 1813" and "Mappa especulativo da esportação dos efeitos entrado [*sic*] pelas estradas de Nazaré Termo de Jaguaripe e feira de 12 de Janrᵒ de 1823," both in BN, II-34,8,29; "Lista das mandiocas que se achão nos lavradores do districto da Villa de Maragogᵉ . . ." (1780), APEB, SH, 187; "Mappa semanario da farᵃ entrada, consumida e existᵉ nos meses de agtᵒ a dezbrᵒ, 1835," the weekly "Relação do nᵒ de alqueires de farinha na presente semana . . ." (9/1/1835–18/6/1836, with interruptions), and "Entradas e descargas dos barcos do Reconcavo" (17/9/1836), all in APEB, SH, 1609; adm. (CP) to the Pres. (28/3/1845), APEB, SH, 1610.

ᵃ Wherever necessary, amounts reported in sources have been converted to annual quantities.

ᵇ For the assumptions made in calculating these estimates (which are based on a yield of 40 alqueires per 1,000 covas), see Chap. 7.

ᶜ Percentages calculated against the average annual volume of flour registered with the granary in a five-year period centered on the year in question.

stead of sending it all to Salvador, undoubtedly smuggled some flour to engenhos across the bay or to other parts of Brazil.

In any event, half a century later, from Jaguaripe alone, the quantity of
flour actually shipped to Salvador exceeded that potentially marketed surplus by fully 30 percent. In a twelve-month period between 1 October 1825
and 31 October 1826, provision boats carried some 235,000 alqueires of flour
from local ports in Jaguaripe to Bahia's capital. Just as they had in the late
eighteenth century, the townships around the Bay of All Saints continued
throughout the first half of the nineteenth century to furnish more than half
of all the flour reaching Salvador's Public Granary. Thus, although export
agriculture spread to all parts of the Recôncavo, farmers in the region apparently succeeded in increasing their output of farinha to meet the growing
demand in Bahia's local market.

The absolute lack of a sustained upward trend in the real price of farinha
between 1770 and 1865 reinforces that conclusion. Figure 8 shows that
when deflated by an index based on the prices of a dozen widely consumed
foodstuffs, farinha prices again display their characteristic volatility from
one year to the next. During this period they at times rose steeply, only to fall
again in the following years. Each fall, in the end, canceled out the previous
increase. As a result, the real price of the single most important staple in
the Bahian diet proved remarkably stable over the long run. The number of
engenhos in Bahia more than tripled between 1780 and 1860; exports of
sugar from the province underwent a fourfold increase. Cane, tobacco, and
coffee went far in reshaping the rural landscape of the southern Recôncavo,
but in Salvador, on average, an alqueire of farinha cost in real terms no more
in the 1850s than it did in the 1780s. Thus, over the long term, the expansion
in the cassava cultivation apparently kept pace with the growth of urban
and rural demand for farinha.[48]

In the same decades that the average price of farinha held steady in real
terms, its price relative to that of sugar underwent a considerable increase
(see Figure 9). Put differently, the price of sugar measured in alqueires of
cassava flour tended to fall over the long term.[49] Planters and cane farmers,
as a result, had to produce more and more sugar to sustain their slaves. With
what they earned from the sale of one arroba of sugar, planters and cane farmers could purchase in the early 1790s the 5 $^1/_4$ alqueires of flour necessary to
feed seven adult slaves for an entire month. The same quantity of sugar six
decades later, in the late 1850s, bought them slightly more than 1 $^1/_2$ alqueires of flour, barely enough to provide two slaves with one month's rations. Yet many planters and cane farmers in the mid-nineteenth century
continued to buy cassava flour rather than rely on home production. They
apparently reckoned that the greater income earned by concentrating the
labor of all hands in the cultivation of cane and the manufacture of sugar
still offset the now higher cost of purchased provisions.

For roceiros and other small farmers, the changing relative prices of farinha and sugar meant that in the first half of the century, cane became an

ever less attractive alternative to cassava. The late-colonial chronicler Vi-lhena, had he lived in the 1850s, certainly would not have written, "there is no one who does not want to be a lavrador de canas." Even in Vilhena's own time, when sugar prices had been the most enticing, a whole series of obstacles stood between most roceiros and the gains in social prestige and income that planting cane seemed to promise.[50]

Yet roceiros, over time, would have found few incentives in the contin-ued cultivation of cassava. Given the long-term stability of farinha prices, they could hope to increase their income from flour sales only by planting more casssava. But expanded production entailed proportionately greater risks. Prices could and did plunge in "good years" when favorable growing conditions prevailed and harvests were bountiful. Roceiros in such years might have to sell their larger output of flour at a loss. Manoel Ferreira da Câmara witnessed the "wretched fate" that overtook cassava growers in Na-zaré when, in 1805, prices sank so low that they did not even cover freight charges. Câmara left Nazaré convinced of the growers' "misery and unhap-piness."[51]

Some four decades later, in 1844, the president of Bahia, Joaquim José Pinheiro de Vasconcelos, took considerable pride in announcing to the pro-vincial assembly that his term in office had seen an end to the "excessive dearth" of previous years. Increased cultivation of cassava had produced "such abundance . . . that, for many years now, the price [of flour] has not stood so low." The farmers who furnished that flour hardly shared the presi-dent's satisfaction. That same year, members of the municipal council of Camamu wrote to the provincial president to "deplore . . . the total deca-dence of agriculture and commerce" that "the diminished price" of farinha had caused their township. Farmers, according to the council, could no longer sustain their families with their earnings from sales of farinha.[52]

All farmers plant their crops knowing that they undertake a risk; when, several months later, the growing season ends, an unanticipated fall in prices may force them to sell their harvest at less than the cost of production. Where, however, the general tendency in prices is upward, increases in real income can compensate farmers for the risks they take from year to year and can encourage them to expand their output. Even though Bahian roceiros in the early nineteenth century could expect no such compensation from the price of farinha, they not only continued to cultivate cassava, but actually increased their production of farinha.

Conclusions

Price movements in Salvador between 1780 and 1860 reveal a local mar-ket that, despite its size and vigor, was vulnerable from one year to the next both to the pull of an emerging modern world economy and to the much more primitive forces of drought and rainfall. Greater participation in that emerging world economy only exacerbated the problems of scarcity that ac-

Constant
mil-réis of 1810

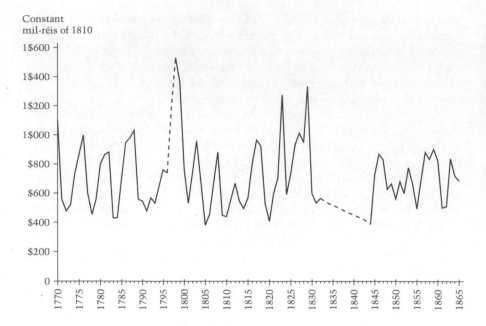

Alqueires
of farinha

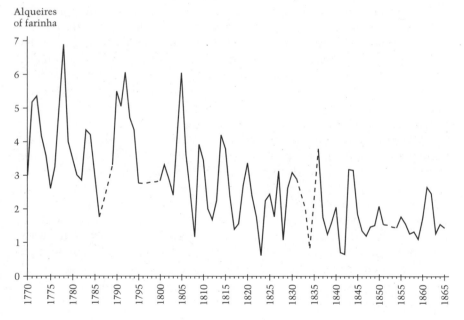

Figure 8 (top left). Salvador. Deflated Price of One Alqueire of Farinha, 1770–1865 (in constant mil-réis of 1810).

SOURCES. Mattoso, "Au Nouveau Monde," Annexes, pp. 445–61; "Conta corrente da despeza e receita que houve no Celleiro Publico . . . " (1834–43, with interruptions), APEB, SH, 1609 and 1610; Bahia, *Falla* (1868, J.B. Nascentes de Azambuja), *Documentos annexos*: Franklin Americo de Menezes Doria, "Relatorio do Chefe de Policia," "Tabella para fornecimento dos presos pobres das cadeias desta cidade," n.p. See n. 7.

NOTE. Farinha prices have been deflated using a price index for the yearly cost of a basket of foodstuffs based on the diet received by poor prisoners held in Salvador's jails as recorded in the police chief's 1868 report (cited above). This is the only the source I located that indicates both the type of foodstuffs consumed and their quantities. The prisoners received weekly: 42 oz. of bread, $1^3/_4$ oz. of coffee, 2 lbs. of fresh beef (*carne verde*), $^7/_{10}$ of a quarter alqueire of cassava flour, 3 oz. of bacon (*toucinho*), 8 oz. of rice, 2 lbs. of jerked beef, 15 oz. of beans, $^1/_{400}$ of a *canada* of olive oil (*azeite doce*), and $^1/_{400}$ of a *canada* of vinegar. (The prisoners also received unspecified amounts of "condiments" [*temperos*] and "fresh green vegetables" [*verduras*]. Because the amounts were unspecified and because Mattoso's price series do not include these items, I have not included them in the index.) Multiplied by 52 and thus converted into figures for annual consumption, these quantities may be used with Mattoso's price series to construct a weighted index for a basket of basic foodstuffs. Since Mattoso collected information on the price of wheat flour rather than bread, I have converted bread to flour with a standard baker's ratio of 13.5 lbs. of flour for 23 lbs. of French bread (*pão francês*). For years before 1810, Mattoso was unable to locate information on the price of coffee. It is unlikely that coffee was widely consumed in Salvador before that date. Therefore, the index does not include coffee for years before 1810. Where Mattoso's other series contained lacunae, the price of the product in question was excluded from calculations for that year. The index can be regarded as reflecting the expenditures made in poorer households on foodstuffs to feed an adult.

Figure 9 (bottom left). Salvador. Price of One Arroba of White Sugar Measured in Alqueires of Farinha, 1770–1865.

SOURCES. Mattoso, "Au Nouveau Monde," Annexes, pp. 445–61; "Conta corrente da despeza e receita que houve no Celleiro Publico . . . " (1834–43, with interruptions), APEB, SH, 1609 and 1610; bills of sale and receipts for white sugar attached to postmortem inventories, APEB, SJ, IT and ARC, IT. See n. 7.

companied delayed or diminished harvests. In the long run, however, Bahia's local market proved resilient to the demands of growth in the province's export economy. The expansion of export agriculture in the first half of the nineteenth century caused neither the disappearance of cassava from the Recôncavo nor any significant upward trend in the real price of farinha.

Instead, export economy and local market shared, in the long run, a complementary relationship. Because Bahian planters relied heavily on the local market to feed their slaves, expanding sugar production in the Recôncavo generated a larger rural demand for farinha and other basic foodstuffs. Increased supplies of locally produced and marketed farinha were, in turn, essential not only in ensuring the well-being of Salvador's growing urban population, but also in making possible the long-term expansion of highly specialized plantation agriculture in the rural Recôncavo. Thus, price movements in Salvador provide further evidence that by the late eighteenth century, the Bahian market for locally produced foodstuffs had become an integral and even crucial part of a broader regional economy dominated by slave-based export agriculture.

To understand how Bahian planters and farmers achieved long-term increases in the production of both export crops and farinha requires that we turn our attention away from the fluctuations of prices in local and overseas markets and look more closely at the countryside that surrounded the Bay of All Saints—at the land planters and farmers cultivated, the slaves they employed, and the agricultural practices they followed. The remaining chapters of this study take up those topics.

CHAPTER 5

Land

Bahians throughout the Recôncavo knew that the rains that fell in late February or early March signaled not only the end of summer but also the start of the planting season. Gangs of slaves began to trudge into the canefields of engenhos on the northern side of the bay. Armed with hoes, they opened trenches in the heavy soil where they would place and cover stalks of planting cane. In Cachoeira, slaves, generally in smaller groups, carefully prepared the seedbeds on the tobacco farms. Farther south, only one or two slaves might be at work in the fields. Together with their masters, they used their hoes to pile the soil into small mounds (covas), where, they hoped, cassava cuttings would take root and flourish. Whatever the crop, agriculture meant opening the earth, working the land. An examination of the Recôncavo's agricultural economy might therefore well begin with the land itself—the rich massapés coveted by sugar planters and the lighter, sandier soils used by tobacco farmers and cassava growers. In dealing with land, this chapter concentrates on two issues: the availability of land for increasing production of both export and subsistence crops, and the patterns of tenure that governed the distribution and use of landed property in the Recôncavo.

An Agricultural Frontier

Contrary to the view held by some historians, Bahia in the late eighteenth and early nineteenth centuries possessed an abundant supply of land for agricultural expansion.[1] A full appreciation of just how plentiful land was requires a broader perspective than the regional focus adopted in this study. Neither the vague limits that contemporary commentators used to define the Recôncavo nor the boundaries that modern geographers trace around the region ever constituted barriers to migration or to the spread of agriculture. For this reason, we must also bear in mind that beyond the Recôncavo stretched a vast and sparsely populated province, equal in area to modern France. Scattered over Bahia's half a million square kilometers were pockets of settlement, separated by great empty expanses of largely uncultivated territory. Although population growth and migration had begun to fill this "hollow frontier," the interior would remain thinly settled throughout the nineteenth century. As late as 1872, fewer than 1.5 million people lived in the entire province. Population density was thus extremely low.[2]

Of course, some regions of the Bahian interior were sparsely populated because their harsh, dry climate discouraged settlement. Few activities besides cattle ranching could prosper in the arid scrub lands of northeastern Bahia. These were the sertões (backlands) later made famous by Euclides da Cunha in his recounting of Canudos, the great messianic rebellion that shook Bahia in the 1890s. Although justly celebrated as a masterpiece of Brazilian literature, da Cunha's narrative has contributed to the mistaken notion that caatinga (scrub land) covered all of the Bahian interior and that all backlanders were ranchers, cowboys, or ranch hands. Da Cunha mentions only in passing the moist bottomlands found in river valleys here and there throughout the sertão. Likewise, he fails to describe the large areas of the interior where enough rain does fall in normal years to make agriculture possible. In such areas, farmers grew a wide variety of crops in the nineteenth century. The cereals they cultivated would, in the last decades of the century, reach coastal markets by rail. They also harvested coffee, tobacco, and cotton; and from their sugarcane, hundreds of tiny engenhocas manufactured rapaduras and distilled cachaça. Cane cultivated closer to the coast, in townships north and northwest of the Recôncavo, supplied engenhos that, after 1800, produced sugar for export.[3]

Low population densities characterized not only the backlands of the interior but also Bahia's long southern coast, where rainfall was in no way lacking. The coast south of the Recôncavo receives at least 1,500 millimeters of rain a year. Townships along this stretch of coastline had begun, by the mid-seventeenth century, to supply farinha for Salvador's market. Nevertheless, even at the end of the eighteenth century, settlement in the two southern comarcas of Ilhéus and Porto Seguro had scarcely breached the coastal forests. From those forests came much of the valuable hardwood timber exported from Salvador and used in the city's shipyards.[4]

The dense woods along the southern coasts also sheltered unconquered Indians, who, from time to time, attacked lone travelers and isolated farmsteads. Population did increase with expanding production of export crops and cassava flour after 1780. Yet the real transformation of this heavily forested frontier region would not come until the 1890s, when the promise of quick and easy wealth from surging cocoa exports drew thousands of migrants to Ilhéus and other nearby townships. In the furious and often violent land rush that followed, most of the migrants would end up as rural laborers, working for the few who had succeeded in establishing themselves as plantation owners.[5] Thus, whether they headed westward into the interior or southward along the coast, Bahians encountered an abundance of unsettled and uncultivated land.

They did not need, however, to endure long journeys into the interior or to brave Indian attacks on the southern coast; in the late eighteenth century, land for agricultural expansion was still available in the townships around the Bay of All Saints. To be sure, the Recôncavo by then already stood apart from other areas of Bahia. Two-and-a-half centuries of colonization had wrought enormous changes. Where the first explorers had found only a few Indian villages surrounded by great stands of primeval forest, Portuguese settlers and African slaves had cleared fields to plant cane, tobacco, and cassava. They had also built a network of villages, hamlets, and towns, separated in most cases by less than a day's walk.[6] This relatively dense pattern of settlement notwithstanding, the Recôncavo still contained a great deal of uncultivated land.

On this matter, we can trust José da Silva Lisboa's testimony. Lisboa wrote in 1781 that in the Recôncavo alone could be found enough land to bring about a fourfold increase in sugar production. He was perhaps thinking of the sizable tracts of good cane land in the northern parishes of Santo Amaro and São Francisco do Conde, which planters would not begin to exploit fully until the second or third decade of the nineteenth century.[7]

Lisboa undoubtedly also had in mind the extensive woodlands that, in his day, still covered large parts of the Recôncavo and that the historiography seldom mentions. Where historians have noticed those woodlands, it has been only to stress the almost constant process of deforestation that the region underwent from the first years of Portuguese settlement. Settlers had, it is true, recklessly destroyed large stands of virgin forests both to open fields for cultivation and, perhaps more devastating, to obtain fuel. Firewood cut from the forests kept alight the furnaces in the boiling houses in the Recôncavo's sugar mills. Using metaphors that would soon become common in the literature on sugar, the Jesuit André João Antonil at the beginning of the eighteenth century described those furnaces as "mouths that truly devour forests, prisons of perpetual fire and smoke." He went on to liken them to erupting volcanos and even to hell itself. The furnaces had indeed devoured entire forests. Already in the mid-seventeenth century, owners of some long-established plantations lacked forested land a convenient distance from their mills, and every year, when the harvest season began, they had to make costly purchases of firewood.[8]

The late colonial resurgence of sugar production both accelerated the deforestation and reduced the amount of uncultivated land available in the northern Recôncavo. As the number of engenhos multiplied and canefields spread out in all directions, shortages of firewood became more widespread. With the support of the colonial government, planters began to search for ways to reduce their consumption of firewood without cutting back their output of sugar. They experimented with designs for more efficient furnaces and with the use of bagasse (cane trash; that is, the refuse of milled cane) as fuel. The improved furnaces and the introduction of a new, more fibrous and more generally productive variety of sugarcane, known in Brazil as Cayenne cane and elsewhere as Otaheite cane, did finally allow many planters to shift from firewood to bagasse after 1816.[9]

Yet the sugar industry, despite its voracious appetite for both firewood and land, never succeeded in entirely deforesting the Recôncavo or depleting the supply of uncultivated land in the region. A report prepared in 1790 by Joaquim de Amorim Castro, crown judge for Cachoeira, makes clear that woodlands survived everywhere in the region. The virgin forests he describes began in the bayshore parish of Santiago do Iguape, a major center of sugar production and the site of more than a dozen engenhos. From Iguape, one branch of woodlands, some 7 leagues (42 kilometers) in length, wound through the sugar-producing township of Santo Amaro, while another branch stretched westward into the main tobacco districts of Cachoeira. Still farther west, according to Amorim Castro's report, lay even more extensive stands of virgin forest.[10] Four decades later, in 1834, Miguel Calmon would note that planters with estates near the bay left large areas of good cane land to lie waste. Nineteenth-century descriptions of plantations bear out Calmon's remarks. Even for estates located close to the bayshore, those descriptions often refer to large reserves of forested land.[11]

Further evidence that the Bahian sugar industry suffered no shortage of land comes from an 1835 census of the parish of Santiago do Iguape. There, as in other traditional cane-growing districts, the sugar trade's recovery from the 1780s on encouraged planters to invest heavily in their estates by repairing dilapidated mills, establishing new engenhos, and planting more cane. If the number of slaves they owned is any measure, then the expansion in cane cultivation was substantial; slaveholdings on some engenhos more than doubled in size between 1780 and 1835.[12]

Perhaps the most spectacular increase occurred at the Engenho Vitória, which, in the mid-1780s, had been a smaller-than-average plantation. By 1814, Vitória had come into the hands of Pedro Rodrigues Bandeira, a wealthy merchant with connections to the slave trade. Bandeira quickly set about building up the engenho's labor force so that at the time of his death in 1835, Vitória counted 242 slaves. That was no less than a fivefold increase over the fewer than 50 slaves who had worked there in 1786. All in all, Iguape, with its numerous engenhos and cane farms and with its large slave population, struck Bahians as a well-cultivated and thickly settled parish.[13]

Nevertheless, when the vicar of Iguape carried out the 1835 census, he recorded the names of 42 sawyers who earned their living by cutting timber and firewood from the parish's forests. Clearly, not all of the woodlands described by Amorim Castro in 1790 had perished in the furnaces of the boiling houses on Iguape's engenhos. Far more numerous than sawyers were small farmers, who cultivated mainly cassava and other food crops; they numbered more than 200. If the planters of Iguape had been hard pressed for land to grow more cane, they would surely not have hesitated to expel poor tenant farmers and squatters from their estates. That more than 200 such farmers continued to live and cultivate roças in the parish strongly suggests that the planters had more land than they themselves could use.[14]

Yet, should the sugar producers of Iguape or any other northern bayshore parish have needed or simply wanted more land, they had only to look across the bay to the cassava-growing townships of Jaguaripe, Nazaré, and Maragogipe. There, on a still-open agricultural frontier, they could readily have found fresh, uncultivated land amid the dense forests that still covered much of the southern Recôncavo at the beginning of the nineteenth century. Those forests sustained a timber industry in Jaguaripe that supplied large quantities of firewood to engenhos on the other side of the bay and hardwood planking to Salvador's shipyards.[15]

The smacks and launches that plied the bay between Jaguaripe and Salvador carried not only firewood and timber but also farinha. Although Jaguaripe and Maragogipe furnished much of the farinha sold in the city's market, cassava farms occupied only a small fraction of the total land area of the southern Recôncavo. In 1780, for example, farmers in the two townships may have produced 224,576 alqueires of flour, both for their own consumption and for sale, from the 5.6 million covas of cassava they planted. To plant that number of covas, they would have needed, by an extremely generous estimate, 18,682 hectares, a scant 7 percent of the total land area of the southern Recôncavo.[16] Sixty-five years later, after cassava cultivation had considerably increased in the Recôncavo, the administrator of the Public Granary reported that Salvador received annually between 260,000 and 312,000 alqueires of flour from the region. The cassava needed to produce 312,000 alqueires of flour would have required, again by an extremely generous estimate, no more than 51,909 hectares; that amounts to less than one-fifth of the entire area of the southern Recôncavo. We could reduce that estimate by half with no risk of understating the area necessary for the production the same amount of flour. As late as 1869, local authorities in Nazaré could report that their township, by then the site of more than one hundred engenhos, still contained large tracts of unexploited land suitable for agriculture.[17]

Land therefore was not a scarce resource in nineteenth-century Bahia. Even within the confines of the Recôncavo, Bahian planters and farmers could bring new areas into cultivation and thereby achieve a more or less simultaneous increase in the production of both export crops for overseas markets and farinha for sale in Salvador.

Cane, tobacco, and coffee did indeed spread into those new areas. Their expansion changed Bahia's agricultural geography and transformed the southern Recôncavo and other coastal cassava-growing districts into centers of export agriculture. That process, already described in Chapter 2, need not be reviewed here. We can instead focus on cassava, for which the documentary record, although thin and often imprecise, leaves little room for doubt. The cultivation of cassava expanded from the late eighteenth century on, even as the production of sugar, tobacco, and coffee also increased. On a still-open frontier, Bahian roceiros, "with axes and fire [a ferro e fogo]," cleared forests in the southern Recôncavo and in the old comarca of Ilhéus to plant larger and larger areas with cassava.[18] The results of that expansion were manifest in Salvador, where the volume of farinha handled by the Public Granary underwent marked growth, and prices, from one decade to the next, held constant in real terms.

Greater production should have pleased local authorities in those southern areas; after all, they constantly received orders to encourage the planting of cassava and to ship as much farinha as possible to Salvador. Yet, perhaps surprisingly, they sometimes regarded cassava's expansion with alarm. In Maragogipe, expansion had pushed cassava production inland and away from the town and port. The township's roceiros increasingly found it more convenient to bypass Maragogipe's weekly fair and market their farinha through Cachoeira or Nazaré.[19] In Jaguaripe and the nearby coastal townships of Ilhéus, areas where logging remained an important industry, local authorities saw roceiros as "incendiaries" who, in their efforts to increase cassava production, wantonly laid waste to valuable stands of hardwood timber. The pace of destruction only sped up when farinha prices rose. In the early 1780s, for example, cassava growers from Nazaré began to expand southward along the River Jiquiriçá into the comarca of Ilhéus. Francisco Nunes da Costa, crown judge for the comarca, complained that in only six years' time they had "reduced precious forests as ancient as the world to ashes." "No manner of accounting," he added, could reckon the damage the roceiros had already done. The only solution was "to guard, defend, and demarcate" the remaining stands of hardwood timber and to force the "rustic and ambitious" roceiros to plant their cassava elsewhere.[20]

At stake here, as Nunes da Costa well knew, were the interests of the crown. Indiscriminate and unauthorized deforestation amounted to nothing less than the destruction of royal property. By law, all hardwood timber, even on private land, belonged to the crown. With planking, beams, and masts cut from that timber, the royal arsenals of Lisbon and Salvador built the ships that made up the Portuguese navy. The crown would, nevertheless, wait more than a decade before acting decisively on Nunes da Costa's recommendation. In 1797, immediately after issuing a decree that revoked all existing land titles in the area, it appointed Baltasar da Silva Lisboa as judge for the comarca and charged him with devising a "plan" to control and restrict logging. Silva Lisboa began by reasserting the crown's rights to all hardwoods and imposing new, restrictive regulations on the felling and marketing of timber.

The reforms immediately brought the crown judge into conflict with all the main local interests in this frontier economy: the *fabricantes* (timbermen) who owned local sawmills, the merchants who dealt in planking and beams, and the cassava growers. Their protests, culminating in a "strike" by the fabricantes in 1799–1800, forced the crown and Silva Lisboa to yield. After that, all serious attempts to enforce the new regulations were abandoned. Fabricantes could once again freely fell hardwood timber; the new restrictions on trade were removed; and the property rights of landowners were restored.[21]

It is particularly revealing that this dispute, the best-documented conflict over land use involving cassava growers, had nothing to do with export agriculture. It did not pit small farmers against sugar planters eager to force them off their land in order to plant more cane. Instead, the roceiros of Ilhéus, pressing against the frontier to produce more farinha for the internal market, found themselves at odds with a royal bureaucracy intent on upholding the crown's rights and on preserving valuable stands of hardwood timber. The dispute thus serves as a fitting conclusion to a discussion of the availability of land for agricultural expansion in early nineteenth-century Bahia.

Patterns of Land Tenure in the Recôncavo

At the same time, the dispute also brings into focus other issues related to land. In nullifying property titles in the comarca, the crown sought greater control over land use to limit further deforestation. Agricultural expansion, as the crown recognized, depended not only on the physical availability of land but also on who controlled the land. Determining who held that control means asking questions about landed property and its distribution in the rural Recôncavo.

PROPERTY, LOCATION, AND SOIL QUALITY

Investigating such questions might at first view appear largely irrelevant or even misguided. After all, what importance could ownership of rural property hold in an area where an open agricultural frontier offered a seemingly endless supply of land?[22] The existence of a frontier certainly did diminish the value of landed property. Land in colonial and early nineteenth-century Bahia never became so precious a resource that mere ownership automatically guaranteed social and economic power. And it definitely did not ensure control over labor. Yet Bahian planters and farmers, far from regarding land as valueless, attached considerable importance to its ownership. Real property always represented a significant share of the wealth that landowners in the rural Recôncavo bequeathed to their heirs, who, for their part, never ceased to entangle themselves in endless litigation and even violent feuds to safeguard their real or presumed rights to that property.[23]

At times, they even flouted the risk of slave rebellion. In the late 1820s, for example, Captain Tomé Pereira de Araújo, proprietor of the Engenho da Cruz in the parish of Santiago do Iguape, asked his neighbors for permission to build a sluiceway for his mill across their estates. All agreed, with one exception: Dona Maria Ana Rita de Meneses, owner of the Engenho Cassucá. Even after Captain Tomé obtained a court order in his favor, Dona Maria Ana Rita steadfastly refused to yield the right-of-way. Captain Tomé nevertheless went ahead with construction, and Dona Maria Ana Rita, in turn, twice sent her slaves to destroy the sluiceway. On the second occasion, in 1830, some two hundred slaves from both sides, supervised only by a handful of drivers and overseers, met at the site of the disputed watercourse. The local justice of the peace, as soon as he heard of the meeting, rushed to Cassucá, hoping to prevent bloodshed. He found the slaves already nearly out of control. Large gatherings of slaves were always dangerous, and the danger, as the justice knew, was greater than ever.[24]

Bahian slaves had, since the beginning of the nineteenth century, carried out a series of uprisings and revolts. By 1830, the generalized climate of fear that gripped the free population elsewhere in the Recôncavo had surely taken hold of Iguape, where plantation slaves had rebelled in 1814, 1827, and 1828. The last uprising had seen the death of an overseer and four freedmen at Captain Tomé's own Engenho da Cruz.[25] Yet in seemingly foolhardy disregard for the very real danger, he and Dona Maria Ana Rita had massed their slaves and led them into a potentially explosive situation. Their willingness to risk a slave revolt amply testifies to the importance Bahians attached to the ownership of real property.

The paradox that land should have been both plentiful and highly valued can be resolved by turning our attention away from land in general or in the abstract. Land is not a homogeneous good; instead, location and soil quality give rise to crucial differences that distinguish one piece of land from another. Squatters whose only goal was to grow enough food to feed themselves and their families might freely ignore those differences. On almost any plot of land, even in the farthest corner of the interior, they could plant a field of cassava, beans, and maize. But agriculturalists who hoped to sell their crops wanted land that lay within easy reach of markets and gave them the greatest yields from the least effort.

The importance of location should be self-evident; to a large extent, it determined the costs of marketing agricultural produce. If an estate lay a great distance from Salvador, the costs of transportation might reduce or even eliminate the returns from selling the crop. The cotton cultivated by farmers in the distant interior of southwestern Bahia, for example, virtually disappeared from the province's export trade after 1830. Burdened by heavy transport costs, it could no longer compete on the world market in a period of falling international prices. Growers of tobacco, cassava, and cane on lands nearer the coast had the same concerns. The colonial government took their concerns into account when it established the system of "discounts" used in assessing the tithe on tobacco after 1768 and on sugar after 1800.

For sugar producers, the botanical properties of cane made proximity to a mill just as important as distance from Salvador. Cane, once cut, begins to rot after 36 hours, its saccharine content declining quickly and hence its value as the raw material for sugar. Thus, whether or not sugar producers owned milling equipment, their canefields could lie no farther from the nearest engenho than the distance that slow-moving oxcarts could cover in a day-and-a-half. The need for ready access to an engenho also restricted the opportunities for roceiros in the southern Recôncavo to participate in the sugar industry until the 1830s. In the last decade of the eighteenth century, when high sugar prices brought many newcomers to the industry, planting cane in the hope of producing sugar for export was simply not practicable for most cassava growers in Jaguaripe and Maragogipe. No more than perhaps a dozen engenhos manufactured sugar in the two southern townships. As late as 1829, engenhos numbered only 36, in contrast to the 141 sugar plantations that bordered one another in the parishes along the northern side of the bay.

Not only should land be conveniently located; the soils on that land should also ideally be as fresh and fertile as possible. More than that, the soils should be of the appropriate type for the crops grown on that land. Bahian authors from the early colonial chroniclers on repeatedly classified, described, and ranked the types of soil found in the Recôncavo. All agreed that for sugarcane, the best soils were the heavy clays known as massapés, which covered only a relatively small part of the region. Second-best were the lighter and more widespread salões. In last place came the sandy areias, soils in which tobacco or cassava might flourish but cane did not grow nearly so well.[26]

The prices assigned to rural property matched this ranking. Land bearing salões fetched only half the price of an equivalent area of massapé; areias went for even less.[27] The available evidence further suggests that the real price of good cane land apparently rose and fell with the changing fortunes of the Bahian sugar industry.[28] Table 11 shows that the price of a tarefa of massapés in constant pounds sterling generally held steady or declined when the industry stagnated. Conversely, in periods when sugar production expanded rapidly, land values increased. Massapé lands could command high prices at those times because they combined the advantages of location and soil type. Over such lands—not over land in general or in the abstract—Bahians fought each other in the courts and in feuds for the rights and privileges of ownership.

PLANTATIONS AND FARMS, SMALL PROPERTIES AND GREAT ESTATES

A broad scholarly consensus has long held that those rights and privileges in colonial and nineteenth-century Brazil belonged almost exclusively to a small class of great landowners. Their enduring monopoly over landed property supposedly originated in the generous land grants of one to three

TABLE 11

Price of One Tarefa of Land Bearing Massapé Soil,
Bahia, Selected Years, 1805–88

(1 tarefa = 4,356m²)

Year	Price in current mil-réis	Price in constant pounds sterling of 1810[a]	Index of price in constant pounds sterling (1810 = 100.0)[b]
1805	Rs. 30$000	£7 18s	94.6
1810	Rs. 30$000	£8 7s	100.0
1832	Rs. 80$000	£32 4s	386.5
1834	Rs. 100$000	£38 11s	462.4
	Rs. 70$000	£26 18s	322.7
1836	Rs. 43$103	£15 5s	182.9
1837	Rs. 30$000	£8 17s	106.4
1839	Rs. 40$000	£13 10s	162.1
	Rs. 80$000	£27 1s	324.5
1848	Rs. 90$000[c]	£32 17s	394.3
1850	Rs. 40$000	£16 17s	201.5
	Rs. 50$000	£21 —s	252.0
	Rs. 70$000	£29 8s	352.6
1852	Rs. 90$000	£37 1s	444.5
1854	Rs. 50$000–Rs. 60$000	£18 14s–£22 9s	224.4–269.3
	Rs. 60$000–Rs. 80$000	£22 9s–£29 18s	269.3–359.1
	Rs. 100$000	£37 8s	448.8
1856	Rs. 70$000	£26 5s	314.3
1857	Rs. 50$000	£17 11s	210.6
1858	Rs. 80$000	£27 12s	331.1
1871	Rs. 50$000	£15 —s	179.8
1874	Rs. 40$000–Rs. 100$000	£11 18s–£29 14s	142.6–356.6
1875	Rs. 80$000[d]	£26 14s	320.5
	Rs. 60$000	£20 —s	240.4
1881	Rs. 60$000	£20 4s	242.3
1883	Rs. 55$000	£18 12s	223.3
1888	Rs. 25$000	£11 4s	134.5
	Rs. 20$000	£8 19s	107.6

SOURCES: Postmortem inventories, APEB, SJ, IT and ARC, IT; surveys of engenhos in the parishes of Matoim, Socorro, N.S. da Purificação, and Rio Fundo (1854), all in APEB, SH, 4597; EL, [Bahia], p. 14; Simonsen, 407–8, 431, 454; and Leff, 2: 246 (for exchange rates); and Imlah, 93–98 (for index of the value of British exports).

[a] Rounded to the nearest shilling.
[b] Index calculated before rounding.
[c] "Price for massapés and salões of the very best quality."
[d] "Price for massapés taking into account the [good] location."

square leagues (44 to 131 square kilometers) that the Portuguese crown gave wealthy and well-connected settlers. With those grants, known as *sesmarias*, sugar planters along the coast and cattle ranchers in the interior established enormous estates, "to be measured in square miles rather than acres," that left little room for the development of any class of smallholders.[29] Although the crown lost its power to grant sesmarias in 1822, latifundia would, throughout the nineteenth century, retain their stranglehold over the countryside.

The parliament of the independent Brazilian Empire failed during the next three decades to approve legislation to replace the colonial land grant

system. The Land Law it finally passed in 1850 proved completely ineffective at controlling the acquisition of public lands by private individuals.
Powerful landowners took advantage first of the absolute lack of legislation
and then of the lax enforcement of the 1850 Land Law to enlarge their estates
by expropriating vast tracts from the public domain. According to the standard argument, for the coastal areas of Northeastern Brazil, this meant that,
just as in the early colonial period, great estates would continue to dominate
the rural landscape.[30]

Recently, however, Katia Mattoso has questioned whether this conventional view of landholding applies to the Recôncavo. Mattoso notes that Portuguese inheritance laws (valid in Brazil until 1917) permitted primogeni-
ture only in a few exceptional cases. In all other instances, partible inheritance was the rule; all recognized children shared equally in the wealth their
parents left at death. Planters could still enlarge the holdings they inherited
through purchase, but their deaths resulted once again in the division of
property among all their heirs. Mattoso argues that by the mid-nineteenth
century, equal division of wealth among all heirs had destroyed the great
estates of the early colonial period and replaced them with a patchwork of
small and fragmented properties. Many engenhos, she asserts, had become
too small even to produce sugar. Only where heirs agreed to joint ownership
did families maintain intact holdings that encompassed more than one
working engenho. Thus, for Mattoso, partible inheritance is an important
element in explaining the decline of the Bahian sugar industry in the second
half of the nineteenth century.[31]

Mattoso has, in effect, reopened the entire topic of landholding in the
Recôncavo and in the other sugar-producing areas of Northeastern Brazil to
new research. In Bahia, that research will involve examining a truly complex pattern of land tenure. The long-established arrangements between senhores de engenho and cane farmers meant that productive units in the
sugar industry did not necessarily coincide with holdings of landed property.
Both in the sugar districts and elsewhere, moreover, ownership of rural property took several different forms. Alongside estates owned outright by individuals either alone or jointly as *bens livres* (that is, under free and clear
titles) stood properties held in two types of entail—*morgados* and *capelas*
(or *encapelados*)—in which an "administrator" enjoyed usufruct rights to
the land during his lifetime. The administrator could not sell or otherwise
permanently alienate the property either in whole or in part. At his death,
the usufruct rights passed to a single designated heir, usually a first-born
son. Bahians also held land under different forms of emphyteusis—that is, as
freely transferable property subject to a perpetual leasehold.[32] No less varied
were the usually unwritten rental agreements that proprietors in the rural
Recôncavo reached with their tenants.

A thorough examination of how this complex pattern of landholding
evolved over time will also have to overcome seemingly insurmountable
difficulties in the source materials. Notarial records, such as deeds of sale

and postmortem inventories, are often widely scattered and frustratingly uninformative. They generally do not mention the amount of land sold, bequeathed, rented, or donated; instead, they often refer simply to "lands." In other instances, they describe the property as having so many *braças* (or fathoms) of frontage and as extending however far back it might extend (*e os fundos que houver de ter*).

Brazilian legislators could have furnished later generations of historians with at least one easily used source to investigate land tenure in Bahia if, in the Land Law of 1850, they had included provisions for a true cadastral survey of rural property. Instead, the law and the ministerial regulations for its implementation required only that landowners "register" their holdings with their local vicar. The registries or surveys compiled by Bahian parish priests in the late 1850s and early 1860s often seem designed to thwart systematic analysis. Landowners rarely mentioned the size of the properties they registered. Although they usually did describe the boundaries and limits of those properties, the descriptions, where they are not cryptic for the modern reader, are frequently vague; they sometimes refer to such "landmarks" as coffee trees, banana groves, and stones that had already disappeared in the landowner's lifetime. Some landowners declared ownership of several, not always adjoining properties in a single registration while, in other instances, they described their holdings as consisting of various pieces (*pedaços*), lots (*sortes*), portions (*porções*), or parts (*partes*) of land which might or might not be contiguous and might or might not form a single farm or plantation.

Consequently, it is seldom possible to do much more than count—count the number of registrations made in a given parish, the number of landowners filing registrations, and the number of holdings that included at least one engenho.[33] The results of this admittedly simple procedure, shown in Table 12, suggest several tentative conclusions. First, the spread of export agriculture during the first half of the nineteenth century did not create a single, uniform pattern of landholding in all parts of the Recôncavo. Strikingly different patterns continued to characterize the region's traditional crop areas in the mid-1850s: large plantations in the long-established sugar districts and generally smaller holdings elsewhere. More than half the registrations filed in six parishes along or near the northern shore of the bay were for sugar plantations. Likewise, 98 of the 182 landowners in those parishes can be identified as senhores de engenho.[34]

Sugar planters also owned land in other parts of the Recôncavo; but there, to a much greater extent, they shared control over rural property with many other landowners. Clearly, despite considerable increases in sugar production, B. W. Higman's description of Barbados as "a vast sugar plantation" would not apply to the Recôncavo. A substantial landowning class of small and middling farmers survived in the western and southern parishes. The survival of that class, which can also be documented in probate records, helps explain the growth in farinha production between the late eighteenth

TABLE 12

*Registrations of Landed Property in the Bahian Recôncavo,
c. 1859, Selected Parishes*

Parish	Number of registrations made[a]	Number of landowners[b]	Number of registrations including at least one engenho[c]
Traditional sugar-producing parishes			
N.S. do Socorro do Recôncavo	23	21	10
N.S. do Monte	45	37	21
S. Gonçalo da Vila de S. Francisco	21	21	14
N.S. da Purificação de S. Amaro	71	49	47
S. Pedro do Rio Fundo	39	38	19
Santiago do Iguape	46	41	23
TOTAL	245	182[d]	131[e]
Traditional tobacco-growing parishes			
N.S. do Rosário do Porto da Cachoeira	70	50	3
N.S. da Conceição da Feira	232	177	3
N.S. do Bom–Sucesso da Cruz das Almas	341	267	8
Traditional cassava-growing parishes			
S. Bartolomeu de Maragogipe	174	164	13
N.S. de Nazaré das Farinhas	172	148	18
S. Antônio de Jesus	590	492	5

SOURCES: RET, APEB, SH, 4661, 4677, 4697, 4701, 4712, 4739, 4748, 4758, 4787, 4795, 4801, 4815.
[a] Excludes registrations for holdings that could be identified as urban and reregistrations of rural properties sold after their first registration.
[b] Defined here as any individual who claimed sole ownership of a rural property or as any distinct group of individuals who jointly owned a rural property.
[c] Does not equal the total number of engenhos in a parish because some planters declared more than one engenho in a single registration.
[d] Excludes double-counting (i.e., instances where a single landowner registered property in more than one parish).
[e] Excludes double-counting (i.e., instances where lands belonging to a single engenho straddled parish boundaries and where, as a result, the same estate was registered in two different parishes.)

and the mid-nineteenth centuries.[35] Not having invested in milling equipment, these landowning farmers had no commitment to the monocultural production of sugarcane. They were free to use their land to grow other crops.

One indication that those farmers owned generally small or medium-sized properties comes from the number of landowners who filed registrations. Here the contrast between the sugar districts and the southern and western parishes is particularly revealing. In no parish on the northern shore did landowners number more than a few dozen. Even in a large parish such as Nossa Senhora da Purificação de Santo Amaro, a center of sugar production since the late sixteenth century, the number of landowners was no greater than in the smaller and more compact parish of Nossa Senhora do Rosário do Porto da Cachoeira, where tobacco was traditionally the main crop. In both Nossa Senhora de Nazaré and São Bartolomeu de Maragogipe, three times as many landowners held rural property as in Nossa Senhora da Purificação. Landowners were even more numerous in the parish of Santo Antônio de Jesus, where land ownership was divided among almost five hundred proprietors.

TABLE I3

Size of Landholdings Registered in the Parish of Cruz das Almas
and in Six Traditional Sugar-producing Parishes, c. 1859

Area in hectares	Parish of Cruz das Almas		Six traditional sugar-producing parishes[a]	
	No.	Pct.	No.	Pct.
<10	74	36.5%	21	13.3%
11–20	18	8.9	14	8.9
21–40	26	12.8	7	4.4
SUBTOTAL	118	58.2%	42	26.6%
41–100	37	18.2%	17	10.8%
101–400	26	12.8	24	15.2
401–1,000	11	5.4	29	18.4
1,001–2,000	9	4.4	39	24.7
>2,000	2	0.8	7	4.4
TOTAL	203	100.0%	158	100.0%

SOURCES: RET, APEB, SH, 4661, 4701, 4712, 4748, 4787, 4795, 4815; Sonneville, p. 39.
NOTE: Includes only holdings for which information on area is available. The size of landholdings in Cruz das Almas are taken from Sonneville's analysis of the land registry for the parish, but his figures have been adjusted to eliminate the small number of urban holdings registered in Cruz das Almas. In the six sugar-producing parishes, just as in other areas of the Recôncavo, many landowners failed to report the size of their holdings. It was, however, possible in a number of cases to locate that information in postmortem inventories from the mid-nineteenth century and in the 1854 surveys of engenhos in the parishes of Rio Fundo and Socorro found in APEB, SH, 4597. Landowners in the sugar-producing parishes (but not in Cruz das Almas) frequently registered several properties at one time. In such cases, the areas for all holdings registered in a declaration have been summed to reach a total area. Where landowners submitted more than one declaration, the properties from different declarations have not been aggregated to reach a grand total. (This is consistent with the procedure used by Sonneville.) The only exception to this rule is in the three instances where a single engenho straddled the boundary between two parishes.
[a] Socorro, Monte, S. Gonçalo da Vila de S. Francisco, N.S. da Purificação de S. Amaro, Rio Fundo, and Santiago do Iguape, all on or near the northern bayshore.

Such disparities point to significant differences in property size that become more apparent in Table I3. This table compares the size of landholdings in six traditional cane-growing parishes and in Cruz das Almas, a center of tobacco production and the one parish outside the sugar districts where proprietors routinely declared how much land they owned.

In Cruz das Almas, smaller and middling properties predominated. Approximately 60 percent of the holdings registered in the parish measured 40 hectares or less; only 23 percent of all properties encompassed more than 100 hectares. By contrast, in the sugar parishes, properties with 40 hectares or less accounted for no more than 27 percent of all holdings, while estates measuring 101 or more hectares comprised more than 60 percent. Table I3 thus demonstrates that landholdings in the traditional bayshore sugar districts represented, by the standards of the mid-nineteenth-century Recôncavo, large properties.

With an average area of approximately 481 hectares, the engenhos found in those parishes were not enormous latifundia (see Table 14). No sugar estate in the Recôncavo could rival the Casagrande plantation in Peru, which controlled more than 40,000 hectares of cane land in the late 1920s.[36] But the fact that Bahian engenhos did not extend over comparable areas does not warrant the conclusion that they had become small or highly fragmented properties. Definitions of small and large are not absolute where agricultural property is concerned; they vary according to the crops grown and the technologies used in cultivation and processing. Before the mid-nineteenth century—when the use of steam power became widespread and, more important, when the introduction of vacuum pans, centrifugals, and other innovations revolutionized the manufacture of sugar—a series of technological constraints limited the amount of land planted with cane that a single mill could handle in a harvest season. Cultivating more land served no purpose unless another mill was built.

In the West Indies, the limit was reached when an estate had 600 acres (243 hectares) in cane. Thus, with allowances for reserves of woodland, provision grounds, pasture, and fallow, the optimal size of a West Indian sugar estate until the mid-nineteenth century was just under 2,000 acres, or about 810 hectares. Such plantations seem, however, to have been rare in most parts of the Caribbean.[37] Even in Jamaica and Cuba before the 1850s, an estate of more than 800 hectares ranked "well above" the average. Planters in the French colony of Guadeloupe in the 1830s found that they could profitably manufacture sugar on estates of between 50 and 100 hectares.[38] These, then, are criteria for judging the size of Bahian plantations: 810 hectares as the optimal size and perhaps 75 hectares as the minimum for profitability. At 481 hectares, the average engenho in the Recôncavo fell squarely within that range.

The size of individual plantations tells, however, only part of the story. Almost a third (29.6 percent) of the 98 planters who held landed property in the six parishes on or near the northern bayshore owned at least two engenhos. A smaller group of 13 planters owned three or more engenhos. In-

TABLE 14

Areas Occupied by Engenhos in Six Traditional Sugar-producing Parishes, c. 1859[a]

Area in hectares	Engenhos		Area in hectares	Engenhos	
	No.	Pct.		No.	Pct.
130–49	4	4.8%	600–99	10	11.9%
150–99	10	11.9	700–99	0	0.0
200–99	11	13.1	800–99	5	6.0
300–99	14	16.7	900–99	1	1.2
400–99	14	16.7	1000+	5	6.0
500–99	10	11.9	TOTAL	84	100.0%

SOURCES: RET, APEB, SH, 4661, 4701, 4712, 4787, 4795, 4815.

NOTE: Where landowners neglected to declare the size of their estates, it proved possible in some cases to locate that information in postmortem inventories from the mid-nineteenth century and in the 1854 surveys of engenhos for the parishes of Rio Fundo and Socorro in APEB, SH 4597. Areas refer only to areas of engenhos and do not include adjoining cane farms where these were registered separately or where registrations specified their area.

[a] Socorro, Monte, S. Gonçalo da Vila de S. Francisco, N.S. da Purificação de S. Amaro, Rio Fundo, and Santiago do Iguape.

cluded in this group were figures like Antônio Pedroso de Albuquerque, the notorious slave trader, as well as representatives of old aristocratic families like Antônio Bittencourt Berenguer César; the second baron of São Francisco, José de Araújo de Aragão Bulcão; the baron of Cajaíba, Alexandre Gomes de Argolo Ferrão; and Inácio Borges de Barros. Partible inheritance made the preservation of large estates difficult but, as these examples show, clearly not impossible.

Indeed, despite the laws that imposed an equal division of wealth among all heirs, some estates grew over time. For example, Captain José Pires de Carvalho e Albuquerque, when he died in 1808, left his heirs three engenhos in the township of Santo Amaro: Nazaré, São Miguel, and Rosário. Of the three, only Nazaré went to Captain José's son Joaquim Pires de Carvalho e Albuquerque, the future viscount of Pirajá. By his death in 1848, the viscount had acquired (probably through inheritance) the Engenho São Miguel as well. His son, the baron of Pirajá, outdid both his father and his grandfather by amassing a fortune in landed property that, already in the 1850s, included São Miguel, four other nearby engenhos, and several fazendas. The baron owned all five sugar plantations outright, not jointly with other heirs. Indeed, joint ownership of engenhos was decidedly uncommon in the Recôncavo.[39]

It is also worth pointing out that an emphasis on partible inheritance and on the size of Bahian engenhos can be misleading. After the middle of the nineteenth century, the modernization of sugar production required, above all else, capital—capital to acquire vacuum pans and centrifugals, to construct small-gauge railroads to carry cane quickly from the field to the mill, and to consolidate landholdings where necessary. At the Casagrande sugar estate in Peru, generous investments by the German firm of Gildemeister helped finance land acquisition; with that capital, the plantation grew from a fairly modest 725 hectares in 1850 to an estate of gigantic proportions after 1900. Similarly, beginning in the 1890s, government subsidies provided Bahian planters with capital to modernize the sugar industry, and they, too, set about consolidating rural properties in the Recôncavo. The usinas (plantations with modern central sugar factories) that gradually replaced the old, semimechanized engenhos would, by the late 1920s, have an average area of 4,010 hectares.[40]

In sum, despite partible inheritance, sugar planters retained firm control over rural property in the northern bayshore parishes. The estates they owned not only ranked as large properties by local standards, but were also of adequate size for profitable sugar production. The concentration of landed property in the hands of a relatively small group of senhores de engenho, in turn, distinguished the traditional sugar districts from the western and southern Recôncavo.

Two Bayshore Sugar Parishes

That highly concentrated pattern of landholding can be better understood by looking closely at two bayshore parishes, Nossa Senhora do Socorro do Recôncavo in the township of São Francisco do Conde and Santiago do Iguape in the township of Cachoeira.[41] In both parishes, sugar production had begun by the last decades of the sixteenth century. Three hundred years later, in the 1880s, the British firm of Dennis, Blair and Company would choose Socorro and Iguape as sites for two of the six central sugar factories (*engenhos centrais*) it proposed to build in the Recôncavo. The firm actually built and briefly operated a central factory in Iguape.[42] Beyond such points in common, the two parishes differed in notable ways. That should not be surprising. Every parish was, by definition, unique; each had its own peculiar history and its own distinct topography. Nevertheless, both Socorro and Iguape displayed many of the features that characterized land tenure in the long-established sugar districts in the mid-nineteenth century.

Socorro, situated at the northeast corner of the Bay of All Saints, was a fairly small parish, bounded on the west by the River Paramirim and on the east by the River São Paulo (see Map 3). Near the bayshore and along the two rivers lay sizable stretches of flat land, which gave way to low hills farther inland. Everywhere, areas of heavy massapé soil alternated with patches of lighter salões and areias. In 1817, nine engenhos milled cane in Socorro, and a tenth would come into operation by the mid-1850s.

As Map 3 makes readily apparent, those ten engenhos, belonging to eight sugar planters, controlled most of Socorro's territory. The largest landowner in the parish was Colonel Miguel José Maria de Teive e Argolo. He owned two engenhos, Almas and Santo Estêvão, with a combined area of 1,220 hectares. Ranking just below Colonel Miguel was Joaquim Egas Moniz Barreto e Aragão, whose two adjoining plantations, the Engenhos do Tanque and Mataripe, formed an estate that measured nearly 1,100 hectares. The plantations belonging to the other six senhores de engenho averaged 394 hectares.

All in all, Socorro's ten sugar plantations left little room for landholding by small and middling farmers. The parish did possess fourteen fazendas and sítios, but even some of these smaller properties were controlled by senhores de engenho. For example, Antônio Moniz Barreto de Aragão, Joaquim Egas's brother, owned not only the fazendas known as Caípe de Fora and da Ponta but also an engenho in the township of Santo Amaro. The Fazenda do Engenho de Baixo belonged to Salvador Moniz Barreto de Aragão, the baron of Paraguaçu, who was one of the greatest landowners in the Recôncavo. At the adjoining Fazendas João Dias and Noviciado, Paulo José de Teive e Argolo, Colonel Miguel's brother, planned to build his own sugar mill. Thus, ownership of land in Socorro rested firmly in the hands of fewer than a dozen, often interrelated senhores de engenho.

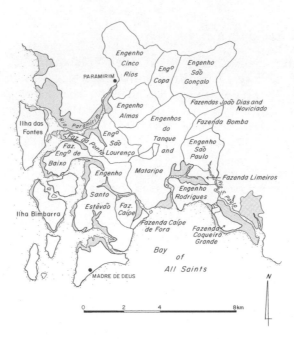

Map 3. Rural Properties in the Parish of Nossa Senhora do Socorro do Recôn-cavo (São Francisco do Conde), 1858

SOURCE. RET, APEB, SH, 4815. Also see n. 41. Also based in part on Brazil . . . , *Carta do Brasil*, folha SD-24-X-A-IV: *Baía de Todos os Santos*; and Sampaio, *Carta*. Property boundaries are approximate.

NOTE. Boundaries have not been drawn between contiguous properties belonging to one owner. Likewise, the names of most smaller properties are not shown. Islands shown did not, for the most part, belong to the parish of N.S. do Socorro. Shaded areas indicate tidal flats. A name in small capitals designates a hamlet or village.

Map 4 (right). Rural Properties in the Parish of Santiago do Iguape (Cachoeira), c. 1859

SOURCE. RET, APEB, SH, 4712. Also see n. 41. Also based on Brazil, . . . , *Carta do Brasil*, folha SD–24–X–A–IV; and Sampaio, *Carta*. Boundaries are approximate.

NOTE. Boundaries have not been drawn between contiguous properties belonging to one owner. Likewise, the names of smaller properties are not shown. The Engenhos Buraco, Vitória, and Conceição all belonged to the baron of Paraguaçu. Conceição was located in the parish of N.S. do Rosário do Porto da Cachoeira; Vitória and Buraco were situated in the parish of Santiago do Iguape. The Engenhos Caimbongo and Brandão were each owned jointly by three proprietors. The Engenhos da Praia and Acutinga and the Fazenda Cassucá were not registered, but were mentioned by other landowners in describing the boundaries of their own properties. Shaded areas indicate tidal flats. Underlined names in capitals designate towns. Names of villages and hamlets also appear in capitals, but are not underlined.

Engenho Santana
dos Patos
?

Engenho
Engenhoca
or
São
José

Engenho
da

Engenho

Engenho
Novo

CACHOEIRA

Engenho
Cabonha

do
Acu

do
Acu

Engenho da Praia

Santa Catarina

Engenho

Cruz

RIO AÇU

RIO

Acutinga

SUCUPEMA

Cassuço

Engenho
do

Desterro

Faz das Ana Pereira
& Pereira Guedes

Engº S.
Domingos

Faz S. Maria

Engenho
Calembá

Faz Caange

de N.S. da
Purificação

RIO JAPARAÍ

Engenhos
Conceição,

Vitória,

and

Buraco

Engenho
da
Embiara

Faz
Grande

Engº Maroim

Engo do Meio

Engo do Meio

Faz. Fojos

Engenho
Campina

Engenho
da
Guaíba

Engº S.
Antônio
da
Guaíba

Faz da Rochela

SANTIAGO DO IGUAPE

Engenho

Brandão

Engenho
Caimbongo

RIO PARAGUAÇU

Engenho
da
Ponta

Fazenda

Santiago

Iguape

Basin

SÃO FRANCISCO DO PARAGUAÇU

Engenho

da

Pena

MARAGOGIPE

RIO GUAÍ

RIO PARAGUAÇU

N

0   2   4   8km

Bay of
All Saints

Kinship ties also linked those senhores de engenho to landowners in the parish of Santiago de Iguape, which became in the nineteenth century something of a showcase for the Bahian sugar industry. At his Engenho da Ponta, Manoel Ferreira da Câmara entertained the German mining engineer Wilhelm Christian Gotthelf von Feldner in 1816 and, two years later, the naturalists Johann Baptist von Spix and Carl Friedrich Philipp von Martius. In the 1850s, Robert Avé-Lallemant, as well as the English Quakers John Candler and Wilson Burgess, spent time at the neighboring Engenhos Vitória and Buraco.[43]

The parish those European travelers visited lay just above the mouth of the Paraguaçu, where, before reaching the Bay of All Saints, the river widens to form a large basin or inland bay (see Map 4). The calm, brackish waters of the basin provided, in the early nineteenth century, a livelihood for perhaps one hundred fishermen, who caught *robalos*, *tainhas*, and *cavalas* with fish traps and dragnets (*redes de arrasto*). Those too poor to afford nets and sailing canoes collected crabs and other shellfish on the flats exposed at low tide.[44] Beyond the tidal flats lay more or less narrow strands of level land that separated the eastern and western shores of the basin from rugged, hilly terrain. Here and there, streams broke through the hills to form steep valleys. Although salões and areias covered most of those hills and valleys, massapés could be found along the western shore and on the two small peninsulas that jutted out into the basin.

North of the basin stretched an "extensive plain," traversed by the rivers Sucupema and Acu, that ended abruptly in an escarpment some six to seven kilometers from the water's edge. This was the area known as the "celebrated valley of Iguape"; Luís dos Santos Vilhena called it "the famous Iguape." The "legitimate massapé soils" found there were, he wrote, "so valiant" that despite many years of cultivation, they had not yet shown any sign of "weakness." He went on to add that Iguape's engenhos produced the "best sugar in the Recôncavo." Echoing Vilhena's praise, José Joaquim de Almeida e Arnizáu in the 1820s described the valley's soils as, "without contradiction, the most appropriate known" for sugarcane. A century later, in 1927, the agronomist Alexandre Grangier judged the same massapés to be of "an extraordinary fertility."[45]

The distribution of those soils, together with the topography, to a large extent determined settlement and landholding patterns in Iguape. Engenhos in the valley occupied long strips of land that extended back from the water's edge toward the escarpment. This arrangement gave planters access to good, level cane land, as well as to wooded hills. Where the forests had been cleared for the timber and firewood they could yield, the uplands served as pasture.[46] Similarly, senhores de engenho from Desterro south found it advantageous to own land both along the shore and in the steep chain of hills known as the Serra da Guaíba. To preserve their holdings intact, some planters in Iguape had entailed portions of their estates. Thus, an entail established before 1790 made parts of the large Engenho Engenhoca (or São José do Acu) an *encapelado* and helped prevent the piecemeal division of its 1,300 hectares. Entails also protected the integrity of the Engenhos da Pena, Santo Antônio da Guaíba, and Embiara.

Such safeguards were, however, exceptional. Most land in Iguape was held as freely disposable property and therefore fell, from time to time, subject to partible inheritance. While the inheritance laws undoubtedly helped create the distinctive striplike pattern of property lines found on the northern plain, equal division of wealth among all heirs did not produce disastrous consequences. Even the least extensive sugar plantations in the parish were not unduly small; the Engenhos do Meio and Maroim each controlled some 140 hectares of good cane land.

In 1839, twenty years before the vicar of Iguape compiled the land registry for his parish, the inheritance laws broke up one of the larger holdings on the northern plain. The Engenhos São Domingos and Santa Catarina had until that year formed a single estate, with two sugar mills, belonging to Colonel Domingos Américo da Silva. Although the two plantations were divided into separate properties after the colonel's death, the division hardly impoverished his heirs. Júlio Américo da Silva now became the owner of Santa Catarina, with its 260 hectares, while his older brother, Domingos Américo, the future baron of Santiago, received some 270 hectares at São Domingos and three nearby or adjoining fazendas.

The parish of Iguape also offers an example of an estate maintained intact because its owner died childless. Pedro Rodrigues Bandeira, having no legitimate children of his own, left his three engenhos, Buraco, Vitória, and Conceição, to a niece and her husband, Salvador Moniz Barreto de Aragão, in 1835. This was the same Salvador Moniz Barreto who, bearing the title baron of Paraguaçu, would also come to own two large plantations and a fazenda in the parish of Monte, as well as another fazenda in Socorro. His holdings, with a combined area of more than 2,400 hectares, made him one of the Recôncavo's leading landowners.[47]

Where the inheritance laws or land sales created smaller properties in Iguape, these, like those in Socorro, often belonged to senhores de engenho or to men well on their way to becoming planters. For example, Egas Moniz Barreto de Aragão, who owned the Fazendas Grande and Capoeira in the 1850s, would later inherit the Engenho Vitória. Neighboring small properties belonged to Tomás Pedreira Geremoabo, owner of the vast Engenho Novo do Paraguaçu in Maragogipe, and to Francisco Ferreira Viana Bandeira, who, through marriage, would inherit the Engenho da Ponta. Some of these apparently independent small properties, moreover, actually remained bound to nearby plantations by *obrigações de encargo real*; that is, they were held under a form of emphyteusis that obligated their owners to mill any cane they grew at a specific engenho. João Francisco de Souza Paraíso, for instance, owned the Fazendas Ana Pereira and Pereira Guedes, as well as his own sugar mill at the Engenho da Guaíba, but the cane he planted at Ana Pereira and Pereira Guedes was "captive"; it had to be milled at the Engenho da Embiara.

Thus, in the mid-nineteenth century, the planters of Iguape, like their counterparts in Socorro, still held a near-monopoly over land ownership in their parish. A total of only 41 landowners had appeared before the local vicar to register holdings of rural property. Of those, 17 were sugar planters, and they owned 19 of Iguape's 23 engenhos. Four individuals, in an arrangement that was altogether unusual in the Recôncavo, jointly owned the Engenhos Caimbongo and Brandão. Of the remaining 21 landowners, 3 possessed sugar plantations elsewhere in the Recôncavo; another 2 would soon become senhores de engenho through inheritance. That left a mere 16 landowners to form a class of smallholders.[48] The contrast between Iguape and any one of the traditional tobacco- or cassava-growing parishes is so striking that it needs no further comment.

Planters, "Tenants at Will," and Cane Farmers

The average size of rural properties, the number of landowners in a parish, and the boundary lines separating engenhos and fazendas are no more than the skeletal components of land tenure, significant only insofar as they shaped the daily lives of planters and farmers in the rural Recôncavo. A comparison of the land registry of Iguape with an 1835 census for the same parish provides an opportunity to explore what the ownership of rural property meant for Bahians who looked to agriculture for their livelihood. Although taken two-and-a-half decades before the land registry was compiled, the census probably reflects with fair accuracy the population of the parish in the middle of the nineteenth century.[49]

That population included 272 small farmers: roceiros, lavradores de mandioca, and those whose occupation was listed as simply "farming" (lavoura).[50] In a parish where all rural property belonged to fewer than 50 landowners, it is obvious that these small farmers seldom, if ever, held titles to the land they and their families worked. Their presence in the parish scarcely interfered with sugar production, because the planters of Iguape enjoyed what Henry Koster in Pernambuco called an "overplus of land that gives room for the habitations of free people in the lower ranks of life." The small farmers cultivated roças on land that, although owned by planters, was usually ill-suited for sugarcane: the hilly uplands of the Serra da Guaíba, the slopes of the northern escarpment, and the rugged terrain extending south from the village of Santiago do Iguape. In fact, almost half the small farmers in Iguape lived in the southeastern corner of the parish on properties that João Calmon du Pin e Almeida and Jerônimo Vieira Tosta would register in 1859 as the Fazenda Santiago and the Engenho da Pena. Both estates, according to their owners, contained "lands appropriate for small crops [pequena cultura]"—that is, cassava, beans, and maize.[51]

In other Northeastern provinces, many of these small farmers would very likely have been classified as *moradores*, a term rarely used in Bahia. Although scholars sometimes translate *morador* as "squatter," the French engineer M. A. de Mornay, who lived in Pernambuco in the 1840s, came closer to the mark when he wrote, "The *Morador* is a kind of tenant at will ...[who] pays no rent." Planters granted their "tenants at will" not just land but also protection in disputes with neighbors or the law. In return, moradores performed various services for their planter landlords: "going on errands, ... seeing that the woods are not destroyed by persons who have not obtained permission to cut down timber, and other offices of the same description." They occasionally paid a "trifling rent" in cash or produce; and at election time, they would be on hand to support the planter's candidate. When necessary, a planter might also call on them to serve as thugs and henchmen in his own feuds with fellow landowners.[52]

Although Bahians seldom used the term *morador*, the small farmers of Iguape must have closely resembled the "tenants at will" who lived on sugar plantations elsewhere in Northeastern Brazil. What is certain is that, like moradores, they lacked written, notarized leases to the land they cultivated.[53] Their tenure was, therefore, always insecure. But in a region where plantations contained ample amounts of uncultivated land and planters could always find use for another retainer, eviction seldom represented more than a passing inconvenience. The small farmer gathered up his family and his meager household goods, left his thatched cabin, and looked for another patch of land on a nearby estate.

Also listed in the 1835 census of Iguape are 98 lavradores de cana.[54] Their occupation as sharecropping cane farmers at an earlier time would have conferred a social rank just below that of senhor de engenho. During the early colonial sugar boom, they had constituted a stratum of "proto-planters." As conditions in the sugar economy changed, so did the lavradores' status; they came to form one of the most thoroughly mixed social groups in Northeastern Brazil. Their heterogeneity drew the attention of de Mornay, who observed that cane farming in Pernambuco was still "considered quite a gentlemanly employment" but promptly added that there were "Lavradores of all grades in colour and respectability; some plant very extensively their plantations [i.e., cane farms], producing as much as 50 tons of sugar yearly, while those of others will produce ... [only] one or two tons."[55]

Only a few examples are needed to show that with equal justice, de Mornay could have been describing lavradores in Bahia. The first examples come from the "Livro da Caixaria," or mill ledger, kept at the Engenho Nossa Senhora do Amparo in Santo Amaro, where, during the harvest of 1795–96, eight lavradores delivered cane for grinding. All eight were by definition sharecroppers, but that, as the ledger reveals, did not mean that they all planted cane on roughly the same scale. At one extreme was José Justino de Freitas, whose cane produced more than 355 arrobas of sugar. At the other was a marginal producer, Pedro Correia Coutinho, whose cane yielded a mere 6 arrobas, 22 pounds of sugar. The parish of Iguape furnishes similar examples. There, in 1827, Manoel Lopes da Paixão succeeded in planting 5 tarefas with cane, but his fields were in such a poor state that the probate assessors deemed them worth no more than 2½ well-cultivated tarefas. Sometime before his death that same year, Lopes da Paixão certainly met his neighbor Manoel Estanislau de Almeida. When Almeida died in 1838, he left his heirs some 65 tarefas planted with cane.[56]

Like those de Mornay observed in Pernambuco, the lavradores of Iguape varied not only according to the size of their canefields but also by color and legal status. Although most were white, their number included freeborn blacks and mulattos and even a few former slaves.[57]

Despite their diversity, most lavradores shared a common trait: they were tenant farmers who planted cane on rented land. Once again, the numbers from Iguape require little explanation. No more than a handful of the 98 lavradores listed in the 1835 census could possibly have owned the land they worked. Postmortem inventories from Iguape and the other main sugar-producing districts reveal much the same pattern of landlessness; only 20.3 percent of all lavradores owned any rural property at all. The great majority of Bahian lavradores were, then, not only sharecroppers but tenant farmers as well.

The sharecropping and rental agreements that lavradores reached with senhores de engenho benefited both parties. By taking on cane farmers, mill-owning planters could increase the output of sugar at their engenhos without having to bear the full cost and risk of expanding cultivation. The number of cane farmers they took on varied from one estate to another and from year to year; an average of two to four cane farmers seems to have been common for engenhos in the northern Recôncavo.[58] At those engenhos, the cane grown by those farmers could in some cases account for as much as two-thirds of all the sugar produced in a harvest season.[59]

Likewise, the sharecropping and rental agreements opened up the socially prestigious and usually profitable sugar industry to men and women who could not afford to establish their own plantations. Even individuals of quite modest means, such as Félix Júlio de São José, could take up cane farming, provided they had access to land near a mill. Probably a former slave or, at the very least, the son of a freed slave woman, Félix Júlio worked as a *feitor* (slave driver or overseer) at the Engenho Novo da Guaíba in the parish of Monte, where he earned Rs.150$000 a year. At his death in 1815, he owned a chest (*arca*), some clothing, a horse, one hoe, one scythe, a few pieces of silver plate, and three African slaves. But because he lived on an engenho and because he was allowed to farm a bit of land, Félix Júlio, by no means the poorest lavrador in the Recôncavo, had managed to plant eight tarefas with cane.[60]

Cane farming attracted men and women like this slave driver because the sugar industry was generally profitable, and because participation in that industry held the promise of social mobility. With a great deal of good luck and hard work, a few better-off lavradores would now and then make the leap from sharecropper to planter and come to own an engenho. But even, as in most cases, when lavradores and their descendants remained share-croppers, they still had possibilities for social mobility. Along with senhores de engenho, lavradores could claim membership in the Recôncavo's socially prestigious sugar sector. Both groups were united around a common interest in the prosperity of the sugar industry. Both also depended on each other. Without access to a mill, it was pointless for lavradores to grow cane; similarly, lavradores who delivered a large crop at harvest time could contribute decisively to the income planters drew from sugar production at their engenhos. This mutual dependence, reinforced in some cases by kinship, showed in the money, oxen, and field hands that planters occasionally lent their cane farmers.[61]

Mutual dependence did not, however, imply equality. Although the balance sometimes shifted, senhores de engenho always held the upper hand, and lavradores paid dearly for the opportunity to participate in the sugar industry. Becoming a lavrador meant entering a branch of agriculture dominated by a relatively small circle of planters; they controlled both the best bayshore cane land and the equipment needed to transform cane into sugar. This double monopoly allowed planters to impose burdensome contracts on cane farmers, especially those who owned no land. Rental agreements in the early seventeenth century required lavradores to turn over all the molasses and one-half the sugar produced from their cane in exchange for processing and then, specifically as rent, either one-fourth or one-third of the remaining sugar. Thus, tenant cane farmers ended the harvest with none of the molasses and only a small part of the sugar produced from their cane: no more than 37.5 percent and as little as 16.5 percent.[62]

Such leases could attract lavradores only as long as sugar prices remained high, prospects for overseas sales good, and engenhos in the Recôncavo few in number. That explains why, in the eighteenth century, senhores de engenho increasingly found that they had to grant leases on more generous terms. Among other concessions, they sometimes allowed lavradores to keep a share of the molasses their cane produced. They also reduced the amount of sugar deducted as ground rent. Antonil in 1711 and Vilhena in the 1790s mentioned rents that came to one-fifteenth of the lavrador's share of the sugar. Accounts attached to inventories from 1801 and the late 1830s show cane farmers in São Francisco do Conde paying rents at precisely that rate. In other cases, senhores de engenho demanded only one-twentieth of the lavrador's share. Some tenant farmers obtained even more liberal leases; at least nominally, they paid no ground rent at all. Their rent was included in the share the planter took for milling the cane.[63] Even so, they still gave up half their crop in an arrangement that had no clear counterpart in either tobacco or cassava production.

Beyond surrendering half or more of their crop, tenant cane farmers also had to deal with the "tyrannical justice" of senhores de engenho, who, as landlords, seldom hesitated to violate unwritten rental and sharecropping contracts. In the 1790s, Vilhena in Bahia, and two decades later, Louis-François de Tollenare in Pernambuco both commented on the abuses cane farmers suffered at the hands of planters. A tenant farmer might have just finished the first of two or three harvests from a canefield, only to learn that his landlord was ordering him to leave the plantation immediately. He would then count himself fortunate if he received full and just compensation for the cane he had planted and the other improvements he had made. Among poorer lavradores, insecure tenure gave rise to an almost nomadic existence. After a few seasons at one engenho, willingly or not, they would leave in search of greater security and more generous leases. Such seems to have been the life of José Torquato de Barros, a cane farmer in São Francisco do Conde. When he died in 1859, he left no household goods of any appraisable value beyond a few silver spoons. His widow explained that the few items of furniture the couple had once owned had all been lost in the moves they had made. After the last forced move, she had had to sell one of the couple's seven slaves to meet "indispensable" household expenses.[64]

When tenant cane farmers remained on engenhos for more than a single harvest, they still had to worry about the timely milling of their crop. Once they had cut their cane, any delay in milling could cause irreparable losses in sugar, and therefore in income as well. But as tenant farmers, they had neither a choice in where they milled their cane nor any control over when milling would take place. Not only did planters, in drawing up milling schedules, favor independent lavradores who held unencumbered titles to their own land over tenant cane farmers; they also rearranged schedules at the last moment to attract more independent lavradores to their mill. A tenant cane farmer might, as a result, "see in a week's time the loss of more than a year's labor." In 1850, for example, Antônio José Correia Cravo, who rented the Sítio do Formigueiro at the Engenho Jiaré in São Francisco do Conde, lost perhaps two-thirds of his crop because Jiaré's owner had failed to mill his cane promptly. Cravo, rather than risk future losses, left Jiaré for another plantation at the end of the harvest.[65]

Even when their cane was milled in timely fashion, lavradores could not always count on receiving their full share of the sugar their cane yielded. Controlling the scales used to weigh the product, senhores de engenho had little difficulty adjusting sugar shares to their own advantage. Sometimes they also arbitrarily retained part of the lavrador's sugar as a forced "loan." Unsettled political conditions could open the way for still greater abuses, as Francisco Manoel da Rocha, a tenant at the Engenho Coité de Baixo, learned. The engenho's Portuguese-born owner wanted nothing to do with Brazilian lavradores in the troubled years just before and after independence. He refused to mill their cane on time, burned their canefields, and had them violently evicted from his estate. The beleaguered Rocha would no doubt have agreed with José da Silva Lisboa, who, four decades earlier, described the landless cane farmers as "absolutely dependent on planters, who, according to their whims, hold them in servile oppression."[66]

Examples of planter abuse can, however, be as misleading as they are revealing. All too easily, they create the image of hapless tenant cane farmers entirely at the mercy of all-powerful planters. Contemporary references to "servile oppression" notwithstanding, cane farmers were not serfs. They were in no way tied to estates owned by planters, nor were they perpetually bound to the sugar industry. They always had alternatives outside that industry. They could obtain a cash income by growing tobacco, cassava, or, later, coffee as well. They could also freely leave the northern Recôncavo to seek land elsewhere in the region, in the interior, or along the southern coast. Given that such alternatives existed, we can only conclude that, throughout the early nineteenth century, planting sugarcane, despite burdensome rental and sharecropping agreements, usually furnished lavradores with at least enough income to break even. Otherwise, no matter how much lingering social prestige may have been attached to sugar production, they would sooner or later have abandoned cane.

The very same José da Silva Lisboa who spoke of "servile oppression" considered cane farming at least as profitable as operating a mill. Much later, in the early 1870s, when lasting decline had taken hold of the Bahian sugar industry, lavradores did withdraw from cane farming. Often they continued to rent land from senhores de engenho, but not to grow cane. Accordingly, they preferred leases that specified a rent paid in cash rather than in sugar. Where senhores de engenho still insisted on rents in kind, lavradores grew only enough cane to satisfy their obligations as tenants. They devoted the rest of their energies to the cultivation of tobacco and cassava.[67]

It is no less important to understand that the planters' power to abuse their tenant cane farmers derived from a double monopoly: planters controlled both the best bayshore cane land and the equipment needed to manufacture sugar. Land ownership by itself would not have allowed them to impose heavy leases and burdensome sharecropping agreements on lavradores. Nor could simple land ownership free a lavrador from a planter's control. To cultivate cane, to participate in the sugar industry, even lavradores with their own land had to reach a sharecropping agreement with a neighboring planter.

No similar double monopoly existed in cassava and tobacco production, and consequently landowners could not charge high rents or impose burdensome sharecropping agreements on their tenants. The sandy soils suitable for those crops were more plentiful than the massapés preferred by sugar planters, and neither cassava nor tobacco required any large investment in processing equipment. As a result, instead of taking half a tenant's crop, landowners in the western and southern Recôncavo had to content themselves with very modest rents. Converting those rents from current mil-réis to alqueires of farinha reveals just how modest they generally were. Often,

TABLE 15

Ground Rents for Sítios and Fazendas
in the Western and Southern Recôncavo, 1788–1859

Year	Property (name where known) and location (parish, where known, and township)	Rent In current mil-réis	In alqueires of farinha[a]
1788	Sítio do Mamucabo, N.S. do Rosário, Cachoeira	Rs. 6$000	10.8
1791	Sítio da Tabua, S. Gonçalo dos Campos, Cachoeira	Rs. 5$000	11.0
1792	Sítio das Almas, S. Estêvão de Jacuípe, Cachoeira	Rs. 4$480	9.2
1798	Sítio do Catete, S. Gonçalo dos Campos, Cachoeira	Rs. 9$280	11.0
1807	Faz. do Buraco nas Bananeiras, S. Gonçalo dos Campos, Cachoeira	Rs. 11$000	17.0
1809	Faz. Cajazeira, N.S. do Rosário, Cachoeira	Rs. 40$000	58.4
1821	Sítio do Bruco, S. Gonçalo dos Campos, Cachoeira	Rs. 60$000	79.6
1823	Faz. do Cumbe, S. Estêvão de Jacuípe, Cachoeira	Rs. 9$000	10.1
1825	Faz. do Oiteiro, N.S. do Rosário, Cachoeira	Rs. 30$000	30.3
1828	Sítio no Vitambum, Muritiba, Cachoeira	Rs. 4$000	3.0
1830	Sítio Gravatá, Muritiba, Cachoeira	Rs. 8$000	6.8
1834	Sítio do Bruco, S. Gonçalo dos Campos, Cachoeira	Rs. 10$000	6.9
1843	Sítio (name unknown), Maragogipe	Rs. 80$000	52.3
1854	Sítio Janeiro, Outeiro Redondo, Cachoeira	Rs. 16$000	8.7
1854	Sítio da Fonte, Outeiro Redondo, Cachoeira	Rs. 5$000	2.7
1859	Sítio do Canta-galo, N.S. de Nazaré das Farinhas, Nazaré	Rs. 3$000	0.9

SOURCES: Postmortem inventories, APEB, SJ, IT and ARC, IT; RET, APEB, SH, 4758, registro no. 14.
[a] Calculated against a five-year average for the price of farinha centered on the year in question.

as shown in Table 15, landowners collected in rent no more than the 9.125 alqueires that Bahians regarded as a standard yearly ration. To lease the land they worked, tenant farmers had to produce and sell only a few more alqueires of farinha than what they needed to feed themselves, their families, and their slaves.

In 1830, for example, Francisco Álvares da Silveira paid Rs.8$000 as rent for the Sítio Gravatá in the parish of Muritiba. At Gravatá, Silveira employed his six slaves in caring for an orchard of fruit trees, a small coffee grove, and fields that contained 12,500 tobacco plants and 28,000 covas of cassava.[68] The cassava Silveira planted would have, even in a bad year, yielded perhaps 560 alqueires of flour, 80 times more than the 7 alqueires he needed to pay his rent. It also seems quite likely that some of the higher rents shown in Table 15 actually represent debts for several years' back rent.[69]

The same sugar planters who routinely evicted cane farmers from their estates sometimes displayed little interest in collecting rent on land outside the traditional cane-growing parishes. In the 1820s and 1830s, for example, Antônio Lopes Ferreira e Souza, who owned the Engenho Preguiça in Santo Amaro as well as several tobacco farms in the parish of São Gonçalo dos Campos, allowed Rosa Maria de Sá, a tenant at one of those farms, to run up a debt for 27 years' back rent. Evidently, Rosa Maria felt secure enough in her tenure to neglect to pay her rent for nearly three decades. The coffee groves planted by tenant farmers in the southern and western Recôncavo provide another indication that such farmers enjoyed relatively stable access to land. Coffee trees require at least five to six years of growth before they bear fruit. For that reason, tenant farmers who lived in fear of sudden eviction or who, if evicted, could not expect compensation for land improvements would not have risked planting coffee.[70]

Conclusions

"For everything," Vilhena wrote in the 1790s, "there is land."[71] And indeed there was enough land not only for sugarcane, tobacco, and coffee, but also for cassava. Bahia in the late eighteenth and early nineteenth centuries possessed a plentiful supply of land for the expansion of agriculture. Planters and farmers, even without leaving the townships around the Bay of All Saints, could bring new areas into cultivation to increase the production of both export crops and cassava. In the long run, the existence of an agricultural frontier prevented any lasting competition between the export economy and the demand for locally grown foodstuffs in the regional market.

No less important than the availability of land were the patterns of tenure that governed the use and distribution of landed property in the Recôncavo. Despite the expansion of export agriculture, the region continued to shelter not only large sugar plantations but also hundreds of generally smaller fazendas and sítios. Along with the senhores de engenho, who have, until now, drawn the attention of most historians, a substantial landowning class of small and middling farmers survived in the western and southern Recôncavo. These were the farmers who cultivated the cassava that met the growing demand for farinha in Salvador's market.

Although separable for the purposes of analysis, the two issues addressed in this chapter—the existence of an agricultural frontier and the patterns of land tenure—are, in the end, closely related. Jerome Blum, in his study of rural Europe in the eighteenth and nineteenth centuries, writes, "In agricultural societies land is the single most valuable commodity and those who control it dominate the society."[72] More than any other group in Bahia, the senhores de engenho approximated the landed aristocracies Blum has studied. Politically and socially, they dominated life in the rural Recôncavo. They owned plantations that, by the standards of the Recôncavo and other sugar-producing regions, ranked as large estates.

They did their best, moreover, to imitate the landed aristocracies of Europe. They gave their children needlessly long surnames to flaunt their real or imagined ties to noble European lineages. After independence, they eagerly accepted titles of nobility in the newly established Brazilian Empire. They continued to rely on property laws imported from Portugal to uphold their rights and privileges as landowners. But in Bahia, where an open frontier offered an abundance of unsettled and uncultivated land, those rights and privileges conferred only limited social and economic power. As a result, Bahian planters achieved and maintained power not through simple ownership of land, but rather by owning and controlling both the best bayshore cane land and the mills that manufactured sugar. It is always worth recalling that, in their own day, they were known not as great landowners or even as planters, but as senhores de engenho—lords of the mill. The social and economic power they derived from this double monopoly was great— but not great enough, as the next chapter will show—for them to command the labor of the many wretchedly poor Bahians who lived in freedom throughout the Recôncavo. On sugar plantations and on many tobacco and cassava farms as well, slaves, not free men and women, worked in the fields and harvested the crops.

CHAPTER 6

Labor

I n this America," the town council of Santo Amaro declared in 1802, "the oxen that pull the ploughs . . . are slaves." The council made this curious declaration in a petition that sought for Brazilian farmers a privilege already enjoyed by their counterparts in Portugal. There, in cases of foreclosure for debt, the law prohibited creditors from seizing livestock on the grounds that without draft animals, a farmer could not hope to sow his fields and pay his debts. The town council of Santo Amaro, in requesting that slaves also be exempt from seizure, applied the same reasoning but adapted it to conditions in the colony. Just as European agriculture could not forgo the use of draft animals, Bahian farmers could not bring crops to harvest without slaves. The aldermen of Maragogipe, in a similar petition, made the very same point: "the slaves of Brazil" should, for all legal purposes, be regarded as "plough oxen . . . [because] they work the earth, plant and harvest the crops, and [do] all the other services necessary for the principal sustenance of the people and of the troops."[1]

Slaves in the rural Recôncavo did indeed perform all the necessary "services" both in the cultivation of export crops and in the production of foodstuffs for local markets. So essential was their labor to the growth and prosperity of the region's economy that no study can chart the changes in that economy without giving them attention. This chapter therefore examines the use of slave labor in the Recôncavo, focusing in particular on the patterns of slaveholding and the composition of the slave population.

Slave Labor in the Rural Recôncavo

The widespread use of slave labor gave rise in the Recôncavo to one of the densest slave populations anywhere in Brazil. As Chapter 1 noted, perhaps as many as 89,000 slaves lived in the region in 1816–17. That number would remain high throughout the first half of the nineteenth century; even as late as 1872–73, it still stood at somewhere between between 72,000 and 81,000.

For the purpose of this study, the total size of the slave population matters less than its geographic distribution. Knowledge of where in the Recôncavo slaves lived helps to clarify which activities in the rural economy employed slave labor. Table 16 therefore brings together information on the slave population gathered from scattered and often fragmentary censuses and surveys for various townships and parishes around the Bay of All Saints. As might be expected, the table indicates that slaves were especially numerous in the traditional sugar parishes on or near the northern bayshore. The first slaves imported from Africa came to Bahia in the mid-sixteenth century to work in the nascent sugar industry, and, over the next three hundred years, the engenhos and cane farms of the Recôncavo would consume enormous quantities of slave labor.

Senhores de engenho and lavradores did not, however, monopolize slaveholding in the Recôncavo. Neither in Bahia nor anywhere else in Brazil was the use of slave labor ever confined to plantation agriculture. As Table 16 shows, slaves generally accounted for between one-fifth and one-third of the population in the tobacco- and cassava-growing districts of the western and southern Recôncavo in the late eighteenth and early nineteenth centuries. The table thus puts to rest the questions some historians persist in raising about whether Bahian tobacco farmers owned slaves. Noting that tobacco farms were generally smaller than sugar plantations, those historians conclude that free family labor predominated in tobacco production and that slavery played no significant role in this branch of agriculture.[2]

Not only does the conclusion ignore contemporary references to the presence of slaves on tobacco farms; it also confuses two quite separate issues: first, whether peasant farmers in the Recôncavo grew tobacco; and, second, whether other farmers used slaves in cultivating this export staple. In any event, a population of nearly four thousand slaves in the parish of São Gonçalo dos Campos in 1835 leaves no room for doubt: tobacco growers did indeed employ considerable amounts of slave labor.[3] Likewise, the sizable slave populations in the southern Recôncavo suggest that the cultivation of cassava was not strictly a peasant activity. More than three-fourths (78 percent) of the roceiros listed in a 1781 survey of Jaguaripe owned slaves. Further evidence for the use of slave labor in the production of cassava and tobacco comes from the probate records of Nazaré, Maragogipe, and Cachoeira, where more than nine-tenths of all farmers with inventoried property were slaveholders.[4]

TABLE 16

Slave Populations of Various Districts of the Rural Recôncavo, 1779–1854

Year and location	Slaves		Observations
	No.	Pct. of total pop.	
1779. Parish of Nazaré.	1,493	40.8%[a]	Mainly cassava. Census returns.
1781. Township of Jaguaripe (including the parish of Nazaré).	725	—	Mainly cassava. Results of a survey of cassava growers.
1816–17. Townships of Jaguaripe and Maragogipe.	11,521	—	Mainly cassava, some sugar, some tobacco. Results of a survey of slaveowners.
1825–26. Hamlet of S. Francisco do Paraguaçu and southeastern corner of the parish of Iguape.	100	19.7%	Mixed sugar and cassava. Results of a partial census.
1846. Parish of Aldeia (township of Nazaré).	278	—	Mixed sugar and cassava. Results of a partial survey of engenhos and cassava farms.
1825–26. Hamlet of Belém da Cachoeira and nearby rural districts (parishes of Conceição da Feira and N.S. do Rosário do Porto da Cachoeira).	295	27.4%	Mainly tobacco. Results of a partial census.
1825–26. Parish of S. Gonçalo dos Campos.	1,179	38.7%	Mainly tobacco. Results of a partial census.
1835. Parish of S. Gonçalo dos Campos.	3,918	34.4%	Mainly tobacco. Census returns.
1825–26. Parishes of Muritiba, Outeiro Redondo, and Cruz das Almas.	930	36.8%	Mixed tobacco and sugar, some coffee. Results of a partial census.
1825–26. Rural districts lying south of the town of Cachoeira and along the Paraguaçu River.	253	42.2%	Mixed sugar and tobacco. Results of a partial census.
1788. Parish of Rio Fundo.	3,977	—	Mainly sugar. Results of a census (?).
1816–17. Townships of S. Amaro and S. Francisco do Conde—parishes along or near the northern bayshore.[b]	18,266	—	Mainly sugar. Results of a survey of slaveowners.
1825–26. Parish of Santiago do Iguape—areas along or near the northern shore of the Iguape basin.	1,340	73.3%	Mainly sugar. Results of a partial census.
1835. Parish of Santiago do Iguape.	3,985	53.8%	Mainly sugar. Census returns.
1854. Parish of Rio Fundo.	2,069	—	Mainly sugar. Results of a survey of engenhos and cane farms.

SOURCES: "Lista das pessoas que se achão assistentes na Freguezia de N. Srª de Nazaré . . ." (1779), APEB, SH, 596; "Ofício do Capitão-mor da Vila de Jaguaripe ao Governo da Bahia que remete as relações dos lavradores empregados na plantação de mandioca, 1781," BN-s/m, I-31,30,52; surveys of engenhos and cassava farms in Aldeia (1846), APEB, SH, 6182; Schwartz, Sugar Plantations, pp. 506, 441; Censos [Cach., 1825–26], ARC, PAE; "Relação do Nº de Fogos . . . de São Gonçallo [dos Campos]" (1835); "Relação do Numero de Fogos . . . Iguape" (1835); survey of engenhos in Rio Fundo (1854) in APEB, SH, 4597.

[a] The census has columns for the number of sons, daughters, agregados, and slaves, but no columns for husbands and wives. I have assumed that, where the census classifies a male head of a household as married, the wife was present. Only after making that adjustment did I calculate the total size of the parish population. This probably results in a slight overstatement of the free population and hence in a slight understatement in the proportion of slaves.

[b] Parishes of Socorro, Monte, S. Gonçalo da Vila de S. Francisco, S. Sebastião do Passé, N.S. da Purificação de S. Amaro, and Rio Fundo.

Wage Workers, Agregados, and Domésticos

Although wage workers provided essential services and skills in the rural Recôncavo's economy, they made up no more than a small fraction of the labor force. Sugar planters, for example, usually kept on their estates a permanent staff of free employees consisting of a *caixeiro* (crater), an overseer or slave driver, and a few workers with the technical skills needed in the boiling house to transform cane into sugar—one or two kettlemen and teache-men, a sugar master, and an assistant sugar master.* Planters also hired artisans and other skilled workers either to complete specific tasks or to work for short periods of time; for example, masons to repair the brick furnaces of the boiling house, sawyers to cut firewood, or wainmen (*carreiros*; that is, wagon drivers) to cart cane at harvest time. Thus, in the sugar industry, wage labor was by and large restricted to the areas of management, technical skill, and craft work.[5]

None of these areas, however, constituted an exclusive preserve for the employment of free workers. On some plantations, slaves held the post of *feitor* (overseer); they worked as craftsmen; and they handled the delicate operations of sugarmaking in the boiling house. Quite typically, the slave population at the Engenho São Gonçalo in the parish of Socorro included in the late 1830s four wainmen, a carpenter, a sawyer, a blacksmith, a potter, a mason, a seamstress, a cobbler, and a lacemaker. A middle-aged slave named Eleutério, as the *feitor do serviço*, supervised the fieldwork of his fellow bondsmen, while the elderly Felisberto oversaw tasks assigned to young children. The engenho hired free employees for the positions of teache-man, kettleman, and assistant sugar master during the harvest of 1838–39 only because the skilled slaves who normally worked in the boiling house had run away to nearby plantations.[6]

More important, at São Gonçalo and on engenhos and cane farms throughout the Recôncavo, slaves, not hired workers, labored in the fields; they did the planting, kept the fields clean of weeds, and harvested the cane. As a result, slaves made up between 85 and 98 percent of the work forces employed on Bahian sugar plantations in the mid-nineteenth century.[7] The occupation of "agricultural laborer," for all practical purposes, did not even exist among the free inhabitants of the cane-growing districts. According to an 1835 census, 25 women in the parish of Santiago do Iguape worked, though not necessarily in the sugar industry, as *ganhadeiras* (day laborers);

---

* *Caldeireiros* (kettlemen) and *tacheiros* (teache-men) worked the large copper *caldeiras* (cauldrons), *paróis* (kettles), and *tachas* (teaches) in which cane juice was boiled down and clarified. The *mestre de açúcar* (sugar master) and *banqueiro* (assistant sugar master) directed operations in the boiling house and supervised the final, critical stages of boiling and clarifying. The *caixeiro* supervised the weighing and packing of finished sugar and kept accounts of the plantation's output with each harvest. See, e.g., Schwartz, *Sugar Plantations*, pp. 145–48; and Antonil, pp. 112–21, 206–23.

another 10 individuals, mostly men, found employment as *enxadas* (literally, hoes; that is, field hands) and as *serventes de engenho* (plantation workers); while one freed slave hauled molasses for a living—a total of 36 unskilled wage workers to be set against the more than 3,900 slaves living in the same parish. When senhores de engenho and lavradores needed extra hands to lay in a new field of cane or to harvest a crop, they often rented slaves from their neighbors instead of hiring free workers.[8]

Use of wage labor was, if anything, even less common outside the sugar industry.[9] Tobacco and cassava farmers, where they did employ free non-family labor, were much more likely to take in *agregados* and *domésticos* (literally, "attached persons" and "domestics") than to pay wages to a free field hand. Throughout the Recôncavo, inequality in the distribution of wealth had created a sizable population of free men and women who survived by "attaching" themselves to a household.[10] It seems safe to assume that many of these "attached" men and women and "domestics" had to work in exchange for the food and shelter they received, and that their work often included lending a hand in the planting and harvesting of crops. They were, in effect, lodgers or boarders who worked for their keep.

At present, however, it is difficult to determine how common such arrangements were in the Recôncavo. Census materials do little more than enumerate agregados and domésticos; they provide no direct information about the obligations that bound an agregado or doméstico to a household. Indeed, to some extent, such materials hinder discussions of free nonfamily labor. Bahian census takers used the terms *agregado* and *doméstico* loosely, inconsistently, and, at times, interchangeably to designate an individual in some way dependent on the head of a household or on the owner of a farm or plantation.[11] Into these catchall categories fell lodgers and boarders, as well as informally adopted children or foundlings like the 3-year-old José Inocêncio listed as a doméstico in an 1835 census of São Gonçalo dos Campos. The same census classifies Maria, a 35-year-old parda, as an agregada; the unwed mother of two children, she lived with José da Silva Machado, a black farmer, 36 years of age. Similarly, in Iguape in 1835, Domingos Ramos, pardo, age 28, whose profession was "farming," headed a household that included the unmarried Marcolina Maria, a 25-year-old parda, and her young daughter. Marcolina Maria, according to the census takers, was a doméstica.

Unless we are prepared to believe that in all such cases, single men like José da Silva Machado and Domingos Ramos had taken in unwed mothers as lodgers, it seems clear that domésticas and agregadas were often simply common-law wives. Wives and children, especially in poorer families, may have had to work long hours, but their contributions to the household economy cannot be equated with any form of nonfamily labor. In other instances, individuals classified as agregados appear to have lived largely on their own; they were married, had children, and might even possess a few slaves. They depended on the household to which they were attached chiefly for access to land. They were, in other words, the "tenants at will" described in Chapter 5, who, by all accounts, only occasionally worked for their landlords.

Even in the case of those agregados and domésticos who, as lodgers and boarders, regularly worked in the fields and performed other services in exchange for food and shelter, it is not at all clear that they should be regarded as a source of *nonfamily* labor. They lived in the households to which they were "attached"; at least in poorer households, they certainly shared meals with the rest of the household; and the type of work they did must often have been indistinguishable from the labor performed by family members. Sometimes, they actually were family members: poorer relatives or adult children who had not yet established their own households. Therefore, one could reasonably argue that such agregados and domésticos served to augment the pool of *family* labor available to a household.

Whatever status we assign to agregados and domésticos, the general conclusion remains that in all branches of agriculture, wherever Bahians confronted a permanent need for more labor than a single family could provide, they almost always turned to the institution of slavery to obtain that labor. In brief, slavery permeated the entire rural economy.

Slave Labor, the Poor Free Population, and Land

Slave labor prevailed in Bahian agriculture not because a free population was lacking in the countryside but because, for routine fieldwork, the planters and farmers of the Recôncavo could not count on any dependable supply of voluntary wage labor. Bahia's great reserves of unoccupied and uncultivated land allowed large segments of the poor free population to avoid permanent and full-time employment as field hands. Access to land gave them the means to secure an often precarious but nonetheless independent subsistence. Planters and farmers therefore had little choice: either they employed slaves or they fell back on the limited amount of labor they and their families could furnish.

The argument advanced here is scarcely new. It derives from the treatises on colonization that Edward Gibbon Wakefield published in the 1830s and 1840s. For Wakefield, the circumstances that gave rise to slavery as a labor system were "not moral, but economical: they relate not to vice and virtue, but to production." Slavery and other forms of coerced labor would take root and develop where "one man finds it difficult or impossible to get other men to work under his direction," where "circumstances . . . stand in the way of combination and constancy of labour." Wakefield argued that those circumstances existed "wherever population is scanty in proportion to the land. . . . Slavery . . . has been confined to countries of a scanty population, has never existed in very populous countries, and has gradually ceased in countries where population gradually increased to the point of density."[12]

If men and women who might otherwise have to sell their labor could find land and cultivate it on their own, Wakefield argued, they would not

willingly hire themselves out as wage workers. A demand for labor performed "with constancy and combination" that exceeded what a single family could furnish would then be met only through some form of coercion.
And the need for coercion would persist until either population growth or
some artificial mechanism restricted access to land.[13]

Other authors have, over the years, endorsed, reformulated, and refined
these arguments; most notably Herman Merivale and Karl Marx in the nineteenth century and H. J. Nieboer, Willemina Kloosterboer, and Evsey Domar
in the twentieth century.[14] To those nineteenth-century European authors,
however, slavery was an unfamiliar labor regime, known only from historical accounts of ancient Greece and Rome or from contemporary descriptions
of distant colonies. It is therefore especially significant that Brazilians, living among slaves and dependent on slave labor for their wealth, also recognized the relationship between slavery and an abundant supply of unappro-
priated land. The clearest statement of that relationship comes from Miguel
Calmon's 1834 essay on sugar production.

> I call forced that labor which can only be had through the subjection or . . .
> servitude of the worker; voluntary [labor] being that which is obtained by
> the ordinary means of a simple wage or salary. . . . In unsettled countries,
> where subsistence is easy, and man can live without great exertion, the first
> type of labor has been established by law or by custom; in those [countries]
> that find themselves in opposite circumstances, the second type prevails.
> And it is for that reason that there are . . . slaves . . . in Brazil.[15]

Such arguments match the evidence both for Brazil as a whole and for
Calmon's native province of Bahia.[16] Chapter 5 has already established that,
in the late eighteenth and early nineteenth centuries, the province possessed
an open frontier. Bahians who held legal titles to land in the sparsely settled
interior or along the southern coast could expect little effective protection
for their property rights from the Brazilian state, which was particularly
weak at the level of local government and all the more so in frontier areas.
Against usurpers and squatters, the state could rarely secure its own rights
to land that belonged to the public domain.[17]

Land was plentiful even in the Recôncavo, where, on unused corners
of fazendas and engenhos, poor free men and women found the means to
survive.[18] As agregados or "tenants at will," they built precarious *ranchos*
(huts or cabins) covered with palm thatch to shelter themselves and their
families. Inside they kept their few household goods—seldom much more
than a hammock, a couple of clay pots, a large hollowed-out calabash for
storing farinha, two or three sharp knives, an improvised trivet for cooking,
and, if they lived close to the bay, a fishing net. Nearby, in a small clearing,
they planted their roças of cassava and, no doubt, beans and maize as well.
A banana grove, a jackfruit tree, and a *dendezeiro* (oil palm) completed what
one British observer generously described as "their quarter acre of mandioca
and banana plantations." They might also have a small patch of tobacco and,

later in the nineteenth century, perhaps even a few coffee trees. Game caught in the forests and shellfish gathered from the tidal flats along the bay provided "Sunday luxuries" and "holiday delicacies."[19]

When a special need arose—when, for example, they had to buy new clothes—these poor propertyless Bahians would, in exchange for wages, lend a hand on neighboring plantations or farms. But, if at all possible, they avoided any employment that involved fieldwork, preferring instead to help in carting harvested crops or to work in and around the sugar mills. Once they had enough money in their pockets to meet the current need, they lost interest in wages and returned to their roças. The owner of the land where they had their hut and quarter-acre of cassava and bananas might now and then, for whatever reason, object to their presence and order them summarily evicted. Yet eviction, for all the inconvenience it caused, would have seldom meant dire and lasting hardship. Thrown off one estate, agregados and other "tenants at will," often described by contemporaries as restless nomads, moved on to another plantation or farm where, again without paying rent, they would construct a new hut and open a new clearing for another roça. Or they could leave the Recôncavo to settle in the interior or along the southern coast.

From Vilhena in the 1790s on, intellectuals, planters, and government officials despaired of ever making this segment of the Bahian peasantry "useful." They saw these poor free men and women as idle, lazy, indolent *vadios* (loafers) who contributed nothing to society and whose existence should not be tolerated. After all, these supposedly shiftless people ate, drank, clothed themselves, and lived without drawing an income from property and without working regularly for those Bahians who owned property. Unlike slaves, moreover, they could not be defined as property. They represented, for that very reason, a threat to society—a source of "vice," "crime," and general lawlessness. Having no interest in property, they could be easily "seduced" by "astute anarchists," and, since they apparently had nothing better to do with their time, they might at any moment take part in violent uprisings and rebellions.

In 1842, Joaquim José Pinheiro de Vasconcelos invoked such fears when, as president of Bahia, he proposed legislative measures to "convince" poor men to take up wage labor on the estates of wealthier men (*na propriedade dos ricos*) and to fulfill thereby "the burden that the Author of Nature imposes on all mankind." His proposal would have forced any man without property or without regular employment to join a "company" of wage laborers that would be subject to judicial supervision.[20] The provincial assembly never approved the law. Indeed, it is doubtful whether local authorities in Bahia, with only limited resources at their disposal, could have ever enforced such legislation.

Later proposals for similar measures likewise came to nothing. In 1857, Manoel Pinto da Rocha, a senhor de engenho, called on the government to pass a law that would "obligate" poor unemployed men to work for wages.

He repeated his demand in 1871 after the end of the Paraguayan War (1864–70). During the war, according to this planter, "immense numbers of day laborers" had hired themselves out "even for low wages." The fear of being conscripted and of "going off to suffer the mortal fatigues of war" had induced them to seek almost any employment. But as soon as the war ended, and with it the "incentive" created by military recruitment, planters once again found it impossible to obtain reliable laborers willing to do fieldwork. Pinto da Rocha could not, of course, suggest that the provincial government declare war; he did, however, demand legislation that would have the same effect.[21]

While Bahians were wont to see stubborn resistance to wage labor as proof of wicked idleness, George Stevens, British consul at Salvador in the 1880s, left a more sympathetic and convincing picture of the poor men and women who, "eking out a miserable but contented existence" on their roças, abounded in the countryside. He pointed out that they refused full-time employment as field hands quite simply because they "prefer poverty to being trampled upon." "Rough as is their present lot," Stevens added, "it is to them independently sweet, and it is envied by many a slave."[22]

In Bahia, where even the poorest peasants generally had access to land and retained a good measure of "the independence they invariably covet and for which they are capable of any sacrifice," planters and farmers had no real choice: either they owned slaves and used them as field hands or they employed no labor "with constancy and combination" at all.[23] Recourse to slavery provided senhores de engenho, tobacco farmers, and even roceiros with a reliable means of securing a permanent year-round labor force.

The Transatlantic Slave Trade and the Supply of Slaves

Slavery offered another advantage: while the transatlantic slave trade was still open (until 1850–51), the importation of African slaves made it possible to achieve quick increases in the size of the agricultural labor force. Hundreds or even thousands of Africans could, in a few months' time, be brought across the Atlantic, landed in Salvador, and shortly thereafter put to work on the plantations and farms of the Recôncavo. Thus, the slave trade created a highly elastic labor supply that was capable, in principle, of meeting any increase in demand.[24]

The expansion of Bahian agriculture from the late eighteenth century on did indeed generate an increasing demand for labor that sustained an intense traffic in slaves between Africa and Bahia. What distinguished that traffic from other, better-known branches of the slave trade was that it was, to a large extent, locally controlled. Merchants based in Salvador, by the mid-1700s if not earlier, had assumed chief responsibility for furnishing the colony with slaves. Over their competitors in Lisbon or Oporto, they had the advantage of ready access to stocks of twist tobacco and cachaça, both of which served as prized trade goods on the West African coast. They could also count on local resources for much of the credit needed to finance slaving ventures.[25]

The profits earned in those ventures returned to Bahia, where, when not ploughed back into the slave trade, they funded investments in the local economy. Thus, Joaquim Pereira Marinho, one of the most notorious slavers of the early nineteenth century, was a founding shareholder in the Banco da Bahia and in a company that, in the early 1870s, attempted unsuccessfully to build the province's first central sugar factory. Other Bahian slavers also invested in the sugar industry. Joaquim Alves da Cruz Rios, the son of a slave trader and a slaver in his own right, bought the large Engenho Cravaçu, with its more than 1,050 tarefas of good cane land, in the parish of Monte, where, at the time of his death in 1862, he employed some 180 slaves. Another slave trader, Antônio Pedroso de Albuquerque, purchased not one but three engenhos in the Recôncavo.[26]

These merchants, who enjoyed esteem and respect in Bahian society, drew their profits from what Miguel Calmon called "a brutal metamorfose de mangotes em nagôs" (the brutal metamorphosis of rolls of twist tobacco into Yoruba [slaves]).[27] Every year, their ships disgorged onto the shores of Bahia thousands of enslaved West Africans, as well as smaller numbers of slaves from Angola, from the area of present-day Zaire, and even from Mozambique—the men, women, and children Bahians knew as *nagôs, tapas, minas, uçás, geges, bornous, angolas,* and *congos.**

Although the true volume of this trade will never be known, a revised set of estimates recently published by David Eltis suggests that between 1786 and 1851, a total of nearly 410,000 slaves were brought to Bahia from various points on the African coast.[28] Of those, perhaps slightly more than half arrived in the 30 years between 1791 and 1820, when the late colonial resurgence of the export economy created a strong and fairly steady demand for slave labor (see Table 17). Bahian merchants imported in those years an average of more than 7,000 slaves a year.

Imports declined briefly during the war for independence but then surged to an annual average of approximately 9,500 slaves in the late 1820s. This sudden increase came at a time when sugar planters in the Recôncavo were building a record number of new engenhos and when, consequently, their need for additional labor must have been particularly great. The surge also coincided with growing fears about the future of the slave trade. Under the terms of an 1826 Anglo-Brazilian treaty, the importation of slaves from any part of Africa would become illegal in March 1830.[29] Many planters and

---

* These terms (by no means a comprehensive list) designated slaves of the following supposed origins: *nagô,* Yoruba; *gege,* Ewe; *tapa,* Nupe; *bornou,* Borno; *uçá* (and its several variants), Hausa. *Mina* referred to a slave obtained at a port on the Mina Coast in West Africa; *angola* and *congo* designated an origin in West Central Africa. Contemporary observers and modern research alike point to the predominantly West African origin of slaves brought to Bahia in the eighteenth and nineteenth centuries. See, e.g., Castelnau, pp. 7–9; Verger, *Fluxo;* J. J. Reis, "População," pp. 145–47; and M. J. de S. Andrade, pp. 97–108.

TABLE 17

Estimated Imports of African Slaves, Bahia, 1786–1851

Years	Nos.	Years	Nos.	Years	Nos.
1786–90	20,300	1811–15	36,400	1836–40	15,800
1791–95	34,300	1816–20	34,300	1841–45	21,100
1796–1800	36,200	1821–25	23,700	1846–50	45,000
1801–5	36,300	1826–30	47,900	1851	1,900
1806–10	39,100	1831–35	16,700	TOTAL	409,000

SOURCE: Eltis, pp. 243–44.

merchants in Bahia may have believed that their government would never enforce the ban. After all, it had made no real efforts to fulfill its commitments under an earlier Anglo-Portuguese treaty that had prohibited slaving north of the Equator from 1815 on. But they also knew that Britain had every intention of bringing to an end the transatlantic slave trade. In 1827, the British Navy began to seize Bahian ships it merely suspected of dealing illegally in slaves north of the Equator.

Fearing that Britain would adopt even more aggressive tactics after 1830, merchants in all parts of Brazil rushed to import as many slaves as possible before the scheduled end of the trade. So successful were they that local slave markets became momentarily overstocked and the trade came to a near standstill in 1831 and 1832. As a result, the Brazilian government was even able to gain parliamentary approval in 1831 for legislation that freed any African illegally introduced into the county and mandated severe penalties for merchants found guilty of importing slaves.

The legislation soon became another law *para inglês ver* (for the Englishman to see); that is, completely ineffective at preventing a revival of the slave trade. Notwithstanding the 1826 treaty and the 1831 law, upwards of two hundred thousand Africans were imported into Southeastern Brazil in the late 1830s to meet the vigorous demand for slaves from the rapidly expanding coffee industry.[30] Recovery was slower in Bahia, where stagnation in the provincial export economy resulted in a diminished demand for slave labor. Imports returned to their former levels only in the late 1840s, in response both to renewed growth in the Bahian export economy and the alarmingly more aggressive tactics employed by the Royal Navy, which now threatened to blockade Brazil's main ports. Having little choice, the Brazilian government finally yielded to British pressure, and in 1850–51, it moved quickly and decisively to close the country to further imports of African slaves.

The end of the transatlantic slave trade redefined the market for slave labor in Brazil. The slave population as a whole had never achieved a positive rate of natural increase. Deaths had always exceeded births, and only the constant influx of newly enslaved Africans had ensured the growth of the slave population. After that influx came to an abrupt end in 1850–51, what had been a highly elastic labor supply began to contract. Now plantations, farms, and even entire regions would have to compete for a dwindling number of slaves.

The competition quickly gave rise to a massive transfer of slaves from towns and cities to the countryside and from regions with declining or less profitable export economies to those where export production was undergoing rapid growth. Between 1851 and the early 1880s, some two hundred thousand slaves were forced to migrate from far Southern and Northeastern Brazil to the coffee-growing provinces of the Southeast, which had, in the previous half-century, emerged as the "dynamic center" of the Brazilian economy. Coffee growers in the Southeast were willing and able to pay higher slave prices than planters and farmers elsewhere.[31]

The new interprovincial slave trade transformed Bahia from a net importer of slaves to a net exporter. In the three-and-a-half decades after 1850, 24,000 slaves left the province, most of them destined for the coffee plantations of Rio de Janeiro, São Paulo, and Minas Gerais. At least 12,000 were exported during the 1850s alone. Indeed, no sooner were Brazilian ports closed to the African trade than dealers began to buy up slaves in Bahia and ship them south. Outside merchants who offered sellers "exorbitant" prices for their bondsmen appeared in Cachoeira as early as August 1851. A few years later, John Morgan, British consul at Salvador, noted, "the great demand from Rio de Janeiro, and the high price paid, is an inducement the small proprietor and the needy cannot resist." Not even a tenfold increase in the tax on slaves exported from the province could effectively counteract that inducement, which only grew stronger in years when droughts struck. Consul Morgan informed the Foreign Office in 1860 that two years of "frightful drought in the interior" had brought famine and had "obliged many families to sell their household slaves at any price." He estimated that as a result, more than 2,700 slaves had been shipped to Rio de Janeiro between 1858 and 1860.[32]

The interprovincial trade accelerated slavery's decline in Bahia and hastened the onset of a long and painful transition to free labor. Yet the extent of that decline in the 1850s must not be exaggerated. Neither as an institution nor as a labor regime could slavery be described as moribund in 1860. Here it is worth recalling that Bahia, as late as 1872–73, still ranked third among all Brazilian provinces in the size of its slave population. More slaves lived and worked in Bahia than in the coffee-growing province of São Paulo. Far more pressing in the 1850s than the need to find alternatives to slavery were the questions of how and where to use a dwindling supply of slave labor—whether in export agriculture or in the production of foodstuffs for local consumption.

Slave Prices in Bahia, 1780–1860

Although, in the quarter-century before 1850, neither the diplomatic pressure of the British Foreign Office nor the gunships of the Royal Navy

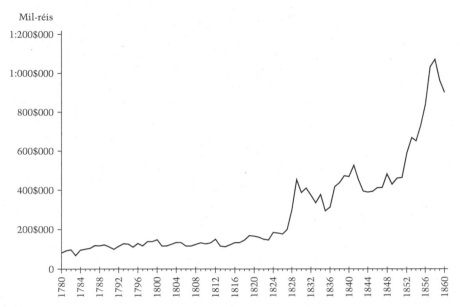

Figure 10. Bahia. Slave Prices, 1780–1860 (price of a healthy male field hand in current mil-réis).

SOURCES. Appraisals of slaves in postmortem inventories, APEB, SJ, IT and ARC, IT.

NOTE. The series shown is based on annual means of values assigned in inventories to 1,484 healthy adult and young adult male slaves employed as field hands. It excludes values assigned to skilled slaves and slaves described as ill, having physical defects, unruly, or rebellious. The general movement of this series matches the movement of prices in Bahia found in other studies, none of which covers the entire period 1780–1860.

succeeded in preventing the forced migration of more than a half-million Africans to Brazil, their efforts did have a discernible impact on the prices paid in current mil-réis for slaves in Bahia. As Figure 10 illustrates, the gradual and relatively smooth upward tendency that had, since 1780, characterized slave prices gave way to much sharper fluctuations after 1825. The price of an adult male field hand rose abruptly at the end of the 1820s and again in the late 1830s and early 1840s. Both of those increases coincided with Great Britain's adoption of more aggressive naval tactics in its ongoing campaign against the transatlantic trade. When, after 1850, the trade finally came to an end, prices soared. A field hand who had fetched less than Rs.480$000 in the early 1850s sold for Rs.1:075$000 by 1858. All in all, slave prices had undergone a more than tenfold increase since 1780.

Had they been able to examine a retrospective series for those prices, British abolitionists in the 1850s would surely have been tempted to congratulate themselves for having struck a tremendous blow against slavery in Bahia. Their strategy had always aimed at raising the price of slaves to a point where planters and farmers everywhere in Brazil would find it cheaper to resort to some form of noncoerced labor. But any self-praise on the part of abolitionists in Great Britain would have overlooked two key points. First, in their willingness to pay higher slave prices, Bahians demonstrated their continuing confidence in the future of both slavery and slave-based agriculture. Slave prices soared in the 1850s not only because the transatlantic trade had been closed but because the decade brought new prospects for growth and prosperity in the Bahian export economy.[33] Second, comparisons of current prices do not take into account variations in the purchasing power of the mil-réis. They therefore yield a distorted view of real price changes. Thus, although the nominal price of a field hand increased enormously in the eight decades after 1780, the cost of acquiring a slave in real terms may have changed very little.

One way to test for that possibility is to convert slave prices from current mil-réis to arrobas of white sugar and alqueires of cassava flour. (Regrettably, information on tobacco prices is not at hand to calculate slave prices in constant units of tobacco.) This conversion allows us to detect and evaluate real changes in the cost of a new slave for planters and roceiros. Figures 11 and 12 chart the movement of slave prices in constant units of cassava flour and sugar. They demonstrate that in real terms, the cost increased considerably less than a review of nominal prices would suggest.

In effect, whereas slave prices in current mil-réis were, on average, more than 600 percent higher in the 1850s than in the 1780s, those prices, when converted to alqueires of farinha, display an increase of less than 85 percent. This means that, annual fluctuations aside, the prices cassava growers received for their farinha rose nearly enough to keep pace with the upward movement of nominal slave prices. As a result, in the first half of the nineteenth century, those growers lost relatively little ground in their ability to purchase slaves.

For sugar planters and cane farmers, the increase in the real cost of acquiring a slave was more substantial. In the early 1780s, they could, with income from the sale of slightly less than 50 arrobas of white sugar, buy a healthy male field hand; seven decades later, in 1855, a comparable slave would cost them the equivalent of 257 arrobas of white sugar. That amounts to a real increase of more than 400 percent.[34]

Bahian senhores de engenho and lavradores were not alone in having to contend with much higher real prices for slaves in the first half of the nineteenth century. Throughout the Americas, in the coffee-growing regions of Southeastern Brazil, in Cuba, and in the southern United States, slave prices exhibited a clear upward trend that contrasted with a no less well defined downward tendency in the prices of export staples. Even so, improvements in the marketing and production of staples, along with access to areas of fresher and more fertile soils, made slave labor more productive during those same years. The net effect of those improvements was to com-

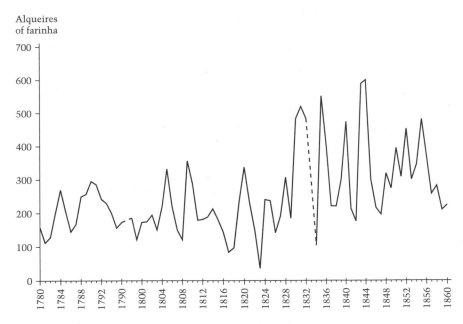

Figure 11. Bahia. Slave Prices Measured in Alqueires of Farinha, 1780–1860 (price of a healthy male field hand).
SOURCES. Appraisals of slaves in postmortem inventories, APEB, SJ, IT and ARC, IT; Mattoso, "Au Nouveau Monde," Annexes, pp. 445–61; "Conta corrente da despeza e receita que houve no Celleiro Publico . . . " (1834–43, with interruptions), APEB, SH, 1609 and 1610. See note to Figure 10 and Chap. 4, n. 7.

pensate planters for the higher prices they had to pay for slaves and to maintain the profitability of plantation agriculture in the U.S. South, Cuba, and Southeastern Brazil.[35] In Bahia, it seems that similar improvements also helped ensure the continuing profitability of slave-based sugar production. The adoption of new technologies for manufacturing sugar and the introduction of Cayenne cane in 1816 apparently resulted in considerable gains in the amount of sugar produced per slave each growing season (see Table 18). The doubling and perhaps even tripling in the output of sugar per slave between the 1780s and the mid-nineteenth century would have gone far in offsetting the rise in slave prices.

Patterns of Slaveholding in the Recôncavo

Sugar planters, tobacco farmers, and cassava growers all purchased slaves, but the number of slaves they bought and the size of their holdings varied greatly. To a large extent, the patterns of slaveholding in the Recôncavo paralleled differences in the distribution of landed property. Because slaves, like land, represented a form of wealth, an appropriate first step in analyzing patterns of slaveholding is to examine Gini coefficients of in-

Figure 12. Bahia. Slave Prices Measured in Arrobas of White Sugar, 1780–1860 (price of a healthy male field hand).
SOURCES. Appraisals of slaves and receipts and bills of sale for white sugar in postmortem inventories, APEB, SJ, IT and ARC, IT; Mattoso, "Au Nouveau Monde," Annexes, pp. 445–61. See note to Figure 10 and Chap. 4, n. 7.

equality. The Gini coefficient is a statistical measure of dispersion or concentration with values ranging from 0.0 to 1.0. The coefficient will equal 0.0 in a hypothetical situation where complete equality characterizes the distribution of wealth; when wealth is absolutely concentrated, its value will be 1.0. Thus, the lower the value of the Gini coefficient, the more evenly distributed the ownership of slaves.

Table 19 shows that when such coefficients are calculated for the population of slaveowners or slaveowning households, they suggest a marked contrast between the sugar-producing districts on the northern side of the bay and the rest of the Recôncavo. Wealth held in the form of slaves was most concentrated in the traditional sugar parishes on the northern side of the bay. Elsewhere, in tobacco- and cassava-growing areas, slave ownership was much more evenly distributed. The same contrast reappears in the mean size of holdings and in the share of slaves belonging to the top 10 percent of slaveowners or slaveowning households. Thus, in 1835, the average holding was nearly three times larger in Santiago do Iguape than in the nearby tobacco-growing parish of São Gonçalo dos Campos. Two-thirds of Iguape's entire slave population belonged to the wealthiest ten percent of slaveowners. In São Gonçalo dos Campos, those slaveowners controlled less than 40 percent of the slaves in that parish.

Yet whether we regard Iguape or any other traditional sugar parish as an example of extreme concentration in slave ownership depends very much on the perspective we adopt. Stuart Schwartz has pointed out that when such a perspective broadens to include the sugar-producing colonies of the West Indies, the most notable features of slaveholding in the Recôncavo are the "relatively smooth" distribution of slaveownership and the small average size of holdings in all parts of the region.[36] Those features become evident when we look more closely at three representative parishes: Nazaré das Farinhas, São Gonçalo dos Campos, and Santiago do Iguape. As Table 20 reveals, medium-sized holdings of 5 to 19 slaves were common in all three parishes. Likewise, in all three parishes, a large share of slaveowners possessed fewer than 5 slaves. Everywhere, men and women whose holdings consisted of a single slave accounted for at least one-fifth of all slaveowners. This was true even in Iguape, where fishermen, artisans, peddlers, seam-

TABLE 18

Estimated Annual Output of Sugar per Slave on Bahian Plantations, 1781–1854

(In arrobas)

Year	Annual output of sugar per slave	Observations
1781	40.0	
c. 1790	44.4	
1832	82.5	
1854	103.5	Average for engenhos in the parish of Matoim.
1854	107.8	Average for engenhos in the parish of Socorro.
1854	110.6	Average for engenhos in the parish of Açu da Torre.
1854	132.3	Average for engenhos in the parish of Rio Fundo (calculated only for slaves employed on engenhos).
1854	88.6	Average for engenhos in the parish of Rio Fundo (calculated for slaves employed on engenhos and cane farms).
1854	118.7	Average for engenhos in the parishes of Matoim, Socorro, Açu da Torre, and Rio Fundo (does not include slaves employed on cane farms in Rio Fundo).
1854	97.2	Average for engenhos in the parishes of Matoim, Socorro, Açu da Torre, and Rio Fundo (includes slaves employed on cane farms in Rio Fundo).
1854	90.0–135.0	

SOURCES: Alden, "Price Movements," p. 342; [Mendes], p. 292; *PP* (1831–2), *Reports from Committees*, 16: "Report . . . on the Commercial State of the *West India* Colonies," pp. 272–73 (testimony of Evanson Alchorne); surveys (1854) of engenhos in the parishes of Matoim, Socorro, Açu da Torre, and Rio Fundo in APEB, SH, 4597; Carson, *Primeiro relatorio*, p. 9.

NOTE: Because a whole series of difficulties beset attempts to measure productivity, the estimates presented in Table 18 should be accepted with caution. Some of the difficulties are common to contemporary sources of information on slave-based sugar production in all parts of the Americas. See Barrett, *Efficient Plantation*, pp. 19–26, esp. p. 20. The sources available for Bahia and the structure of the Bahian sugar industry, where lavradores generally owned about one-third of all the slaves permanently employed in sugar production, create additional difficulties. For more detail, see Barickman, "Slave Economy," pp. 395–98.

TABLE 19

Distribution of Slaveholdings in the Rural Recôncavo, 1779–1835

Year	Location	Gini coefficient of inequality[b]	Average slaves per owner	Percentage of slaves owned by the top 10% of owners
		MAINLY CASSAVA		
1779	Parish of Nazaré	.50	4.4	36.2%
1816–17	Township of Jaguaripe (including the parish of Nazaré)	.38	4.5	—
1816–17	Township of Maragogipe	.45	4.8	—
		MAINLY TOBACCO		
1835	Parish of S. Gonçalo dos Campos	.56	6.5	39.7
		MAINLY SUGAR		
1816–17	Parish of Rio Fundo	.62	10.5	53.0
1816–17	Parish of S. Gonçalo da Vila de S. Francisco[a]	.64	10.4	54.0
1816–17	Parish of S. Sebastião do Passé	.65	16.1	63.0
1816–17	Parish of N.S. da Purificação de S. Amaro	.67	10.0	54.0
1816–17	Parish of Socorro	.70	11.9	58.0
1816–17	Parish of Monte	.77	16.1	78.0
1835	Parish of Santiago do Iguape	.74	18.6	67.6

SOURCES: "Lista das pessoas que se achão assistentes na Freguezia de N. Srª de Nazaré . . ." (1779), APEB, SH, 596; Schwartz, *Sugar Plantations*, p. 443; "Relação do Nº de Fogos . . . São Gonçallo [dos Campos]" (1835); "Relação do Numero de Fogos . . . Iguape" (1835).

[a] Includes the parish of N.S. Madre de Deus do Boqueirão.

[b] Calculation of Gini coefficients from the censuses of Nazaré (1799), Iguape (1835), and S. Gonçalo dos Campos (1835) used the number of slaves present in a household as a unit of ownership. The coefficients for 1816–17 were calculated by Stuart Schwartz from a survey of slaveowners. See *Sugar Plantations*, p. 565, n. 7, and chap. 6. Although my discussion largely agrees with his, Schwartz does not deal with the tobacco-growing districts of the western Recôncavo. Also note that the Gini coefficients in the table exclude the population that did not own slaves. When households without slaves are included, the coefficients are substantially higher: 0.71 for Nazaré in 1779, 0.84 in S. Gonçalo dos Campos in 1835, and 0.95 in Iguape in 1835.

stresses, priests, and roceiros as well as sugar planters and cane farmers owned slaves.

Slaveholding in these parishes and elsewhere in the Recôncavo crossed racial lines. Free blacks, pardos, and cabras, some of whom were themselves former slaves, headed nearly half (46.5 percent) of the slaveowning households in Iguape and roughly 30 percent of all such households in São Gonçalo dos Campos. Although free blacks and mulattos often possessed only a few slaves, they were still slaveholders.[37]

The main differences between the three parishes lay not in the presence of small or medium-sized slaveholdings but at the top end of the scale. While no household in Nazaré employed more than 34 slaves, and in São Gonçalo, units of 40 or more slaves could be found in only 1.7 percent of the slaveowning households, more than one-tenth (11.2 percent) of the holdings in Iguape comprised at least 40 slaves. Eleven households in the sugar-producing parish could claim control of 100 or more slaves. The differences are all the more striking when the focus shifts from slaveowners to slaves. The great majority of slaves in Iguape (79 percent) lived and worked in units of 20 or more; roughly two-thirds (69.7 percent) were held by owners with at least 40 slaves. In both São Gonçalo dos Campos and Nazaré, by contrast, more than two-thirds of the slaves belonged to households with fewer than 20 slaves. A substantial share of the slave population in the two parishes (approximately 32 percent in Nazaré and 19 percent in São Gonçalo) lived in units of 4 or fewer.

ENGENHOS AND CANE FARMS

These differences not only indicate disparities in wealth among parishes; they point to a hierarchy in the size and scale of agricultural establishments. At the head of that hierarchy were, beyond any doubt, the engenhos—plantations that combined the cultivation of cane with the manu-

TABLE 20

Slaveowners, Slaves, and Size of Slaveholdings
in Three Parishes

Size of slaveholdings	Nazaré das Farinhas, 1779[a]	São Gonçalo dos Campos, 1835[b]	Santiago do Iguape, 1835[c]
PERCENTAGE DISTRIBUTION OF SLAVEOWNERS BY SIZE OF SLAVEHOLDINGS			
1	30.9%	22.5%	21.0%
2–4	38.8	35.5	27.6
SUBTOTAL	69.7%	58.0%	48.6%
5–9	17.8	22.0	20.1
10–19	10.8	14.0	13.1
20–39	1.7	4.3	7.0
40–59	–	1.7	2.8
60–99	–	–	3.3
100–199	–	–	3.7
≥200	–	–	1.4
TOTAL	100.0%	100.0%	100.0%
PERCENTAGE DISTRIBUTION OF SLAVES BY SIZE OF SLAVEHOLDINGS			
1	7.1%	3.4%	1.1%
2–4	25.0	15.7	3.9
SUBTOTAL	32.1%	19.1%	5.0%
5–9	25.7	22.1	7.1
10–19	31.3	29.9	8.9
20–39	10.9	17.5	9.3
40–59	–	11.4	7.0
60–99	–	–	13.2
100–199	–	–	31.3
≥200	–	–	18.2
TOTAL	100.0%	100.0%	100.0%

SOURCES: "Lista das pessoas que se achão assistentes na Freguezia de N. Srª de Nazaré . . ." (1779), APEB, SH, 596; "Relação do N⁰ de Fogos . . . São Gonçallo [dos Campos]" [1835]; "Relação do Numero de Fogos . . . Iguape" (1835).
ᵃ 343 slaveowners; 1,493 slaves.
ᵇ 600 slaveowners; 3,918 slaves.
ᶜ 214 slaveowners; 3,985 slaves.

TABLE 21

The Size of Slave Work Forces on Bahian Engenhos, 1788–1854

No. of slaves	Rio Fundo, 1788		S. Amaro and S. Francisco do Conde, 1816–17[a]		Santiago do Iguape, 1835		Socorro, Matoim, and Rio Fundo, 1854	
	No.	Pct.	No.	Pct.	No.	Pct.	No.	Pct.
20–39	12	34.3%	35	24.0%	2	9.5%	7	17.1%
40–59	5	14.3	27	18.5	2	9.5	14	34.1
60–99	13	37.1	59	40.4	6	28.6	14	34.1
100–149	4	11.4	21	14.4	3	14.3	6	14.6
≥150	1	2.9	4	2.7	8	38.1	0	0.0
TOTAL	35	100.0%	146	100.0%	21	100.0%	41	100.0%
Ave. slaves per engenho	61.5		67.7		122.8		59.7	

SOURCES: Schwartz, *Sugar Plantations*, pp. 306, 450, 454; "Relação do Numero de Fogos . . . Iguape" (1835); surveys of engenhos in the parishes of Matoim, Socorro, and Rio Fundo (1854) in APEB, SH, 4597.
    [a] Traditional sugar parishes of Socorro, Monte, S. Sebastião do Passé, S. Gonçalo da Vila de S. Francisco, N.S. da Purificação de S. Amaro, and Rio Fundo. Schwartz in Table 16-4 (*Sugar Plantations*, p. 450) provides the distribution of slave work forces on engenhos in all parishes in S. Amaro and S. Francisco do Conde. In Table 16-6 (ibid., p. 454), he lists, for each parish, the number of slaves employed on engenhos. Working with the original survey lists for the outlying parishes of N.S. da Oliveira, S. Domingos da Saubara, and Santana do Catu (in APEB, SH, 233) I have adjusted the frequencies in Schwartz's Table 16-4 to exclude slaves on engenhos in those parishes.

facture of sugar and that consequently had to maintain slave work forces large enough to meet the need for labor both in the fields and in the mill during the nine-month harvest season. Although, in the 1750s, a parish priest in Santo Amaro had claimed that no planter could hope to manufacture sugar with fewer than 40 slaves, some Bahian engenhos did operate with smaller work forces. An 1854 survey, for example, records a total of 632 slaves on 36 engenhos in the parish of São Pedro do Açu da Torre, north of Salvador; that comes to an average of fewer than 18 slaves on each plantation.[38] Açu da Torre was, however, an outlying parish that had been been opened up to sugar production only since about 1800 and was, therefore, not representative of Bahia's traditional cane-growing districts. Most senhores de engenho who had estates on or near the northern bayshore did in fact employ more than 40 slaves; those with the largest properties could claim ownership of more than 100 (see Table 21). The average size of plantation work forces in the traditional cane-growing districts ranged from 53 slaves in São Pedro do Rio Fundo in 1854 to nearly 123 in Santiago do Iguape in 1835. Thus, in the core area of the Recôncavo's sugar zone, engenhos typically had direct control over 50 to 100 slaves.[39]

Cane farms, because they did not manufacture sugar, were, as a rule, much smaller establishments. Not even exceptionally wealthy cane farmers such as Manoel Estanislau de Almeida and Father Anselmo Dias Rocha, both of Iguape, could match the great sugar planters. In the early 1830s, Almeida employed 64 slaves at the Fazenda da Capela de Santa Maria, which he rented, and Father Anselmo had 77 slaves at his Fazenda Cassinum—

holdings that seem almost modest when compared with the 233 slaves who lived at the Engenho da Ponta or with the 250 enslaved workers that Manoel Inácio de Lima Pereira kept at his Engenho da Praia in the same parish. Whereas for all practical purposes, operating an engenho presupposed ownership of slaves, cane farming did not. It was entirely possible for an impoverished lavrador, working on his own, to plant and harvest cane. The 1835 census of Iguape lists twenty lavradores who owned no slaves at all and whose only help came from family members and, in some cases, a few domésticos. But these would have been at best marginal producers; the cane they grew could have yielded no more than a negligible fraction of the sugar manufactured at the engenhos in that parish.[40]

Of the 66 lavradores in Iguape who did own slaves in 1835, more than half employed between 5 and 19 slaves; another 18 percent had holdings of 20 to 39 slaves. Sources from various parts of the Recôncavo indicate that, in the late eighteenth and early nineteenth centuries, Bahian lavradores owned, on average, 10 to 17 slaves (see Table 22). Therefore, cane farming can be identified as an activity characterized by medium-sized slaveholdings.

TOBACCO FARMS

It is far more difficult to determine any typical size for the slaveholdings on the Recôncavo's tobacco farms. The difficulty stems in part from the uneven history of tobacco exports between 1780 and 1860. Although, for sugar producers, the eight decades after 1780 represented generally a period of prosperity, the tobacco trade suffered a prolonged slump in the early nineteenth century. The 1815 ban on slaving north of the Equator and the loss, after 1822, of privileged access to the Portuguese market resulted in a steady

TABLE 22

The Size of Slave Work Forces on Bahian Cane Farms, 1780–1860

No. of slaves	S. Amaro, S. Francisco do Conde, and Iguape, 1780–1860		S. Amaro and S. Francisco do Conde, 1816–17		Santiago do Iguape, 1835	
	No.	Pct.	No.	Pct.	No.	Pct.
1–4	16	13.2%	117	24.5%	11	16.7%
5–9	27	22.3%	156	32.6%	20	30.3%
10–19	41	33.9	139	29.1	18	27.2
SUBTOTAL	68	56.2%	295	61.7%	38	57.6%
20–39	29	24.0%	63	13.2%	12	18.2%
⩾40	8	6.6	3	0.6	5	7.6
TOTAL	121	100.0%	478	100.0%	66	100.0%
Ave. slaves per farm	17.2		10.5		14.2	

SOURCES: Postmortem estate inventories, APEB, SJ, IT and ARC, IT; Schwartz, *Sugar Plantations*, p. 452; "Relação do Numero de Fogos . . . Iguape" (1835).

decline in tobacco exports after 1816. Overseas sales remained depressed until the late 1840s, when Bahian growers began to produce large amounts of leaf tobacco. The shift entailed more than the mere substitution of one variety for another. The preparation of cured leaf tobacco, which could be used in making cigars and cigarettes, involved less elaborate processes and less labor than the manufacture of twist tobacco. The long depression in exports and the shift in production brought changes in tobacco farming: as large slaveholdings were broken up, the crop attracted a growing number of peasant farmers. Nevertheless, farmers who could afford to do so would continue, until abolition in 1888, to depend on slave labor.

In tracing the changes in tobacco farming, it is perhaps best to begin by recalling that tobacco, because it could be cultivated almost as efficiently on a one- or two-acre plot as on a large fazenda, was always a far less prestigious crop than sugarcane. Although the proper cultivation of tobacco involved a number of delicate and labor-intensive operations—from transplanting seedlings to careful pruning and leaf-by-leaf harvesting—the growing season was short, only six to eight months. Newly planted cane, by contrast, took as long as a year-and-a-half before it was ready for cutting. Tobacco grew well in the same light, sandy soils that were suitable for cassava, making it easy for farmers to combine the cultivation of an export crop with the production of farinha. The processing of tobacco, furthermore, required no heavy investment in equipment or outbuildings.[41]

Thus, Francisco Adolfo de Varnhagen, in a report on tobacco farming in Bahia, wrote in the early 1860s,

> of all the intertropical industries, tobacco requires the least capital. . . . [T]he poor man who has nothing more than a hut [rancho] of mud walls and palm thatch that he has built for himself and a small bit of land for a roça of cassava that he has been given or that he has rented already possesses everything he needs to become a tobacco grower.[42]

Peasant production of this export staple, which can be traced back at least to the 1770s, appears to have become widespread by the early nineteenth century. In 1835, almost two-thirds (64 percent) of all farm households in São Gonçalo dos Campos, in the very heart of the famous tobacco-growing "fields of Cachoeira," owned no slaves. The shift to leaf tobacco a decade later made it even easier for such households to plant the crop. Indeed, as observers from the 1850s onward increasingly came to associate tobacco with peasant farmers, they helped establish its enduring reputation as a *lavoura do pobre* (poor man's crop) and a *lavoura de quintal* (backyard crop).[43]

Not only did the cultivation of tobacco make it possible for poor farmers, agregados, and other "tenants at will" to take part in the export economy; it also allowed them in some cases to accumulate the wealth needed to become slaveholders—not, to be sure, masters of great gangs of captive workers, but slaveholders nevertheless. That such opportunities existed is clear

TABLE 23

The Size of Slave Work Forces on Tobacco Farms in the Township of
Cachoeira, 1780–1860

No. of slaves	1780–1815		1816–1845		1846–1860	
	No.	Pct.	No.	Pct.	No.	Pct.
1–4	12	11.8%	20	20.4%	16	28.6%
5–9	29	28.4%	29	29.6%	24	42.9%
10–19	42	41.2	28	28.6	11	19.6
SUBTOTAL	73	69.6%	57	58.2%	35	62.5%
20–39	14	13.7%	10	10.2%	5	8.9%
40–59	5	4.9	5	5.1	0	0.0
60	0	0.0	6	6.1	0	0.0
TOTAL	102	100.0%	98	100.0%	56	100.0%
Ave. slaves per farm	14.7		20.0		8.7	

SOURCE: Postmortem estate inventories, APEB, SJ, IT and ARC, IT.

from the 1835 census of São Gonçalo dos Campos. Of the 551 farmers who employed slave labor in that parish, more than half (55 percent) owned fewer than five slaves; one-third had only one or two slaves.[44] The presence of so many farmers with small slaveholdings blurred the distinction between peasant and slave-based agriculture in the tobacco districts of Cachoeira.

For better-off farmers, those who possessed enough appraisable property to warrant the expense of a postmortem inventory, the surviving probate records can be used to compare the size of slaveholdings over time. Table 23 shows that in the years 1780 to 1815, when overseas sales of Bahian tobacco were strong, nearly 70 percent of better-off farmers in Cachoeira left their heirs between 5 and 19 slaves. The average holding was just under 15 slaves. In size, then, these farms resembled the cane farms of Iguape, Santo Amaro, and São Francisco do Conde. They were medium-sized rural establishments that stood apart from the great majority of farms worked by peasant growers with or without the help of a few slaves.

The tobacco districts also had their share of truly wealthy farmers. Encouraged by the high prices their staple fetched before 1815 and the easy credit merchants then offered, they expanded production and built up large slave work forces. João Ferreira de Melo, for example, employed 64 slaves on his farms near the hamlet of Belém da Cachoeira while, farther north, no fewer than 90 slaves worked on the fazendas owned by Francisco Machado da Silva and his wife, Dona Ana Rosa de Santa Maria. Some of these wealthy lavradores de fumo operated what were, in effect, very large tobacco farms, comparable in size to the engenhos of the northern bayshore. Dona Úrsula Maria das Virgens kept 50 slaves at her Fazenda da Terra Dura in São Gonçalo dos Campos. Larger still was the work force of 79 slaves at Antônio Lopes Ferreira e Souza's Fazenda da Vargem in the same parish.[45] But with only limited economies of scale in tobacco production, most wealthy farmers, it seems, chose to divide their holdings into medium-sized units. João Ferreira de Melo's 64 bondsmen cultivated tobacco, cassava, maize, and beans at his three fazendas, Quilombo, Laranjeira, and Cajazeira. Similarly, Francisco Machado da Silva and his wife employed their 90 slaves at three different farms.

These four prosperous tobacco growers belonged to a generation that profited from the brisk trade in Bahian tobacco at the beginning of the nineteenth century. They also lived long enough to see the onset of depression after 1815. Their deaths and those of other wealthy lavradores de fumo in the 1820s and 1830s explain a paradox: postmortem inventories carried out between 1816 and 1845 indicate not a decline but an increase in the mean size of slaveholdings in Cachoeira's tobacco-growing parishes. That increase is misleading; it obscures a tendency toward smaller work forces, and therefore toward smaller farms as well. Already, the proportion of tobacco growers who left their heirs fewer than 5 slaves had almost doubled, rising from just under 12 percent before 1815 to over 20 percent between 1816 and 1845. Prosperity would return to the tobacco districts of the Recôncavo in the late 1840s. But unlike the earlier boom, the mid-nineteenth-century recovery, based on growing sales of leaf tobacco, would not give rise to large slaveholdings. Not a single inventory from 1845 on registers a work force of 40 or more slaves.

Much more noteworthy in the end, however, is that despite the long depression in exports and the shift to leaf tobacco, the farmers of Cachoeira continued to employ slave labor. In the mid-nineteenth century, three-fifths (62.5 percent) of all farmers with inventoried wealth could still claim ownership of medium-sized slaveholdings. Slave-based production of tobacco would survive in the Recôncavo for another three decades. In 1887, one year before Brazil finally abolished slavery, Antônio de Cerqueira Pinto Brandão kept a work force of 17 slaves at his Fazenda Tibiri near Belém da Cachoeira, not far from the farms where, 60 years earlier, João Ferreira de Melo had employed his 64 slaves. And the Fazenda Tibiri was not unique; in the 1880s, slaves still planted and harvested tobacco on farms throughout the township of Cachoeira.[46]

CASSAVA FARMS

Of all rural establishments in the Recôncavo, cassava farms were the smallest. João Rodrigues de Brito spoke in 1807 of "the wretched farinha growers [lavradores de farinhas] . . . who, because of their poverty, deserved pity."[47] Indeed, when compared with senhores de engenho or even with well-to-do tobacco farmers, the roceiros of the southern Recôncavo do appear wretchedly poor. A 1781 survey of the township of Jaguaripe (including the parish of Nazaré), for example, lists 170 slaveowning cassava farmers. Of those, only 13 (7.6 percent) employed ten or more slaves, while 68 percent owned fewer than five slaves and more than one-third (37.6 percent) had only one or two slaves.[48] Various censuses and surveys suggest that in the late eighteenth and early nineteenth centuries, a typical cassava farmer in the southern townships and elsewhere in coastal Bahia might employ between two and eight slaves.[49]

Clearly we are dealing here with the use of slave labor on a very small scale and with correspondingly small rural establishments. Yet it was not necessarily what Caio Prado Júnior, drawing on late colonial descriptions of Bahia, called a "paltry" form of husbandry, practiced by "decadent" and "degenerate" roceiros, the "residual" elements in Brazilian society. It is true that among the roceiros of Jaguaripe, Nazaré, and Maragogipe in the 1780s were farmers like Rodrigo *por sobrenome não perca* (Rodrigo whose surname doesn't matter) and former slaves, such as Inácia Gege (Ewe) and Luís *preto forro* (black freedman). Yet they, together with the other roceiros of the southern townships, produced large surpluses of cassava flour for sale in a growing regional market.[50]

Caio Prado's characterization ignores, moreover, the finer gradations of wealth, status, and political power. The roceiros of Jaguaripe were often impoverished, but not all of them were equally poor. The owner of eight or ten slaves, who would warrant little attention in any of the sugar parishes of the northern bayshore, ranked in the southern Recôncavo of the late eighteenth century as a well-to-do farmer. Thus, Pedro José Barreto, who owned ten slaves and whose cassava fields in 1789 may have yielded as much as four thousand alqueires of flour, was a lieutenant in the local militia. In the 1790s, he served as inspector of farinhas for Nazaré, a position that gave him both the responsibility of supervising trade in the staple and the chance to manipulate that trade for his own benefit. His predecessor in the post, Francisco da Silva de Andrade, a militia captain, was also a farmer, as well as a merchant who lent money to other cassava growers and bought the stocks of farinha they brought to Nazaré's weekly fair. To market those stocks, Captain Francisco had two launches that could carry some 1,300 alqueires of flour weekly to Salvador.[51]

These men certainly were not peasants, but neither were they typical of Bahian roceiros who owned slaves. For the majority of those roceiros, who owned only a few slaves, we need to ask whether it makes any sense to insist on a radical distinction between slave-based agriculture and peasant farming. Consider, for example, a pair of roceiros from the 1781 survey of Jaguaripe: Francisco Antônio, the owner of two slaves, and Manoel Ferreira, who owned no slaves at all. Manoel Ferreira, perhaps because he had a larger family and older children or because he had taken in an agregado, planted in 1781 five thousand covas of cassava, the same number as Francisco Antônio. Take another pair of roceiros, from the 1835 census of Iguape: Tomé Pereira de Carvalho and Pedro José. Pereira de Carvalho headed a household that included his wife, Maria Joaquina, their two young sons, and Bernardo, an African slave. Pedro José, who lived with his wife, Ana Rita, and their three children, owned no slaves.

All four roceiros and their families must have led very similar lives. Francisco Antônio and Tomé Pereira de Carvalho had slaves that they could employ in planting and harvesting cassava, but both men must have also done fieldwork. Likewise, although both possessed in their slaves property that their children would inherit, their status as slaveholders was at best precarious. A sequence of bad harvests might force them to sell their slaves for needed cash, or their slaves might suddenly take ill and die. Conversely, with a few good harvests sold at high prices, Manoel Ferreira and Pedro José just might be able to scrape together the money to buy a field hand.

We gain a glimpse into the lives of slaveholders like these in *O juiz de paz na roça* (The Country Justice of the Peace), a comedy by the Brazilian playwright Luís Carlos Martins Pena, first performed in 1838. The play opens with Maria Rosa, the wife of Manoel João, and her daughter, Aninha, sewing. Maria Rosa worries out loud that her farmer husband works too hard, to which Aninha responds, "Mother, you know very well that he has only Agostinho." Agostinho, it soon becomes clear, is the family's one slave. "Father said," continues Aninha, "that when he harvests the big cassava field, he is going to buy me a little black slave girl [*uma negrinha*]." Her mother answers that she knows about those plans, but she has already reminded Aninha that slaves are expensive.

A few scenes later, Manoel João makes his appearance, dressed in trousers of coarse blue cloth (*ganga azul*), one leg rolled up, and a short blue baize jacket. Barefoot, he carries a hoe slung over his shoulder. Accompanying Manoel João is Agostinho, also with a hoe on his shoulder and a basket of coffee berries on his head. Agostinho wears no jacket but just a shirt and a pair of trousers, both made of cotton cloth. In his stage directions, Martins Pena does not bother to say that Agostinho is also barefoot; the playwright could safely assume that no director in nineteenth-century Brazil would put shoes on an actor portraying a rural slave.[52]

Manoel João, after greeting his wife, begins to complain about how hard he has worked. "I weeded the cassava . . . I opened a clearing for a new field . . . I cleaned the ditch . . . and soon I plan to do some coffee picking." He goes on to order his daughter to grab a basket after dinner and go gather coffee berries from the bushes around the house. In a later scene, he reminds his wife to feed the chickens and to finish preparing the farinha made from cassava grown in the family's roça.

Then, Manoel João, Maria Rosa, Aninha, and Agostinho all sit down to a common meal—master and slave, who work side by side in the fields, eat at the same table. Although Manoel João ranks, no less than any wealthy senhor de engenho, as a slaveholder and is committed to the survival of slavery in Brazil, he lives in close and constant contact with his single bondsman. Neither in the fields, where he handles a hoe, nor at the dinner table, where he eats with his fingers and licks them clean, could he pass himself off as a lordly patriarch and master of the type described by Gilberto Freyre in his many studies of slavery in Northeastern Brazil.[53]

For the many Bahian roceiros and tobacco farmers who, like Manoel João, owned only one slave, it is hard to imagine how their daily lives could radically differ from those led by their nonslaveowning neighbors. It is equally difficult to see how the purchase of one or two more slaves would introduce fundamental changes. Ownership of two or three slaves would not free a farmer and his family from house- and fieldwork; at most, it reduced their drudgery. What is more likely and more important is that it gave the family a greater measure of economic security by making possible increases in production both for home consumption and for sale.

In some cases, close daily contact in the fields and at common meals may have fostered a sense of camaraderie between small slaveholders and their bondsmen. Yet, intimacy, as Martins Pena shows us, did not imply equality. In the play, Manoel João wears a jacket; Agostinho does not. When both men return from work, Agostinho, not Manoel João, carries the basket of freshly harvested coffee berries. Maria Rosa has lemonade (*jacuba*) ready for her thirsty husband, but none for the no less thirsty slave. As the family sits down to eat, we learn that the household's supply of carne seca has run short. What little is left ends up on Manoel João's, Maria Rosa's, and Aninha's plates; Agostinho has to make do with a meatless meal of farinha and oranges. Inequalities such as these, although they may appear trifling when set against those that distinguished sugar planters and well-to-do tobacco farmers from their bondsmen, were nevertheless real; they reaffirmed the authority of masters over their slaves.

The Composition of the Slave Population in the Rural Recôncavo

On small farms and large plantations alike, the perpetuation of that authority depended not only the daily display of inequalities, but also on the long-term reproduction of an enslaved work force. Quite simply, without slaves, there could be neither masters nor any slave economy. Historians have long known that the slave populations of most American plantation societies were not self-sustaining, and that the only important exceptions to this rule were the southern United States and, in the early nineteenth century, the island of Barbados. Everywhere else, to increase or even just to maintain the size of their holdings, planters constantly had to import newly enslaved Africans. For this reason, the end of the transatlantic trade generally resulted in a lasting decline in the slave population.[54]

Scholarly discussions have now moved beyond these fairly straightforward observations toward trying to explain why most slave populations failed to reproduce themselves. Although the topic remains the subject of considerable debate, it is already clear that, where planters depended chiefly on the transatlantic trade for labor recruitment, two features generally characterized slave populations.[55] First, Africans, rather than creoles (i.e., American-born slaves), made up, if not the majority, then a large share of the slave population.[56] Second, males outnumbered females. The second feature stemmed directly from the first, because males were exported from Africa in much greater numbers than females. Both features, in turn, contributed to the failure of slave populations to undergo natural increase. A deficit of females lowered the overall birthrate and thereby worked against reproduction; and, because they were exposed to unfamiliar diseases in their new environment, recently arrived African slaves suffered higher rates of mortality, resulting in an excess of deaths over births. Over time, as slave societies matured and as the population of creole slaves gradually grew, the imbalance between the sexes and the proportion of Africans tended to diminish.[57] But as long as planters continued to rely heavily on the transatlantic slave trade for labor recruitment, males would outnumber females and African-born slaves would make up a substantial share of the population.

All of this is certainly true both for Brazil generally and for Bahia. The forced migration of more than 400,000 Africans to Bahia between 1786 and 1851 left the province with a slave population of fewer than 175,000 in 1872–73. Although information for earlier periods is perhaps less trustworthy, it offers nothing to alter the general conclusion: the growth of the slave population in Bahia as a whole always depended on the transatlantic trade. Contemporary observers, from José da Silva Lisboa in the early 1780s to Miguel Calmon in the 1830s and João Monteiro Carson two decades later, had no doubts about the matter. Their views match the conclusions reached more recently by historians, who, taking the long view, argue that in the Recôncavo, reliance on the transatlantic trade determined demographic patterns in the slave population from the late sixteenth to the early nineteenth century: a majority of slaves were always African by birth, and men always outnumbered women by a wide margin.[58]

In taking the long view, however, historians have also necessarily taken a very broad view. As a result, like contemporary observers, they have overlooked the significant differences that emerged in the Bahian slave population by the late eighteenth century. The cassava and tobacco farms of the Recôncavo did not replicate the demographic patterns found on the region's sugar plantations. Only by looking closely at each type of rural establishment can we gain a better understanding of the different ways slavery met the need for labor in the Bahian countryside.

CASSAVA FARMS

Because the evidence is scant, those differences are perhaps less clear in the case of cassava production. Unfortunately, the census materials that might provide detailed information on the slave population of the southern Recôncavo in the late colonial period have not yet been discovered. All we have at present is a 1788 census from the area that would later become the township of Taperoá, on the coast just south of the Recôncavo. It lists slaves by name, making it possible to determine their sex; but it fails to record their place of birth. Farmers in Taperoá, who had long produced farinha for Salvador's market, began in the early 1780s to grow rice as well as cassava. Nevertheless, cassava remained, even at the end of that decade, the area's most important crop.[59] We can therefore cautiously use the 1788 census to help establish the demographic patterns in the southern Recôncavo.

For the years after 1825, postmortem inventories yield information on the sex and birthplace of 650 slaves owned by 106 farmers in the townships of Nazaré and Maragogipe. But those inventories date mostly from the 1840s and 1850s, when farmers in the southern Recôncavo grew not only cassava but also tobacco and coffee. Once again, the cultivation of crops other than cassava makes tentative the conclusions based on the available evidence.

Yet if we were expecting the slave population on these farms to show the characteristic imbalance between the sexes and the predominance of Africans, the 1788 census and the inventories do not bear out that expectation. On farms in Taperoá, the sex ratio was only 118 males per 100 females.[60] The inventories from Nazaré and Maragogipe point to an even lower ratio: 108 males for every 100 females. These inventories also indicate a surprisingly small percentage of Africans: less than one-fourth (22.4 percent) of all the slaves who worked on those farms. One possible explanation lies in the different prices paid for male and female slaves. Women usually sold for 10 to 20 percent less than men. Perhaps, because cassava farmers drew only a relatively modest income from farinha sales, they had from a very early date consistently purchased more female than male slaves.[61]

ENGENHOS AND CANE FARMS

A much more plentiful body of evidence allows for a greater measure of confidence in describing the demographic patterns that characterized the Recôncavor's engenhos and cane farms. A convenient starting point is the 1835 census of Santiago do Iguape. The census lists 3,518 slaves employed on 21 sugar plantations and 66 cane farms. More than half of those slaves (56.1 percent) had been born in Africa. This population as a whole displayed a ratio of 152 males for every 100 females, a disparity that resulted directly from dependence on the transatlantic slave trade for the reproduction of the labor force. Thus, while the sex ratio for creole slaves was 104, the ratio for Africans was 208.

The imbalance between the sexes tended to be larger on engenhos than on cane farms. Sugar planters needed not only field hands but also a large number of skilled and semiskilled workers, who were usually male. Indeed, the parish of Iguape included estates with truly unnatural populations, such as the adjoining Engenhos São Domingos and Santa Catarina, both owned by Colonel Domingos Américo da Silva; and the Engenho da Cruz, which belonged to Captain Tomé Pereira de Araújo. The sex ratio was 193 at São Domingos and Santa Catarina. It was even more unbalanced at the Engenho da Cruz: for every 2 female slaves Captain Tomé employed, he possessed 5 male bondsmen. Together, these three sugar plantations had a combined work force of 401 slaves, 70 percent of whom were African by birth.[62]

The very same demographic patterns reappear in the slave listings for engenhos in Iguape and elsewhere in Cachoeira found in partial censuses

TABLE 24

Composition of the Slave Population on
Bahian Engenhos and Cane Farms, 1780–1860

Location and date	No. of slaves	Males per 100 females[a]	African-born slaves as pct. of total[b]
Iguape, 1835			
Engenhos	2,579	155	57.9%
Cane farms	939	143	50.9
Engenhos and cane farms	3,518	152	56.1
Cachoeira, 1825–26[c]			
Engenhos	1,029	189	54.9
S. Amaro, S. Francisco do Conde, and Iguape, 1780–1860[d]			
Engenhos	3,208	147	50.1
Cane farms	2,084	138	45.7
Engenhos and cane farms	5,292	143	48.7

SOURCES: "Relação do Numero de Fogos . . . Iguape" (1835); Censos (Cach., 1825–26), ARC, PAE; postmortem inventories, APEB, SJ, IT and ARC, IT.

[a] Ratios do not take into account slaves whose sex cannot be determined.

[b] Percentages do not take into account slaves whose place of birth cannot be determined.

[c] Nine engenhos in the parish of Iguape and five in other parishes.

[d] Includes one engenho in suburban Salvador and another in the township of Abrantes, both owned by planters who also had properties in S. Francisco do Conde.

from 1825–26 and also in inventories from Santo Amaro, São Francisco do Conde, and Iguape. The probate records indicate that in the years 1780 to 1860, Africans accounted for fully one-half (50.1 percent) of all slaves on the sugar plantations of the northern Recôncavo, and that males outnumbered females by a ratio of 147 to 100 (see Table 24).

These figures are remarkably high for a region where the production of sugar using slave labor dated back to the mid–sixteenth century, some 70 years before English settlers established the first "sugar works" in Barbados. Philip Curtin has argued that "in the sugar colonies themselves, demographic history tended to fall into a regular pattern over time." In those colonies, after an initial period of settlement and heavy dependence on the Atlantic slave trade, the predominance of Africans and males would gradually give way to a mainly creole slave population with a more balanced sex ratio. Yet parishes like Santiago do Iguape, which, if anything, should have closely resembled the oldest colonies—islands such as Barbados, St. Kitts, or Antigua—matched instead the newest sugar colonies in the West Indies, such as Trinidad. There, the newly established sugar industry expanded rapidly after the late 1780s, and by 1813, the island could claim 221 sugar estates. The more than twelve thousand slaves who worked on those estates were 58.2 percent African by birth and had a sex ratio of 141—figures virtually identical to those for the engenhos and cane farms of Iguape in 1835.[63] Thus, more than two centuries after African slaves first began to labor in the canefields and sugar mills of the Recôncavo, Bahian planters and cane farmers continued to rely heavily on the transatlantic slave trade to replenish and expand their work forces.

TOBACCO FARMS

In 1835, the same year Father Pedro Antônio de Campos Turipaz, the vicar of Santiago do Iguape, counted his parishioners, another vicar, Father Vicente Ferreira Gomes, compiled a census of the neighboring parish of São Gonçalo dos Campos, at that time probably the most important center of tobacco cultivation in the Recôncavo. The farmers of São Gonçalo dos Campos, according to Father Vicente's census, owned 3,762 slaves, roughly the same number as owned by the senhores de engenho and lavradores de cana of Iguape.[64] Beyond their comparable size, however, the two slave populations thoroughly differed. African-born slaves, who made up fully 70 percent of the working-age population owned by the sugar planters and cane farmers of Iguape, accounted for less than one-fourth (23.6 percent) of slaves of working age (15 to 45) on the neighboring parish's tobacco farms. The contrast remains just as sharp when the focus expands to include slaves of all ages. Whereas Africans constituted more than half the slave population found on Iguape's sugar plantations and cane farms, they represented a mere 19.1 percent of all slaves on the farms of São Gonçalo dos Campos. The great majority (80.9 percent) of the enslaved men, women, and children who worked in the tobacco fields of this parish had been born in Brazil.

The differences did not end there. The sex ratio for this largely creole slave population was nearly balanced, with no more than 106 male slaves for every 100 female slaves. The slave women in São Gonçalo dos Campos also seem to have been considerably more fertile than their counterparts in Iguape. For farm households, the census lists a total of 811 Brazilian-born slave children under the age of 10, or a ratio of 85 children for every 100 slave women between the ages of 15 and 44. That ratio, known as the child-woman or general fertility ratio, is low; too low, in all likelihood, to allow for any positive rate of natural increase. Even so, it is fully 35 percent higher than the comparable ratio for sugar plantations and cane farms in Iguape (62.9). These child-woman ratios can also be used to estimate a rough average of how many surviving children were born to slave women during their reproductive lives. While slave women on Iguape's sugar plantations and cane farms bore an average of only 1.89 children who survived, the average for tobacco farms in São Gonçalo dos Campos was just over 2.5.[65] A naturally self-sustaining population would require an average of only 2.

These admittedly rough estimates do not take into full account infant and adult mortality and therefore certainly overstate the average number of surviving children in both parishes. They suggest nevertheless a marked contrast in slave fertility levels between the sugar plantations and tobacco farms of the Recôncavo. They also point to the possibility that, by the 1830s, the slave women of São Gonçalo dos Campos may have been giving birth to nearly enough children to maintain, over time, the total size of the slave population in that parish.

TABLE 25

Composition of the Slave Population in Tobacco-growing
Parishes of Cachoeira and in the Parish of Santiago
do Iguape, 1835 and 1825–26

Location and date	No. of slaves	Males per 100 females	African-born slaves as pct. of total
Parish of São Gonçalo dos Campos, 1835			
Slaves owned by farm households	3,762	106	19.1%
All slaves	3,918	106	19.0
Parish of São Gonçalo dos Campos, 1825–26	1,179ᵃ	104	24.2
Hamlet of Belém da Cachoeira, 1825–26ᵇ	376ᵃ,ᶜ	112	21.5
Parishes of Outeiro Redondo, Muritiba, and Cruz das Almas, 1825–26	779ᵃ,ᵈ	121	38.9
Parish of Santiago do Iguape, 1825–26ᵉ	1,440ᵃ	155	45.6
Parish of Santiago do Iguape, 1835ᵉ	3,985	147	53.6

SOURCES: "Relação do Nº de Fogos . . . São Gonçallo [dos Campos]" [1835]; Censos (Cach., 1825–26), ARC, PAE; "Relação do Numero de Fogos . . . Iguape" (1835).
NOTE: Santiago de Iguape is included here to facilitate comparisons.
ᵃ Results of partial censuses.
ᵇ Includes rural districts surrounding Belém da Cachoeira in the parishes of N.S. do Rosário do Porto da Cachoeira and Conceição da Feira, as well as areas along or near the River Paraguaçu south of the town of Cachoeira.
ᶜ Excludes slaves employed on engenhos and one slave of unknown sex.
ᵈ Excludes slaves employed on engenhos.
ᵉ Includes the hamlet of S. Francisco do Paraguaçu.

These findings, which are completely at odds with established arguments about slavery and export agriculture both in Brazil as a whole and in Bahia, necessarily raise questions about the reliability of the 1835 São Gonçalo census. Could Father Vicente and his census takers, for example, have repeatedly mistaken Africans for Brazilian-born slaves, and men for women? Or could the farmers of São Gonçalo dos Campos have misreported the birthplaces of their slaves? A series of partial censuses from 1825–26 allows us to dismiss those possibilities as highly improbable (see Table 25). True, these censuses do indicate a higher sex ratio and a higher proportion of African slaves for the more thinly settled parishes south of the River Paraguaçu, such as Muritiba and Cruz das Almas, where tobacco was less well established and where, in the 1820s, the production of coffee was expanding. Even so, both the sex ratio and the percentage of Africans are well below the comparable figures for Iguape in either 1825–26 or 1835.

In the well-established tobacco-growing districts north of the Paraguaçu, parishes such as São Gonçalo dos Campos and Conceição da Feira, moreover, creoles in 1825–26 made up a large majority of all slaves. Then and in 1835, the sex ratios were low (ranging from 104 to 112). It therefore seems very unlikely that error or willful misreporting can explain the nearly balanced sex ratio and the small percentage of Africans in the 1835 slave population of São Gonçalo dos Campos.

Could the explanation lie in the depression that overtook the tobacco trade after 1816, and especially after 1822? Perhaps, as exports of tobacco declined, the farmers of Cachoeira sold off large numbers of slaves, especially African and male slaves.[66] The township's probate records offer little support for that hypothesis. A sample of postmortem inventories for the eight decades between 1780 and 1860 furnishes information on the sex and birthplace of more than 3,500 slaves employed on tobacco farms in all parts of Cachoeira. As Table 26 reveals, the imbalance between the sexes did decrease between the periods 1800–19 and 1820–39; the ratio of males to females fell from 116 to 109. The proportion of Africans in the slave population also fell after 1819. Far more important, however, is that at all times, even in the generally prosperous years before 1820, creoles were a clear majority of all slaves on the tobacco farms of Cachoeira. Africans never represented more than 30 percent of the enslaved work forces on those farms. Likewise, even at their highest, the sex ratios were quite low. The ratio of 116 male slaves for every 100 female slaves for the first two decades of the nineteenth century cannot match the ratios of 140 or 150 that characterized Bahian engenhos during the entire period 1780–1860.

Together, the probate records and the censuses from 1825–26 and 1835 allow for only one conclusion: Bahian tobacco farmers, quite unlike their neighbors, the sugar planters, did not depend primarily on the transatlantic slave trade to guarantee the long-term reproduction of the slave work forces they employed. Although it is unlikely that the slave population in the tobacco districts ever achieved a positive rate of natural increase, the evidence does suggest that that population may have been largely self-sustaining. It is otherwise difficult to account for the high proportion of creoles and the nearly balanced sex ratios that characterized the slave population in the tobacco districts at all times between the late eighteenth and mid-nineteenth centuries. Farmers in São Gonçalo dos Campos and other tobacco-growing parishes still imported African slaves, but those imports served mainly to enlarge their slaveholdings rather than to replenish work forces diminished by a large and constant excess of deaths over births.

TABLE 26

Composition of the Slave Population on Tobacco Farms in the Township of Cachoeira, 1780–1860

Period	No. of slaves	Males per 100 females[a]	African-born slaves as pct. of total[b]
1780–99	853	107	29.2%
1800–1819	861	116	29.6
1820–39	1,136	109	21.5
1840–60	731	99	11.3
1780–1860	3,581[c]	108	23.2%

SOURCE: Postmortem estate inventories, APEB, SJ, IT and ARC, IT.
[a] Ratios do not take into account slaves whose sex cannot be determined.
[b] Percentages do not take into account slaves whose place of birth cannot be determined.
[c] Does not include two slaves whose sex was not identified.

A few recent studies have uncovered broadly similar patterns for slave populations elsewhere in Brazil. Most of those studies, however, focus on poorer and more remote regions that lacked well-developed export economies.[67] Cachoeira, by contrast, was not an isolated backwater but a township firmly linked to the broader Atlantic economy. Its farmers produced nearly all the tobacco exported from Brazil in the late eighteenth and early nineteenth centuries. By value, their tobacco accounted for up to one-fourth of the overseas trade in Brazil's second- or third-largest provincial export economy. All the more remarkable is that much of the tobacco went to the coast of West Africa, where merchants used it to barter for slaves—slaves they seldom sold to Bahian tobacco farmers.

We can assume that at one point in time, Africans outnumbered native-born slaves on tobacco farms, and later a transition toward a predominantly creole population took place. How and when that change came about are questions that cannot be settled here. Postmortem inventories from the 1780s and 1790s reveal that by the late eighteenth century, creoles already represented 70 percent of the slave population, and that a near parity had been achieved in the numbers of male and female slaves. Future research will perhaps locate the transition in the 1750s and 1760s, when tobacco exports stagnated. This may have led farmers to cut back the number of new slaves they bought. As merchants delivered fewer and fewer Africans to buyers in the tobacco districts, the slave population on the sítios and fazendas of Cachoeira would have become increasingly creole, and the sex ratio would have fallen.[68]

Alternatively, future research may show that from the very beginning, tobacco farmers tended to buy fewer male slaves than sugar planters did, not only because female slaves sold for lower prices, but also because farmers found women and even children useful in tobacco production.[69] Differences in diet stand out as another possible explanation. As Chapter 7 will demonstrate, tobacco farmers, unlike sugar planters, employed their slaves in producing for home consumption not only cassava but also maize and beans. If those same slaves received significant amounts of maize and beans to supplement their rations of farinha and jerked beef, they would have had a much healthier diet, which, by lowering infant mortality, could have fostered the growth of a predominantly creole slave population in the tobacco-growing districts.[70]

Although these hypotheses await future research, it is already clear that sugar production subjected slaves to the harshest and the most brutal working conditions. The backbreaking and dangerous task of cutting cane and the long hours of night work inside the mills and boiling houses during the nine-month harvest season had no counterparts in either tobacco or cassava production. As in the West Indies, sugarcane was in Bahia the deadliest of crops.[71] To maintain or increase the number of enslaved workers they employed in its production, planters and cane farmers, year after year, imported thousands of African men and women; they relied, in other words, on an "extensive" pattern of labor recruitment. Tobacco farmers and also, it seems, roceiros relied far less on the transatlantic slave trade and much more on the natural growth of the slave population.

Conclusions

In Bahia, where a plentiful supply of land made it possible even for poor, propertyless peasants to survive without regularly hiring themselves out for wages, sugar planters, tobacco farmers, and cassava growers alike faced the problem of retaining a permanent and reliable work force. Slavery offered a solution that proved both flexible and adaptable. So long as the transatlantic slave trade lasted, planters and farmers could increase fairly quickly and easily the size of the agricultural work force. Men and women enslaved in Africa could, in a few months' time, be brought across the Atlantic and put to work on the plantations and farms of the Recôncavo. By ensuring an elastic supply of labor, the slave trade worked against any lasting competition for labor between export agriculture and production for internal markets.

Just as important, the trade permitted the widespread use of slave labor in the Bahian economy and the equally widespread ownership of slaves in Bahian society. By no means confined to plantation agriculture, slavery pervaded the entire rural economy. Slaveholdings ranged in size from the gangs of one hundred or two hundred workers employed by wealthier senhores de engenho to the one or two slaves that tobacco and cassava farmers owned. The small size of such holdings blurred the distinction between peasant and slave-based agriculture. Slaveholdings also differed in composition, revealing, in turn, distinct patterns of labor recruitment. For the long-term reproduction of their work forces, planters and cane farmers relied on the transatlantic slave trade. Tobacco farmers and, apparently, cassava growers depended far less on the importation of African slaves and much more on the natural growth of the slave population.

For the slaves themselves, this meant equally different life experiences. The majority of the slaves who planted cane and worked in the millhouses of the Recôncavo were foreigners. Enslavement had robbed them of their freedom, torn them from their kin, and brought them to a foreign land, where, if they were male, they had few chances of ever forming a stable family. They could, however, share those experiences with their many fellow workers. By contrast, the slaves on the fazendas and sítios of Cachoeira and the roças of Nazaré and Maragogipe were, for the most part, slaves in their own land. Brought up speaking Portuguese or at least a patois, they lived and worked among men and women who often must have been kin. Yet they may have had few opportunities to create a life apart from their masters. Like Agostinho in Martins Pena's play, they might not even have had the chance to eat alone. The lives slaves and their masters led were also shaped by the daily tasks and work routines of planting sugarcane, tobacco, and cassava. The next chapter examines those tasks and routines.

CHAPTER 7

Production

In October 1821, Luís Paulino d'Oliveira Pinto da França, owner of the Engenho de Aramaré in the parish of São Pedro do Rio Fundo, Santo Amaro township, sailed from Salvador for Lisbon. Luís Paulino had been elected one of the delegates who would represent Bahia at the Cortes, an assembly charged with drawing up a single constitution for what had since 1815 been the United Kingdom of Portugal, the Algarves, and Brazil. The letters he received over the next two years from his wife and sons, who remained in Bahia, told alarming news: attacks by political opponents on Luís Paulino's reputation and honor; hastily convoked meetings of authorities, who issued decrees only to reverse them soon thereafter; an increasingly bitter rivalry between native "Brazilians" and "Europeans" (Portuguese-born residents of Brazil) that led to skirmishes in the streets of Salvador; and finally, open warfare in the Recôncavo between troops loyal to the Portuguese crown and an army raised by supporters of Brazilian independence. The same letters also brought Luís Paulino news of Aramaré.

> It has rained constantly for two months. I was coming along with a beautiful crop, but now everything has gone awry. . . . One canefield [*tabuleiro*] has dried out, and I am going to take care of another one. . . . I have already bought 34 oxen and am now waiting for horses. . . . I am going to start milling; the lavradores will help in sawing firewood. . . . The [only] good slaves are those from the Coast [of West Africa]; the rest are hell. . . . The harvest this year is small. The next one will be better if the newly planted canes can

be milled. . . . At last, the next harvest, if there are enough oxen and horses, will be very large, for we have cane enough for 1,800 loaves of sugar. What an awful slave that overseer is. . . . What a meager harvest! . . . With the war, sugar has yielded nothing; the chests [of sugar], with the rains, could not be sent down over the roads.[1]

Rainfall, fieldwork, slaves, overseers, firewood, oxen, and horses—even in the midst of political upheaval and war, the attention of Luís Paulino's wife and sons remained firmly fixed on Aramaré. For the planters, farmers, and slaves who lived in the rural Recôncavo, life centered on the daily and yearly routines of planting fields, bringing crops to harvest, and preparing produce for market. In those routines, labor systems and patterns of land tenure came together to set in motion the agrarian economy. Knowledge of the routine practices that governed crop production in the Recôncavo therefore is crucial in explaining how the region's economy evolved between the late eighteenth and the mid-nineteenth centuries. This chapter examines those practices; it looks at how planters and farmers in the Recôncavo organized the production of cassava, sugar, and tobacco.

Cassava

To meet a large and growing regional demand for basic foodstuffs, Bahian roceiros had at their disposal one of the most valuable plant tools of the tropics: cassava, a hectare of which could supply several million more calories than the same area planted with any other major food crop.[2] The cultivation of cassava allowed farmers in the southern Recôncavo to satisfy a major part of their own subsistence needs and, at the same time, to market sizable surpluses of farinha. Evidence of those surpluses comes not only from the "small fleets" that filled Salvador's harbor, but also from a series of surveys that local officials carried out in the southern townships in the 1780s (see Table 27). A survey of Jaguaripe (including the parish of Nazaré), for example, lists 310 farmers who, in 1780, had planted almost three million covas of cassava. If yields that year fell as low as 15 alqueires of flour for every thousand covas, the cassava fields of this township would have provided 44,829 alqueires of flour—more than twice as much flour as the farmers needed to feed themselves, their families, and their slaves.[3]

On average, however, harvests would have been more abundant. José da Silva Lisboa claimed in 1781 that a farmer could wrest 20 alqueires of flour from one thousand covas of cassava grown in "the most mediocre" soils. Later, in the early nineteenth century, Manoel Ferreira da Câmara observed that a yield of 30 alqueires from every thousand covas would not be at all surprising. The town council of Camamu quoted the same yield for cassava planted in "the worst" soils.[4]

A court decision from 1785 suggests that normal yields were even higher. A farmer in Jaguaripe lost his roça when cattle from a neighboring farm got loose and destroyed the four thousand covas he had planted. The

TABLE 27

Cassava Production and Marketable Surpluses
of Farinha in the Southern Recôncavo, 1780–89

Location and year; no. of farmers	Subsistence needs (alqueires)	No. of covas planted	Yields of 20 alqueires per 1,000 covas		
			Est. total output of farinha (alqueires)	Marketable surplus (alqueires)	Marketable surplus as pct. of total output
Jaguaripe,[a] 1780 310 farmers	19,418	2,988,600	59,722	40,354	67.5%
Maragogipe, 1780 402 farmers	25,194	2,625,800	52,516	27,322	52.0%
Jaguaripe,[a] 1781 218 farmers	13,651	2,505,700	50,114	36,463	72.8%
Nazaré,[b] 1789 305 farmers	19,108	4,711,000	94,220	75,112	79.7%
Jaguaripe,[a] 1789 299 farmers	18,725	—[c]	—[c]	—[c]	—[c]

SOURCES: Lista dos lavradores de mandiocas de Jaguaripe (1780), APEB, SH, 199; "Lista das mandiocas que se achão nos Lavradores do distrito da Villa de Maragog[e] . . ." (1780), APEB, SH, 187; "Ofício do Capitão-mor da Vila de Jaguaripe ao Governo da Bahia que remete as relações dos lavradores empregados na plantação de mandioca, 1781," BN, I-21,30,52: "Lista dos Lavradores de mandioca das Rossas de Nazareth . . ." (1789) and insp. de f. (Estiva) to the Câm. de Jaguaripe (25/2/1789) and enclosure, both in BN, II-34,5,28.

NOTE: See note 3 in the text.

[a] Including the parish of Nazaré.

[b] Including Aldeia.

[c] The 1789 survey of Jaguaripe lists the amount of farinha made each week by farmers. The estimate of production shown in the table was obtained by multiplying the total amount of farinha made weekly by all farmers by 52.

town judge appointed "two of the most competent appraisers with sufficient knowledge of cassava farming" to place a monetary value on the damage. The two appraisers in their estimate assumed that one thousand covas would furnish enough cassava for 40 alqueires of flour. At this ratio, the 310 farmers in the 1780 survey would have harvested enough cassava to make more than 119,000 alqueires of flour, which would have provided them with a marketable surplus that amounted to 84 percent of total output. The other surveys of Jaguaripe, from 1781 and 1789, and of Maragogipe, from 1780, all indicate that by the late eighteenth century, the cultivation of cassava in the southern Recôncavo was firmly tied to an expanding regional market for farinha.[5]

The roceiros who provisioned that market followed relatively primitive agricultural practices and techniques, which differed little from those that, according to legend, Saint Thomas, the wandering apostle, had taught the Indians and that the Indians had passed on to the first Portuguese settlers in Brazil.[6] The cultivation of cassava began with *ferro e fogo*, iron and fire— an iron axe to open a clearing on land with low, brambly secondary growth, *capoeiras*, or, wherever possible, virgin land with the much more impressive first-growth *matas* (forests); and fire to clean the field of underbrush. When the nutrient-rich ashes had cooled, roceiros and their slaves set about pre-

TABLE 27 (*continued*)

Yields of 30 alqueires per 1,000 covas			Yields of 40 alqueires per 1,000 covas		
Est. total output of farinha (alqueires)	Marketable surplus (alqueires)	Marketable surplus as pct. of total output	Est. total output of farinha (alqueires)	Marketable surplus (alqueires)	Marketable surplus as pct. of total output
89,658	70,240	78.3%	119,544	100,126	83.8%
78,774	53,580	68.0%	105,032	79,838	76.0%
75,171	61,520	81.8%	100,228	86,577	86.4%
141,330	122,222	86.5%	188,440	169,332	89.9%
—[c]	—[c]	—[c]	175,136[c]	156,411	89.3%

paring the soil. They used hoes to heap the earth into small mounds known paradoxically as covas (pits or hollows). "Hillocks," Henry Koster called them, while John Mawe, another early nineteenth-century traveler, thought they looked like mole hills.[7] Rising from one-half to three-quarters of a meter above the ground, the covas improved drainage and helped protect the all-valuable cassava roots from becoming waterlogged and rotting during the rainy winter months. Into each cova went two or three *manivas*, pieces of stalk, about ten to fifteen centimeters long, freshly cut from the roceiro's own plants. Then, depending on the season, maize or beans or both might be sown in the rows between the covas. The cassava cuttings would quickly take root, and in two weeks, a shoot would push through the soil to appear atop each cova.

Over the next several months, the field would require periodic hoeing to keep it free of weeds. The first hoeing took place four weeks after planting and the second four to five months later; thereafter, light weedings would be necessary every two months. All the while, farmers watched for any sign of pests, especially caterpillars and ants. "So voracious and harmful" were ants, according to Manoel Ferreira da Câmara, that in a single day they could ruin "the most promising crop." When ants did attack, farmers tried to drown or burn their colonies. Escaped cattle represented another threat; unless chased away, cows would feast on the leaves of "young cassava plants, pull up the stalks, and leave them on the floor of the ground." A royal decree of 1701, intended to protect cassava and other crops, prohibited cattle raising within 10 leagues (approximately 60 kilometers) from the bayshore; but the legislation was seldom, if ever, rigorously enforced. At least a half-dozen cases in which farmers declared that foraging cattle had destroyed their roças came before the town judge of Jaguaripe in 1784 and 1785 alone. Farmers also had to contend with thieves who would sneak into fields at night and dig up ripening cassava.[8]

If the crop survived all these threats and if the weather provided fair growing conditions, then, after nine to eighteen months, the fields would look something "like a nursery of hazels."[9] From central stalks that had grown to about one meter spread small branches with palmated leaves. Below ground, each plant had put down five to ten bulbous roots that were ready for harvesting.

Cultivating cassava, although certainly not easy work, did not demand great amounts of arduous labor. On an already cleared field, a roceiro working with a single able-bodied slave could, in a month's time, prepare and plant ten thousand covas, which might yield as much as four hundred alqueires of flour. The farmer and the slave would invest another two months of labor in weeding and harvesting. As long as the soil did not harden from lack of rainfall, cassava plants could generally be uprooted by hand. The author of one nineteenth-century agricultural manual even advised slaveowning farmers to assign the task of harvesting to pregnant women or slaves recovering from illnesses.[10]

Much more labor-intensive than cultivation was the preparation of farinha. Ridding cassava roots of their poisonous prussic acid and transforming them into the coarse flour that was the chief staple in the Bahian diet involved six tasks: scraping, washing, grating, pressing, sifting, and toasting. All of this took place inside or around the casa de farinha, a small outbuilding or a shed attached to the farmer's house. There, all available hands gathered to scrape the roots with blunt knives or shells and then wash them. Next the roots had to be grated or shredded against the roda de ralar (grating wheel). "The wheel," Koster explained in 1816,

> is placed in a frame, and a handle is fixed to it on each side, by which it may be turned by two men, one of them working at each of the handles. A trough stands under the wheel, and the wheel is cased in copper, which is made rough by means of holes punched in it. . . . The mandioc is thrust against the wheel whilst it is turned with great velocity, and being by this means ground it falls into the trough underneath.[11]

Farmers in the Recôncavo employed the single-wheeled roda Koster described, as well as moendas and bolandeiras, which consisted of a large, hand-driven wheel linked by a pulley to a smaller grating wheel. This arrangement, which provided a faster grating wheel, reduced the time needed to shred the cassava roots. Work time could be further shortened if the farmer invested in a horse- or water-powered wheel. Although the farinha wheel, whatever the power source, represented an advance over the original method of grating roots against a stone-encrusted board, the design of wheels apparently did not undergo any significant changes in the nineteenth century.[12]

The pulp (massa) that fell into the trough below the wheel was next pressed or "dried" overnight to remove the prussic acid. Bahian farmers "dried" the pulp with either a beam press or a screw press, both cumbersome contraptions made of wood. The first resembled a large weighted nutcracker, and the second was modeled after European wine and olive presses. "Drying" might also take place in a *tipiti*, a long cylindrical basket in common use in the first half of the nineteenth century. Into one end of the tipiti, farmers placed the grated pulp; at the other end, they attached a log or stone that would serve as a weight. When hung from a rafter or the sturdy branch of a tree, the weighted tipiti contracted; as it tightened, it pressed out the poisonous liquid that slowly dripped into a trough below. The tipiti, borrowed by Portuguese settlers from the Indians, so impressed Thomas Ewbank, a North American who visited Brazil in the 1850s, that he decided to buy one as a souvenir. "If there is a current primitive invention evincing closer and happier reasoning out of common tracks, and which exhibits neater and cheaper results," wrote Ewbank, "we do not know where to look for it."[13] Farmers took care to keep livestock away from the troughs below the tipiti or the press not only because the animals would die if they drank the liquid, but also because it contained a valuable product. The fine white sediment that collected at the bottom of the trough, when dried, washed, and sifted, was tapioca, which found buyers both in Brazil and abroad.

The grated pulp of the cassava root, once pressed, had a crumbly texture that sifting by hand transformed into a coarse grain somewhat like moist sand. After sifting, the most unpleasant task in making farinha began. The sifted pulp was placed on an *alguidar*, a large griddle made of glazed clay or copper, and then lightly toasted over an open hearth. Toasting improved the flavor and removed the remaining traces of prussic acid. But, to prevent burning, the farmer or a slave had to stand next to the hot hearth and constantly stir the sifted pulp with a wooden spatula. "When quite crisp," as Koster observed, the toasted flour was "taken off the hearth and . . . suffered to cool."[14] Sifted once again and placed in sacks that held two or three alqueires, the farinha was now ready for sale.

Cassava was in many ways an ideal crop for small farmers, whether they owned slaves or relied solely on family labor. First and foremost, by growing cassava, they took a major step toward ensuring their own subsistence. Roceiros knew all too well that the price and supply of farinha fluctuated greatly from one year to the next and even from month to month. Although other crops might bring in a greater cash income, farmers could not make *pirão* (cassava flour porridge) from cash. In years when farinha supplies fell short in local markets and prices soared, all the extra income that other crops provided might have to go toward purchasing flour. Even then, a small farmer's household might have to make do with less than the customary three-fourths of an alqueire every month. Thus, to abandon cassava and buy farinha meant entrusting household survival to a highly uncertain and unreliable market.

Over and above subsistence concerns, cassava cultivation allowed small farmers to utilize the few slaves they owned and family members efficiently year-round. Cassava has no inherent seasonality. Although March and April were the best months for planting, farmers could take advantage of a good rainfall any time of year to lay in a few hundred covas. They were thus able to distribute fieldwork evenly throughout the entire year. The 1780 survey of cassava farms in Maragogipe illustrates this staggered pattern of planting particularly well. When the town council of Maragogipe carried out the survey, farmers in that township had in their fields a total of 2,625,800 covas: 45,500 newly planted, 1,284,400 described as "green," 307,500 *a chegar* (nearly ripe), and 980,000 ripe covas.[15]

Not only did planting and weeding go on throughout the year, but so did harvesting. Once ripe, cassava roots need not be harvested immediately; they can remain in the ground for a year or longer before turning woody. As the author of one nineteenth-century agricultural manual pointed out, cassava's "storehouse is the earth in which it is sown." Farmers drew on the supplies kept in that natural storehouse during the entire year, spreading out the undoing (*desmancha*) of a cassava field and the preparation of farinha from the harvested roots over several months' time. Each week or two, after taking into account the other tasks to be done and the number of hands they could count on, roceiros decided how much cassava to harvest.[16] Thus, the cultivation of cassava, quite unlike the growing of most cereals, presented no seasonal peaks or troughs in the demand for labor. There was no need to hire extra hands at planting or harvest; nor were there long stretches of "dead time" when slaves, roceiros, and their families remained idle.

Weekly or biweekly sales of farinha would have resulted in a relatively even year-round flow of income. They could eliminate one of the most serious problems that so often besets small farmers: the seasonal "lumpiness" in income that forces those farmers into the hands of moneylenders to take out loans against the uncertain results of a harvest still many months away. The flexibility that characterized cassava cultivation also allowed farmers to adjust output to short-term price movements. If prices fell, farmers who were not too hard pressed for cash could cut back on harvests and reduce the amount of farinha they sold every week. Conversely, in crisis years, growers whose fields had escaped drought or excessive rainfall harvested as much cassava as possible to take advantage of the high prices; at times, they even uprooted cassava that was not yet fully ripe.[17]

That same flexibility worked against larger growers. They had the resources to rent slaves at planting and harvest time and to build true granaries on their farms to store stocks of farinha. But those advantages counted for very little in the cultivation of a crop that had no inherent seasonality and that had the earth itself as a storehouse.[18] For that very reason, larger growers would look for other crops, especially export crops, that allowed them to make better use of their greater resources. The long-term stability in the movement of real farinha prices also pushed them toward export agriculture. Here, however, they, too, could take advantage of cassava's flexibility to produce both crops for export and flour for sale in local markets. Without abandoning cassava, they could adjust work schedules on their farms to the labor requirements of export crops.

Sugar

From start to finish, the production of sugar demanded a great deal more labor than cultivating cassava and preparing farinha. Around 1790, Luís Antônio de Oliveira Mendes described planting cane and making sugar as "the most laborious and costly [activity] so far discovered on the face of the earth and the most difficult and, at the same time, the most ingenious enterprise to which men have ever devoted themselves."[19] This enterprise began in February, when gangs of slaves lined up in fields on Bahian cane farms and engenhos and struck their hoes into the ground to open a trench or furrow. As soon as the trench was about fifteen centimeters deep, the overseer would order the slaves to take a few steps back and start over. They would repeat the same operation until they had opened trenches across the entire field. Later, the slaves would place cut pieces of cane stalk into these trenches, known as *regos*, and then bury the stalks with a light covering of soil. Planting continued from February to May, when torrential rains made fieldwork all but impossible. A second round of planting began in July or August and ended in early September. During all these months, weekly or sometimes almost daily rainfall rendered the heavy massapé soils of the northern Recôncavo "frankly soft, pasty, and sticky" and made the work of opening trenches with hoes all the more difficult.[20]

Not until the 1930s or 1940s would the plough completely replace hoe gangs in fieldwork on Bahian sugar plantations. In the late eighteenth and early nineteenth centuries, the use of the plough remained quite localized, restricted for the most part to districts like the parish of Santiago do Iguape, which had sizable stretches of fairly flat land. More than half (52 percent) of the planters and cane farmers in Iguape used ploughs to trench their fields, but fewer than one-tenth (8 percent) did so in the generally hillier township of São Francisco do Conde.[21]

On a trip through the Recôncavo in 1847, the French diplomat Baron Forth-Rouen observed one of those ploughs at work. *"Eighteen oxen and three or four blacks,"* he wrote, "pulled the plough, and they were barely able to cut a furrow a few inches deep." The plough Forth-Rouen watched was probably very similar or perhaps identical to the *arado Pai Adão* (Father Adam plough) Bahian planters used in the first half of the twentieth century. A large and heavy implement, crudely fashioned from wood, the arado Pai Adão had wheels and an iron-tipped share but no moldboard; like the plough described by Forth-Rouen, it was drawn by six to ten teams of oxen. Two ploughmen guided it while at least one young boy walked alongside to keep the oxen in line.[22]

Agricultural reformers in the nineteenth century insisted that ploughing brought savings in labor and reduced the time spent in dressing the soil. According to Manoel Ferreira da Câmara, "a well-built and ably handled plough will do the work of from 30 to 40 hoes." Antônio Calmon du Pin e Almeida, who employed a plough at his Engenho Santo Antônio da Patativa in the 1830s, agreed with Câmara. But Calmon's engenho was located on an admirably flat plain west of the town of Santo Amaro, not on hilly terrain where the use of a heavy plough would have been much more difficult. Moreover, although ploughing no doubt did save labor, it did little else. Bahian ploughs, lacking moldboards, did not turn the soil; they simply loosened the earth as they broke open a relatively shallow furrow. The end result was virtually the same as a trench opened by a gang of slaves using hoes.[23]

That planters in the Recôncavo should have relied throughout the nineteenth century on such a primitive implement might seem to be proof of great backwardness. European farmers, after all, had used moldboard ploughs since the Middle Ages. From the late eighteenth century on, those farmers could choose from a wide variety of ploughs with improved designs that turned the soil even more thoroughly. Yet in Bahia, planters continued well into the twentieth century to employ a plough with a name that, as the agronomist Adrião Caminha Filho noted in the 1940s, suggested "prehistoric" origins. Caminha Filho condemned the Father Adam plough as "incapable of meeting the needs of rational agriculture and . . . of properly turning the celebrated massapés of the Recôncavo." Alexandre Grangier, another agronomist, took a more positive view. He admitted in 1926 that at first glance, the techniques of field preparation used by Bahian sugar planters might seem primitive, but he added that it took only "a little observation" to discover that the planters were "not so backward as might be thought" and that they were "in part right." In the rainy winter months, smaller teams of oxen drawing lighter, more modern ploughs "easily get mired in the mud," while "in the summer . . . the massapés dry up in such a way that no modern implement can withstand the traction." The soil, Grangier noted, "becomes so hard that only the old Father Adam plough can open a furrow and even so a shallow one." Indeed, Baron Forth-Rouen reported in the late 1840s that a Frenchman who owned land in the Recôncavo had tried out ploughs imported from Europe on his estate, but the implements had proved "altogether useless."[24]

Even if that Frenchman had succeeded in tilling his fields with the European ploughs, he might have done more harm than good. Soils such as massapés, and tropical soils in general, do not stand up well against deep ploughing and thorough turning. On the contrary, such techniques, although appropriate for the cultivation of cereals in temperate climates, can produce disastrous results in the tropics. The soils become hardened and compacted, making planting nearly impossible. Thus, senhores de engenho and cane farmers in the Recôncavo had sound reasons for not abandoning the hoe and the Father Adam plough for more modern implements.[25]

Trenching, whether done by hoe or by plough, remained the only method of soil preparation used on Bahian engenhos. Planters in the Recôncavo never adopted the system of cane holing that became widespread in parts of the West Indies after the early 1700s. This system called for the excavation of a square "hole" that measured two to three feet across and five to six inches deep. The narrow ridges separating the cane holes formed a neat and orderly grid completely different in appearance from the roughly cut trenches seen on Bahian plantations. Both before and after placing pieces of cane stalk in the center of each hole, West Indian slaves filled and lined the holes with dung and whatever plant waste was at hand. The entire system worked to halt erosion and to maintain or restore soil fertility.[26]

By contrast, even though they kept large numbers of oxen on their estates and, in some cases, raised livestock as well, Bahian senhores de engenho took no special steps to prevent soil exhaustion. A few well-read and wealthy reformers did experiment with manuring and, impressed by the results, urged other planters to do the same. But their advice went unheeded. As Antônio Calmon pointed out in 1834, most planters and cane farmers believed that "allowing the land *to rest*" was "as good as manuring." They continued year after year to harvest cane from the same field until yields began to show a marked fall. They then let the land lie fallow for three or more years before burning off the wild vegetation that had grown up and replanting the land with cane.[27]

The failure to adopt manuring and other more intensive practices did not reflect any blind adherence to tradition. Not only was land more plentiful in Bahia than on most of the islands in the West Indies, but also, it seems, the soils in the traditional sugar districts of the Recôncavo proved more resistant to erosion and nutrient depletion. It therefore made little sense to divert slaves from other tasks and employ them in digging cane holes, gathering dung from cow pens, and spreading it over fields. Cane holing required much more labor than trenching; so much more that some planters in Barbados spared their own bondsmen from this exhausting work by renting slaves to dig the holes.[28]

Although planting took place yearly on Bahian engenhos and cane farms, it was not necessary to resow each field every year. Sugarcane, once cut, grows back and yields a new crop. Bahians referred to newly planted cane as *canas de rego* (trench cane), to the second-year growth as *socas*, and to the third crop as *ressocas*. Cane would produce more crops, but with such greatly diminished saccharine content that, after the third or fourth year, fields were generally replanted. For the slaves who did that replanting, fieldwork did not end once they had buried pieces of cane stalk in the trenches. All fields, whether they contained canas de rego, socas, or ressocas, had to be weeded at least three times during the growing season.

The routine of trenching, planting, and weeding changed little, if at all, between 1780 and 1860. One of the very few differences a senhor de engenho from the late eighteenth century would have noticed 50 years later would have been the variety of cane cultivated in the Recôncavo. Sometime between 1810 and 1820, first in Iguape and then elsewhere in the region, the so-called Cayenne cane began to replace the creole cane that Portuguese settlers brought from the Atlantic islands of Madeira and São Tomé in the early sixteenth century. Some historians have doubted whether the new variety gained acceptance in Bahia.[29] But contemporary observers such as Miguel Calmon in 1834 and George Fairbanks in the 1840s did not share those doubts; they ranked the introduction of Cayenne cane as a major innovation. Over creole cane, it had a number of advantages: it grew taller; it had a higher sacccharine content, which meant greater yields; it withstood drought better; and its more fibrous stalk made its trash better suited for use as a fuel. For all these reasons, Cayenne cane soon became the most widely cultivated variety of sugarcane in Brazil.[30]

The pace of work on Bahian plantations quickened in early August. The heavy winter rains had ceased; planting had resumed; and now the harvest season, which would last a full nine months, began. Canes sown the year before, as well as socas and ressocas, were ripening and had to be cut. Gangs of slaves armed with scythes marched into the fields. They cut the cane stalks close to the ground and stripped them of their outer leaves while an overseer, whip in hand, stood nearby, watching for any sign that work was slowing down. Meanwhile, another gang of slaves gathered bundles of cut cane and placed them on ox-drawn wagons. If the estate was located near the bay or a navigable stream, small boats might take the place of the wagons.

As soon as the wagons or boats arrived at the estate's headquarters, still another group of slaves unloaded the bundles of cane and readied them for milling. They arranged them in piles beneath the covered verandas (*picadeiros*) that surrounded the millhouse.[31] Inside, more slaves fed the canes into the rollers of a crushing mill powered either by teams of oxen or horses or by a water wheel. The juice extracted from the canes flowed by way of a wooden channel from a trough beneath the mill into another trough in the boiling house, a large room adjoining the millhouse.

Along the walls of the boiling house stood a battery of "coppers": cauldrons (*caldeiras*), kettles (*paróis*), and teaches (*tachos*), each smaller than the last and all fitted into the brickwork over a series of furnaces. Slaves ladled the juice from the receiving trough into the first copper and, while skimming off the impurities, let it heat to a temperature just below boiling. They then transferred the juice to the next copper, where they "tempered" it with wood ashes or lime to aid the process of granulation. As the juice passed into progressively smaller coppers, more and more heat was applied, so that by the time it reached the last and smallest teache, it had taken on the consistency of syrup. A quick boiling in this last teache brought the syrup to the "striking" point—the point at which crystallization occurred. On the sugar master's orders, what had now become a thick mixture of molasses and sugar crystals was removed from the heat and ladled first into a trough and then into bell-shaped earthenware molds.

The work inside the boiling house, which lasted all day and into the night, required both skill and endurance. The slaves who tended the coppers, while they constantly stirred and skimmed the juice, had to watch it carefully to prevent burning. All their care would serve no purpose if, at the end of the process, the sugar master failed to make his "strike" at the right moment; an entire batch of sugar would then be lost. All this went on amid heat, smoke, and steam that, as Koster noted, "increas[ed] greatly the violence of the exertion."[32]

Two more steps were necessary to manufacture white sugar: purging and claying. The molds filled with the molasses and sugar mixture were taken to a large, adjoining room, the purging house, where they were set on racks and left to dry for about two weeks. The molds were then punctured to allow the molasses to drain. At the same time, slaves, generally women, covered the open face of the molds with moist clay and poured water into them. As the water percolated through the mold, it displaced the molasses and other impurities. Two weeks later, the process yielded an inverted cone, consisting of clayed white sugar at the top and yellowish brown muscovado at the bottom. Once this cone of sugar was removed from the mold, a knife easily separated the white from the muscovado. Then, after pounding with a hammer, the sugar was ready for weighing and crating.[33]

The beginning of the harvest season signaled the start of nine months of intense labor on Bahian engenhos. Slaves, both the skilled and the unskilled, braced themselves for days and nights of work at an unrelenting pace. For planters, the harvest demanded careful planning and coordination. Fields had to be cut as soon as the cane they held reached maturity; any delay might lead to lower yields. Even greater losses resulted from the failure to mill the harvested cane within 48 hours. Likewise, the juice extracted from that cane had to be boiled almost immediately to prevent the onset of fermentation. Thus, only constant attention to scheduling could guarantee the continuity of work and the greatest possible output of sugar.

In Bahia and elsewhere in the Americas, the art of sugarmaking at the end of the eighteenth century had scarcely changed since European settlers first transplanted cane to the New World in the 1500s. The differences that distinguished an engenho in Northeastern Brazil from a sugar works in Barbados or an *ingenio* in Cuba amounted to little more than minor variations.[34] Everywhere, the processes were essentially the same: milling, boiling in open coppers over direct heat, and purging. Not until the first half of the nineteenth century would a fundamentally new technology become available. The vacuum pan, centrifugals, and a series of other innovations, completely transforming the long-established processes of sugarmaking, brought into existence the first fully mechanized sugar mills.

Planters in Northeastern Brazil certainly did not take the lead in developing or adopting that new technology. They had, on the contrary, a reputation for backwardness and unwillingness to consider change. Historians have repeatedly quoted the testimony of Louis-François de Tollenare and Henry Koster, who commented on the "extreme ignorance" of senhores de engenho in Pernambuco. "They continue," wrote Koster in 1816, "year after year the system which was followed by their fathers, without any wish to improve, and indeed without the knowledge that any improvement could be made."[35]

Manoel de Vasconcelos de Souza Bahiana, the owner of an engenho in the Recôncavo, two decades later encountered the same resistance to change among Bahian planters. When he proposed innovations, the planters answered, "The old ones knew more than we do; whatever there was to be discovered they discovered. . . . We don't want inventions. Don't bother us with philosophy."[36] Reformers like Souza Bahiana increasingly used the term *routine* as a code word for what they regarded as the appalling backwardness of the Bahian sugar industry. In his 1834 essay on sugar production in Bahia, for example, Miguel Calmon lashed out against "those time-honored *habits* that have enshrined the worst errors" and "that cruel *routine* that, like Milton's Satan, walks about everywhere without ever escaping the darkness." Less literary in his style, João Monteiro Carson observed in 1854 that the province's sugar industry clung to "its old routine; resting, it remains stationary."[37]

Such remarks were deliberate exaggerations, made by writers who hoped to encourage greater and more rapid change in the province's sugar industry. All three authors knew that some progress had been made in the past three or four decades and that not all planters opposed innovation. Indeed, in the late eighteenth and early nineteenth centuries, Bahia could lay claim to some of the best minds in Brazil, many of whom took a keen interest in technological change and innovation. The province also possessed the famous Engenho da Filosofia, described by some scholars as a "model farm" or "experimental plantation" that symbolized the bold, "modernizing" attitudes of Bahian planters. From about 1812 on, the engenho supposedly served the "express purpose" of disseminating the most recent information on methods of sugar production and trying out new technologies.[38]

These exceptions notwithstanding, all three authors correctly recognized that the interest shown in innovation and change by a small, well-educated elite did not by itself guarantee either change or the widespread adoption of new technologies. They also knew that Bahia no longer stood at the forefront of modernization in sugar production. The technological gap separating the Recôncavo's engenhos from the mills in the most advanced sugar-producing regions in the Americas would only widen as the province's sugar industry edged toward nearly complete collapse in the late 1880s.[39] Technological change did take place in Bahia in the first half of the nineteenth century, but that change often met resistance and remained within strict limits. Bahian planters adopted only those new technologies that offered proven results and that could be easily adapted to the existing system of production.

Two main areas of innovation stood out. The first was the millhouse, where steam engines began to replace teams of oxen and horses as the source of power. In 1815, the *Idade d'Ouro do Brasil*, Bahia's first newspaper, announced with great fanfare that the governor of the captaincy had visited the estate of Pedro Antônio Cardoso on the island of Itaparica, opposite Salvador at the mouth of the Bay of All Saints. There, accompanied by a group of senhores de engenho, the governor witnessed the working of Bahia's first steam-powered mill. The steam engine, ordered from the English firm of Walsh and Bolton, had cost Cardoso three contos de réis, a sum he could have spent on the purchase of twenty or more young male field hands. Walsh and Bolton had been unable to furnish Cardoso with a technician to install the machinery properly. Apparently as a result, problems soon arose. One year later, the *Idade d'Ouro do Brasil* informed its readers that Cardoso had put his steam engine up for sale. That same year saw the installation of Bahia's second steam engine at the Engenho Pimentel in São Francisco do Conde, owned by Bento de Araújo Lopes Vilas Boas, the future baron of Maragogipe. A decade-and-a-half later, the engine was still providing power to turn the engenho's crushing mill. Its success convinced other planters to invest in steam engines, so that Bahia in 1834 possessed 46 steam-powered mills. That number increased to 282 by 1873, when approximately two-fifths of the engenhos in the Recôncavo employed steam engines.[40]

The application of steam power to the milling process did not in any fundamental way transform the manufacture of sugar. More cane could be crushed in a shorter time than with a mill powered by oxen or horses, but the yield of sugar from a given amount of cane remained the same. A steam-powered mill in the early nineteenth century was, at bottom, no better than a well-built water-powered mill. Thus, only where planters could not harness the flow of a quick-running stream to their mills could they achieve substantial gains by installing a steam engine.[41]

Much more important in increasing sugar yields from cane was the adoption of horizontal crushing mills, known in Brazil from 1800 on. In 1820, Felisberto Caldeira Brant Pontes, owner of a large plantation in the comarca of Ilhéus, ordered two such mills from the English firm of Graham, Buxton and Company. Brant Pontes was following the example of his brother-in-law, Pedro Antônio Cardoso, who in 1815 had equipped his engenho on Itaparica with a horizontal mill as well as the steam engine. Bahian artisans had, by that date, already learned to assemble these mills, and their skill was known as far away as São Paulo. The new mills differed from those then in use in the arrangement of the rollers, which were now aligned horizontally rather than vertically. This arrangement, especially when the rollers were made of iron, crushed cane more efficiently; that is, it extracted more juice from the cane. It also allowed planters to employ more workers in feeding cane stalks into the mill, thereby decreasing the time needed to crush a given amount of cane. The horizontal mills had another advantage: they worked well no matter what type of power was used to turn the rollers— teams of oxen or horses, a water wheel, or a steam engine.[42]

The other main site of technological change was the boiling house, where Bahian innovators in the late eighteenth and early nineteenth centuries focused on the search for more efficient furnaces. The search proved successful: improvements in furnace design brought savings in the consumption of firewood and, with the introduction of Cayenne cane, permitted the burning of cane trash. From the 1820s on, cane trash fueled the furnaces on more than half the engenhos in the northern Recôncavo. To rebuild furnaces and to fit them with the iron doors that controlled drafts, planters, of course, had to hire masons familiar with the new designs and a blacksmith. Yet they did not need to sink vast amounts of additional capital into their estates. Nor did they have to carry out a full-scale reorganization of work routines. Slaves already worked at clearing trash from the millhouse floor, hauling firewood, and stoking furnaces. Those same slaves could remove moist trash to a *bagaceira* (drying shed) and bring dried trash back to the boiling house to be burned.[43]

The adoption of steam power in milling, the installation of horizontal mills, and the improvements in the design of furnaces defined the extent of technological change in the Bahian sugar industry between 1780 and 1860. Such innovations, as F. W. O. Morton has pointed out, were not enough to ensure competitiveness on the world market. The first half of the nineteenth century saw a true revolution in sugarmaking technology that led to the establishment of fully mechanized mills in Cuba. These mills employed steam power not only to crush cane but also to transform cane juice into sugar. By 1860, the Spanish colony had 64 fully mechanized mills. Bahia had no more than 2—one at the Engenho São Lourenço, owned by Francisco Gonçalves Martins, and the other at Tomás Pedreira Geremoabo's Engenho Novo do Paraguaçu. Both planters experienced financial difficulties after installing the new equipment. Even as late as 1926, fully mechanized mills in Bahia numbered only 22, of which 5 were closed at the time. Another 230 engenhos in the Recôncavo continued to manufacture sugar with the traditional methods.[44]

The failure to modernize stemmed not from a reliance on slave labor or from any deeply engrained atavism, but rather from the limited financial resources available to planters. Lacking an adequate banking system and with few other sources of capital for long-term investment, planters could not afford the enormous expense of purchasing vacuum pans, centrifugals, and pneumatic curing machines. Cost stood out as the sole obstacle to the use of such equipment, in the view of the Junta da Lavoura (Board of Agriculture). In 1853, this semiofficial organization responsible for promoting improvements in Bahian agriculture acknowledged the superior results that could be obtained with vacuum pans, but nevertheless recommended that the provincial government not attempt to encourage their use; the cost was simply too great. Instead, according to the board, the government should seek ways to perfect the production methods already in use.[45]

Only the wealthiest planters could afford to lose income from one or two harvests while they experimented with new technologies. The others waited for proof that the innovations were genuine and not fraudulent, like the *sácaro-motriz*, a mill that, its inventors claimed, needed no power source at all to crush cane. A strong sense of caution characterized even the wealthiest senhores de engenho and those most interested in technological change. Thus, in 1859, when João Maurício Wanderley, the owner of large sugar estates in the Recôncavo, had the chance to purchase a steam-powered plough, he declined the offer. Wanderley wanted the promise of "immediate results, *not* ruinous experiments."[46]

What had become of the bold "modernizing attitude" that, according to some scholars, had led Bahians at the beginning of the nineteenth century to establish the "experimental plantation" at the Engenho da Filosofia? How is it that experiments at this "model farm" did not provide planters like Wanderley with proof that new technologies would bring "immediate" advantages? In reality, the Engenho da Filosofia eloquently illustrates once again the limits of those modernizing attitudes. Experiments did take place there, but the engenho was not in any conventional sense either a model farm or an experimental plantation. Nor did it even formally bear that name. It was actually a private estate, the Engenho São Carlos in the township of Cachoeira, owned by Manoel Jacinto de Sampaio e Melo. Sampaio e Melo, who also happened to hold an appointment as a regius professor of philosophy, spent several years trying to perfect a design for a more efficient furnace. He also spent, from his own fortune, more than four contos de réis, a sum then equal to the value of 30 young, able-bodied field hands. His efforts won him the disdain of his fellow planters, who saw that instead of making sugar with proven methods and profiting, Sampaio e Melo busied himself with failed experiments. Mockingly, they took to calling his estate the Engenho da Filosofia. Sampaio e Melo did, in the end, succeed; in 1816, he published a design for a more efficient furnace that would burn cane trash.[47]

Sampaio e Melo's furnace represented an important advance, but it was not a vacuum pan. Relying on what was quickly becoming an antiquated technology, Bahian planters found themselves poorly prepared to handle the difficulties they faced in the decades after 1860. Between 1866 and 1871, a disease known as the *moléstia* attacked sugarcane in Bahia and even forced some senhores de engenho to buy sugar for their own household needs. Increased production of beet sugar in Europe created a more serious and more lasting problem. At the same time, planters in Bahia had to contend with a dwindling supply of slave labor. The result was not a steady march toward modernization but a dismal decline in exports from the province that had, at the beginning of the century, ranked first in sugar production.[48]

Tobacco

Tobacco was, like sugar, an export staple, one of the mainstays of overseas trade in Bahia. Yet although both might be expected to fit a common pattern of extensive monoculture, the production of sugar and tobacco presented striking differences.

The best-known and most obvious differences were in processing, the one area of tobacco production that, before the 1830s, depended almost exclusively on slave labor.[49] Farmers who processed their own crops needed one or two specially trained slaves known as *fumeiros*. Seldom did Bahian farmers grow enough tobacco to warrant the ownership of more than three fumeiros. Even then, field hands and other slaves had to help in what Vilhena called the "sordid work" of twisting tobacco into tightly woven cords.[50]

That work began when, after being left a day in the sun to wilt, harvested tobacco leaves were brought from the fields to the *casa de fumo* (tobacco house or barn). Unlike the engenho that united under a single roof the mill-house, the boiling house, and the purging house as well as a storeroom for crated sugar, the casa de fumo was merely a good-sized shed. Sometimes it consisted of nothing more than a room attached to the farmer's house. There the slaves strung the leaves onto vines or poles and hung them to dry. After about a week, they took the leaves down and went through them one by one, carefully tearing off the stems. A farmer might at this point set aside some of the better leaves and have them ground into snuff. Most of the crop would, however, be made into long, ropelike cords.

The farmer now counted on the special skills of the fumeiro, who, together with three or four other slaves, operated the *banco de engenho*, a device that consisted of a wooden rod mounted on a bench and fitted with a handle for turning at one end. One of the slaves tightened the cord by turning the rod while the others added leaves until the cord had achieved a suitable length, thickness (three fingers thick, according to Antonil) and weight.[51] Then the slaves, after taking the cord off the rod, wrapped it around a sturdy stick or pole to form a *bola* (ball) of tobacco.

The next day, the slaves undid the bola, subjected the cord to a new twisting, and wrapped it around another stick. Repeated twistings, known as *viraduras*, produced a cord with a more uniform and tighter weave. The bola between each viradura was left standing upright in a rack with a trough underneath. By the third day, it began to secrete the oils still contained in the imperfectly dried leaves. *Mel de fumo* (tobacco honey), the farmers called the oils. When, after a month or more of twisting, the cords had attained the proper consistency, the slaves joined three of them to form a longer rope. They then brushed onto the rope a generous coating of a tarlike syrup made by mixing the "tobacco honey" with molasses, anise, other herbs, and sometimes lard—a concoction that gave Bahian tobacco its sweet aromatic flavor. One last set of tasks remained: the coated ropes were wound around light sticks into tight rolls weighing as much as 25 arrobas (367.5 kilograms). The slaves wrapped the finished rolls in the leaves of the banana plant or the gravatá, a local shrub, and placed them in leather casings.

Although time-consuming, the manufacture of twist tobacco did not require a large number of workers. Much more important were the skill and dexterity those workers brought to the casa de fumo. Beyond the costs of acquiring and maintaining slaves, tobacco farmers had to make only a modest investment in equipment and installations. They needed little more than a shed, racks, poles, a few other simple wooden implements, and a copper cauldron to boil the mixture of "tobacco honey," herbs, and molasses they applied to the ropes of twisted tobacco. But not even this investment was absolutely necessary. Farmers who lacked the resources to equip a casa de fumo and buy a trained fumeiro paid merchant-processors, known as *enroladores*, to twist and roll their tobacco. Or they grew leaf tobacco, which, after harvesting, they simply hung to dry in makeshift open-air sheds or from the rafters inside their homes.[52] Leaves hung from rafters—nothing could be further from the complexities of an engenho with its crushing mill, battery of coppers, furnaces, and racks of earthenware molds.

The differences between tobacco and sugar extended beyond processing to the daily and yearly routines of fieldwork.[53] Tobacco was above all a demanding crop. Of the soil, it demanded a rich supply of nutrients; of farmers, their slaves, and their families, it demanded not so much endurance or strength as constant care and diligent attention to detail. Indeed, strength counted for very little when, from March or April on, slaves began to take handfuls of tiny seeds and bury them in shallow holes dug by hand or with a hoe in a specially prepared seedbed (*canteiro* or *viveiro*). Nor did strength enter into the care the young plants received in the seedbed. There they were watered at least once a day and kept shaded from the sun. Farmers and their slaves constantly watched for the "terrible insects" that might attack the seedlings: ants, caterpillars, crickets, and grasshoppers. They even went out with lights "on dark and gloomy nights" to pick insects off the plants.[54]

A full month would pass before the seedlings would be mature enough to be transplanted. Slaves gently uprooted the plants by hand, placed them in baskets, and carried them off to a nearby field, where covas that resembled those used in growing cassava stood ready to receive the plants. Here, timeliness became important. If the replanted seedlings were to flourish, the transfer to the field could take place only after the young plants had reached the right height and rains had moistened the soil. Poorer farmers depended on each other's help to complete the task of transferring the seedlings in time. They invited their neighbors for a day's work, followed by a large meal and a celebration known in the nineteenth century as a *boi-de-cova* (ox in the pit).[55]

Once the seedlings had been transplanted, constant hoeing kept the field clear of weeds and gave farmers and slaves the opportunity to detect early attacks by the dreaded caterpillars. When caterpillars did attack, farmers in Bahia sometimes let loose in their fields flocks of turkeys that would "avidly swallow up" the pests. They also counted on children, who were especially adept at picking caterpillars from the stalks and leaves.[56] Two months after transplanting, when the plants had reached the height of about one meter, capping or "gelding" (*capação*) took place. The slaves removed the topmost shoot of each plant. Capping prevented the plants from flowering and thereby increased the growth of the leaves, but it also led to the appearance of suckers or secondary shoots. These, too, had to be removed in an operation known as *desolha* (suckering).

With September came the first harvest. Instead of uprooting the entire plant, slaves picked each leaf individually, taking care not to disturb the shoots nearest the ground. These shoots, later capped, produced a second growth of leaves, *socas*. In picking the socas, slaves once again left untouched the shoots at the base of the plant. In this way, farmers might obtain as many as three or four harvests from each plant before the end of the season in December, when they allowed their fields to go to seed.

Great amounts of labor went into bringing a tobacco crop to harvest, but that labor was more painstaking than backbreaking. Where sugar planters wanted strength and endurance in their field hands, tobacco farmers looked for dexterity, expertise, and diligence. The example of tobacco production in Bahia thus refutes the argument that slavery was incompatible with "care-intensive" activities and that only "effort-intensive" activities could employ slave labor. Indeed, in the cultivation of tobacco, as Antonil wrote in 1711, "everyone works . . . the old and the young, men and women, overseers and slaves." Women and even older children could, just as well as adult men, handle the delicate tasks of sowing seedbeds, transplanting, capping, pruning, and leaf-by-leaf harvesting. In the twentieth century, women have often taken full charge of the daily work on the tobacco farms of the Recôncavo while their husbands held down jobs in town or on nearby sugar plantations.[57]

The quality of the rolls of twist tobacco that merchants in Cachoeira and Salvador received at the end of the growing season depended not only on the care given to the crop in the field and in the casa de fumo, but also on whether the leaves in those rolls came from the first or from later harvests. In general, only the first and the second growth of leaves produced rolls that would meet the standards of the Board of Inspection for export to Europe. The rest the board rejected as *refugo* (refuse) and as unfit for shipment to Portugal.[58] Rolls of refugo had, however, a ready market. Merchants in the West African trade could not legally purchase tobacco approved by the board; they had to use refugo in bartering on the coast of Africa for the slaves they shipped to Brazil. The regulations of the Board of Inspection thereby encouraged Bahian farmers to produce rolls of tobacco from the second- and third-growth socas.

But, even without the regulations, farmers had their own sound reasons for harvesting socas. On the one hand, freezing temperatures never cut short the growing season; on the contrary, farmers had to worry much more about the blistering summer heat, which could "burn" the tobacco plants, than about frost, a near impossibility in Bahia. When, in September, the leaves of plants sown in March or April ripened, three to four months of good growing weather were still left before the start of summer—not enough time to put in another crop, but long enough for a second or a third growth of leaves to appear on mature plants. On the other hand, socas, even if they fetched a lower price, still added to the size of the overall harvest and to the farmer's total cash income from tobacco.

That larger overall harvest came, however, at the cost of damage to the soil. Tobacco as a crop tends to exhaust soils quickly. Farmers in colonial Virginia and Maryland, who did not harvest second-growth leaves, found that, if yields were to be maintained, a field would bear no more than three successive years of cultivation. The land then had to lie fallow for a full twenty years. In Bahia, the harvesting of socas only worsened the problem of soil depletion. Three harvests in one growing season would do nearly as much harm as three years of planting with a single harvest each year. Carried out three years in a row, repeated harvesting would do vastly more damage.[59] To offset that damage, the farmers of Cachoeira manured their fields and rotated tobacco with other crops.[60]

The example of Bahian tobacco has, in this regard, a broader significance for an understanding of slave-based agriculture. It belies the claim made, without qualifications, by Ferndando Henrique Cardoso that "a slave economy . . . is by its very nature an *economy of waste*." Likewise, the field techniques used by tobacco growers in the Recôncavo do not serve as evidence to support Eugene Genovese's argument that slave labor is in itself incompatible with more intensive practices such as crop rotation and manuring.[61]

Against such arguments, nearly every author who dealt with tobacco farming in Bahia, from Antonil in 1711 on, called attention to the practice of regularly manuring tobacco fields. "The farmer's first task," Joaquim de Amorim Castro, an experienced tobacco grower, wrote in the late 1780s, "is to prepare the land with the dung necessary for its fertility." That generally meant using what José da Silva Lisboa appropriately called portable paddocks (*currais portáteis*). Beginning in February or March, farmers had a small paddock set up in a corner of a field where they intended to replant tobacco seedlings; there they kept their cattle penned overnight for a week or until the ground had received an adequate amount of dung and urine. Farmers then had the paddock moved to another part of the field, where, to speed up fermentation, their slaves had already spread cuttings of brush and whatever other plant material happened to be at hand. Once again the cattle "slept" seven or more nights in the paddock. Thus, after several weeks' time, a layer of dung would cover the entire field. With the soil later worked up into covas, the *malhada* (manured field) would be ready for the month-old tobacco plants sown in the seedbed.[62]

Manuring obviously required cattle. Sugar planters sometimes ran cattle on unused portions of their engenhos, but that was a parallel activity, not directly linked to the cultivation of cane and therefore not a necessary part of good estate management. The better-off tobacco farmers of Cachoeira, by contrast, practiced a form of mixed husbandry: on their sítios and fazendas, raising livestock was an integral part of tobacco production. Miguel Calmon accurately described the relationship in 1835: "The more cattle a farmer has . . . the more tobacco he reaps."[63] Roughly three-fifths (58.6 percent) of the better-off tobacco growers in Cachoeira did, in fact, raise at least a few head of cattle. The wealthiest among them kept 30 or more head of breeding stock (*gado de criar*), occasionally described in postmortem inventories as "manuring cattle" (*gado de estrumar*). Sometimes they also owned ranches in the interior with much larger herds that could replenish the breeding stock on their farms in the tobacco districts. Farmers too poor to afford their own cattle had to make do with whatever manure they could beg, borrow, or buy from their neighbors.[64]

All farmers, even those without cattle, could practice crop rotation (which also served to control pests). Instead of planting tobacco in the same field until the soil was worn out and then clearing new ground for another field, farmers alternated tobacco with other crops. The exact sequence of crops remains unclear; no doubt, just as no one rotation is followed everywhere in the tobacco districts of the Recôncavo today, crop sequences also varied in the eighteenth and nineteenth centuries from parish to parish and perhaps from farm to farm. Among the possible sequences were a first crop of either beans or peanuts, followed by tobacco and, in turn, by cassava; tobacco the first year, maize or beans or both the second year, and then two years of cassava; and a crop of tobacco followed by one to four years of cassava. All these sequences included at least one year of cassava. Where cassava immediately followed tobacco in a field, it benefited from the residues left from the previous year's manuring. Thus, as a result of crop rotation, the cultivation of cassava as well as other food crops constituted, like the raising of livestock, an integral part of tobacco production. For every malhada of tobacco on a well-managed sítio or fazenda, there would be another field of comparable size planted with cassava.[65]

Two examples, both drawn from probate records, illustrate the close association of tobacco with food crops. The first comes from the inventory of João Ferreira de Melo, owner of the Fazendas Quilombo, Laranjeiras, and Cajazeira near the hamlet of Belém da Cachoeira. The probate assessors who visited those farms in 1827 found 64 slaves, 2 houses, outbuildings, wagons, and implements, such as hoes and axes, along with more than 80 head of cattle (not counting oxen) and extensive fields of cassava. In storage were 30 alqueires of harvested beans, 2 alqueires of dried maize, and 2 wagons filled with maize still on the cob. Returning one year later, the assessors had to evaluate more cassava, a manured field ready for tobacco seedlings, a manured seedbed, and 20,000 covas recently planted with beans. Between 1826 and 1827, according to affidavits attached to the inventory, Melo's farms had produced more than 600 arrobas of twist tobacco.[66]

The second example comes from the inventory of Francisco Moreira de Freitas. Freitas possessed 14 slaves, whom he put to work at the Sítio do Caranguejo, a rented farm in the parish of Nossa Senhora do Rosário do Porto da Cachoeira. There, after Freitas's death in 1818, his widow showed the probate assessors a modest house, some furniture, tools (mainly axes and hoes), and a small orchard of fruit trees, bananas, and coconut palms—all worth less than one-third the value assigned to the livestock the couple owned: 2 horses, 15 oxen to pull the couple's wagon, and 17 head of "manuring cattle." Freitas's widow also presented for appraisal a complete set of equipment for manufacturing rolls of twist tobacco and a thatched shed that held a wheel and the other "accessories" needed to make farinha. When the assessors inspected the rest of the Sítio do Caranguejo, they found a field with 22,000 covas of tobacco and another field with 3,000 covas ready to receive replanted seedlings; two fields of cassava, one with 80,000 covas of ripe cassava and the other with 14,000 recently planted covas; a third field with 10,000 covas raised and ready to be planted with cassava; a field of beans with 13,000 covas already nearing harvest; and a field with 9,000 covas where Freitas's slaves had planted peanuts (*mandubis*), beans, and maize.[67]

Unless a devastating drought struck or torrential rains drenched the fields for several weeks on end, the 94,000 covas already planted with cassava at the Sítio do Caranguejo would have provided Freitas's family and slaves with far more farinha than they could possibly consume in a year or even two. Yields could fall below twenty alqueires for every thousand covas and Dona Rosa Silvéria, Freitas's widow, would still have an ample surplus of farinha for sale in local markets. Not only would such sales add to total farm income, they could also shelter the household from hardship in years when tobacco fetched low prices or when overseas markets for Bahian tobacco contracted. Table 28 shows that the fazendas and sítios of the tobacco-growing parishes of Cachoeira often produced sizable and, in some cases, truly large marketable surpluses of farinha.[68]

More than a mere technical adaptation to the specific requirements of tobacco production, the cultivation of food crops amounted to a strategy that aimed at household self-sufficiency and diversification of output, in sharp contrast to the highly specialized monoculture that led senhores de engenho and lavradores de cana to purchase farinha rather than grow cassava. The tobacco farm was, in effect, also a cassava farm. Few, if any, tobacco farmers would have cared to call themselves roceiros; they preferred the more digni-fied title of lavrador de fumo. Yet like the roceiros of the southern Recôn-cavo, the lavradores de fumo of Cachoeira harvested large surpluses of cas-sava. Fully four-fifths (82 percent) of the better-off farmers in that township invested in the equipment necessary to make cassava into flour.[69] Indeed, so closely was tobacco associated with cassava that a single shed sometimes served as both casa de fumo and casa de farinha.

Tobacco, Coffee, and Agricultural Diversification

Between 1780 and 1860, sugarcane, tobacco, and coffee expanded into the cassava-growing townships of Maragogipe, Nazaré, and Jaguaripe. The expansion of export agriculture into the southern Recôncavo had varied con-sequences. In the case of sugarcane, it often meant the establishment of large monocultural plantations like the Engenhos Sururu and Vira-saia in Mara-gogipe, both owned by Francisco de Oliveira Guedes. The one hundred slaves who worked at these two engenhos in the late 1850s depended almost

TABLE 28

Cassava Production on Tobacco Farms in
the Township of Cachoeira, 1788–1857

Year	Name of farm(s)	No. of slaves	Estimated output of farinha[a]		
			No. of covas	In alqueires	In yearly rations[b]
1788	Sítio do Cocão	18	20,000[c]	400	43.8
1796	Faz. da Velosa	14	26,000	520	57.0
1798	Sítio da Vargem	10	27,000	540	59.2
1800	Faz. do Saco	17	13,000	260	28.5
1809	Faz. da Cajazeira	21	18,000	360	39.5
1813	Sítio Olhos d'Água	17	76,000	1,520	166.6
1817	Faz. do Acu	15	48,000	960	105.2
1818	Sítio do Caranguejo	14	94,000	1,880	206.0
1819	Sítio do Candeal	3	14,000	280	30.7
1819	Faz. da Capianga	10	56,000	1,120	122.7
1823	Faz. da Terra Dura	50	40,000	800	87.7
1825	Faz. Taquaris	58	90,000	1,800	197.3
1826	Faz. da Tucaia, Bananeira, and Genipapo	71	60,000	1,200	131.5
1827	Faz. Quilombo, Cajazeira, and Laranjeiras	64	195,000	3,900	427.4
1830	Sítio do Gravatá	6	28,000	560	61.4
1834	Faz. da Vargem	43	100,000	2,000	219.2
1839	Faz. do Cocão	5	20,000	400	43.8
1840	Faz. da Jaqueira	9	50,000	1,000	109.6
1842	Faz. Gravatá, Tabuleiro, and Terra Dura	71	205,000	4,100	449.3
1843	Faz. Terra Dura	4	42,000	840	92.1
1844	Faz. Capoeira	27	20,000[c]	400	43.8
1846	Faz. Murundu	4	16,000	320	35.1
1846	Faz. Areal	19	50,000	1,000	109.6
1846	Faz. Coqueiro	15	135,000	2,700	295.9
1854	Faz. Vargem Grande	15	60,000	1,200	131.5
1854	Faz. Caminhoá	15	30,000	600	65.8
1855	Faz. Sergi	22	110,000	2,200	241.1
1857	Faz. do Roçado	5	25,000	500	54.8
1857	Faz. Caracanha	7	20,000	400	43.8

SOURCES: Postmortem inventories, APEB, SJ, IT and ARC, IT.
NOTE: See note 68.
[a] Yield of 20 alqueires of farinha per 1,000 covas.
[b] Yearly rations of 9.125 alqueires.
[c] Does not include covas of cassava specifically set aside for the consumption of the household and slaves.

entirely on purchased farinha for their daily meals.[70] Few roceiros, however, had the resources to establish such plantations. At most, they might become cane farmers. But not only did cane farming mean turning over half or more of the crop to a senhor de engenho, it also meant that the former roceiros subjected their few slaves and perhaps family members as well to the exhausting work of planting and weeding canefields and then to the even more arduous task of cutting cane. The hard labor might leave no time to plant enough cassava to meet household needs. Although sugar would certainly provide a larger average income, roceiros with only a few slaves or with no slaves at all ran households as much as business concerns.[71] What use was a greater cash income if, in some years, it all went toward buying farinha?

Tobacco, by contrast, required fewer hours of backbreaking labor and far more attention to detail and diligent care in fieldwork. The small farmers of the southern Recôncavo who took up tobacco cultivation did not need to surrender half their crop to a senhor de engenho for processing; instead, they simply strung the harvested leaves onto poles and hung them up to dry. At the same time, they could continue to grow cassava both for their household needs and for sale in local markets.

The same was true of coffee. All the farmer needed for shelling dried coffee berries was a good-sized *pilão* (mortar) and a sturdy pestle, both made of wood. The famous aromatic "Maragogipe coffee" came from farms that seldom had more than a few hundred coffee trees. The largest groves, containing four thousand to nine thousand trees, would not even have ranked as small plantations in the major coffee-growing regions of Southeastern Brazil. Planting a portion (*porção*) or a backyard orchard (*quintal*) of coffee trees furnished small farmers with another source of cash income and allowed them to take part in the export economy without abandoning cassava.[72] Indeed, postmortem inventories indicate that more than three-fourths of the farms in Maragogipe and Nazaré had casas de farinha. Thus, the expansion of tobacco and coffee into the southern Recôncavo resulted not in the spread of export monoculture but in the diversification of output on small and middle-sized farms.[73]

That pattern of diversification extended even to some of the smaller sugar plantations in the southern townships, such as the Engenho do Mocambo in Maragogipe, owned by Dona Hilária Maria de Jesus until her death in 1857. Three years later, the executor who took over the administration of the engenho and its twenty slaves presented his accounts to the probate authorities. The accounts show that during the drought years 1857 to 1859, when a plague of caterpillars also struck, the executor had to purchase farinha to make up for the shortfall in the cassava harvests. Better growing conditions in 1859 permitted the executor to rely solely on the engenho's own output of farinha from the beginning of 1860 on. Despite the drought, the engenho's slaves, according to the executor's accounts, produced 416 arrobas of sugar and 26 *cargas* (wagon- or packloads) of rapaduras (cakes of unrefined brown sugar) between February 1857 and October 1860. The engenho also harvested and *sold* 151 arrobas of leaf tobacco, 171 arrobas of coffee, and 259 alqueires of maize. When, in October 1860, the executor closed his accounts, the engenho had in the ground 25,000 covas of ripe cassava—enough to feed Dona Hilária Maria's one daughter and twenty slaves for an entire year and, even if harvests were poor, to supply at least 250 alqueires of flour for sale in local markets.[74]

With fair growing conditions, those 25,000 covas could have easily yielded a surplus of more than 400 alqueires for sale. Just as the distinction between slave-based and peasant agriculture was often far from clear-cut on the roças of Maragogipe and Nazaré, no hard-and-fast distinction separated export agriculture from production for local markets in the daily work done by the slaves at the Engenho do Mocambo, or on tobacco and coffee farms throughout the southern and western Recôncavo.

CHAPTER 8

Conclusions

I n 1940, a scant seven years after Gilberto Freyre published his first major work on Northeastern Brazil, Fernando Ortiz wrote his now-classic study of sugar and tobacco in Cuba. Ortiz was, like Freyre, a pioneering social scientist in Latin America. Both authors, moreover, took up similar tasks: they sought to understand how slavery and export agriculture had historically shaped the societies in which they lived. Ortiz's study drew a sharp contrast between sugar production and tobacco farming in Cuba, a contrast he called a "Cuban counterpoint." Often betraying strong nationalist sentiments, his language now sounds dated, and even at times excessively literary for a serious sociological and anthropological study. Some of his arguments are also questionable. Yet among the many enduring merits that have made Ortiz's study a classic is its wide-ranging exploration of the possible diversity in a society and economy permeated by slavery and dominated by export agriculture.[1]

That possible diversity has, by contrast, seldom received anything more than passing attention from historians and other social scientists interested in colonial and nineteenth-century Northeastern Brazil. That is—to borrow Ortiz's analogy—they have largely failed to investigate the interlocking relationships that, in contrapuntal fashion, may have linked the daily lives of planters, urban consumers, rural slaves, and small farmers to both local and overseas markets, creating a complex and varied social and economic landscape in the Northeastern countryside. Instead, those scholars have more often than not accepted as a received truth the view that plantation agriculture completely shaped and defined the society that developed in the Recôncavo and in the other coastal areas of Northeastern Brazil during the colonial period and throughout most of the nineteenth century.

The historical development of the Recôncavo was, indeed, intimately linked to sugar production and to plantation agriculture. For more than three hundred years, slaves, both those brought from Africa and their Brazilian-born descendants, worked in the canefields and millhouses of Bahian engenhos to produce sugar for foreign markets. Trade in sugar and in such staples as tobacco, cotton, and coffee brought renewed prosperity to Bahia in the late eighteenth century. The eight decades between 1780 and 1860 witnessed real growth in the export economy; the volume of goods shipped abroad increased, and earnings from overseas trade rose. The sugar planters who owned engenhos in the townships around the Bay of All Saints and the merchants in Salvador who handled the export trade enjoyed great prestige in Bahian society; they also wielded equally great political influence.

Yet to focus solely on the plantations, on the senhores de engenho, and on the trade in export staples—to adopt the narrowly plantationist perspective that has for so long dominated the historiography—not only results in a gravely distorted image of social and economic life in the Recôncavo in the early nineteenth century, but also hinders any deeper understanding of the features that distinguished plantation agriculture in the townships surrounding the Bay of All Saints. Even when applied to this archetypical plantation region, the plantationist perspective proves woefully inadequate.

That perspective fails to account for the large urban *and rural* market for basic foodstuffs that had emerged in the Recôncavo by the end of the eighteenth century. Indeed, by accepting without reservation a plantationist perspective of Brazil's past, Frédéric Mauro and Francisco de Oliveira can dismiss even the possibility that a significant internal market could have developed in the Bahian countryside. Mauro and Oliveira assume that the engenhos of the Recôncavo must have been self-sufficient and that plantation slaves could not have contributed to any demand for locally produced foodstuffs. Thus, Francisco de Oliveira boldly asserts that "no exchange between units of production" took place in rural Bahia; the problem of obtaining essential provisions on the supposedly "closed" estates of the Recôncavo was strictly an "internal matter," solved within the boundaries of the plantation.[2]

But where, according to Mauro and Oliveira, no market could have developed, the small fleets of barcos vivandeiros that filled Salvador's harbor testify to a thriving trade in basic foodstuffs. Into the city's market flowed the produce of far-flung supply regions to meet a vigorous urban demand for fruits and vegetables, jerked beef, salted fish, rice, maize, and beans, and above all farinha de mandioca, the chief breadstuff in the Bahian diet. The demand for farinha extended beyond the city's limits and into the neighboring countryside, where sugar planters and cane farmers regularly purchased large quantities of farinha to feed their slaves.

The existence of a rural market in the Recôncavo for cassava flour and other essential provisions points to the high degree of specialization that characterized Bahian sugar plantations in the late eighteenth and early nineteenth centuries. Closely tied to an emerging world economy, senhores de engenho and lavradores as well tended to concentrate all their resources in the cultivation of cane and in the manufacture of sugar and sugar byproducts. They came, as a result, to depend on the local market to guarantee the day-to-day reproduction of their slave work forces. The most fundamental components of the diet slaves ate—cassava flour, jerked beef, and salt cod— as well the cotton goods that clothed them reached the plantations and cane farms after passing through the market.

Thus, the local production and marketing of foodstuffs, so often dismissed as marginal, peripheral, or simply subsidiary activities, emerge as crucial and even fundamental in the broader regional economy dominated by export agriculture. The expansion of sugar production in Bahia from the late eighteenth century on required and depended on a growing and generally reliable local supply of basic provisions. In turn, any lasting and serious shortfall in the supply of provisions available in local markets would have threatened the further growth and development of highly specialized plantation agriculture in the Recôncavo.

It likewise becomes clear that the use of slave labor in export agriculture did not constitute, in itself, an insurmountable barrier to the development of an internal market. Plantation slaves occasionally sold surplus produce from their roças; more often, and with a far greater impact on the internal economy, those slaves, through purchases made by their masters, contributed to the demand for locally produced foodstuffs. It would, however, be shortsighted to liken the Bahian market to markets found in mature capitalist economies. Planters and cane farmers bought for their slaves only a narrow range of commodities—limited, for all practical purposes, to a few essential provisions and cheap cotton goods. More important, perhaps, for the long-term reproduction of their work forces, planters and cane farmers relied not on purchases of farinha made in the local market but on the transatlantic slave trade.

Specialization in the sugar industry did, nevertheless, foster and even require specialization elsewhere in the Bahian economy. The combined rural and urban demand for farinha encouraged hundreds of roceiros in the southern Recôncavo and all along Bahia's coastline to cultivate cassava. Far from being isolated peasants with only negligible ties to a monetary economy, these roceiros often owned slaves and used them to produce impressive surpluses of flour. Perhaps as much as 80 percent of the flour prepared on the roças of Jaguaripe, Nazaré, and Maragogipe was, already in the 1780s, intended for sale. In no way, then, does it advance our understanding of colonial and nineteenth-century Brazil to follow Caio Prado Júnior in characterizing Bahian roceiros as "decadent" and "degenerate" farmers practicing a "paltry" form of agriculture.[3]

Although they have been neglected in the historiography, slaveowning roceiros stand out as one of the most interesting segments of rural society in colonial and nineteenth-century Brazil. Outside the boundaries of the plantation, they employed slave labor; and outside the more familiar circuits of international trade, they marketed sizable surpluses of agricultural produce. Ownership of slaves created, between these cassava growers and the sugar planters of the Recôncavo, a bond founded on a common interest in the preservation of slavery as an institution and as a labor regime. Sales of flour to senhores de engenho and lavradores strengthened that bond. Yet from one day to the next—when they worked in the fields and in the casa de farinha; when they sat down to meager meals of jerked beef, farinha, and oranges; when they and their sons dodged military press gangs—roceiros with only one or two slaves led lives that very much resembled those led by their neighbors who did not own slaves.[4]

The demand for basic foodstuffs in the rural Recôncavo introduced competition into the otherwise complementary relationship that Salvador shared with its immediate hinterland. Urban consumers, sugar planters, and cane farmers all competed in the same regional market for the same supplies of farinha. Official attempts to mitigate this competition through the creation of the Public Granary, a controlled market, and through laws requiring planters and cane farmers to cultivate cassava met with little success. Senhores de engenho and cane farmers openly defied the laws by refusing to grow adequate amounts of cassava; they quite simply found it more profitable to buy farinha.

Competition for supplies of marketed farinha only grew worse when sugar prices rose. To take advantage of higher prices, planters cut back on whatever cassava they did cultivate, acquired more slaves, and increased their purchases of farinha. Thus, prosperity in the export economy often exacerbated the periodic problems of scarcity. It would, however, be simplistic to explain those problems as nothing more than a consequence of rising sugar prices. More often than not, crises—years when the price of farinha peaked and shortages were most acute—coincided with droughts or excessively wet winters; that is, with seasons when poor growing conditions brought about a temporary shortfall in cassava production.

The regional market for farinha proved more resilient over the long run to the pressure it received from an increasing urban population and the growth of the export economy. That growth spread the cultivation of sugarcane, tobacco, and coffee into the townships on the southern side of the Bay of All Saints. Yet the transformation of Nazaré and Maragogipe into centers of export agriculture did not lead to the disappearance of cassava from the Recôncavo; on the contrary, production of farinha for the regional market increased in the first half of the nineteenth century. Nor did the growth of the export economy provoke any lasting and extraordinary rise in the price of farinha; in real terms, an alqueire of farinha cost, on average, no more in the 1850s than it did in the 1780s. The absence of any sustained upward trend in the price of farinha strongly suggests that, over the long run, expansion in cassava cultivation kept pace with growth in the urban and rural demand. Expanding cultivation of cassava, in turn, translated into the larger supplies of farinha that were vitally necessary for the continued growth of highly specialized plantation agriculture.

To understand how Bahian planters and farmers achieved, between 1780 and 1860, increases in the production of both export and subsistence crops, we must first abandon the common assumption that during the colonial period and throughout the nineteenth century, sugar planters monopolized the ownership and use of land in Northeastern Brazil. In truth, it makes little sense, in dealing with an area that possessed an open agricultural frontier, to speak of monopolistic control over land. Beyond the Recôncavo, in the interior and along the southern coast, lay vast reserves of unsettled land fit for agriculture. Fresh land could be found even within the Recôncavo, where, in the late eighteenth century, extensive stands of virgin forest still covered much of the countryside. A plentiful supply of land made it possible to expand cultivation and thereby increase the production of both export crops and cassava.

Agricultural expansion depended not only on the physical availability of land, but also on the patterns of land tenure. Here, too, the documentary record fails to bear out the view that planters monopolized the ownership and use of land. Senhores de engenho did retain firm control over rural property in the traditional sugar parishes located on or near the northern bayshore. They did so despite inheritance laws that promoted the equal division of property among all heirs. With an average area of roughly 481 hectares, engenhos in the bayshore parishes were large estates by the standards of the nineteenth-century Recôncavo; they were also large enough for the profitable production of sugar.[5] Through their ownership of the best land for cane near the bay and, just as important, through their control of the equipment needed to manufacture cane into sugar, senhores de engenho were able to impose burdensome sharecropping and rental agreements on tenant cane farmers. The geographic expansion of the sugar industry after the 1790s did not, however, recreate this highly concentrated pattern of landholding in other parts of the Recôncavo. Even in the 1850s, hundreds of small and middling farmers who had not invested in equipment to mill cane divided among themselves ownership of land in the southern and western townships. These were the farmers who met the growing demand for farinha in the regional market.

Recognizing that land was abundant and that sugar planters never monopolized its use is also fundamental in explaining the widespread reliance on slave labor in the Bahian countryside. On a still-open frontier and on unused portions of fazendas and engenhos in the Recôncavo, poor, propertyless free men and women found the means to survive without regularly hiring themselves out as wage workers. Access to land allowed them to hold on to a good measure of the "independence" that, as George Stevens, British consul in Salvador, observed in the 1880s, "they invariably covet and for which they are capable of any sacrifice." Their lives were, no doubt, often marked by wretched poverty. But as Stevens also noted, their independent poverty was "envied by many a slave."[6] Unable to count on these poor men and women as workers, sugar planters, tobacco farmers, and cassava growers all faced the problem of maintaining a permanent and reliable labor force. In slavery, they found a common solution. The use of slave labor provided them with field hands they could depend on throughout the agricultural year. As long as the transatlantic slave trade lasted, moreover, it was possible to achieve relatively quick increases in the size of the rural work force. That possibility lessened competition for labor between export agriculture and production of foodstuffs for local markets.

Slavery also proved quite flexible. It could meet the need for labor on both plantations and small farms. Slaveholdings in the Recôncavo varied enormously in size, from the gangs of 50, 100, or even 200 enslaved workers on the engenhos of the northern bayshore to the work forces of only 2 or 3 slaves that roceiros and tobacco farmers often owned. The small size of such holdings undermines attempts to draw a hard-and-fast distinction between slaved-based production and peasant agriculture in the Bahian countryside.

Slaveholdings in the rural Recôncavo differed not only in size but also, and perhaps more important, in composition. The slave population on Bahian engenhos and cane farms remained, throughout the period 1780–1860, heavily African, and males always outnumbered females. Such a population could not grow or even maintain its numbers without the constant importation of African slaves. The reproduction of the labor force in the sugar industry was thus doubly tied to the market: planters relied on a regional market in Bahia for the daily rations they fed their slaves and on a transatlantic market for the recruitment of new generations of enslaved workers. By contrast, the tobacco farmers of the Recôncavo—and also, it seems, the roceiros—depended far less on the transatlantic slave trade and much more on the natural growth of the slave population. As a result, already in the late eighteenth century, the great majority of slaves on Bahian tobacco farms were Brazilian-born, and a near-parity between males and females had been achieved. The long-term reproduction of this work force took place not primarily in Africa but on the fazendas and sítios of Cachoeira.

The daily and yearly routines of sugar, tobacco, and cassava production help explain these different patterns of labor recruitment. In Bahia and elsewhere, sugar production subjected slaves to an unrelenting routine of backbreaking and often dangerous labor, both in the fields and in the millhouses. In neither tobacco nor cassava production could comparable working conditions be found. Indeed, from their slaves, tobacco farmers demanded not so much brute strength as dexterity, skill, and experience. They could usefully employ women and even children in the many delicate tasks needed to bring a tobacco crop to harvest.

The steps those farmers took to preserve soil fertility further distinguished the cultivation of tobacco from sugar production. Practicing a form of mixed husbandry, they regularly manured their fields. They also rotated tobacco with food crops, such as maize, beans, and cassava. For the slaves who worked on the farms in the tobacco districts, crop rotation may well have provided a healthier diet. For the farmers, rotating tobacco with food crops amounted to a strategy aimed at both household self-sufficiency and diversification of output. The cassava they harvested yielded large surpluses that, once made into flour, could be sold in local markets.

Tobacco and sugar production thus displayed fundamental differences. In landholding, in labor recruitment, in land use, in field techniques, in provisioning, and in work routines—in all these areas, tobacco and sugar differed radically. Taken together, these differences point to the existence of distinct agrarian systems *within* slave-based export agriculture. The tobacco farm, in short, was not simply a smaller version of the sugar plantation; it was not a plantation at all.

Efforts to present tobacco as a plantation crop, to fit it into a common pattern of extensive export monoculture, are therefore just as misleading as the claim that "from the colonial period on," tobacco in Bahia "was a family crop, cultivated by free farmers."[7] Such efforts necessarily turn a blind eye to all the characteristics that distinguished the sítios and fazendas of Cachoeira from the engenhos and cane farms of the northern bayshore. Yet those differences are the key to explaining how a class of slaveowning tobacco farmers survived the prolonged depression in tobacco exports between roughly 1815 and the early 1840s. Those farmers survived as slaveholders because they did not rely chiefly on the transatlantic slave trade for labor recruitment. They survived also because, on their farms, they harvested enough cassava to feed themselves, their families, and their slaves and to sell a surplus of flour in local markets. Even in good years, when prices for tobacco were high and the overseas trade was flourishing, cultivation of cassava both reduced out-of-pocket expenses and helped meet household needs. Sales of flour, in turn, provided Bahian tobacco farmers in those years with an additional source of income that could be used in expanding tobacco production.

Today, tobacco growers in the Recôncavo continue to recognize the close connection between their staple crop and cassava. "The profit of the tobacco," they claim, lies in cassava.[8] In the late eighteenth and early nineteenth centuries, that "profit" helped both to ensure household survival and to sustain the slave-based production of Bahia's second most important export staple. Here again, the production and marketing of basic foodstuffs played a crucial and even central role in a broader regional economy dominated by export agriculture.

The expansion of tobacco into the southern Recôncavo therefore did not result in the unbridled spread of export monoculture. The same holds true for coffee. What took place was not the transformation of small farms into large monocultural plantations but rather the diversification of output on small and middling farms. Roceiros in the southern townships began to combine production of farinha for local markets with the cultivation of export crops.

Bahian tobacco stands out as something of an anomaly in the agrarian history of colonial and nineteenth-century Brazil. In no other major export crop did Brazilian-born slaves make up the majority of all workers. Everywhere else, planters and farmers depended heavily on the transatlantic slave trade for labor recruitment. Nowhere outside the tobacco districts of Bahia did planters or farmers practice mixed husbandry, regularly manure their fields, and systematically rotate crops.

Such field techniques have, in fact, remained quite rare even in recent times. Leo Waibel, a German agricultural geographer who carried out research in southern and western Brazil in the 1950s, was quick to recognize just how exceptional in this regard Bahian tobacco growers were. Everywhere, Waibel found farmers exploiting the land with little concern for the preservation of soil fertility; they rotated fields, not crops. He concluded that the intensive techniques that had long been a part of farming in Europe would not, for many years to come, take hold in Brazilian agriculture. Then, at the end of his stay in Brazil, Waibel visited Bahia, where, to his amazement, he saw tobacco growers manuring their fields and rotating crops. He was all the more astonished to learn that these growers were not European or Japanese immigrants but Brazilian-born farmers who were often of mixed Portuguese and African ancestry.[9]

Precisely because tobacco production in Bahia did not conform to the more familiar pattern of extensive monoculture, it reveals the possibilities that existed within slave-based export agriculture. The broad generalizations that have sustained more than two generations of scholarship can no longer be accepted without question. Historians cannot now simply assume that slave-based export agriculture in Brazil meant plantation agriculture and that land use was always extensive. They cannot take it for granted that production for export was necessarily incompatible with a largely self-sustaining slave population.

The coffee industry that developed in the provinces of Rio de Janeiro and São Paulo after 1800 in many ways recreated the structures already established in the sugar-producing areas of Northeastern Brazil. Wealthy planters laid claim to large estates, where, with no concern for the preservation of soil fertility, they had their slaves cultivate row after row of coffee trees. Like senhores de engenho in Bahia, they depended heavily on the transatlantic slave trade for the long-term reproduction of their enslaved work force. But the example of Bahian tobacco production shows that no simple continuity linked those coffee estates with the engenhos of Northeastern Brazil. *Within* slave-based export agriculture, there were alternatives to the plantation.

Explaining how and why those alternatives were discarded will require more than vague references to an earlier history of plantation agriculture in Brazil or to the demands of an emerging world capitalist economy; it will require close attention both to the strategies that guaranteed the daily, yearly, and long-term reproduction of slave-based export agriculture in Southeastern Brazil and to the connections between that region's local markets and its plantations. A full explanation, moreover, will require the careful investigation of Brazilian social and political life in the early nineteenth century.[10]

The diversity that characterized the slave economy of the rural Recôncavo and the complex and varied links between export agriculture and local markets in the region have even broader implications. The evidence for the Bahian Recôncavo suggests how the plantationist perspective might be replaced with a better paradigm for interpreting Brazil's past, and especially its agrarian history. Efforts to devise a new paradigm must, for example, attach as much importance to food production—whether for the market or not—as to export agriculture. Whatever weight the export sector carried in the economy as a whole, the continued flow of agricultural staples to overseas markets ultimately depended on adequate supplies of foodstuffs in Brazil. For this reason, the production and marketing of foodstuffs cannot be dismissed as peripheral, secondary, or even subsidiary activities; nor should those activities be regarded merely as evidence that the economy and society of colonial and nineteenth-century Brazil were more complex than the plantationist perspective might suggest. Instead, such activities must be seen as fundamental to the growth and development in Brazil of an economy dominated by slave-based export agriculture.[11]

The task at hand is thus no longer simply to demonstrate an internal network of exchanges linking various supply areas with Brazil's larger cities and towns. Nor is it to show that, both socially and economically, areas where production for export failed to become firmly established in colonial and nineteenth-century Brazil differed significantly from the main centers of plantation agriculture. A narrow focus on the internal economy can indeed be just as misleading as older views that dismiss as irrelevant all activities and social groups not directly tied to the plantation and the export trade. Instead, the current challenge is to explore and analyze, for different regions of Brazil, the evolving relationships between production for export, the internal economy, and slavery.

Efforts to replace the plantationist perspective must also take into account that, well into the present century, Brazil possessed an open agricultural frontier. The availability of unsettled and uncultivated land shaped to a considerable extent the agricultural practices, labor regimes, and social relationships in the Brazilian countryside. Recognizing that land was plentiful will necessarily mean questioning the all-too-familiar and often vague references to the virtual monopoly that wealthy planters and large ranchers held over land use and landed property in colonial and nineteenth-century Brazil. More carefully nuanced and better-documented studies that begin by acknowledging the existence of an agricultural frontier will no doubt reveal a countryside with ample room for small and middling farmers who owned rural property and for agregados, moradores, and other "tenants at will" who may, at times, have enjoyed more or less stable customary rights to the land they cultivated. Those studies will, in turn, reopen for investigation questions about how wealthy planters, ranchers, and other large landowners did eventually gain a stranglehold over land use in many regions of Brazil.[12]

Likewise, the search for a new and better paradigm will require close attention to agricultural practices. Information on how planters and farmers used the land and how they produced the crops they grew is indispensable for an understanding of the social and economic structures that prevailed in rural Brazil. Questions about labor regimes and, to a lesser extent, about land tenure have long been standard in historical studies of rural Brazil. Far too often, however, those studies have neglected the actual production of crops or, at most, have relegated the topic to a brief introductory chapter.[13] Yet it was in the routine tasks of preparing the soil, planting, and harvesting that land tenure and labor regimes—component parts of a system of crop production—came together and set in motion the agrarian economy. To focus only on selected parts of a system necessarily means losing sight of the system as a whole and can easily result in an incomplete and even faulty understanding of landholding and labor relations.

In conclusion, we might return to the parish of Santiago do Iguape. For Luís dos Santos Vilhena, it was "the famous Iguape"; José da Silva Lisboa described the parish as a "garden of engenhos."[14] Of those engenhos little now remains. The country houses where wealthy planters once resided and the mills where slaves once produced "the best sugar in the Recôncavo" are today crumbling ruins.[15] Gone, too, for the most part, are the canefields, replaced by seemingly endless rows of oil palms (*dendezeiros*). Yet not everything has changed. Forests still cover the escarpment that separates Iguape from the "fields of Cachoeira"—the tobacco-growing districts of Belém da Cachoeira, Conceição da Feira, and São Gonçalo dos Campos. Farmers in those districts continue to plant tobacco and cassava. Launches and sailing canoes still glide across the calm, brackish waters of the Iguape Basin. From some of the small boats, fishermen cast their nets and set their traps, hoping to catch *robalos, tainhas, cavalas*, oysters, and shrimp, while other launches and canoes head for the nearby port of Maragogipe. There, packhorses and mules still arrive every Saturday, burdened by heavy sacks of farinha brought from neighboring roças for sale in the market fair.

The physical distances between Iguape and São Gonçalo dos Campos or Maragogipe are small, no greater today than they were 150 years ago. But in the early nineteenth century, those distances both separated and linked the vastly different worlds that, within the slave economy of the rural Recôncavo, formed a Bahian counterpoint of sugar, tobacco, and cassava.

Reference Matter

Appendix: Postmortem Inventories and Manuscript Censuses

Postmortem Estate Inventories

This study relies for many of its conclusions on a sample of more than five hundred postmortem estate inventories. The greater part of this documentation is housed in the collection of Inventários e Testamentos in the Seção Judiciária of the Arquivo Público do Estado da Bahia, Salvador (APEB, SJ, IT). The Arquivo Regional da Cachoeira in Cachoeira also has holdings of such inventories, similarly catalogued as Inventários e Testamentos (ARC, IT). Both collections are organized by district: by municipalities at the APEB and by parishes at the ARC. At both archives, however, each *maço* (bundle or packet) contains complete inventories with various initial dates, often mixed with incomplete processes and surviving fragments of other inventories (consisting, in some cases, of little more than a cover sheet). All this means that the researcher must examine each inventory in a *maço* to determine whether a particular process is complete (or at least nearly complete) and to identify the type of property owned by the deceased.

For the present study, I worked with all the postmortem inventories from the two sugar-producing townships of Santo Amaro and São Francisco do Conde from the years 1780 to 1860 that were available for consultation from 1986 to 1988 at the APEB. At the same archive, I also worked with the entire set of holdings from 1780 to 1860 for the township of Cachoeira to locate inventories from the parish of Santiago do Iguape, a traditional center of sugar production in the Recôncavo. Similarly, I examined all the then-available inventories for Santiago do Iguape from 1780 to 1860 at the ARC. Furthermore, without attempting any exhaustive search, I was able to locate among the probate records for the city of Salvador (housed in the APEB) a few postmortem inventories for sugar planters who owned properties in São Francisco do Conde, Santo Amaro, and Iguape, but who, at the time of their death, resided in Salvador.

After gathering information from these collections, I proceeded to eliminate those inventories that were too incomplete for use and those that were not for sugar producers—that is, for either planters or cane farmers. These eliminations left a sample of 162 postmortem inventories for sugar producers.

The holdings for the township of Cachoeira (a traditional center of tobacco production) at the APEB are much more extensive than the collections for any other municipality in the Recôncavo except Salvador. In part, the size of those holdings forced me to adopt different procedures. Once again, I examined all maços that contained inventories carried out between 1780 and 1860; but instead of working with all processes, I attempted to gather, for each decade, information from at least 35 inventories for tobacco farmers.

I systematically excluded those inventories in which the deceased could not be identified as a tobacco grower. I made other exclusions as well. The township of Cachoeira in the late eighteenth century included inland parishes such as São José das Itapororocas (modern Feira de Santana) that, in the early nineteenth century, would be dismembered to form separate townships. I systematically excluded inventories from these inland parishes and restricted my research to probate records from parishes that, in the mid-nineteenth century, belonged to the township of Cachoeira (see Map 2). It was impossible for some decades, especially the earlier ones, to obtain a total of 35 inventories. In these cases, I attempted to supplement my sample with inventories from the holdings of the ARC for the parishes of São Gonçalo dos Campos, Nossa Senhora do Rosário do Porto da Cachoeira, and Conceição da Feira. In the end, time constraints cut short my work, so the final sample used here consists of 260 postmortem inventories for tobacco farmers.

In working with inventories from the townships of Maragogipe and Nazaré, I also encountered difficulties. It was again necessary to examine each inventory in order to exclude those for estates of sugar planters. Furthermore, the available holdings for the two southern townships include virtually no records before the mid-1820s; most of the documentation dates from after 1840. Once again, time constraints cut short my work. Nevertheless, I was able to collect information from a total of 116 inventories carried out between 1825 and 1860.

The end result of my work with Bahian probate records was a core sample of 538 postmortem inventories for sugar planters, cane farmers, tobacco farmers, and cassava growers from the townships of São Francisco do Conde,

Santo Amaro, Cachoeira, Nazaré, and Maragogipe. This does not, however, represent the total number of inventories used in preparing this study. Fragmentary inventories, which were excluded from the core sample, often contained valuable information. Likewise, I have made occasional use of inventories for sugar producers from Maragogipe, Nazaré, and the predominantly tobacco-growing parishes of Cachoeira. Work with another 53 postmortem inventories at the ARC allowed me to increase the number of observations used in constructing the series for slave prices presented in Chapter 4. (From these inventories, I collected only information on the appraised value of slaves.)

I also examined more than 380 postmortem inventories carried out between 1861 and 1888 in the townships of São Francisco do Conde, Santo Amaro, Cachoeira, Maragogipe, and Nazaré, several of which are cited in the notes. Even when there was no reason to cite these inventories, the information gathered from them proved valuable; it often confirmed patterns and tendencies I had observed in working with the inventories from 1780 to 1860. Thus, this study draws, in various ways, on research with a total of nearly 1,000 postmortem inventories.

Manuscript Censuses

This study also makes extensive use of manuscript censuses from the last decades of the eighteenth century and the years 1825–26 and 1835. The 1825–26 and 1835 censuses deserve special comment. In April 1835, the vicars of Bahia received orders from the provincial president to take a complete count of their parishioners, both slave and free. Each vicar was to prepare, by 31 December 1835, lists that recorded the name, age, color, civil status, occupation, and birthplace of every man, woman, and child in his parish. Vicars who did not comply were threatened with the loss of their stipends. The vicars of Bahia apparently did not take that threat seriously. A few offered excuses for not carrying out a population count; most, it seems, simply ignored the orders.[1]

In any event, only four parish censuses from 1835 have survived. Fortunately, two of those are from the rural Recôncavo: one from the parish of São Gonçalo dos Campos, one of the most important tobacco-growing districts in Bahia, and the other from the parish of Santiago do Iguape, a major center of sugar production.

> "Relação do Numero de Fogos, e moradores do Districto da Freguezia de Sant-Iago Maior do Iguape, da Comarca da Villa da Cachoeira da Provincia da Bahia" (1835), APEB, SH, 6175–1 (cited in this book as "Relação do Numero de Fogos . . . Iguape" (1835))

> "Relação do Nº de Fogos e moradores do Districto da Freguezia de São Gonçallo da Vª da Cachoeira" [1835], APEB, SH, 5683 (cited as "Relação do Nº de Fogos . . . São Gonçallo [dos Campos]" [1835]).

Unfortunately, the entire last section of the census of São Gonçalo dos Campos (with the lists for the district of the Capela dos Humildes) was too fragile for use, as were several sheets for the other districts, and a few other sheets were missing. Thus, the figure of 11,406 used in this study as the population of São Gonçalo dos Campos refers only to the number of residents present in the 1,760 households on sheets in the volume that could be examined, and is based on a direct count of the nominal lists for those households.

Like the 1835 censuses, a series of partial censuses from 1825–26 for the township of Cachoeira represents the results of a failed attempt to carry out a population count for the entire province.[2] These lists were located among loose, uncatalogued papers (Papéis Avulsos e Encaixotados, PAE) in the ARC. None of them covers an entire parish or even, it seems, an entire district (*capela*) in a parish. Except when referring to a specific list, in notes and tables I have generally cited these census lists collectively as Censos (1825–26), ARC, PAE.

The use of these censuses posed a number of difficulties. On the one hand, the surviving lists vary greatly in format and in the type and quality of information they contain. On the other, unlike the 1835 censuses, the population lists from 1825–26 are organized not by parish but apparently by militia district. Only occasionally did the census takers include any clear indication of the area covered by those lists. The titles they attached to the lists, moreover, often make no mention of any parish, referring instead to the names of specific farms or plantations. In other cases, the titles are, for all practical purposes, meaningless. One list, for example, bears the title "Alistamento das pessoas compreendidas no mesmo alistamento com suas individuações" (Listing of the persons included in the same listing with their individual traits). Some lists have no titles at all. Thus, to use these census lists, it was first necessary to determine the areas they covered. This involved matching the names of persons and properties in the lists with names that appear in contemporary probate and notarial records.[3]

The fourteen lists used in this study cover a large part of the main tobacco-growing districts of Cachoeira and perhaps one-third of the sugar-producing parish of Santiago do Iguape in the same township.

Parishes of Conceição da Feira and Nossa Senhora do Rosário da Cachoeira (hamlet of Belém da Cachoeira and nearby rural areas)

"Alistam^to das pessoas que Abitão Neste Arraial de Belem e Seo Serconvizinho da Terra da Capella . . . "

"Alistam^to das pessoas que habitão desde a Fazenda do Acu te a porteira do Eng° dos Pattos . . . "

"Alistamento das pessoas que habitão desde o Tibiri te o Porto . . . "

"Rol de Joaquim Ignacio."

Parish of Nossa Senhora do Rosário da Cachoeira (areas near and along the River Paraguaçu south of the town)

"Alistamento das pessoas que habitão desde o principio da ladeira que sobe para Bellem té a Manga a confinar no Engenho do Navarro."

Parish of São Gonçalo dos Campos

"Freg^a de S. Gonçalo dos Campos . . . no prez^e anno de 1825. Alistam^to das pessoas q. morão nos Humildes . . . "

"Lista dos abitantes q. izistem desde o Disteirro Tabua e vargem te o taboleiro do gandu . . . "

Untitled census list that begins with "Faz^da da faca" (with a cover sheet that reads "Pedro Alz. Roiz. 4").

Parishes of Outeiro Redondo and Cruz das Almas

"Relação do Alistamento das peças que morão desde o Oiteiro Redondo . . . the ttermo de Maragogipe"

"Relação Nominal ou exacto alistamento das pessoas que se comprehendem desde a Cruz das Almas . . . Freguezia de Nossa Senhora do Desterro do Oitr° Redondo, e Cruz das Almas."

Parish of Muritiba

Untitled census list with a cover sheet that bears a poem praising the judge.

Parish of Iguape (areas along or near the northern shore of the Iguape basin)

"Alistamento das pessoas que habitão dés do Engenho da Crûz athê o Engenho Novo"

"Alistam^to das peçôas comprehendidas no mesmo alistamento com suas individuaçoens."

Parish of Iguape (hamlet of São Francisco do Paraguaçu and nearby rural areas)

"Alistam^to das pessoas q. habitão desde o Sitio do Paraguassu the o Eng° Velho."

Notes

For complete authors' names, titles, and publication data for works cited in short form in the Notes, see the Bibliography. Dates for manuscript materials are given in numerals in parentheses in the following order: day, month, year. Thus, 7/2/1786 refers to 7 February 1786.

In citing the addresses and reports (*Falas* and *Relatórios*) delivered by the presidents and vice presidents of Bahia to the provincial assembly, I have provided only a short title (either *Falla* or *Relatorio*) followed by the year when the address or report was delivered and the name, in brief form, of the president or vice president who delivered the address or report. Both the year and the abbreviated name of the president or vice president are enclosed in parentheses.

CHAPTER I

1. Freyre, *Casa-grande e senzala*; and *Nordeste*, esp. pp. 12–13.

2. Linhares, "Subsistência," p. 748. Also see C. F. S. Cardoso, "O trabalho," p. 69.

3. *Plantation* has been defined in various ways. See Graves, "Plantation." In the literature on colonial and nineteenth-century Brazil, the term is usually understood to be equivalent to what Caio Prado Júnior called *a grande lavoura* (roughly, large-scale agriculture). The characteristics that distinguished *a grande lavoura*, which Caio Prado equated with the English term *plantation*, were the large estate, extensive export monoculture, and, until the late nineteenth century, slave labor. See his *Formação do Brasil*, pp. 119–56. The present study uses *plantation* and *plantation agriculture* with this meaning. In dealing with Brazil, it makes more sense to employ this rather imprecise definition than to resort to other formulations such as Curtin's *plantation complex* (derived from the experience of the West Indies) in *Rise and Fall*, pp. 11–13; or Moreno Fraginals's definition in "Plantation economies," p.

187, n. 1 (which, on the whole, does not differ greatly from Caio Prado's *grande lavoura*).

4. See, e.g., Lobo, *História do Rio de Janeiro*; Linhares, *História do abastecimento*; Martins Filho and Martins, "Slavery"; Brown, "Internal Commerce"; Marcílio, *Caiçara*; Kuznesof, *Household Economy*; Karasch, *Slave Life*; Libby, *Transformação*; Alden, "Price Movements"; F. C. T. da Silva, "A morfologia"; Metcalf, *Family*; Schwartz, *Slaves*, Chap. 2; and Fragoso and Florentino, *O arcaísmo*. To some extent, the recent literature builds on older, pioneering studies, most of which deal with Southeastern Brazil. See, e.g., Hermann, *Evolução*; Zemella [vianna], *O abastecimento*; Franco, *Homens livres*; and Forman, Chap. 2.

5. Freyre, *Nordeste*, pp. 42–43, specifically includes the Recôncavo in his definition of the Northeast. Recent studies by Schwartz (*Sugar Plantations* and *Slaves*), dealing broadly with the sugar industry in the colonial period, and Mattoso (*Bahia: A cidade* and *Bahia, século XIX*), focusing mainly on the city of Salvador in the nineteenth century, have transformed the social and economic historiography of Bahia. Among the newer works see esp. J. J. Reis, "Slave Rebellion"; and Borges, *Family*. The best general history of Bahia in the early nineteenth century remains Morton's "Conservative Revolution."

6. See, e.g., Furtado, chaps. 7–11; Novais, pp. 109–12; F. Fernandes, pp. 25, 110; Gorender, *O escravismo*, Chap. 12; Ianni, pp. 11–22, 47–48; J. G. da Silva, pp. 13–25; F. de Oliveira, "A emergência," pp. 402–3.

7. Prado Júnior, *Formação*, pp. 125, 158–61. Also cf. Lapa, *O antigo sistema*, pp. 46–47; and F. C. T. da Silva, Chaps. 2–3.

8. The concept of reproduction has gained wide currency in several disciplines and has, in many cases, been usefully expanded to include even cultural issues. Although today the concept has found its way into a variety of theoretical approaches, it can, in all likelihood, be traced ultimately back to Marx (p. 711), who wrote, "Whatever the social form of the production process, it must periodically repeat the same process. A society can no more cease to produce than it can cease to consume. When viewed, therefore, as a connected whole, every social process of production is at the same time a process of reproduction." Also see, e.g., Goody, *Production and Reproduction*; Meillassoux, *Anthropologie*; Garcia Jr., *O sul*; Fragoso and Florentino, *O arcaísmo*.

9. See Chaps. 4–7 below. For the view that tobacco in Bahia was a plantation crop, see, e.g., Arruda, "A produção económica," p. 106; and Dowbor, p. 51. On tobacco cultivation as a peasant activity, see Galloway, "Northeast Brazil," p. 27; Nardi, pp. 10–11; and Mattoso, *Bahia, século XIX*, p. 463. Also see Lugar, "Portuguese Tobacco Trade," pp. 27, 52–53, 55–57; and cf. Flory, pp. 179–81.

10. Ortiz, p. 5. But note that, for Ortiz, a major difference between the two crops in Cuba was the use of slave labor in sugar production; tobacco production, he claims, relied exclusively on free labor. That contrast would not apply to Bahia. Furthermore, although information on the matter is scant, it is clear that at least some Cuban tobacco farmers did employ slaves. Slave labor was also used in manufacturing cigars and processing tobacco. See Knight, p. 65; and Bergad, Iglesias García, and Barcia, pp. 83–84.

11. To date, perhaps the most sustained effort to deal both empirically and theoretically with issues related to the reproduction of slavery and slave-based economies and societies is Meillassoux, *Anthropologie de l'esclavage*, a wide-ranging study of slavery in Africa.

12. It is also clear from the available records that the heirs of many small slaveholders and landowners did not bother to go to the expense of having an inventory

carried out. Or, if they did, most of those inventories have not survived. For a useful summary of the main features of inheritance law in Brazil and references to the relevant legal literature, see Lewin, pp. 352–96.

13. Lowenthal, *Past*.

14. For the series, see Figs. 1–4 and Barickman, "Slave Economy," pp. 526–51. Some revisions have been added for this book.

15. The best discussion of the export economy in this period is Lugar, "Merchant Community," Chap. 2. Lugar, however, was unable to locate information on the trade in specific export staples after 1810. For the years 1850–89, see Bahia, CPE, *A inserção da Bahia*.

16. On the physical geography of the Recôncavo, see Bahia, . . . , CONDER, *Estudos básicos*, tomo 2, vol. 1: *Recursos naturais*; Haskins, Chap. 2. Also see Mattoso, *Bahia: A cidade*, pp. 5–61. On the early settlement of the region, see Schwartz, *Sugar Plantations*, Chaps. 2–4.

17. See, e.g., Haskins, Chap. 1, esp. pp. 6–8; M. Santos, pp. 3–4; Costa Pinto, *Recôncavo*; Machado Neto, *Quadro sociológico*.

18. Despite the creation of new comarcas and name changes after independence, this study refers to the regions along the southern coast of Bahia as the comarcas (or old comarcas) of Ilhéus and Porto Seguro. The colonial designations remain useful because the broad division of the coast into two regions corresponds to settlement patterns that persisted throughout the first half of the nineteenth century.

19. Vilhena, 2: 477–86 and 2: table betw. pp. 460 and 461; Aires de Casal, p. 232; Denis, *Brésil*, p. 232. Also see J. da S. Lisboa, "Descripção" (1799), p. 123. The Public Granary in Salvador used a similar definition of the Recôncavo in classifying stocks of cassava flour coming into the city. See, e.g., adm. (CP) to Pres. (13/12/1844), APEB, SH, 1610.

20. Bahia, . . . , CONDER, *Estudos básicos*, tomo 2, 1: 21–27. Also cf. Mattoso, *Bahia: A cidade*, pp. 29–59; and Schwartz, *Sugar Plantations*, Chap. 4. Note, however, that sources often provide information on townships and parishes as they existed in the eighteenth and nineteenth centuries, forcing me, at times, to use a slightly broader definition.

21. None of the sources for this study contained any map showing eighteenth- or nineteenth-century parish or township boundaries in the Recôncavo, with the exception of the crudely drawn "Mapa do Termo de Marag^e" (n.d. [mid-1840s?]), APEB, SH, 1346. Even detailed descriptions of such boundaries are rare. Therefore, preparing Map 2 entailed reconstructing those boundaries by working backward from current municipal divisions. Using current municipal boundaries to reconstruct nineteenth-century boundaries presents certain problems since the limits of townships have often been re-arranged and redrawn. Current townships, moreover, do not always correspond to nineteenth-century parishes of the same names.

22. "Quadro dos engenhos das vizinhanças da Bahia, com os nomes dos possuidores" [ca. 1790–95], BN, 7,3,27; J. da S. Lisboa, "Descripção" (1799), pp. 122–23; Vilhena, 2: 479–81, 483–84. Throughout this study, Santiago do Iguape is referred to as a bayshore parish even though it borders not the bay but the estuary of the River Paraguaçu. The parish was, however, a traditional center of sugar production with ready access to water transport and to the bay. It thus makes sense to classify Iguape among the bayshore parishes.

23. Morton, "Conservative Revolution," pp. 13–16; Schwartz, *Sugar Plantations*, Chap. 10; Flory, Chap. 4; Flory and Smith, pp. 571–94; Kennedy, pp. 415–39; Borges, esp. Chaps. 2 and 7. On the architecture of Bahian engenhos, see E. B. de Azevedo, *Arquitetura*.

24. Antonil, pp. 292, 324, and pp. 292–93, n. 2–3 (by Mansuy), p. 324 n. 1 (by Mansuy); Flory, Chap. 5; Lugar, "Portuguese Tobacco Trade," pp. 57–61, esp. p. 60; Vilhena, 2: 482; J. de A. Castro, "Memoria sobre a manufactura do Tabaco," pp. 113, 115; "Representação dos lavradores de tabaco" (1814), BN, II-34,8,18.

25. J. da S. Lisboa, "Carta" (1781), p. 503; Vilhena, 1: 41–42 and 2: 484, 486; Schwartz, *Sugar Plantations*, p. 83. Also see Chaps. 4 and 7.

26. See, e.g., Schwartz, *Sugar Plantations*, p. 83; Prado Júnior, *Formação*, p. 160.

27. Haskins, pp. 167–69; Conceição, p. 100.

28. Ouv. (Bahia) to Gov. (4/9/1785), *ABN*, 34 (1912): 9–10; Domingos Alves Branco Moniz Barreto, "Planta da Aldêa de Massarandupio" (1794) and "Planta da Villa de Abrantes" (1794), *ABN*, 34 (1912): 330–31; ouv. (Cach.) to Gov. (23/1/1804), *ABN*, 37 (1915): 178–79; militia recruitment lists for districts in the parishes of Rio Fundo and Oliveira dos Campinhos (1809) in APEB, SH, 417-1; "Requerimentos e ofícios referentes ao pedido dos habitantes de Santana do Catu" (1809–1811), BN, II-34,8,14; Câm. de S. Amaro, "Representação" (28/4/1802), *ABN*, 37 (1915): 479; idem to Pres. (1/9/1821 and 6/10/1821), APEB, SH, 244.

29. Partial censuses of the parishes of Rio Fundo and N. S. da Purificação de S. Amaro (1788) in APEB, SH, 596; militia recruitment lists for districts in the parishes of Rio Fundo and Saubara (1809) in APEB, SH, 417-1; Câm. de S. Amaro, "Representação" (28/4/1802), *ABN*, 37 (1915): 479; idem to Pres. (1/9/1821 and 6/10/1821), APEB, SH, 244; jz de fora (SA e SFC) to Gov. (25/9/1814), APEB, SH, 226.

30. "Quadro dos engenhos" [ca. 1790–95], BN, 7,3,27; João da Costa Carneiro de Oliveira, "Breve compendio de reflexões sobre a villa de Jaguaripe" (1799), *ABN*, 36 (1914): 182–83; J. da S. Lisboa, "Descripção" (1799), p. 123; Flory, pp. 177–80; Antonil, p. 324 n. 1 (by Mansuy); jz ord. [?] (Marag.) to Gov. (3/7/1788), APEB, SH, 187; Câm. de Maragogipe to Gov. (26/5/1779), APEB, SH, 199; idem to Gov. (12/7/1766), APEB, SH, 201–13; idem, "Representação" (4/8/1802), BN, II-34,5,100; Câm. de Jaguaripe to Gov. (12/7/1766), APEB, SH, 199; idem to the ouv. da comarca (1/12/1807), BN, II-34,3,11; Vilhena, 2: 486; Morton, "Royal Timber," p. 44 n. 10. Also see Chap. 7 below. On the sales of Bahian pottery in Rio de Janeiro, see Brown, p. 66; and Ewbank, p. 357.

31. Vilhena, 2: 459–60; Wetherell, p. 95. Also see Alden, "Population," pp. 173–205; Th. de Azevedo, pp. 184, 190; and J. N. de S. e Silva, p. 79.

32. Alden, "Population," p. 186; and "Mappa da enumeração da gente e povo desta Capitania da Bahia" (1780), *ABN*, 32 (1910): 480, which reports a total population of 219,243 for Bahia alone (i.e., excluding the subordinated captaincies of Sergipe and Espírito Santo). The census indicates that 150,096 inhabitants, or 68.5 percent of Bahia's entire population, lived in the Recôncavo. A military census carried out five years before (which did not include young children) reports a population of 120,548 for the Recôncavo (67.5 percent of the captaincy's total population). (In calculating the figures for 1775, I have excluded those outlying parishes in the township of Cachoeira that would be dismembered to create new townships by 1860, as well as S. Gonçalo do Pé do Banco, located in Sergipe and incorrectly classified as a parish in Bahia.) See "Mapa de tôdas as freguesias" in Vilhena, 2, betw. pp. 460 and 461; and "Instrucção para o Marquez de Valença" (1779), *ABN*, 32 (1910): 437.

33. Brazil, . . . , *Recenseamento* (total taken from the tables summarizing the parish returns on unnumbered pages). See, however, note 36 below.

34. According to an 1810 census cited by Alden ("Late colonial Brazil," p. 607), whites represented 19.8 percent of the entire population of Bahia. An 1848 count revealed that whites constituted only one-third (33.9 percent) of the *free* population in Salvador, Maragogipe, Jaguaripe, Nazaré, and Itaparica. Bahia, *Falla* (1848, J. J. de

Moura Magalhães), "Quadro numerico da população livre de 14 municipios," n.p. Similarly, in 1835, whites represented 19.1 percent of the population in the tobacco-growing parish of S. Gonçalo dos Campos and no more than 8 percent of the population in the neighboring sugar parish of Santiago do Iguape. For sources, see the Appendix.

35. An 1816–17 survey of slaveholders in the townships of S. Francisco do Conde, S. Amaro, Jaguaripe, and Maragogipe registered 33,750 slaves. Schwartz, *Sugar Plantations*, p. 440. Schwartz quite plausibly estimates that another 55,000 slaves lived in the city of Salvador and the township of Cachoeira in 1816–17. That estimate, when added to the results of the survey, points to a slave population of roughly 89,000 for the region as a whole.

36. The 1872 national census and the 1872–73 *matrícula* (or slave registry) provide, for the early 1870s, two independent and almost simultaneous counts of the slave population. For the Recôncavo, the matrícula records a slave population of 80,776—a figure 12 percent larger than the total recorded in the census (72,030). The discrepancies between the two sources are often much larger in the municipal-level returns and, when expressed as a percentage of the figures in the census, vary from −63 percent to +212 percent. For details, see Barickman, "Persistence," pp. 596–600. Until further research explains these discrepancies, we can do little more than conclude that the Recôncavo had a slave population of between 72,000 and 81,000 in the early 1870s.

CHAPTER 2

1. [Mendes], pp. 308–17.

2. Schwartz, *Sugar Plantations*, pp. 171–201, 418–19; Alden, "Late Colonial Brazil," pp. 620–22; Russell-Wood, pp. 593–95.

3. J. da S. Lisboa, "Carta" (1781), p. 501. On Brazilian intellectuals and their efforts at agricultural and economic reform, see Jobim, *Reforma*. On Portuguese colonial policy, see Falcon, *A época*; Alden, "Late Colonial Brazil," pp. 612–27; Novais, *Portugal e Brasil*; Schwartz, *Sugar Plantations*, pp. 416–22.

4. Apparently the first author to apply this now-common expression to late colonial Brazil was Caio Prado Júnior. See *História econômica*, p. 79.

5. The most detailed study of Brazil's export trade in this period is Arruda, *O Brasil*. Also see Novais, pp. 287–303; Alden, "Late Colonial Brazil," pp. 627–53; and, specifically on Bahia, Schwartz, *Sugar Plantations*, pp. 422–38; and Lugar, "Merchant Community," pp. 66–131.

6. Lugar, "Merchant Community," p. 97–98; [Mendes], p. 315; Gov. to D. Rodrigo de Sousa Coutinho (25/8/1798), ABN, 36 (1914): 37; Junta da Real Fazenda da Bahia to the Queen (18/5/1799), AN, Códice 91, fols. 33–36, esp. fol. 34.

7. The price index used to adjust the series, compiled by Imlah (pp. 93–98), is the only index available that covers the entire period 1796–1860. When deflated against the "purchasing-power-parity index" calculated by Leff (1: 244), available only for years after 1821, the series for the total value of Bahian exports (for years after 1821) matches closely the series adjusted by Imlah's index. For an index based on the price of foodstuffs in Salvador, 1780–1860, to deflate the price of cassava flour, see Chap. 4. Because the index charts price movements for a limited range of commodites purchased by urban consumers in poorer households in Salvador, its use here would not be appropriate.

8. See Araújo and Barreto, pp. 31–89; and the discussion at the end of this chapter.

9. See, e.g., Arruda, *O Brasil*, p. 207; Bahia, *Falla* (1854, J. M. Wanderley), "Mappa . . . da exportação . . . " n.p.; and Soares, *Notas*, pp. 225–26; and, on the West Indies, see Higman, pp. 52–53, 59.

10. On this point, also see Lugar, "Merchant Community," p. 120.

11. Alden, "Late Colonial Brazil," pp. 635–39; Koster, p. 66.

12. Alden, "Late Colonial Brazil," p. 636 (for exports in the 1770s); Barickman, "Slave Economy," p. 538 (for exports between 1796 and 1860).

13. Bethell and Carvalho, p. 722; Sampaio et al., pp. 194–96.

14. J. da S. Lisboa, "Descripção" (1799), p. 122; Rebello, p. 166; "Mappa Statistico da Freguezia de Santo Estevão de Jacuipe . . . 1826 e 1827" and "Mappa Statistico da Freg^a de St^a Anna do Camizão . . . 1828," ARC, PAE; Bittencourt [e Accioli], p. 59; Spix and Martius, 2: 597–602, 663–64; Henderson, p. 344; Bahia, *Falla* (1847, A. I. d'Azevedo), pp. 22–23. In the late 1840s, Bahia's incipient textile industry found it cheaper to import raw cotton from Alagoas than to use cotton grown in the interior of the province. Sampaio et al., p. 189. Cotton elsewhere in Northeastern Brazil was grown mainly in the *agreste*, the intermediate zone between the humid coast and the drier interior. M. C. de Andrade, pp. 132–40.

15. J. da S. Lisboa, "Descripção" (1799), p. 122; Henderson, p. 343. For cotton production, see Soares, *Notas*, p. 235; and the tables for annual "harvests" of sugar, cane brandy, cotton, coffee, and tobacco on unnumbered pages in Bahia, *Falla* (1853, J. M. Wanderley); idem, *Falla* (1854, J. M. Wanderley); idem, *Falla* (1855, J. M. Wanderley); idem, *Falla* (1856, A. T. de Moncorvo e Lima); and idem, *Falla* (1857, J. L. V. Cansanção de Sinimbu). Contemporary observers measured "production" by the amount of cotton brought annually to warehouses in Salvador.

16. Taunay, vols. 1–2; Arruda, *O Brasil*, pp. 351–52; Bethell and Carvalho, pp. 719–21.

17. Taunay, 2: 35–69; Amaral, 2: 219–21; Alden, "Late Colonial Brazil," p. 644.

18. "Sobre as terras não cultivadas pertencentes aos ex-jesuítas na Comarca dos Ilhéus" (1783), APEB, SH, MNC; "Officio dos Governadores interinos . . . da Bahia" (23/8/1783), *ABN*, 32 (1910): 539; Domingos Alves Branco Moniz Barreto, "Relação que contém a descripção . . . da Comarca dos Ilhéos" (1790), BN, 14,1,10, fol. 6; Vilhena, 1: 58 and 2: 497; [B. da S. Lisboa], "Memoria sobre o corte das madeiras," fol. 4; [Campos], pp. 434, 436–37; Spix and Martius, 2: 664; J. A. de S. Vianna, pp. 77–79.

19. Spix and Martius, 2: 659, 661; Arnizáu, p. 132; Rebello, pp. 175, 180; "Mappa especulativo dos efeitos entrados pellas estradas territorios da Povoação de Nazr^e . . . na Semn^a de 15 d8br° de 1813" [1823], BN, II-34,8,29.

20. Bahia, *Falla* (1847, A. I. d'Azevedo), p. 22; idem, *Falla* (1852, F. Gonçalves Martins), p. 30; idem, *Falla* (1855, J. M. Wanderley), p. 40; idem, *Falla* (1866, M. P. de Souza Dantas), tables of exports from Ilhéus for 1864 and 1865, n.p.; idem, Commissão da Exploração, . . . , *Interesses*, "Quadros" of exports from Caravelas (1845–48) and Vila Viçosa (1849) and of "agricultural establishments" at the Colônia Leopoldina, n.p.; MacGregor, 4: 198; Mouchez, 2: 65, 75, 108, 161, 163; Hartt, p. 217, 261, 265; Santos and Dultra, pp. 132–42; Câm. de Valença to Pres. (?/5/1849), APEB, SH, 1454; idem to Pres. (22/12/1856), APEB, SH, 1455; jz de direito (Valença) to Pres. (30/5/1849), APEB, SH, 2630; Câm. de Maragogipe to Pres. (25/3/1849), APEB, SH, 1347; Câm. de Nazaré to Pres. (3/12/1855) and Resposta ao circular sobre a produção (1856), both in APEB, SH, 1367; *EL*, [Bahia], p. 55.

21. Postmortem inventories from parishes north of the Paraguaçu contain almost no references to coffee groves. Also see Haskins, p. 206. On Maragogipe coffee, see Ferreira, p. 82; Laërne, pp. 322–23; and Ukers, pp. 140, 345, 367.

22. Further research is required to explain the surge in exports in the mid-1850s,

recorded in both official provincial sources and unofficial sources; likewise, provincial records for "production" (see note 15) also register a surge in the mid-1850s. Changes in the way authorities calculated exports cannot account for the surge. For a more detailed discussion, see Barickman, "Slave Economy," pp. 68–69.

23. Bahia's average share of total Brazilian exports between 1852 and 1860 was 1.9 percent, calculated by comparing Bahian exports to the volume of coffee exported through ports in the province of Rio de Janeiro and through the national capital (coffee from the provinces of Rio de Janeiro, São Paulo, Minas Gerais, and Espírito Santo; Bahian coffee was excluded), as shown in Taunay, 6: 316. In the years 1871–76, Bahia supplied on average 2.5 percent of all the coffee exported from Brazil. Calculated from Laërne, pp. 338–39. On coffee plantations in Southeastern Brazil, see, e.g., E. V. da Costa, *Da senzala*; and Stein, *Vassouras*.

24. "Relação dos Lavradores da Colonia Leopoldina" (1840), APEB, SH, 2329; *EL*, [Bahia], p. 55; H. Mathéo to the Diretores da Estrada de Ferro Tram-road de Nazaré (20/1/1885), APEB, SH, 4976; *PP* (1884), *A&P*, 35: 1599. Also see Chap. 7.

25. Lugar, "Portuguese Tobacco Trade," pp. 28–36; Schwartz, "Colonial Brazil," p. 455; Price, 1: 77, 183; Alden, "Late Colonial Brazil," p. 633; Arruda, *O Brasil*, pp. 381–82.

26. Câm. da Bahia to the Queen (1787), *ABN*, 34 (1912): 61; J. R. de Brito, pp. 14–17, 23–24; Henderson, pp. 342–43; Lugar, "Portuguese Tobacco Trade," pp. 35–50; Nardi, *O fumo*.

27. See sources cited in n. 26; Verger, p. 28 and passim; and Alden, "Late Colonial Brazil," p. 634, who estimates that about a third of Bahia's entire output was consumed in Brazil.

28. Bahia, *Falla* (1828, J. E. Gordilho de Barbuda), fol. 1.

29. Lugar, "Portuguese Tobacco Trade," pp. 36–40; Verger, chaps. 1–5; Schwartz, "Colonial Brazil," p. 459; Alden, "Late Colonial Brazil," p. 634.

30. M. Calmon, *Memoria*, pp. 23–25. On the peak of the 1790s, see Lugar, "Portuguese Tobacco Trade," p. 49; and Gov. to D. Rodrigo de Sousa Coutinho (25/8/1798), *ABN*, 36 (1914): 37. The peaks in the early and mid-1810s may have been related to the fall in tobacco exports from the United States. For these, see Ocampo, p. 214.

31. Henderson, p. 341; Spix and Martius, 2: 718–21; M. Calmon, *Memoria*, p. 28; Camara, *Memorias*, "Memoria N. 2, Sobre o Carrapato"; Bahia, *Falla* (1830, J. E. Gordilho de Barbuda), fol. 5. On droughts, also see Chap. 4.

32. See Chap. 6; for slave imports between 1830 and 1850, Eltis, p. 244.

33. Henderson, p. 342; Lugar, "Portuguese Tobacco Trade," pp. 47–48, 52; Verger, pp. 33–38, 226–28; [Mendes], p. 340; cap.-mor (S. Tomé e Príncipe) to Gov. of Bahia (10/5/1793), APEB, SH, 201–22; diretor (Fortaleza de Ajudá) to Gov. of Bahia (10/9/1790), APEB, SH, 193.

34. On the slave trade to Bahia, see Chap. 6.

35. "Registro de Rolos e Fardos de Tabacos: Cachoeira, 1821–1829," ARC; M. Calmon, *Memoria*, pp. 25–26; Lugar, "Portuguese Tobacco Trade," p. 55; J. J. Reis, "Slave Rebellion," p. 40. The value of exports from Bahia to Portuguese India, consisting almost exclusively of tobacco, fell from an average of over Rs.14:000$000 between 1798 and 1816 to only Rs.35$000 by 1834. "Mappa Geral da Exportação q. fez a Bahia ... 1798 a 1807," BN, I-17,12,4; *Almanach*, pp. 244–45; Lugar, "Merchant Community," p. 112; M. Calmon, *Memoria*, pp. 40–41.

36. Renewed but slow growth in leaf exports seems to have begun in the mid-1830s during the decline in the slave trade to Bahia. See Sturz, p. 103. For leaf tobacco's share of total exports, see Barickman, "Slave Economy," p. 81. On changing pat-

terns of tobacco consumption, see Price, 1: 113, 188; J. E. Brooks, Chap. 9; and Lugar, "Portuguese Tobacco Trade," p. 55.

37. Lapa, *Economia colonial*, pp. 180–81; Lugar, "Portuguese Tobacco Trade," p. 43; José da Silva Lisboa to Martinho de Mello e Castro (11/2/1784), *ABN*, 32 (1910): 553; J. de A. Castro, "Memoria sobre as especies de Tabaco," pp. 211–12; Conde de Aguiar to Gov. (19/1/1810), BN, II-33,21,24; Sturz, p. 103; Bahia, *Falla* (1844, J. J. Pinheiro de Vasconcelos), p. 9; idem, *CL*, 4: 305; idem, *Falla* (1846, F. J. Sousa Soares d'Andréa), p. 60; pres. (Junta da Lavoura) to the Vice Pres. (7/8/1853), APEB, SH, 4593; and, for the shipment of cigars, "Registro de Rolos e Fardos . . . ," ARC, fol. 263. On tobacco "factories," see M. Calmon, *Memoria*, p. 34; and Borba, p. 35.

38. For international tobacco prices in the 1840s and 1850s, see Ocampo, p. 220. For leaf tobacco's share of total exports, see Barickman, "Slave Economy," p. 81. On the link between leaf tobacco and the increase in exports, see Bahia, *Falla* (1851, F. Gonçalves Martins), p. 36.

39. Câm. de Maragogipe to Pres. (25/3/1849), APEB, SH, 1347; Câm. de Nazaré to Pres. (3/12/1855), and idem, Resposta ao circular sobre a produção (1856), both in APEB, SH, 1367; Bahia, *Falla* (1849, F. Gonçalves Martins), p. 41; idem, *Falla* (1852, F. Gonçalves Martins), p. 54; Epifânio José de Meireles, "Esboço descriptivo da Cidade da Cachoeira" (1866), BN, I-3,3,31, fol. 17; Borba and Santos, p. 83 (for exports of cigars and cigarettes); Barickman, "Persistence," p. 616 (on tobacco exports after 1860).

40. Moreno Fraginals, *O engenho*, 1: 35–40; Williams, pp. 226–27; Schwartz, *Sugar Plantations*, p. 423; [Mendes], p. 315. For prices in Salvador, see Fig. 6 in the text. For prices in London, see Deerr, 2: 531. Later references in the text to sugar prices are based on these sources.

41. [Mendes], p. 315; Antonil, p. 280.

42. Gov. to D. Rodrigo de Sousa Coutinho (25/8/1798), *ABN*, 36 (1914): 37.

43. The tithe was a tax amounting to one-tenth of all production received by the church. In Brazil, however, the tithe was paid to the crown, which was supposed to use the revenues to support the church in Brazil. After independence, the right to collect the tithe devolved, in practice, on provincial governments. In Bahia, it became little more than a tax on exports. On the complicated legal history of the tithe, see O. Oliveira, *Os dízimos*. Also see Schwartz, *Sugar Plantations*, p. 173.

44. Gov. to D. Rodrigo de Sousa Coutinho (24/5/1797) and Provedor da Fazenda (Bahia) to idem (23/10/1797), *ABN*, 34 (1912): 447, 466; Gov. to idem (5/6/1799) and Junta da Real Fazenda da Bahia to the Queen (18/5/1799) as well as "Noticia do Plano da Administração . . . , que a Junta da Fazenda Real . . . tem feito praticar" [ca. 1801], all in AN, Códice 91, esp. fols. 21, 24, 33–36. The new system of assessing and collecting the tithe on sugar, and especially the "discounts" based on distance, have been poorly understood by historians. See e.g., Schwartz, *Sugar Plantations*, p. 425; Mattoso, *Bahia: A cidade*, p. 52; and Morton, "Conservative Revolution," pp. 203–4. For a more detailed discussion of the system, see Barickman, "Slave Economy," pp. 100–105. The system was abolished in 1842, when the tithe was replaced by a simple 4 percent tax on sugar exports. Bahia, *CL*, 4: 73. On the tithe on tobacco, which was a "half-tithe" (equal to 5 percent, rather than 10 percent, of its market value), see "Petição dos Lavradores de tabaco da Cachoeira" (1807), BN, II-33,20,2; "Representação dos plantadores de tabaco da Bahia a S.A.R." (1810), BN, II-33,17,6; Francisco Gomes de Souza, Parecer (1810), BN, II-33,17,7; and the bills of sale of tobacco attached to inventories of farmers from Cachoeira.

45. See, e.g., the accounts and bills of sale included in the invs. of João Manoel dos Santos (1787) and of Manoel Dias Rocha (1789), both in ARC, IT; of Antônio Alves da Encarnação (1787) and of Antônio Freitas da Cunha (1794), both in APEB, SJ, IT.

46. "Matrícula dos Engenhos da Capitania da Bahia pelos Dízimos Reais administrados pela Junta da Real Fazenda" [1807–1874], APEB, SH, 632. The Treasury Board began in 1807 to register all existing engenhos and new engenhos as they made their first shipments of sugar to Salvador. The dates, however, were recorded irregularly. The board recorded no dates before 24 July 1818; it stopped dating the registrations after 18 December 1820 and did not regularly record dates until after 18 October 1828. F. W. O. Morton has made the plausible suggestion that of the 469 engenhos registered between 1807 and 1818, perhaps 200 or 300 had existed before registration began, and the rest had been built after 1807. "Conservative Revolution," p. 205.

47. Góes Calmon, p. 47; R. de Almeida, p. 29; Mattoso, *Bahia, século XIX*, p. 572; Pang, *O Engenho Central*, pp. 26, 28–29; Pinho, *História*, p. 321. An earlier version of this argument is found in *A lavoura da Bahia* (1874).

48. Between 1822 and 1830, the price of a hundredweight of sugar in London fell from 31s to 24s, but, because of the declining exchange rate, this amounted to an increase in sugar's price in mil-réis from Rs.7$595 to Rs.12$624. Prices for sugar in Salvador also increased in these years. For exchange rates, see Leff, 1: 246. Later references in the text to exchange rates are based on this source.

49. Morton, "Conservative Revolution," pp. 327–30; M. Calmon, *Ensaio*, p. 173. Also see the three requests for licenses (all dated 1826) in APEB, SH, 4597. Curiously, Mattoso regards the construction of new engenhos as evidence of decline in the province's sugar economy. *Bahia, século XIX*, p. 572.

50. Morton, "Conservative Revolution," p. 330.

51. *PP* (1831–32), *Reports from Committees*, 16: "Report . . . on the Commercial State of the *West India* Colonies," pp. 236, 257–58, 272–73 (testimony of John Brownwell Boothby, George Timothy Sealy, and Evanson Alchorne); Deerr, 2: 430. For an assessment of the negative impact of British duties on Brazilian exports, see Batista, Jr., pp. 203–39. The value of the pound against the mil-réis fell from Rs.10$520 in 1830 to Rs.6$240 in 1836.

52. *A Missão especial*, 1: 134, 192; Delson, pp. 63–67; Deer, 2: 437–42; Bethell, pp. 273–74.

53. *PP* (1867), *A&P*, 29: 187. Also see Bahia, *Falla* (1874, A. C. da Cruz Machado), pp. 178–79. On the process of claying sugar, see Chap. 7. Note, however, that the term *muscovado* could apply to either raw (i.e., unclayed) or darker clayed sugar. Deer, 2: 109 n. On Bahia's specialization in clayed sugar, see Schwartz, *Sugar Plantations*, p. 162. For the proportions of white and muscavado sugar exported, see Barickman, "Slave Economy," pp. 547–49.

54. On this point, see Bahia, *Falla* (1853, J. M. Wanderley), p. 75; and *EL*, [Bahia], p. 42. Although the system of tithe "discounts" was abolished in 1842, the register was maintained until 1874, probably because its numbering of engenhos remained useful in identifying the ownership of chests and sacks of sugar in Salvador's warehouses. See "Relação dos Engenhos . . . da Bahia cujos assucares . . . tem sido depositados nos Trapiches Alfandegados" (1869), BN, II-33,32,3.

55. Unlike what took place in the tobacco-producing region of Güines, Cuba, there is no evidence that Bahian sugar planters made widespread use of violence to expel tobacco farmers from their lands to establish new engenhos. On Güines, see Moreno Fraginals, *O engenho*, 1: 59–66.

56. E.g., the Engenhos Cassucá and S. Domingos in the parish of Iguape (Cachoeira), both registered in 1830, with 76 and 170 slaves respectively in 1835; and the Engenho S. Antônio do Pastinho in the parish of N. S. da Purificação (S. Amaro), registered in 1831, with 95 slaves in 1852. "Relação do Numero de Fogos . . . Iguape"

(1835); inv. of Manoel Bernardo Calmon du Pin e Almeida and Maria Rosa de Araújo Calmon (1852), APEB, SJ, IT.

57. This periodization generally matches the one proposed by Mattoso (*Bahia: A cidade*, pp. 349–51), based on her study of prices in Salvador. Although Mattoso does not analyze exports, she does show that the long-term price movements in Bahia corresponded broadly to Kondratieff cycles in European economies.

58. On the unrest, see J. J. Reis, "A elite baiana," pp. 341–84.

59. Araújo and Barreto, pp. 50, 52; Barickman, "Persistence," pp. 616–25.

60. Barickman, "Persistence," pp. 588–95. For sugar exports in 1889, see Great Britain . . . , *Report for the Years 1885–89 on the Trade of Bahia*, p. 2; and Jancso, p. 356. For sugar exports from other Northeastern provinces, see Galloway, "Last Years," p. 603; Eisenberg, p. 15; M. da G. S. de Almeida, p. 112.

61. Schwartz, *Sugar Plantations*, p. 97.

CHAPTER 3

1. Vilhena, 1: 57, 61, 126–27, 130; Lindley, pp. 103–4, 152–53, 217, 259–61, 267; Spix and Martius, 2: 646, 650; Tollenare, 3: 702–4, 765; Sturz, p. 106; Arnold, pp. 68–70; Wetherell, pp. 91–92, 116–17; Michelena y Rójas, p. 658; Mouchez, 2: 40–41; Th. de Azevedo, pp. 270, 275, 318–40; Alden, "Price Movements," pp. 342–46; Mattoso, *Bahia: A cidade*, pp. 53–54, 255–57, 301. Also see Fish, pp. 69–89; and Querino, pp. 166–225.

2. Mintz, *Sweetness*, pp. 9–12; Braudel, pp. 66–120, esp. pp. 87–91, 103–4. But on Braudel's views on cassava, see F. C. T. da Silva, pp. 70–71.

3. Vilhena, 1: 159. Also see Th. de Azevedo, pp. 358–66; Alden, "Price Movements," pp. 353–54. The experiences of Baud and Ver Huell, two Dutch naval officers who lived in Salvador between 1807 and 1810, bear out Vilhena's remarks on this matter. See Baud, pp. 190–91; and Ver Huell, pp. 196–99.

4. Rice, 5.0 percent; maize, 6.0 percent; beans, 1.3 percent; and cassava flour, 87.7 percent. These percentages, for the volume of grains handled by the granary, are taken from records for complete years for 1786–1848 and 1850 and from the incomplete records for 1785, 1849, and 1851. For sources, see Chap. 4.

5. J. da S. Lisboa, "Carta" (1781), p. 503; monthly "Conta corrente da despeza e receita que houve no Celleiro Publico . . . " (1834–1849, with interruptions) in APEB, SH, 1609, 1610, and 1611; Bahia, *Relatorio* (1868, J. B. Nascentes de Azambuja), *Documentos annexos*: Franklin Americo de Menezes Doria, "Relatorio do Chefe de Policia," "Tabella para fornecimento dos presos pobres das cadeias desta cidade," n.p. Note that farinha in the eighteenth and nineteenth centuries was always measured by volume rather than weight. The standard units were the alqueire (36.27 liters) and fractions thereof. One liter of medium-fine farinha weighs approximately 625 grams; therefore, an alqueire would weigh 22.67 kilograms and a quarter-alqueire 5.67 kilograms. See Barickman, "Slave Economy," p. 122–23.

6. Benci, pp. 54–64; Antonil, pp. 126–29; M. Calmon, *Ensaio*, pp. 59–63; Werneck, pp. 63–65. For modern assessments, see, e.g., E. V. da Costa, p. 230; Schwartz, *Sugar Plantations*, pp. 137–38; J. de Castro, pp. 145–46; and Kiple, "Nutritional Link." For recent discussions of the slave diet in the southern United States and the Caribbean, see, e.g., Kiple and King, chap. 5; Fogel, pp. 132–38; and Kiple, *Caribbean Slave*, pp. 66–88.

7. Schwartz, *Sugar Plantations*, p. 138.

8. The following discussion is based chiefly on the plantation records cited in Table 7; Vilhena, 1: 185–86; [Denis], *Lettres*, p. 253; Regis, pp. 17, 19–20; Câm. de S.

Amaro to Pres. (5/3/1858), APEB, SH, 1427; Naeher, pp. 112, 204; and *EL*, [Bahia], p. 49.

9. "Conta das despezas, que tenho feito com os Engenhos Passagem, Caxoeirinha, Santa Ignez, e fazendas annexas" [1823], APEB, SH, 247.

10. Inv. of Francisco de Oliveira Guedes (1860), APEB, SJ, IT.

11. Banco do Nordeste do Brasil S.A., p. 30; and, for the slave diet in Southeastern Brazil, Stein, *Vassouras*, pp. 173–76; E. V. da Costa, pp. 230–31; Werneck, pp. 64, 75–77; Imbert, pp. 366–68. The contrast in diet between Northeastern and Southeastern plantations reflects the different mix of subsistence crops grown in the two regions. J. de Castro, pp. 59, 113–73, 265–78; Fish, pp. 71–75; F. C. T. da Silva, pp. 103–4.

12. Naeher, pp. 112, 204. Also see the references to daily rations amounting to 1.3 liters in the inv. of Clara Maria do Sacramento and Joaquim da Costa e Melo (1832), APEB, SJ, IT; and Barickman, "Slave Economy," p. 131.

13. Torres, pp. 158, 204–11; Ramos, pp. 62–63. Also see Conceição, p. 74; Saint, Jr., p. 58; and [M.] P. de Aguiar, *A mandioca*, p. 90.

14. Hill, "Remarks" to "Table E," n.p.; Comissão do Celeiro, Parecer (27/4/1847), APEB, SH, 1611; Bahia, *Falla* (1855, J. M. Wanderley), "Mappa . . . dos predios urbanos," n.p.; D. V. de Aguiar, pp. 231, 238; Fish, p. 77; Banco do Nordeste do Brasil S.A., pp. 13, 30, 41. For the prison diet, see note 5. For wheat imports, see, e.g., Soares, *Elementos*, 2: 70; and Bahia, *Relatorio* (1866, M. P. de Souza Dantas), "Quadro . . . artigos importados," n.p.

15. Wetherell, p. 92.

16. [M.] P. de Aguiar, *Abastecimento*, pp. 61–107; and, for bread consumption of slaves, see the purchases of bread for slaves sent to Salvador to recover from illnesses, in the accounts attached to the inv. of Luísa Rosa de Gouveia Portugal (1839), APEB, SJ, IT. On farinha's continuing importance throughout the nineteenth century, see Maximiliano de Hapsburgo, pp. 123–24; Naeher, p. 105; *PP* (1884–85), *A&P*, 35: 1642; Pereira, pp. 74–75; and F. A. dos S. Souza, pp. 1–4.

17. This expression is often found in the sources. On farinha consumed in the form of *pirão*, see Baud, p. 191; Ver Huell, p. 197; Marjoribanks of Marjoribanks, p. 97; Naeher, pp. 112, 203–4; Maximiliano de Hapsburgo, p. 124; Pereira, p. 74; F. A. dos S. Souza, p. 1.

18. For the term *demand for marketed food*, see Tilly, p. 397.

19. On suburban roças, see, e.g., "Lista das roças . . . na 2ª divizão da Freguezia de Santo Antonio Além do Carmo" (1804), BN, I-31,30,39; and [Sargent], p. 165. The classic text on nonmarket exchanges remains Meuvret, pp. 15–28.

20. Câm. da Bahia to Gov. (19/11/1788), APEB, SH, 198; Vilhena, 1: 48–49; "Lista das roças . . . na 2ª divizão da Freguezia de Santo Antonio Além do Carmo" (1804), BN, I-31,30,39; Lindley, pp. 107, 109, 190; Rebello, pp. 157, 162–63; Dundas, pp. 237–40; RET, APEB, SH, 4675, 4829, and 4797. On Salvador's demographic history and the available sources, see Th. de Azevedo, pp. 181–206; and Mattoso, *Bahia: A cidade*, pp. 115–49.

21. Estimates include Lindley, p. 252: 100,000 for 1803; Prior, p. 105: 80,000 for 1813; Feldner, 1: 74: 80,000–100,000 for 1816; Spix and Martius, 2: 639: 115,000 for 1819; Bahia, *Falla* (1855, J. M. Wanderley), p. 34: 124,000–125,000 for 1855; Avé-Lallemant, p. 42: 180,000 for 1859; Mouchez, 2: 50: 152,000 for 1861; and Soares, *Elementos*, 1: 50 and 2: 65: 185,000 for 1865. For a general discussion of such estimates, see Mattoso, *Bahia: A cidade*, pp. 130–33.

22. See Mattoso, *Bahia: A cidade*, pp. 132–33, 137–39.

23. Ibid., pp. 142–47; Lindley, p. 261; Mouchez, 2: 50; and Chap. 6 (for the volume of the slave trade).

24. Câm. da Bahia to the King (8/5/1765), APEB, SH, 132, fols. 160–61; J. da S. Lisboa, "Carta" (1781), p. 503; Gov. to Martinho de Mello e Castro (5/2/1789), *ABN*, 34 (1912): 103; jz ord. (Marag.) to Gov. (29/6/1786), APEB, SH, 187; Câm. de Maragogipe to Gov. (20/2/1796), BN, II-33,27,27; Vilhena, 1: 158; J. R. de Brito, p. 3; *ST*, 26: 330; Th. de Azevedo, pp. 283–87. A 1701 decree requiring slave traders to grow their own cassava rather than purchase flour had become dead letter by the second half of the eighteenth century. For exports of farinha, see, e.g., Arruda, *O Brasil*, p. 207; and Soares, *Notas*, p. 226.

25. Avé-Lallemant, p. 10.

26. Bernardo José de Lorena to Martinho de Mello e Castro (20/4/1788), *ABN*, 34 (1912): 80. The proportion of blacks and mulattos from censuses that provide this information was 68 percent in 1775, 72 percent in 1807, 74 percent in 1848, and 67 percent in 1872. See the sources cited in Table 6; for 1848 (limited to the free population), Bahia, *Falla* (1848, J. J. de Moura Magalhães), "Quadro numerico . . . ," n.p.

27. J. da S. Lisboa, "Carta" (1781), p. 505. J. J. Reis ("Slave Rebellion," pp. 8–9) has estimated that slaves accounted for two-fifths of the city's inhabitants in the mid-1830s. Also see B. da S. Lisboa, "Memoria sobre a Provincia da Bahia," fol. 14; and Nascimento, pp. 95–97. On slaveholding more generally, see M. J. de S. Andrade, esp. pp. 127–49; J. J. Reis, "Slave Rebellion," pp. 33–34; M. I. C. de Oliveira, pp. 41–47.

28. Tollenare, 3: 754. Also see Lindley, p. 268. On the distribution of wealth in Salvador, see Mattoso, *Bahia, século XIX*, pp. 602–51; and J. J. Reis, "Slave Rebellion," pp. 21–36, esp. 21–23. On the insurrections and riots of the 1820s and 1830s, see J. J. Reis, "A elite baiana," pp. 341–84.

29. Alden, "Late Colonial Brazil," p. 606; M. Santos, pp. 3, 13–15; Schwartz, *Sugar Plantations*, p. 442.

30. Vilhena, 2: 483; Lindley, p. 265; Spix and Martius, 2: 617–18; Tollenare, 3: 771; M. Graham, pp. 154–55; Arnizáu, pp. 129–31 and p. 139 n. 1; "Representação dos habitantes de Cachoeira" (1826), BN, II-34,8,17; Rebello, pp. 173–74; Avé-Lallemant, pp. 65–66; Candler and Burgess, p. 59; Univ. Federal da Bahia, Faculdade de Arquitetura, . . . , 2: 19–53, 56–98; D. V. de Aguiar, pp. 104–5, 237–39; F. V. Vianna, pp. 452–54, 457–59, 461–66.

31. On cassava production on tobacco farms, see Chap. 7.

32. [Mendes], pp. 291–92, 319–20.

33. Berlin and Morgan, Introduction, p. 3; Higman, p. 204.

34. F. C. T. da Silva, pp. 364–65; Vilhena, 1: 158; J. R. de Brito, p. 3; "Bahia de outros tempos," p. 53.

35. Vilhena, 1: 158; jz de fora (SA e SFC) to Gov. (8/6/1817), APEB, SH, 241. Also see J. R. de Brito, pp. 3–4, 68; "Termos de vereações . . . de Santo Amaro," pp. 111, 180, 204–5, 216, 221.

36. Lapa, *Economia colonial*, p. 155; jz de fora (SA e SFC) to Gov. (8/6/1817), APEB, SH, 241. Also see the discussion of yields in Chap. 7.

37. Survey of the engenhos in the parish of S. Pedro do Açu da Torre (1854), APEB, SH, 4597. Inventories from Nazaré, Maragogipe, and Cachoeira (excluding Iguape) yielded appraisals of 49 engenhos and engenhocas, 19 of which had fields planted with cassava; roughly half had equipment for making farinha. On agricultural practices, see Rocha, p. 38; Schwartz, *Sugar Plantations*, p. 108; Gorender, *O escravismo*, p. 244.

38. M. Calmon, *Ensaio*, pp. 67–68. Eight references to the ownership of such farms appear in probate records from S. Amaro, S. Francisco do Conde, and Cachoeira, and in RET, APEB, SH, 4739, registro no. 164. Planters, however, did not always use the cassava grown on those farms to feed their slaves. See, e.g., the inv. of Antônio Lopes Ferreira e Souza (1834), APEB, SJ, IT and the attached accounts.

39. J. R. de Brito, p. 3; Camara, "Carta II," pp. 80–81, 84–85 (p. 84 for quoted passage); idem, *Memoria* (1834), esp. pp. 8–9, 11, 18–19; Requerimento dos moradores de Santo Amaro enclosed in jz de fora (SA e SFC) to Gov. (8/6/1817), APEB, SH, 241; M. Calmon, *Ensaio*, pp. 66–75. Also see Fairbanks, p. vii; and *EL*, [Bahia], p. 49.

40. An ongoing debate has in recent years focused considerable attention on the role of provision grounds in Brazilian slavery. See, e.g., C. F. S. Cardoso, *Escravo*; Gorender, *O escravismo*, pp. 258–67; idem, *A escravidão*, pp. 70–81; Schwartz, "Resistance," pp. 69–81; idem, *Slaves*, pp. 49–55, 83–84; and Reis and Silva, chaps. 1–2. On this debate and Bahia, see Barickman, "Bit of Land." For other areas of Brazil and the Americas, see note 41.

41. On the West Indies and the U.S. South, see, e.g., Berlin and Morgan, "Slaves' Economy"; Mintz, *Caribbean Transformations*, chap. 7; Scott, pp. 149–50, 259. For Brazil, see, e.g, Schwartz, "Resistance"; M. R. M. F. Mattos, pp. 124–27, 139–41; Fragoso, "Sistemas," pp. 67–69; Fragoso and Florentino, "Marcelino," pp. 166–71; Lara, pp. 208–20; Galliza, pp. 148–50; Funes, pp. 122–25.

42. Berlin and Morgan, Introduction, pp. 5–6; Kiple, *Caribbean Slave*, p. 67; C. F. S. Cardoso, *Escravo*, pp. 87–90; and Higman, pp. 204–14.

43. Gorender, *O escravismo*, p. 259; idem, *A escravidão*, pp. 72–74.

44. J. da S. Lisboa, "Carta" (1781), p. 501; [Mendes], p. 321; Vilhena, 1: 185–86; Camara, *Memoria* (1834), pp. 6–7.

45. M. Calmon, *Ensaio*, p. 60. Cf. E. Silva, "O Barão," pp. 35–37; and Berlin and Morgan, Introduction, pp. 19–20.

46. Before 1871, slaves in Brazil could not legally own anything. Widespread custom did, however, acknowledge in practice a slave's "right" to a peculium. M. C. da Cunha, p. 5 and passim.

47. Invs. of Manoel Estanislau de Almeida (1838), ARC, IT; and of Maria de Assunção Freire de Carvalho (1848), APEB, SJ, IT, to which Argolo had the accounts for his engenho attached to help settle a dispute among Carvalho's heirs; Candler and Burgess, p. 57. Also see the inv. of Matilde Flora da Câmara Bittencourt e Chaby (1864), ARC, IT.

48. Survey of the engenhos in the parish of Matoim (1854), APEB, SH, 4597; Fragoso and Florentino, "Marcelino," p. 171; M. C. da Cunha, p. 5 and passim. Note that Fragoso and Florentino do not imply that the absence of evidence in probate records proves the existence of provision grounds. Rather, it suggests that neither appraisers nor heirs insisted on asserting the dead slaveowner's legal rights to crops planted in roças.

49. Forth-Rouen, p. 121.

50. Ibid, pp. 120–21; C. F. S. Cardoso, *Escravo*, p. 95 and passim; Berlin and Morgan, Introduction, p. 15. Although there is no reason to believe that provision grounds were less common on tobacco farms than on engenhos and cane farms, evidence is still scarce.

51. J. da S. Lisboa, "Carta" (1781), p. 501; Vilhena, 1: 185–86; Camara, *Memoria* (1834), pp. 6–7; and, for complaints by the church, Vainfas, p. 109; Schwartz, *Sugar Plantations*, pp. 137–38.

52. M. Calmon, *Ensaio*, pp. 59–60 (emphasis in the original).

53. Antonil, pp. 126–28; Benci, pp. 55–64. On these reformist writers, see Vainfas, pp. 107–10, 149–59; and C. F. S. Cardoso, *Escravo*, pp. 94–95, 121.

54. On Santana, see Schwartz, "Resistance" (who first brought the treaty to light); Barickman, "Bit of Land," pp. 664–66; and the works on Brazil in notes 40 and 41. On independent slave marketing in the West Indies (including sales of cassava flour) and elsewhere, see, e.g., Berlin and Morgan, Introduction, pp. 7–8, 11–14; Mintz, *Caribbean Transformations*, pp. 194–206; C. F. S. Cardoso, *Escravo*, pp. 77–79, 88, 108.

55. M. R. M. F. Mattos, pp. 124–27, 139–41; Fragoso, "Sistemas," pp. 67–69; Fragoso and Florentino, "Marcelino," p. 170; Galliza, pp. 148–51. The decision to rely here on probate records is based on the lack of references to slave marketing activities in municipal laws and manumission records. On this matter, see Barickman, "Bit of Land," esp. pp. 666–69, 685–87.

56. Inv. of José Manoel (1825), ARC, IT.

57. Estimates of the purchasing power of Rs.37$680 based on judicial evaluations in other inventories from 1823–26 and on the price of farinha as recorded in Mattoso, "Au Nouveau Monde," Annexes, pp. 445–61.

58. Inv. of Félix Alves de Andrade (1791), APEB, SJ, IT. Price of beans from Mattoso, "Au Nouveau Monde," Annexes, pp. 445–61. Mattoso did not collect information on the price of palm oil.

59. Inv. of José Francisco das Neves (1837), APEB, SJ, IT. Area under cultivation estimated from contemporary appraisals of cassava fields in other inventories, and the number of plants with ratios in Chap. 7. I have assumed here a conservative yield of 20 alqueires per 1,000 covas. See Chap. 7. The only other example I was able to locate in accounts attached to Bahian inventories was the sale in 1843 of a *capado* by a slave named Álvaro at the Engenho Buranhém. Inv. of Joaquim Ferreira Bandeira (1842), APEB, SJ, IT.

60. E. Silva, "Entre Zumbi e Pai-João," p. 3.

61. Fragoso, "Sistemas," pp. 67–69; Fragoso and Florentino, "Marcelino," p. 170.

62. [Mendes], pp. 319–20; Vilhena, 1: 158; Camara, *Memoria* (1834), pp. 3–6; and M. Calmon, *Ensaio*, pp. 68–70. Although planters regarded cassava as a much less prestigious crop than sugarcane, none of these authors invoked social prestige in explaining why planters bought farinha. Here production of flour for home consumption, which might be compatible with a planter's social pretensions, should be distinguished from cultivation of cassava as a commercial crop, which was indeed a far less socially prestigious activity.

63. For purchases of farinha by Câmara's heirs, see the accounts, covering the years 1860–65 and 1882–83, in the invs. of Matilde Flora da Câmara Bittencourt e Chaby (his widow) (1864), ARC, IT; and of Francisco Ferreira Viana Bandeira (his son-in-law) (1882), APEB, SJ, IT.

64. Camara, *Memoria* (1834), p. 3.

65. See, e.g., jz ord. (Jag.) to Gov. (1/9/1785), APEB, SH, 188; idem to Gov. (24/1/1786), APEB, SH, 408; Câm. de Maragogipe to Gov. (15/9/1788), APEB, SH, 199; ouv. (Ilhéus) to Gov. (24/3/1793), APEB, SH, 184; jz de fora (Marag.) to Pres. (17/2/1827), APEB, SH, 2470; jz mun. int. (Marag.) to Pres. (3/12/1837), APEB, SH, 2471; adm. (CP) to Pres. (27/7/1836, 26/7/1838, and 9/11/1838), APEB, SH, 1609; idem to Pres. (26/5/1842 and 13/10/1844), APEB, SH, 1610; idem to Pres. (22/2/1849) and vereador encarregado (CP) to Pres. (31/1/1854), both in APEB, SH, 1611; Câm. de Valença to Pres. (6/6/1850), APEB, SH, 1455; Câm. de Nazaré to Pres. (22/3/1852), APEB, SH, 1367; Câm. de Salvador to Pres. (11/8/1853), APEB, SH, 1401; and Chap. 4.

66. Alternatively, planters could simply cut back on rations; no doubt some did. See M. Calmon, *Ensaio*, pp. 59–60. But over longer timespans, reductions could endanger slaves' health, resulting in production shortfalls or the loss of slaves in whom planters had invested a considerable sum; and might also make master-slave relationships tenser and even help set off rebellions.

67. Estimate assumes that 1) in 1818, only 53 percent of Bahia's 315 engenhos met part or all of their needs for flour through purchases and that the remaining engenhos were entirely self-sufficient; 2) only 50 percent of the 478 lavradores in S. Amaro and S. Francisco do Conde purchased any flour at all; and 3) no lavradores in the parish

of Iguape or suburban Salvador purchased flour. For a more detailed discussion, see Barickman, "Slave Economy," pp. 193–94. That the estimate is conservative is clear when it is recalled that only 23 percent of all engenhos had equipment to make flour from cassava. Excluded from this estimate are full-time free employees (overseers, craters, etc.).

68. Between 1814 and 1824 (excluding 1823, when, during the war for independence, a blockade of the city interrupted normal trade), the amount of flour entering the granary averaged 382,916 alqueires a year. See Chap. 4 for sources.

69. Mauro, "Ultimes réflexions," p. 273 (for quotations); and F. de Oliveira, *O elo*, pp. 22–27. Also see Best, pp. 283–324; Beckford, pp. 45–52; Furtado, Chap. 9; and Taylor, *Sugar*. My conclusions on this matter broadly match those reached, for colonial Bahia, by Schwartz, *Sugar Plantations*, pp. 239–40.

70. Câm. de Jaguaripe to Gov. (12/7/1766), APEB, SH, 199; Câm. de Maragogipe to Gov. (12/7/1766), APEB, SH, 201–13; and, on cassava farms, Chap. 7. For the concept of "rationality" as used here, see W. Kula, chap. 6.

71. Berlin and Morgan, Introduction, p. 6; Barickman, "Bit of Land," pp. 677–80.

72. Even where wage relationships have begun to take hold in rural areas, workers must often supplement their earnings with homegrown foodstuffs. For such situations in Brazil, see, e.g., Stolcke, pp. 45, 68–69; and Cabral, pp. 17–56.

73. A small textile industry did develop in Bahia after 1840, but its production of coarse cottons merely substituted for similar goods imported from Europe and from the province of Minas Gerais. No other new industry emerged to meet a demand for the market formed by slaves in the sugar districts. On the early textile industry in Bahia, see Stein, *Brazilian Cotton Manufacture*, pp. 20–24. For items purchased by freed slaves in the U.S., see Ransom and Sutch, pp. 4–5.

CHAPTER 4

1. J. da S. Lisboa, "Carta" (1781), p. 503. Even in the decade 1800–1809, Salvador's Public Granary seldom handled more than three hundred thousand alqueires a year. See note 8 and Figure 7.

2. Lindley, pp. 103–5, 261–62.

3. Wetherell, pp. 26–27, 29–30; Wilberforce, pp. 91–92; Maximiliano de Habsburgo, pp. 138–39; Mouchez, 2: 40–41, 52–53; Naeher, p. 74. The iconographic evidence and other sources confirm the travelers' references to small "fleets" and "flotillas." See, e.g., Quirijn Maurits Rudolph Ver Huell's watercolor "Vue de la Rade de St. Salvador . . . " (1808 or 1809), reproduced in Graaf (ed.), 2, plate no. 3, between pp. 210–11; and Câm. de Jaguaripe to Gov. (2/8/1788), BN, II-33,21,64.

4. Here I have tried to indicate only those areas that regularly supplied Salvador's market with farinha in the late eighteenth and early nineteenth centuries and have, therefore, used only sources from the years 1775–1810. These include: J. da S. Lisboa, "Carta" (1781), pp. 503–4; Vilhena, 1: 58, 156 and 2: 495–97, 505, 518, 526–30, 571–72; ouv. (Porto Seguro) to the King (12/5/1775) and idem to Martinho de Mello e Castro (1/7/1776), *ABN*, 32 (1910): 294, 325; Lindley, pp. 228–29; [Campos], pp. 437, 444–45; Domingos Alves Branco Moniz Barreto, "Relação que contém a descripção . . . da Comarca dos Ilhéos" (1790), BN, 14,1,10, fols. 5, 12; ouv. (Ilhéus) to D. Rodrigo de Sousa Coutinho (20/3/1799), *ABN*, 36 (1914): 107–8, 113; [B. da S. Lisboa], "Memoria sobre o corte das madeiras"; idem, "Memoria sobre a Comarca dos Ilhéos" (1802), pp. 13–15. Also see the sources cited in Table 10 as well as Chap. 1. For the location of these areas, see Maps 1 and 2.

5. Gov. to D. Rodrigo de Sousa Coutinho (31/12/1796), *ABN*, 34 (1912): 406; "Pro-

ductos exportados da Cidade do Rio de Janeiro," p. 203; Brown, "Internal Commerce," pp. 116–17; Marcílio, *Caiçara*, p. 95; Barickman, "Tame Indians."

6. For the series (which span the years 1749–1931), see Mattoso, "Au Nouveau Monde," Annexes, pp. 445–61. Also see idem, *Bahia: A cidade*, pp. 296–338, for the assumptions and methods used in constructing the series. I have found it more convenient to convert Mattoso's prices from metric measures back to the measures used in nineteenth-century Brazil, relying on the same equivalencies she used to transform the original prices into prices for metric units.

7. Monthly prices for the three-fourths alqueire of flour issued to the granary's one slave, found in the "Conta corrente da despeza e receita que houve no Celleiro Publico . . . " (1834–43, with interruptions), in APEB, SH, 1609 and 1610, were converted to values for a full alqueire; then simple yearly averages were calculated. The nine averages are based on 69 observations. Prices for white sugar for several years between 1833 and 1843 were located in the bills of sale attached to inventories of planters and cane farmers. Again, I have averaged all the available prices for a given year to obtain an annual price for one arroba of white sugar. The bills of sale yield a total of 101 observations for eight years.

8. Summary statements for the volume of grains handled yearly by the granary for different periods can be found in several published and archival sources. Here I have relied mainly on the "Mapa da farinha, arros, milho e feijão q. introu no Celeiro publico da Bahia . . . " (1813) (for 9 Sept. 1785–31 Dec. 1813), AN, Códice 623; and on the "Mappa demonstrativo do numero d'alqueires" (1849) (for 9 Sep. 1785–31 May 1849), and on an annual summary statement for 1850, both in APEB, SH, 1611. Also see Figure 7.

9. For the granary's original charter, see Accioli, 3: 73–77. Day-to-day operations were also governed by later decrees and customary practices, which were never codified. The following description therefore draws on widely scattered sources, including correspondence of the granary's administration with the provincial president, APEB, SH, 1609, 1610, and 1611; documentation in BN, II-33,24,40; "Representação dos donos, mestres de embarcações, . . . que traficam em farinha . . . " [1808?], BN, II-34,8,20; "Memória dos condutores de mantimentos . . . " [1808?], BN, II-34,4,1; and correspondence concerning the flour trade from judges, farinha inspectors, municipal councils, and various local officials in supply areas and in Salvador to the governors and presidents of Bahia, in APEB, SH, and BN.

10. See, e.g., Schwartz (*Slaves*, p. 86), who states that all grains "had to be sold to the *celeiro*, which then charged a tax of twenty *réis* for the service it provided."

11. The granary's efforts to supervise grain sales were consistent with traditional Portuguese laws (summarized by Brown, "Internal Commerce," pp. 102–7) and with similar laws and policies elsewhere in eighteenth-century Europe. On the Portuguese *terreiros*, see F[aria], "Terreiro." I thank Francisco Carlos Teixeira da Silva for this reference. Note that the granary's administration was directly subordinated to the governors of Bahia and, from 1822 to 1856, to the provincial government, when it became a municipal institution and its authority over the grain trade was severely curtailed. On the legal maximum price for farinha, see, e.g., cap.-mor (Jag.) to Gov. (7/5/1781), BN, I-31,27,29; tenente (Jag.) to Gov. (24/1/1786), APEB, SH, 408; Câm. da Bahia to Gov. (24/4/1793), APEB, SH, 198; Royal orders of 24 Sept. and 4 Oct. 1798, APEB, SH, 86, fols. 125, 188. Also note that flour reaching the city by land from suburban parishes and elsewhere was not subject to the granary's controls. But information on the marketing of that flour is scant.

12. The distinction between the markets inside the granary and "in the sea" reappears throughout the documentation. In 1853, the method of collecting the contribu-

tion was altered; the contribution was abolished in 1857; and the granary itself was closed in 1866. Bahia, *Falla* (1853, J. M. Wanderley), pp. 26–27; idem, *CL*, 9: 78; idem, *Relatorio* (1866, P. Leão Velloso), pp. 24–26; Câm. de Salvador to Pres. (20/2/1857), APEB, SH, 1403. Thus, the surviving granary records after 1853 are not a valid guide to the volume of farinha entering the city's market. For these, see AMS, 55.1, 55.2, and 63.1.

13. See adm. (CP) to Pres. (27/7/1837), APEB, SH, 1609; jz mun. int. (Marag.) to Pres. (3/12/1837), APEB, SH, 2471; Câm. de Valença to Pres. (6/6/1850), APEB, SH, 1455. Some planters nevertheless continued to purchase farinha at the granary. Examples of printed granary receipts from 1807, 1808, and 1835 can be found in "Representação dos donos, mestres de embarcações . . . que traficam em farinha" [1808?], BN, II-34,8,20; and in APEB, SH, 1609.

14. Decrees in the late eighteenth century had permitted free trade in foodstuffs within Brazil. Brito, p. 8; Brown, "Internal Commerce," pp. 115–16; Royal order of 24 Sept. 1798, APEB, SH, 86, fol. 125. But the granary, even in the 1840s, required merchants to obtain export licenses and routinely refused requests for licenses.

15. Ouv. (Ilhéus) to Gov. (28/5/1793 and 23/2/1797), APEB, SH, 184.

16. Maximiliano (Príncipe de Wied-Neuwied), p. 180. In 1808, a royal order (*aviso régio*) specifically permitted exports of farinha from the comarca of Porto Seguro to Rio de Janeiro. Pres. (Câm. de Caravelas) to Pres. (26/5/1826), APEB, SH, 4631 (which includes an official copy of the order). But the order merely legalized an established trade in farinha. On that trade, see Brown, "Internal Commerce," pp. 350–53.

17. Vilhena, 1: 125. On the problems caused by recruitment, see, e.g., ouv. (Ilhéus) to Gov. (18/5/1793), APEB, SH, 184; cap.-mor (Jag.) to Gov. (10/7/1788), APEB, SH, 408; Camara, "Carta II," p. 87; adm. (CP) to Pres. (27/7/1836), APEB, SH, 1609; Câm. de S. Amaro to Pres. (21/1/1837), APEB, SH, 1426; Bahia, *Falla* (1844, J. J. Pinheiro de Vasconcelos), p. 9; Comissão do Celeiro, Parecer (27/4/1847), APEB, SH, 1611.

18. But see Dundas, pp. 204, 395–96 on conditions in Salvador in 1822–23, 1825, and 1837–38 when the city was under siege.

19. See, e.g., "Termos de vereações . . . da Camara de Santo Amaro," pp. 111, 180, 204–5, 221; Câm. de S. Luzia do Rio Real to Gov. (30/11/1781), APEB, SH, MNC; "Lista das pessoas que plantão mandiocas . . . nesta Villa Real de Santa Luzia" (1786), APEB, SH, 192; cap.-mor (Sergipe) to Gov. (2/4/1786), APEB, SH, 191. On "farinha inspectors" and their duties, see, e.g., Câm. de Jaguaripe to Gov. (24/2/1796), BN, II-33,18,37; insp. de f. (Aldeia) to Patrício de S. Amaro (19/2/1789), BN, II-34,5,28; cap.-mor (Jag.) to Gov. (20/5/1788), BN, II-33,20,15; the documentation in APEB, SH, 201–31; and "Posturas, 1650–1787," AMS, 119.1, fol. 122. In Salvador before 1785, most sales of flour took place "in the sea." Vilhena, 1: 124; "Discurso sobre o Cell^{ro} publico" [1807 or 1808], BN, II-33,24,40; Accioli, 3: 72–73 n. 113.

20. J. J. Reis, "A elite," pp. 347–51; idem, "Slave Rebellion," pp. 42–44; P. C. Souza, pp. 131–35; Mattoso, "Conjoncture," pp. 33–53; Kraay, p. 503; Barickman, "Tame Indians," pp. 359–62. On the "spasmodic" interpretation of food riots, see Thompson, pp. 76–136.

21. J. J. Reis, "A elite," p. 372; jz de paz (Naz.) to the Pres. (21/2/1832), APEB, SH, 2501; idem to the Pres. (19/1/1825), APEB, SH, 2502; Arnizáu, esp. pp. 133–35.

22. J. J. Reis, "Slave Rebellion," p. 96. On runaway slaves in Camamu, see the more than a dozen letters from local authorities to the provincial president, various dates, 1825–37, in APEB, SH, 1282 and 2298.

23. Câm. de Maragogipe to Pres. (29/11/1827), APEB, SH, 1349; Bahia, *Falla* (1828, J. E. Gordilho de Barbuda), p. [1]; idem, *Falla* (1830, L. P. de Araújo Basto), fol. 3; Câm. de Cachoeira to Pres. (19/12/1832 and 8/4/1834), APEB, SH, 1269; jz de paz (Camamu)

to Pres. (9/1/1833), APEB, SH, 2298; jz de paz (Naz.) to Pres. (14/1/1834), APEB, SH, 2501; "Posturas, 1825–1859," AMS, 119.5, fol. 62; Representação dos lavradores e negociantes de Caravelas (1834), APEB, SH, 2328; Accioli, 4: 231–37, 242–43, 338 n. 13; J. J. Reis, "Slave Rebellion," pp. 45–46. The name *xenxém* (or *xanxã*), an example of onomotopaeia, was meant to represent the sound of coins in a purse. M. J. M. de Carvalho, p. 256.

24. Câm. de Salvador to Pres. (14/11/1857), APEB, SH, 1403; and idem to Pres. (25/1/1858), APEB, SH, 1404; [M.] P. de Aguiar, *Abastecimento*, pp. 61–70.

25. Linhares, *História do abastecimento*, pp. 126–29. The authors who put forward a version of the model are too numerous to be cited here. But see M. Kula, pp. 69–71; and Gorender, *O escravismo*, pp. 248–54; and, for efforts to use the documentary record in applying the model, Schwartz, *Slaves*, pp. 84–93, and *Sugar Plantations*, pp. 435–36; and F. C. T. da Silva, chaps. 6–10. While Schwartz's discussion of crises in the late colonial period endorses the model, Silva, focusing on crises in Salvador between 1650 and 1712 and in Rio between 1724 and 1790, rejects it as inadequate. Neither author makes any extensive use of information on prices. Also see, on related issues, Alden, "Price Movements."

26. Vilhena, 1: 157–58. Also see, e.g., ouv. (Ilhéus) to Gov. (10/2/1780 and 30/2/1787), APEB, SH, 182 and 184; Câm. da Bahia to Gov. (24/4/1793), APEB, SH, 198; Gov. to D. Rodrigo de Sousa Coutinho (31/12/1796), *ABN*, 32 (1912): 406; Comissão do Celeiro, Parecer (27/4/1847), APEB, SH, 1611; Câm. de S. Amaro to Pres. (5/3/1858), APEB, SH, 1427; and Soares, *Notas* (1860), who put forth for Brazil as a whole one of the earliest published versions of the model.

27. Schwartz, *Slaves*, pp. 84–93 (p. 88 for quotations). In dealing more broadly with the issues at stake here, however, Schwartz does suggest a possible positive relationship between production for export and the development of an internal economy in colonial Brazil. See ibid., pp. 65–101, and *Sugar Plantations*, p. 240.

28. For an econometric test of the relationship between sugar and farinha prices with data from Mattoso's series, see Barickman, "Slave Economy," pp. 231–32, where I use a mathematical specification derived from "partial adjustment" models to estimate the relationship's parameters.

29. Camara, "Carta II," pp. 83–85; idem, *Memoria* (1834), esp. p. 6.

30. Câm. de Cachoeira to Pres. (10/3/1834), APEB, SH, 1269; Gardner, p. 78. Also see Góes Calmon, p. 54.

31. Although chronologies of drought years are available (see, e.g., R. H. Brooks, p. 41; and Mattoso, *Bahia: A cidade*, p. 343), they are vague on droughts' geographic incidence, timing, duration, and severity. Therefore, Table 8 draws on widely scattered primary and secondary sources. For Salvador's market (1650–1712) and Rio's market (1724–1790), F. C. T. da Silva (Chaps. 6 and 10) also found a close correspondence between crises and years of either drought or heavy rainfall.

32. See, e.g., Abel, esp. pp. 9–13; Florescano, chap. 9; and Van Young, pp. 94–103.

33. Saint, Jr., p. 85; Conceição, pp. 51–52; and Roosevelt, pp. 118–39.

34. Invs. of Manoel Dias de Amorim (1819), ARC, IT; and of Ana Francisca (1835), APEB, SJ, IT. The probate records yielded six other instances of accounts or debts indicating that tobacco farmers had to purchase farinha during crisis years.

35. "Productos exportados pelo Rio de Janeiro"; Brown, "Internal Commerce," pp. 116–17; Marcílio, *Caiçara*, p. 95; ouv. (Ilhéus) to Gov. (12/5/1793 and 28/5/1793), APEB, SH, 184; the correspondence in APEB, SH, 210–40; Câm. de S. Francisco do Conde to Pres. (5/4/1826), APEB, SH, 1433; Câm. de Cachoeira to Pres. (10/3/1834 and 8/4/1834), APEB, SH, 1269; Góes Calmon, p. 54; Francisco J. Godinho to Pres. (27/10/1853), APEB, SH, 4631; vereador encarregado (CP) to Pres. (22/12/1853, 7/1/1854, and 9/2/1854), APEB, SH, 1611; Bahia, *Falla* (1854, J. M. Wanderley), p. 15.

36. See adm. (CP) to Pres. (8/10/1849), APEB, SH, 1611. Also cf. Florescano, pp. 89–92.

37. Câm. de S. Luzia do Rio Real to Gov. (7/12/1792), APEB, SH, 201–8; João Gomes da Cruz to Gov. (1/6/1793 and 17/6/1793), APEB, SH, 201–40; ouv. (Sergipe) to Gov. (31/3/1817), APEB, SH, 235; Spix and Martius, 2: 718–21; atestado do vig. colado (Santana do Catu) (1810), BN, II-34,8,14; Aufderheide, pp. 173–84; Cunniff, pp. 34–35.

38. See the urgent requests for farinha, dating from the late 1780s and early 1790s, from Portuguese Angola (suffering at the time severe droughts) in APEB, SH, 195. For requests from Lisbon because of shortages of breadstuffs in Portugal, see Royal order of 20 June 1795, APEB, SH, 80, fol. 187; ibid. of 16 Aug. 1797, APEB, SH, 83, fol. 130; ibid. of 3 Sept. 1801, BN, II-33,25,27; Gov. to D. Rodrigo de Sousa Coutinho (31/12/1796), *ABN*, 34 (1912): 405–6; D. Rodrigo de Sousa Coutinho to Gov. (7/9/1801), BN, I-31,30,104. Exports of farinha to Angola and Portugal may have contributed to the price rises of the mid- and late 1790s that so impressed contemporary observers.

39. References to the problems caused by exports to other parts of Brazil, especially to Pernambuco, recur throughout the documentation. See, e.g., Vilhena, 1: 159; "Discurso" [1807 or 1808], BN, II-33,24,40; Pres. (Bahia) to the Ministro do Império (17/12/1833), APEB, SH, 681, fol. 41; Comissão do Celeiro, Parecer (27/4/1847), APEB, SH, 1611. Also see Table 8.

40. Vilhena, 1: 159.

41. In calculating the trend rate of growth, I have excluded 1823 as an "outlier." The exceptional conditions created by the siege of the city during the war for independence prevented normal trade in farinha.

42. *A lavoura da Bahia*, pp. 30–31; Bahia, *Falla* (1871, Barão de São Lourenço), *Documentos annexos*: "Relatorio do Imperial Instituto Bahiano de Agricultura," p. 16 (of the "Relatorio").

43. See, e.g., Rebello, pp. 172, 180–81, 191–94, 205, 207; Asschenfeldt, pp. 55–58; Câm. de Valença to Pres. (?/5/1849), APEB, SH, 1454; Câm. de Camamu to Pres. (3/10/1860 and 19/7/1875), APEB, SH, 1281 and 1282; Câm. de Taperoá to Pres. (1/7/1875), APEB, SH, 1447; Câm. de Nazaré to Pres. (7/9/1869), APEB, SH, 1368; idem to Pres. (31/10/1887), BN, II-33,33,16; MacGregor, 4: 198; Mouchez, 2: 75, 80, 123, 161; Hartt, p. 261; Câm. de Salvador to Pres. (23/3/1878), APEB, SH, 1412; D. V. de Aguiar, pp. 237–38, 245, 256–57, 261; F. V. Vianna, pp. 423, 434, 436, 453, 458, 466, 469, 477, 507, 513; and adm. (CP) to Pres. (13/12/1844), APEB, SH, 1610.

44. Information on production and trade in farinha and coffee in these four townships for various years between 1808 and 1820 can be found in [Campos], pp. 445, 449; Maximiliano (Príncipe de Wied-Neuwied), pp. 180, 202, 211, 217; and "Mapas estatísticos da comarca de Porto Seguro, 1816–1820," BN, I-31,19,15: and, for years between 1845 and 1860, in Bahia, Commissão de Exploração, . . . , *Interesses*, "Quadros" of exports for Caravelas (1845–48), Viçosa (1849), Alcobaça (1845–48), and Prado (1845–48), n.p.; Câm. de Caravelas to Pres. (19/11/1860), APEB, SH, 1296; surveys of "agricultural establishments" in Prado and Alcobaça (1852) in APEB, SH, 2228; and Bahia, *Falla* (1852, F. Gonçalves Martins), p. 44.

45. Bahia, *Falla* (1851, F. Gonçalves Martins), pp. 43–46; idem, Commissão de Exploração, . . . , *Interesses*; Mouchez, 2: 103, 108, 124, 161–64; D. V. de Aguiar, pp. 280–94; Barickman, "Tame Indians."

46. B. da S. Lisboa, "Memoria sobre a comarca dos Ilhéos" (1802), pp. 13–15; ouv. (Ilhéus) to Gov. (10/2/1780, 30/2/1787, and 24/9/1807), APEB, SH, 182, 184 and 212; idem, "Edital," (1780), APEB, SH, 569-1; "Sobre as terras não cultivadas pertencentes aos ex-jesuítas na Comarca de Ilhéus" (1783), APEB, SH, MNC; "Officio dos Governadores interinos da . . . Bahia" (23/8/1783), *ABN*, 32 (1910): 539.

47. See, e.g., ouv. int. (Ilhéus) to Gov. (27/2/1796), APEB, SH, 184; B. da S. Lisboa, "Memoria sobre a comarca dos Ilhéos" (1802), p. 9; idem, "Memoria sobre o corte das madeiras," fol. 4; Maximiliano (Príncipe de Wied-Neuwied), p. 339; Spix and Martius, 2: 677. For shipments of sugar, cocoa, and other products, see tables of exports from Ilhéus for 1864 and 1865 in Bahia, *Falla* (1866, M. P. de Souza Dantas), n.p.

48. This conclusion is justified only if demand did not decline and if no process of technological innovation worked to bring about a steady fall in production costs that, in turn, prevented an upward movement in real prices. For the first necessary condition, see Chap. 3, which shows that demand, on the contrary, increased. For the second condition, see Chap. 7.

49. Here it should be remembered that, in large part, the world market set sugar prices and that, in the first half of the nineteenth century, international sugar prices followed a generally downward trend.

50. See Chaps. 5–8.

51. Camara, "Carta II," p. 85.

52. Bahia, *Falla* (1844, J. J. Pinheiro de Vasconcelos), p. 9; Câm. de Camamu to Pres. (14/9/1844), APEB, SH, 1281. Also see cap.-mor (Sergipe) to Gov. (20/10/1819), APEB, SH, 238; and cf. Maia, pp. 140–44.

CHAPTER 5

1. For the view that, by the early nineteenth century, land had become scarce in Northeastern sugar provinces, including Bahia, and that wealthy proprietors in those provinces enjoyed a near-monopoly over land use, see, e.g., Smith, pp. 301–8; Reis and Reis, pp. 314–18; and Furtado, p. 138.

2. Alden, "Population," p. 93, who uses the expression *hollow frontier*, first applied to Brazil by the geographer Preston James; Brazil, . . . , *Recenseamento* (1872).

3. E. da Cunha, esp. p. 95; Bahia, Instituto de Economia e Finanças, *Atlas*, maps for rainfall, crop distribution, and agricultural production, n.p.; M. L. de Melo, maps betw. pp. 100 and 101 and 106 and 107; L. dos Santos Filho, *Uma comunidade*; Great Britain, . . . , *Report for the Years 1885–89 on the Trade of Bahia*, esp. the foldout map; F. V. Vianna, pp. 419–560; Levine, Chap. 2; and Table 4 in this book. For shipments of "cereals" (which probably included farinha) as well as tobacco by rail to the coast, see the freight records from 1880 in APEB, SH, 4953. On engenhocas, see the 1854 surveys of Jiquiriçá and Jacobina in APEB, SH, 4597; Grangier, p. 54; and Jambeiro, *Engenhos de rapadura*.

4. Bahia, . . . , *Atlas*, maps for climate and rainfall, n.p.; Silva Campos, pp. 105–6; Morton, "Royal Timber," pp. 42–47.

5. Barickman, "Tame Indians"; A. L. Wright, "Market." Also see forthcoming research by Mary Ann Mahony. For the continuing importance of the timber industry along the southern coast, see the more than 250 requests for licenses (dated between 1825 and 1889) to cut timber, preserved in APEB, SH, *maços* (packets) 4616–22.

6. M. Santos, pp. 3, 14–15.

7. J. da S. Lisboa, "Carta" (1781), p. 502; and Table 5 in this book. Also see Carson, *Primeiro relatorio*, p. 19; and the comments included in the 1854 survey of engenhos in the parish of S. Pedro do Açu da Torre in APEB, SH, 4597.

8. Antonil, pp. 196–98, 200–202; Pinho, *História*, pp. 218–26; Ferlini, p. 122.

9. Gov. to D. Rodrigo de Sousa Coutinho (28/3/1798), *ABN*, 36 (1914): 16; Vilhena, 1: 193–94; Camara, "Carta II," p. 80; Bulcão, pp. 101–2; J. R. de Brito, pp. 61–62; M. J. de S. e Mello, *Novo methodo*; M. Calmon, *Ensaio*, pp. 88–91; Gama, pp. 167–68; Morton, "Conservative Revolution," pp. 160–62. Also see Chap. 7.

10. Joaquim de Amorim Castro, "Relação ou memoria sobre as madeiras . . . nas

mattas do termo da Villa da Cachoeira . . ." (1790), *ABN*, 34 (1912): 160–72. Also see Câm. de S. Amaro to the ouv. da comarca (5/12/1807), BN, II-34,3,11.

11. M. Calmon, *Ensaio*, pp. 103–4; Forth-Rouen, p. 120; descriptions of rural properties in the "Registros eclesiásticos de terras" (RET), APEB, SH, and in probate records. See, e.g., the inv. of Joaquim Ferreira Bandeira (1842), APEB, SJ, IT. Also see the references from the 1870s to large stands of "virgin forest" in the northern Recôncavo in Naeher, pp. 96, 123–24, 129, 164–65, 231–39; and the woodlands shown in Sampaio, *Carta*.

12. Based on a comparison of slave listings in the 1835 census with the resident slave populations on nine plantations in earlier years, as recorded in probate records and the Censos (1825–26), ARC, PAE. See Barickman, "Slave Economy," pp. 281–82.

13. Inv. of Manoel Francisco Barreto (1784), ARC, IT; "Relação do Numero de Fogos . . . Iguape" (1835). On Iguape, see Vilhena, 1: 231–32 and 2: 483–84; J. da S. Lisboa, "Descripção" (1799), p. 123; and Arnizáu, pp. 133–34.

14. Also see the references to woodlands in deeds of sale and leases in "Livro de Notas de Escrituras: Iguape, 1831–1845," ARC, fols. 3–5, 7–8, 10–12, and 40–41; and the forests shown in Sampaio, *Carta*. The conditions described here for the northern Recôncavo match those found in the early nineteenth century in the Zona da Mata of Pernambuco, the other main sugar-producing region in Northeastern Brazil. Tollenare, 2: 406; Koster, pp. 194, 358–60; Galloway, "Sugar Industry," p. 290; Eisenberg, pp. 126–27. Also see M. J. M. de Carvalho, pp. 128–48.

15. Vilhena, 2: 486; Câm. de Jaguaripe to the Provedor Geral da Comarca (1/12/1807), BN, II-34,3,11; Morton, "Royal Timber," p. 44 n. 10 and p. 45; Rebello, p. 179.

16. The total number of covas planted in the townships of Jaguaripe and Maragogipe in 1780 was 5,614,400 (for sources, see Table 10). The first step in estimating from this number how much land cassava farmers used is to determine the area given over to each cassava plant. On this matter, contemporary and modern sources cite areas ranging from 3.025 m² to 0.400 m²; but most sources suggest that farmers used roughly one square meter per plant, which is today regarded as the "traditional" area for a cova in the Recôncavo. Camara, *Memoria* (1834), p. 16; jz mun. (Caravelas) to Pres. (24/4/1856), APEB, SH, 2332; Estrella, p. 27; Rocha, p. 34; Antônio José da Conceição, Departamento de Fitotecnia, Escola de Agronomia da Univ. Federal da Bahia, Cruz das Almas (BA), interview, June 1988; Ramos, p. 71; and G. C. Caldas, p. 272.

Note that the figure of 3.025 m² (almost five times the currently recommended area) comes from far southern Bahia. Thus, although it probably does not reflect agricultural practices in the Recôncavo, it can be used to bias the estimate upward. Multiplied by the number of covas planted in 1780, 3.025 m² yields an area of 1,698.356 cultivated hectares.

The next steps involve determining the number of successive harvests farmers obtained from the same field and the length of the fallowing period. Unfortunately, information on these matters is largely lacking. Even in the 1950s, Haskins (p. 257) found it difficult to determine the length of fallowing periods. But see João da Costa Carneiro de Oliveira, "Breve compendio" (1799), *ABN*, 36 (1914): 182–83, which mentions in passing that roceiros in Nazaré obtained three successive harvests. Again, to ensure an upward bias in the estimate, we can assume that farmers obtained only two successive harvests from each field and that fields lay fallow for twenty years. We can then calculate the total area used by cassava farmers with the formula

$$a_t = a_c + (a_c/h \times f)$$

where a_t = the total area used, a_c = the area under cultivation in a given year, h = the number of successive harvests drawn from the same field, and f = the length of the fallowing period. (This formula differs from the one proposed by Waibel [p. 257] to calculate the *minimale Ackernahrung* because it includes the variable *h* for the number of successive harvests.) For the case at hand, a_t equals 18,681.916 ha. Finally, this figure must be compared with the total land area of the southern Recôncavo. Here we have to rely on the areas currently occupied by the municipalities that have been created from the late eighteenth-century townships of Jaguaripe and Maragogipe: 2,675 km². Bahia, SEPLANTEC, . . . , *Informações básicas*.

17. Again, to ensure an upward bias, this estimate assumes a low yield of 20 alqueires per 1,000 covas. (See Chap. 7.) In that case, farmers in the Recôncavo would need to plant 15.6 million covas to produce 312,000 alqueires of flour. Under the same assumptions and with the same formula as in note 16, the amount of land needed to produce 312,000 alqueires of flour for sale in Salvador can be estimated at 51,909 hectares. The estimate is based on the amount of flour received by the granary and not on the total volume of flour produced. But given the upward biases built into the estimate, it seems unlikely that it understates the area used by farmers. For the volume of farinha from the Recôncavo entering the city's market in the mid-1840s, see adm. (CP) to Pres. (28/3/1845), APEB, SH, 1610. On Nazaré, see Câm. de Nazaré to Pres. (23/9/1869) and idem to Pres. (26/1/1876), APEB, SH, 1368. Also see D. V. de Aguiar, p. 245.

18. For the expression *a ferro e fogo* and variants thereof, see, e.g., ouv. (Ilhéus) to the Queen (20/1/1785), *ABN*, 32 (1910): 568; idem to the Gov. (27/1/1789), *ABN*, 34 (1912): 116; and Baltasar da Silva Lisboa to the Gov. (2–4/9/1799), *ABN*, 36 (1916): 232.

19. Câm. de Maragogipe to Gov. (26/5/1779 and 15/9/1788), APEB, SH, 199. The problem was apparently an enduring one. See, e.g., idem to Pres. (25/3/1849), APEB, SH, 1347; idem to Pres. (19/4/1877), APEB, SH, 1350.

20. Ouv. (Ilhéus) to the Queen (20/1/1785), *ABN*, 32 (1910): 568; idem to Gov. (27/1/1789), *ABN*, 34 (1912): 116; Câm. de Jaguaripe to Pres. (2/7/1829), APEB, SH, 1334.

21. Morton, "Royal Timber," discusses in detail the "plan" and the dispute it engendered.

22. For examples of historical approaches that implicitly ask this question, see, e.g., J. de S. Martins, pp. 25–26; Kowarick, pp. 84–85; and Furtado, p. 120.

23. Postmortem inventories from the northern Recôncavo, Cachoeira, Maragogipe, and Nazaré indicate that on average, landed property accounted for 33.8 percent of the total gross wealth that landowners left their heirs. Calculation includes all types of rural property and excludes urban property. On feuds, see, e.g., Bahia, *Falla* (1847, A. I. d'Azevedo), p. 3.

24. Tomé Pereira de Araújo to Pres. [1826?], APEB, SH, 4957; jz de paz (Iguape) to Pres. (4/10/1830), APEB, SH, 2934. Water rights were not an issue in this dispute, which centered on Captain Tomé's "right" to build a sluiceway across Dona Maria Ana Rita's estate.

25. Jz de fora (Marag.) to the Gov. (20/3/1814), BN, II-33,24,22; jz de fora (Cach.) to Pres. (25/3/1827 and 24/9/1828), APEB, SH, 2270; jz de paz (Iguape) to Pres. (24/9/1828), APEB, SH, 2934.

26. See, e.g., G. S. de Sousa, pp. 72–82; Antonil, p. 148; J. da S. Lisboa, "Carta" (1781), p. 499; idem, "Descripção" (1799), p. 123; Vilhena, 1: 175–76; José Carlos de Carvalho, Relatório (20/10/1889), copy sent to Pres., APEB, SH, 4596.

27. This statement is based on the appraisals for land (on the same properties) bearing different types of soil in postmortem inventories; estimates of land prices in the 1854 surveys of engenhos in APEB, SH, 4597; and those in *EL*, [Bahia], p. 14.

28. Once again, for lack of any more appropriate deflator covering the entire period

1805–88, I have relied on the index of the value of British exports found in Imlah, pp. 93–98, to adjust nominal prices of land. Information on land prices is surprisingly scarce. Prices in deeds of sale and probate records, more often than not, refer to entire properties without specifying their area or fail to distinguish lands bearing different types of soil. To ensure a minimum of homogeneity, Table 11 includes in all but one case only values assigned to unforested land bearing massapé soils held under free and clear titles, and excludes appraisals for massapés specifically described as "worn-out."

29. Galloway, "Sugar Industry," p. 290 (for quoted passage).

30. The assumption that landholding was extremely concentrated during this period runs through virtually the entire historiography. See, e.g., Guimarães, *Quatro séculos*; Diégues Júnior, pp. 99–116; Gorender, *Escravismo*, pp. 362–64; Reis and Reis, p. 315; and Freyre, *Nordeste*, passim. On the Land Law of 1850, see Dean, "Latifundia"; J. M. de Carvalho, *Teatro de sombras*, chap. 3; and Smith, pp. 303–38.

31. Mattoso, *Bahia: A cidade*, pp. 41–43 and *Bahia, século XIX*, pp. 462–63, 521. Also see Morton, "Conservative Revolution," pp. 24–28. Neither author's remarks concern the joint ownership of property (*comunhão de bens*) by married couples, which was common in colonial and nineteenth-century Brazil.

32. On entails in Bahia, see Schwartz, *Sugar Plantations*, pp. 292–93; Morton, "Conservative Revolution," pp. 25–27. An 1835 law abolished the privilege of entail in Brazil and determined that existing entails would be freely divisible property at the death of those administrators alive in 1835. Although no study has yet determined the number of entails granted in Bahia, Schwartz and Morton believe that they were uncommon. In probate records, land registries, and "Vínculos e capelas," AN, Caixa 133, pacote 2: "Bahia," I located references to fewer than 40 entails, which would seem to confirm the views of Schwartz and Morton. The forms of emphyteusis found in Bahia included *terras foreiras* and *terras obrigadas*. See Barickman, "Slave Economy," pp. 302–03.

33. Apparently the land registries for the Recôncavo are of generally poorer quality than those for some other parts of Brazil. Although it is unlikely that any of the surviving Bahian registries is complete, there is no reason to believe that they are particularly biased. On the one hand, they include minute rural properties (as small as 0.22 ha); on the other hand, a careful reading of the property descriptions reveals that, in some parishes, large landowners occasionally neglected to register their holdings. See, e.g., note in Map 4.

34. This number includes the 94 proprietors (defined as in Table 12) who owned engenhos in the six parishes, as well as 4 individuals who, in parishes elsewhere in the Recôncavo, registered holdings that included at least one engenho. A more thorough search through the land registries for other parishes might well reveal other such examples.

35. Higman, p. 52. In inventories from Maragogigpe and Nazaré (1825–1860), 66.4 percent of farmers left at least some landed property to their heirs; in probate records from the tobacco-growing parishes of of Cachoeira (1780–1860), the proportion was 61.6 percent. In calculating both percentages, I have included all types of real property except urban holdings; I have likewise excluded inventories of sugar planters.

36. On the Casagrande estate, see Gonzales, pp. 44–47.

37. Craton, p. 6; Barrett, "Caribbean Sugar Production Standards," pp. 147–70. For the size of sugar plantations in various parts of the West Indies at various dates before the late nineteenth century, see Sheridan, pp. 139, 157, 175, 219, 231; Dunn, pp. 90–96; Geggus, p. 75; Schnakenbourg, *Histoire*, 1: 22–26, 30–31; Hall, pp. 185–203; Handler and Lange, pp. 39–40; Watts, pp. 328–51, 488; Bergad, pp. 145–54.

38. Craton, p. 6; Schnakenbourg, *Histoire*, 1: 31. In Cuba, until the 1850s, most newly established sugar estates had ranged in size from six hundred to seven hundred hectares. Watts, p. 488. Also see Bergad, pp. 145–54.

39. Invs. of José Pires de Carvalho e Albuquerque (1808), of the Visconde (Joaquim Pires de Carvalho de Albuquerque) and Viscondessa de Pirajá (1855), and of the Baronesa de Pirajá (1869), all in APEB, SJ, IT; RET, APEB, SH, 4795, registros nos. 33–37, 42. Only 8 (or 6.0 percent) of the 133 engenhos registered in the six traditional sugar-producing parishes were, according to the declarations filed, owned *em comum* (jointly).

40. Galloway, *Sugar Cane Industry*, pp. 135–39; Schnakenbourg, "From Sugar Estate," esp. pp. 86–87; Gonzales, pp. 44–47. On the scarcity of capital for such modernization in nineteenth-century Brazil, see, e.g., Eisenberg, pp. 63–84; and E. C. de Melo, pp. 95–154. Average area of Bahian usinas calculated from information on fifteen estates (all in the northern Recôncavo) in Grangier, pp. 27–41.

41. Although each in its own way might be considered a representative bayshore parish, Socorro and Iguape were selected for closer analysis chiefly for convenience. The land registries for both parishes contain relatively detailed descriptions of holdings, and other sources were at hand to complement them. These included the "Rol das pessoas que tem escravos no distrº da Fregª de Nossa Srª do Socorro" (1816 or 1817), APEB, SH, 233; the 1854 survey of engenhos in Socorro in APEB, SH, 4597; Censos (1825–26), ARC, PAE; "Relação do Numero de Fogos . . . Iguape" (1835); "Livro de Notas de Escrituras: Santiago do Iguape, 1831–1845," ARC; and postmortem inventories. The following discussion is, unless otherwise noted, based on these sources.

42. G. S. de Sousa, pp. 75–77; *PP* (1884), *A&P*, 35: p. 1600; Góes Calmon, p. 105; and Antônio Joaquim da Costa Couto to Pres. (19/1/1887), APEB, SH, 4596.

43. Feldner, 2: 217–19; Spix and Martius, 2: 618–20; Candler and Burgess, pp. 55–62; Avé-Lallemant, pp. 63–65.

44. The 1835 census of Iguape lists 86 fishermen and 6 men and women who lived by gathering shellfish. Also see "Lista de . . . todos os Senhores de Bracos [*sic*] . . . e Pescadores desde o Brandão athe o Engº da Vitoria" (1824), ARC, PAE.

45. Vilhena, 1, map betw. pp. 44 and 45, 1: 231–32, 2: 483–84; Arnizáu, pp. 133–34; Grangier, p. 7. Also see J. da S. Lisboa, "Descripção" (1799), p. 123; and Sampaio, "Excursões," p. 3050.

46. C. da Silva, pp. 399–400.

47. In registering the Engenhos Vitória and Conceição, Moniz Barreto neglected to declare their areas. Therefore, to estimate the total area of his holdings, I have relied on the declared area of the Engenho Buraco, 1,200 tarefas (522 hectares), and on the number of slaves present on that plantation in 1835: 170, or approximately 3.1 slaves per hectare. Assuming that the slave–land ratio was the same at Vitória (with 242 slaves in 1835) and Conceição (with 35 slaves in 1825–26), their combined area would be roughly 860 hectares, which, when added to the known areas of the baron's other properties in Iguape and elsewhere in the Recôncavo, yields a total of more than 2,400 hectares.

48. The numbers in the text add up to 42 because Jerônimo Vieira Tosta, one of the four joint owners of the Engenhos Brandão and Caimbongo, also owned the Engenho da Pena. He is therefore also included with the seventeen sugar planters. Missing from this number are the owners of the Engenhos da Praia and Acutinga, who neglected to register their properties.

49. Land no doubt did change hands between 1835 and 1859, but neither probate records nor the other notarial records preserved in "Livro de Notas de Escrituras:

Santiago do Iguape, 1831–45," ARC, suggest that any process of fragmentation or concentration radically altered the distribution of landed property in that quarter-century. It also seems unlikely that population of the parish underwent major changes during that period.

50. This is the total of all individuals with those occupations. Households headed by such individuals numbered 225. It is unclear what distinctions the census takers were attempting to record by using these three terms. *Lavoura* could, at least in principle, apply to cane farmers. But analysis of variance (using the size of slaveholdings as the dependent variable) indicates statistically that roceiros, lavradores de mandioca, and household heads with the occupation of "lavoura" formed a single group; and also that household heads with those three occupations can be regarded as a group distinct from cane farmers.

51. Koster, p. 360. Once I had prepared Map 4, it became possible to retrace the path taken by the vicar of Iguape and the agents he employed in carrying out the census. Although the census supplies information on location only for planter households, the names of engenhos provided an initial, very rough idea of the path. To refine that idea, I was able to link names of residents recorded in the census with information contained in probate records and with names in the partial censuses of Iguape from 1825–26. See the three relevant lists in Censos (1825–26), ARC, PAE.

52. MacGregor, 4: 179, citing de Mornay; Koster, p. 360; Tollenare, 2: 412–13. More generally, see R. Graham, pp. 23–38; and Naro, pp. 485–517. In this context, the term *agregado* is more common in Bahian sources than *morador*. Also see Chap. 6.

53. For the lack of written leases, see "Livro de Notas de Escrituras: Santiago do Iguape, 1831–1845," ARC.

54. This is the number of individuals whose recorded occupation was either "lavrador" or "lavrador de cana." The number of cane-farming households was 86. But note that the census generally does not record multiple occupations, and it is probable that at least one household head identified as a "proprietor," some professionals, and perhaps some artisans and fishermen also planted cane.

55. MacGregor, 4: 179, citing de Mornay.

56. Invs. of Antônio Freitas da Cunha (1794), APEB, SJ, IT, to which a copy of the "Livro de Caixaria" is attached; of Manoel Lopes da Paixão (1828), and of Manoel Estanislau de Almcida (1838), both in ARC, IT. The households of the two cane farmers from Iguape are listed consecutively in "Alistamt° das peças comprehendidas no mesmo alistamento com suas individuaçoens" [1825 or 1826], ARC, PAE. On lavradores in the colonial period, see Schwartz, *Sugar Plantations*, Chap. 11; Gorender, *O escravismo*, pp. 403–4; and Ferlini, Chap. 5.

57. Of the 98 lavradores listed in the 1835 census, 40 were mulattos (pardos) and 3 were black. The rest were white. The 43 nonwhite lavradores included 5 former slaves.

58. An 1816–17 census of slaves in S. Amaro and S. Francisco do Conde indicates an average of 3 slaveowning lavradores per engenho. Schwartz, *Sugar Plantations*, p. 454. For Iguape in 1835, the average was 3.1 cane-farming households with slaves per engenho or, including households without slaves, 4.1.

59. Cane grown by lavradores accounted for 68.5 percent of all the sugar produced at the Engenho Amparo in S. Amaro in 1795–96 and 1796–97 and for 72.1 percent at the Engenho do Meio in Iguape in 1830–31 and 1831–32. Invs. of Antônio Freitas da Cunha (1794), and of Clara Maria do Sacramento and Joaquim da Costa e Melo (1832), both in APEB, SJ, IT. But I suspect that these represent extreme cases. Also see Eisenberg, p. 192.

60. Inv. of Félix Júlio de São José (1815), APEB, SJ, IT.

61. See the sources cited in note 56, as well as Vilhena, 1: 181; and the accounts and declarations attached to the inventories of cane farmers.

62. Ferlini, p. 217; Schwartz, *Sugar Plantations*, pp. 297–98; Gorender, *O escravismo*, pp. 403–4.

63. Antonil, p. 260; Vilhena, 1: 181; invs. of José Francisco da Silva Serra (1801), of José Francisco da Costa Lobo (1832), of Luís da Costa Ribeiro Correia (1804), and of Guilhermina Galo Gomes (1850), all in APEB, SJ, IT; of José Manoel dos Santos (1782), of João Pereira de Magalhães (1789), and of Manoel Dias Rocha (1789), all in ARC, IT. Also see Tollenare, 2: 411; MacGregor, 4: 179, citing de Mornay; and, more generally, Schwartz, *Sugar Plantations*, p. 298.

64. Vilhena, 1: 181–82; Tollenare, 2: 411–12; inv. of José Torquato de Barros (1859), APEB, SJ, IT.

65. J. da S. Lisboa, "Carta" (1781), p. 500; Vilhena, 1: 180–81; inv. of Maria Vitória de Meneses (1850), APEB, SJ, IT; M. C. de Andrade, p. 73.

66. J. da S. Lisboa, "Carta" (1781), p. 500; Francisco Manoel da Rocha to the Junta do Governo [1824?], APEB, SH, 4597.

67. J. da S. Lisboa, "Carta" (1781), p. 501; Tollenare, 2: 401; Bahia, *Falla* (1871, Barão de São Lourenço), *Documentos annexos*: "Relatorio do Imperial Instituto Bahiano de Agricultura," p. 15; Barickman, "Persistence," pp. 616–26, esp. pp. 621–22.

68. Inv. of Maria Sabina do Sacramento (1830), APEB, SJ, IT.

69. This seems likely because most of the information on rents in Table 15 comes from declarations of debts attached to inventories. In the 1870s, Naeher (p. 204) reported that a roceiro could rent three tarefas of land in the Recôncavo for Rs.10$000 and could draw an annual income of Rs.900$000 (gross) from sales of farinha made from cassava grown on those three tarefas.

70. Inv. of Antônio Lopes Ferreira e Souza (1834), APEB, SJ, IT. On coffee and security of tenure, see Scott, pp. 256–57. In the 1880s, the British consul in Bahia observed that the province's coffee producers included many "small planters or squatters, who, for the most part, . . . pay no ground rent." *PP* (1884–85), *A&P*, 35: 1641–42.

71. Vilhena, 1: 188.

72. Blum, p. 17.

CHAPTER 6

1. Câm. de S. Amaro, "Representação" (28/4/1802), *ABN*, 37 (1915): 479; Câm. de Maragogipe, "Representação" (4/8/1802), BN, II-34,5,100. Also see ouv. (Cach.), Parecer (1809), BN, II-34,5,105.

2. Galloway, "Northeast Brazil," p. 27; Mattoso, *Bahia, século XIX*, p. 463; Nardi, pp. 10–11. Also see Lugar, "Portuguese Tobacco Trade," pp. 53, 57.

3. See, e.g., Antonil, pp. 310–12; J. de A. Castro, "Memoria sobre as especies de Tabaco," p. 197; José da Silva Lisboa to Martinho de Mello e Castro (11/12/1784), *ABN*, 32 (1910): 553; Câm. de S. Amaro, "Representação" (28/4/1802), *ABN*, 37 (1915): 479; "Representação dos Lavradores de Tabaco a S.A.R." (1814), BN, II-34,8,18; Arnizáu, p. 134; M. Calmon, *Memoria*, p. 30.

4. In a sample of 260 inventories (1780–1860) from the tobacco districts of Cachoeira, 98.5 percent of the farmers owned slaves. Likewise, in a sample of 116 inventories (1825–1860) from Maragogipe and Nazaré, 91.3 percent of the farmers owned slaves. Samples based on probate records contain a built-in upward bias. Also see notes 48 and 49.

5. These statements are based chiefly on the accounts attached to postmortem

inventories of sugar planters and cane farmers, many of which are cited in Table 7. On wage labor in the colonial period, see Schwartz, *Sugar Plantations*, chap. 12.

6. Inv. of Luísa Rosa de Gouveia Portugal (1839), APEB, SJ, IT.

7. Survey of engenhos in the parish of Aldeia (1846), APEB, 6182; and the 1854 surveys of engenhos in the parishes of Socorro, Rio Fundo, Açu da Torre, and Matoim, APEB, SH, 4597. Also see *ST*, 26: 333; ibid., 44: 97; *PP* (1867), *A&P*, 29: 186; ibid. (1871), *A&P*, 30: 812; Bahia, *Falla* (1871, Barão de São Lourenço), *Documentos annexos*: "Relatorio do Imperial Instituto Bahiano de Agricultura," p. 22; and idem, *Falla* (1872, J. A. de Araújo Freitas Henriques), p. 139.

8. The census also lists two *criados* and five *campônios*. *Criado* would normally mean servant, but it is not clear what type of servants these were. It is also unclear what the vicar of Iguape meant by *campônio*, an unusual term that might be translated as rustic, countryman, or even peasant. Accounts and declarations attached to inventories of sugar planters and cane farmers yielded eight instances in which slaves were rented, but only one ambiguous reference, before 1860, to the hiring of free workers for fieldwork. Also see Barickman, "Persistence," pp. 605–12.

9. The 1835 census of S. Gonçalo dos Campos does not list a single day laborer or hired field hand among the 7,488 free and freed residents of that tobacco-growing parish. Only 6 *fâmulos*, who were probably domestic servants, appear in the census.

10. In censuses from 1779, the 1780s, 1825–26, and 1835 for various parts of the Recôncavo, the proportion of agregados and domésticos (including their spouses and children) ranged from just under 7 percent of the free population in the District of Afligidos (S. Gonçalo dos Campos) in 1835 to over 50 percent in the hamlet of Belém da Cachoeira and nearby rural areas in 1825–26. See Barickman, "Slave Economy," pp. 363–64.

11. The chief distinction in meaning between *agregado* and *doméstico* would seem to be their semantic range: both were used (by census takers) to refer to lodgers or boarders, common-law wives, etc., but only *agregado* had the additional meaning of tenant at will.

12. Wakefield, *View*, pp. 323–25 (for quotations); idem, *England and America*, 2: esp. pp. 1–46, 118–262. Also note that Wakefield's arguments apply to and assume the use of labor (whether slave or free) in production for commercial purposes.

13. Hence Wakefield's elaborate schemes for creating a class of rural wage laborers in newly settled areas by restricting access to land and making it available only through purchase at high prices. *View*, pp. 331–451; *England and America*, 2: 118–262.

14. Merivale, part 3, esp. pp. 260–69; Marx, pp. 931–40; Nieboer, *Slavery*; Kloosterboer, *Involuntary Labour*; Domar, pp. 18–32. Kolchin (pp. 17–20) ably and succinctly points out the flaws in common criticisms of Nieboer's and Domar's arguments and, by extension, Wakefield's arguments.

15. M. Calmon, *Ensaio*, p. 5.

16. For Brazil, see, e.g., Martins Filho and Martins, "Slavery"; Reis and Reis, "As elites"; Lago, "O surgimento"; J. de S. Martins, *O cativeiro*; and Smith, pp. 121–351. Slenes, *Os múltiplos*, the best-informed critic of Martins Filho and Martins "Slavery," focuses on exports and does not dispute a link between an open frontier and the use of coerced labor. Also see Kolchin, pp. 19–31; and Mintz, "Slavery."

17. Dean, "Latifundia"; J. M. de Carvalho, *A construção*, pp. 122–24; and idem, *Teatro de sombras*, pp. 26–28, 84–106.

18. The remainder of this and the next two paragraphs are based chiefly on Vilhena, 3: 925–30; Arnizáu, pp. 133, 140 n. 1; Bahia, *Falla* (1842, J. J. Pinheiro de Vasconcelos), pp. 4–5; idem, *Falla* (1871, Barão de São Lourenço), *Documentos annexos*:

"Relatorio do Imperial Instituto Bahiano de Agricultura," pp. 7–9, 22; idem, *Falla* (1872, J. A. de Araújo Freitas Henriques), p. 139; Manoel Pinto da Rocha to Pres. (26/12/1857), APEB, SH, 4631; idem to Pres. (28/9/1871), APEB, SH, 4594; *ST*, 44: 97–98; *PP* (1871), *A&P*, 30: 812; ibid. (1884), *A&P*, 35: 1595, 1613–14; *A lavoura da Bahia*, pp. 29–30; D. de Carvalho, pp. 25, 52–54; Pinto, pp. 55–57. All quotations in the text come from these sources. More generally, see R. Graham, pp. 23–38; Franco, *Homens livres*; and H. M. M. de Castro, *Ao sul*.

19. Access to the bay and to rivers and streams was, for a large part of the poor free population, perhaps almost as crucial as access to land. See, e.g., "Lista dos Pescadores . . . nesta Vª . . . da Cachoeira" (1824), "Lista dos pescadores . . . ffreguezia doiteiro Redondo" [1824], and "Lista de . . . todos os Senhores de Bracos [sic] . . . e Pescadores desde o Brandão athe o Engº da Vitoria" (1824), all in ARC, PAE.

20. Bahia, *Falla* (1842, J. J. Pinheiro de Vasconcelos), pp. 4–5.

21. Manoel Pinto da Rocha to Pres. (26/12/1857), APEB, SH, 4631; idem to Pres. (28/9/1871), APEB, SH, 4594.

22. *PP* (1884), *A&P*, 35: 1595, 1613.

23. Ibid., p. 1613 (for quotation referring to independence).

24. Slenes, *Os múltiplos*, pp. 21–22; Fragoso and Florentino, *O arcaísmo*, pp. 43–60; Lovejoy, pp. 51–52; Eltis, pp. 135 (on the average duration of a roundtrip slaving expedition from Bahia to Africa) and 367.

25. Verger, esp. chaps. 1 and 12; Alencastro, pp. 132–33, 142–43; Eltis, pp. 150–51, 153; Miller, chaps. 12–14.

26. Verger, pp. 451–53, 456; inv. of Joaquim Alves da Cruz Rios (1863), APEB, SJ, IT; RET, APEB, SH, 4795, registros nos. 9–10; 4661, registro no. 14; and 4748, registro no. 38; *Contracto . . . para o estabelecimento de uma fabrica central de assucar no Municipio de Santo Amaro . . .* [Salvador, 1874?], p. 2, a copy of which can be found in APEB, SH, 4596. The contract also lists as shareholders Antônio Pedroso de Albuquerque and José de Cerqueira Lima Filho, son of Bahia's most important slaver in the early nineteenth century. On Cerqueira Lima the elder, see Verger, pp. 449–51.

27. M. Calmon, *Memoria*, p. 27.

28. Although some slaves were reexported to other parts of Brazil, Eltis (p. 373, n. 38) concludes that Bahian export agriculture absorbed "the vast majority" of African slaves imported into Bahia.

29. The following discussion of British efforts to end the transatlantic slave trade to Brazil is based on Eltis, esp. chaps. 6–7; Bethell, *Abolition*; and Verger, chaps. 7, 10, 11.

30. Eltis, pp. 243–44.

31. The best analysis of this trade remains Slenes, "Demography," chaps. 3–5.

32. Delegado (Cach.) to the Chefe da Polícia da Provincia (17/7/1851), APEB, SH, 6184; Bahia, *Falla* (1852, F. Gonçalves Martins), p. 53; idem, *CL*, 6: 60; ibid., 8: 154–55; ibid., 14: 96; *ST*, 42: 221; ibid., 47: 55; Slenes, "Demography," p. 603.

33. Eltis, pp. 81–82; Slenes, "Demography," chap. 4.

34. Nevertheless, slave prices in arrobas of sugar remained until the late 1830s below the levels they had reached in the early eighteenth century, when the price of a slave rose from 73 arrobas in 1712 to 188 arrobas in 1738. Alden, "Price Movements," pp. 340–41, 343.

35. Eltis, pp. 186–90; Fogel and Engerman, 1: 59–66 and 2: 54–87; Ransom, pp. 42–47; Bergad, pp. 203–28.

36. Schwartz, *Sugar Plantations*, pp. 438–67, esp. pp. 444, 459–65.

37. The average holding for free and freed blacks and mulattos in both Iguape and S. Gonçalo dos Campos was approximately four slaves. The 1779 census of Nazaré does not provide information on color or race.

38. "Relação da Freguezia de N. Srᵃ da Purificação de Santo Amaro" (1757), *ABN*, 31 (1909): 203; survey of the engenhos in S. Pedro do Açu da Torre (1854), APEB, SH, 4597. Similarly, an 1846 survey of twelve engenhos in Aldeia (in the southern Recôncavo) indicates an average of just under 21 slaves. APEB, SH, 6182.

39. A sample of planter inventories from S. Francisco do Conde, S. Amaro, and Iguape yields an average of 74.6 slaves per engenho. The average includes slaves employed on cane farms where these adjoined engenhos, but excludes slaves at other properties (e.g., nonadjoining cane farms, ranches in the interior, or townhouses in Salvador). Similar exclusions were made with inventories for cane farmers, inventories from the tobacco districts of Cachoeira, and inventories from Nazaré and Maragogipe.

40. Inv. of Cônego Anselmo Dias Rocha (1834), APEB, SJ, IT; "Relação do Numero de Fogos . . . Iguape" (1835). Schwartz (*Sugar Plantations*, p. 452) classifies lavradores with fewer than five slaves as marginal producers.

41. Lugar, "Portuguese Tobacco Trade," pp. 33–35. Also see Flory, pp. 348–49; Schwartz, *Sugar Plantations*, pp. 85–86; Fogel, p. 36; and Chap. 7.

42. Varnhagen, pp. 98 (for quoted passage), 101–2.

43. Manoel Pinto da Rocha to Pres. (26/12/1857), APEB, SH, 4631; *PP* (1877), *A&P*, 35: 1185; *EL*, [Bahia], p. 52; Bahia, *Falla* (1871, Barão de São Lourenço), *Documentos annexos*: "Relatorio do Imperial Instituto Bahiano de Agricultura," p. 15; idem, *Falla* (1872, J. A. de Araújo Freitas Henriques), p. 139. For tobacco's reputation in the twentieth century as a "poor man's crop," see, e.g., Barros, p. 78; Egler, p. 681; and G. C. Caldas, p. 259. For early indications of tobacco production by peasant farmers, see Lugar "Portuguese Tobacco Trade," p. 44; Flory, pp. 202–5; Nardi, pp. 10–11; [Mendes], pp. 322–23; and M. Calmon, *Memoria*, p. 30.

44. The average number of slaves for farm households was 6.8.

45. Invs. of João Ferreira de Melo (1827), of Ana Rosa de S. Maria (1819), Francisco Machado da Silva (1826), all in APEB, SJ, IT; and of Úrsula Maria das Virgens (1823), ARC, IT; "Lista dos Abitantes q. izistem desde o Disteirro Tabua e vargem te o taboleiro do gandu . . . "[1825 or 1826], ARC, PAE. Antônio Lopes Ferreira e Souza, who appears in this census as living at his Fazenda da Vargem, later became the owner of an engenho in S. Amaro and took up residence there. See his inv. (1834) in APEB, SJ, IT.

46. Inv. of Antônio de Cerqueira Pinto Brandão (1887), APEB, SJ, IT. In a sample of 114 postmortem inventories from the tobacco-growing parishes of Cachoeira between 1861 and 1888, estates that included slaves accounted for 90.4 percent of the total.

47. J. R. de Brito, p. 8.

48. "Ofício do Capitão-mor da Vila de Jaguaripe . . . que remete as relações dos lavradores . . . de mandioca" (1781), BN, I-31,30,52. The average holding was 4.2 slaves. The average and the percentages cited in the text exclude 48 growers who did not own slaves as well as 2 slaveowners listed in the survey who had not planted cassava.

49. "Lista da Compᵃ das Ordenᶜᵃˢ da povoação de Taperagoa" (1788), APEB, SH, 596; Schwartz, *Sugar Plantations*, p. 446; postmortem inventories of farmers in the townships of Nazaré and Maragogipe (1825–60), APEB, SJ, IT (which indicate an average of 6.1 slaves per farmer); "Relação do Numero de Fogos . . . Iguape" (1835); survey of farms in the parish of Aldeia (1846), APEB, SH, 6182; surveys of farms in the townships of Alcobaça and Prado on the southern coast (1854), APEB, SH, 2228.

50. These examples are taken from "Ofício do Capitão-mor da Vila de Jaguaripe . . . que remete as relações dos lavradores empregados na plantação de mandioca" (1781), BN, I-31,30,52; "Lista das mandiocas que se achão nos Lavradores do distrito

da Villa de Maragoge" (1780), APEB, SH, 187; and Lista dos lavradores de mandioca de Jaguaripe (1780), APEB, SH, 199. On marketable surpluses, see Chap. 7. For Caio Prado Júnior's characterization, see his *Formação*, p. 161.

51. Cap.-mor (Jag.) to Gov. (30/11/1781) and enclosures, BN, I-31,30,52; insp. de f. (Naz.) to Patrício de S. Amaro (26/1/1789), BN, II-34,5,28; idem to Gov. (17/3/1793), APEB, SH, 201–31; Câm. de Jaguaripe to Gov. (5/7/1788), APEB, SH, 199; idem to Gov. (2/8/1788), BN, II-33,21,64. Also see H. M. M. de Castro, *Ao sul*; and Morton, "Conservative Revolution," pp. 33–34.

52. Martins Pena, pp. 37–66. On slaves' going barefoot and on shoes as a "badge of freedom," see Karasch, pp. 130–31, 362.

53. E.g., *Casa-Grande e senzala, Sobrados e mocambos*, and *Nordeste*.

54. This has been fully and ably demonstrated for the British West Indies by Higman, *Slave Populations*; and by John, *Plantation Slaves*.

55. Much of the relevant literature is summarized and reviewed by Mörner, pp. 37–81. Specifically on Brazil, see Marcílio, "Sistemas demográficos," pp. 201–2; Gorender, *O escravismo*, pp. 320–46; C. F. S. Cardoso, "Escravismo," pp. 45–53; Slenes, "Demography," chaps. 6–8; and Schwartz, *Sugar Plantations*, chap. 13. In Brazil, manumissions also contributed to the slave population's failure to achieve a positive rate of natural increase, but no study suggests that manumissions were a decisive factor in that failure.

56. Throughout this discussion, the term *creole* should be understood as applying to slaves born in the Americas, whatever their color; i.e., not as an English equivalent of *crioulo*, which in eighteenth- and nineteenth-century Brazil designated a Brazilian-born black.

57. Curtin, *Atlantic Slave Trade*, pp. 29–30. Also see Craton, p. 77; and Higman, *Slave Populations*. The preponderance of males in the slave trade reflected preferences in American slave markets for male slaves as well as African preferences for female slaves. See, e.g., Eltis, p. 69.

58. J. da S. Lisboa, "Carta" (1781), p. 502; M. Calmon, *Ensaio*, pp. 8–10; Carson, *Primeiro relatorio*, pp. 7–8; Schwartz, *Sugar Plantations*, p. 350. Also see, e.g., J. J. Reis, "População," pp. 146–49; Marcílio, "Sistemas demográficos," pp. 201–2; Gorender, *O escravismo*, pp. 320–46; C. F. S. Cardoso, "Escravismo," pp. 45–53.

59. "Lista da Comp^a das Orden^ças da povoação de Taperagoa" (1788), APEB, SH, 596. On rice and cassava in Taperoá, see "Sobre as terras não cultivadas pertencentes aos ex-jesuítas na Comarca dos Ilhéus" (1783), APEB, SH, MNC; Domingos Alves Branco Moniz Barreto, "Relação que contém a descrição . . . da Comarca dos Ilhéos" (1790), BN, 14,1,10, fol. 5; B. da S. Lisboa, "Memoria sobre a Comarca dos Ilhéos," p. 18; and Chap. 4.

60. This is the sex ratio for the 444 slaves belonging to individuals identified as "lavradores" (i.e., farmers). The census also lists another 209 slaves in households headed by individuals with various other recorded occupations (one senhor de engenho, several boatsmen, sawyers, tavernkeepers, etc.). The sex ratio for the entire slave population was 123. On the relationship between export agriculture and changes in the composition of slave population, see Marcílio, *Caiçara*, p. 104; Motta, pp. 287–311, esp. 289, 298–99; Wood, pp. 142–66, esp. 163; and, more generally, C. F. S. Cardoso, "Escravismo," p. 48.

61. The sex ratio for African slaves (who necessarily were purchased) on farms in Nazaré and Maragogipe was 158, which is well below comparable ratios calculated for African slaves on cane farms and engenhos. Future research will also need to consider other possible explanations for the relatively large number of female slaves: e.g., women may have been as efficient as men in cultivating and processing cassava, and

some African women may have had experience with the crop in Africa. Today, farm women in the Recôncavo do play a major role in processing cassava into flour. Maia, pp. 69, 121. On prices of female slaves, see, e.g., Mattoso, Klein, and Engerman, p. 69.

62. "Relação do Numero de Fogos . . . Iguape" (1835).

63. Curtin, *Atlantic Slave Trade*, pp. 28–30; John, pp. 8–19, 40, and p. 55. The sex ratio for the entire slave population of Iguape (147 males per 100 females) is almost exactly the same as the ratio for Guadeloupe in 1730 and higher than the ratio for Saint-Domingue in 1754. Mörner, p. 68. Also see Geggus, p. 79. But all such ratios fall well below those cited by Moreno Fraginals (*O engenho*, 2–3: 110–11) for Cuban plantations in the early nineteenth century.

64. "Relação do N° de Fogos . . . São Gonçallo [dos Campos]" [1835].

65. These estimates, which use the child–woman ratio, a cross-sectional measure, to approximate a cohort measure, are calculated by multiplying the child–woman ratio (e.g., 85/100 for S. Gonçalo dos Campos) by 30 (i.e., the number of years from ages 15 to 44, representing 30 years of reproduction) and then dividing the product by 10 (i.e., the number of years between 0 and 9, representing the number of children born during the previous ten years who were alive at the time of the census). I am grateful to Prof. Gillian Stevens, Dept. of Sociology, Univ. of Illinois at Urbana-Champaign, for her advice on this matter.

66. This hypothesis would imply sales on a truly large scale over a fairly short timespan. Farmers in S. Gonçalo dos Campos alone would have needed to sell off, in just a few years, at least 2,000 African-born slaves. But it is unlikely that farmers would have sold only African-born slaves; so the true volume of sales would have been even larger. A similar hypothesis, that tobacco farmers had recently manumitted large numbers of African-born and mainly male slaves, is not borne out by the 1835 census of S. Gonçalo dos Campos, which lists 276 freed slaves—that is, a mere 6.6 percent of the total population of slaves and freed slaves in the parish. The corresponding figure for Iguape is 7.8 percent. Of the 276 freed slaves in S. Gonçalo dos Campos, less than half (44.2 percent) were males and only 58 were African by birth.

67. E.g., Gutiérrez, pp. 297–314; Libby, p. 58; Libby and Grimaldi, "Equilíbrio"; Metcalf, pp. 161–63; Marcílio, *Caiçara*, p. 104. A particularly curious case is the slave population in the sugar-producing area of Ribeira de Vazabarris (Sergipe), which, in 1785, was 66 percent creole and had a sex ratio of 119. Schwartz, *Sugar Plantations*, pp. 352–53.

68. Research on colonial Maryland and Virginia suggests that such a transition could take place over a short period. See Menard, pp. 27–54; and Kullikoff, "A 'Prolifick' People."

69. See Chap. 7. Some evidence for this hypothesis comes from the sex ratios of African slaves calculated from postmortem inventories of tobacco farmers (1780–1860) and from the 1835 census of S. Gonçalo dos Campos: 171 and 162, respectively—well below the ratios of 200 to 220 for African slaves found on engenhos and cane farms. But it seems that price alone did not determine whether tobacco farmers purchased more females or males. If that were the case, then wealthier farmers should have owned proportionately more male slaves than less wealthy farmers. Regression analysis using the size of slaveholdings as recorded in the 1835 census of S. Gonçalo dos Campos as a proxy for wealth does not indicate a significant relationship between the number of slaves owned and sex ratios.

70. See Kiple, "Nutritional Link," who argues that where slaves in Brazil consumed a diet based mainly on farinha and carne seca, the result was a serious deficiency in thiamine, leading to "pervasive" beriberi and increased infant mortality. Kiple's argument might also help explain the anomaly of a largely creole slave popula-

tion on sugar plantations in Ribeira de Vazabarris (Sergipe) in 1785. See note 67; on the diet of plantation slaves in Sergipe, see Mott, p. 38.

71. Higman (esp. pp. 374–78) and John (Chap. 8) demonstrate that in the West Indies, mortality rates were much higher on sugar plantations than on estates producing coffee, cotton, cocoa, pimento, or provisions. The differences in fertility (which was not in itself especially low) were less important. Unfortunately, because no estates in the British West Indies specialized in tobacco in the late eighteenth and early nineteenth centuries, neither Higman nor John presents comparisons between sugar and tobacco.

CHAPTER 7

1. França, *Cartas baianas*, pp. 9, 16, 19, 38, 54, 68, 84.
2. Roosevelt, pp. 123–24.
3. Most of the surveys provide information on the number of covas planted rather than on output of flour. Therefore, to estimate marketable surplus, I first converted the number of covas into alqueires of flour, using the yields reported by contemporaries, discussed in the text. Second, I compared total output of farinha with subsistence needs for the total farm population, which required estimating the size of farm households. Here I used an average of 3.564 free individuals per household, calculated from "Lista das pessoas que se achão assistentes na Freguezia de N. Srª de Nazaré . . ." (1779), APEB, SH, 596. From the 1781 survey of Jaguaripe (for citation, see Table 27), I calculated the percentage of farmers who owned slaves (78) and the average number of slaves owned (4.229). Combining all figures yields an estimate of the total size of the farm population, which, multiplied by 9.125 alqueires (the standard yearly ration), provides an estimate of subsistence needs. Throughout, I have excluded farmers in the surveys who did not plant cassava and those for whom information on the number of covas planted was lacking. The method used here resembles that used by Schwartz in *Slaves*, p. 91.
4. J. da S. Lisboa, "Carta" (1781), p. 503; Camara, *Memoria* (1834), p. 16; Câm. de Camamu to the Pres. (3/10/1860), APEB, SH, 1281 (which also cites instances of much higher yields).
5. Jz ord. (Jag.) to the Gov. (10/4/1785), APEB, SH, 188. Colonial laws requiring planters to cultivate at least five hundred covas for every slave in their service assumed that planters could maintain their families and their slaves with one-third of the farinha produced from the 500 covas; the rest was to be sold in local markets. Jz de fora (SA e SFC) to the Gov. (8/6/1817), APEB, SH, 241. In that case, yields would have to surpass 55 alqueires per thousand covas. Also see Ramos (p. 56), whose field research in the 1970s revealed that small farmers in the southern Recôncavo marketed roughly 70 percent of their total output. The technologies used in the 1970s did not differ greatly from those employed in the late eighteenth century.
6. The following discussion of the cultivation of cassava and preparation of farinha is based chiefly on J. da S. Lisboa, "Carta" (1781), p. 503; idem, "Descripção" (1799), pp. 121–22; João da Costa Carneiro de Oliveira, "Breve compendio" (1799), *ABN*, 36 (1914): 182–83; Vilhena, 1: 200–202; Naeher, pp. 203–5; Estrella, pp. 25–41; Rocha, pp. 23–36; Werneck, p. 78; and postmortem inventories; as well as descriptions of the practices currently used in Bahia and elsewhere in Northeastern Brazil: Ramos, pp. 56–76; Saint, Jr., pp. 53–56, 59–64, 102–15; Bahia, . . . , CONDER, *Estudos básicos*, tomo 4: *A produção*, pp. 99–106; and Garcia, Jr., *Terra*, pp. 121–26, 129–33; and on Schmidt, chaps. 2–4.
7. Koster, p. 370; Mawe, p. 73.

8. Camara, *Memoria* (1834), pp. 19–20; jz ord. (Jag.) to the Gov. (2/10/1784, 29/1/1785, 10/4/1785, 23/10/1785, 12/5/1785, and 9/8/1785), all in APEB, SH, 188; Lapa, *Economia colonial*, p. 167. Also see Bahia, *Falla* (1871, Barão de São Lourenço), *Documentos annexos*: "Relatorio do Imperial Instituto Bahiano de Agricultura," pp. 16–17; and the inv. of Padre Francisco Ribeiro Barbosa (1807), APEB, SJ, IT, which includes an appraisal of a cassava field "destroyed" by cattle and thieves.

9. Ewbank, p. 379.

10. Jousselandière, p. 213. From field observations in the Recôncavo in the early 1970s, Saint, Jr. (p. 103) reports 166.5 days of labor to cultivate and harvest one hectare of cassava on already cleared land. Here I have assumed one square meter per cova. See Chap. 5. On labor requirements, also see J. da S. Lisboa, "Carta" (1781), p. 503.

11. Koster, pp. 372–73.

12. In their appraisals, probate assessors in Maragogipe and Nazaré often merely recorded a value for "the accessories for making farinha" without any further description. But 76 inventories in the sample do supply some information on equipment; of those, 51 describe the wheels as moendas. Fewer than one-third of the moendas were horse-powered, and only one was attached to a water wheel. Also see the 1846 survey of 23 cassava farms in the parish of Aldeia in APEB, SH, 6182. Contemporary depictions of wheels can be found in Kidder, 1, plate betw. pp. 242 and 243; and in Ribeyrolles, 2, plate 56. With the exception of the power source, the wheels used currently in making farinha appear to be virtually identical to those described in eighteenth- and nineteenth-century sources; today small gasoline motors are often attached to the wheels.

13. Ewbank, p. 381. Although references to both screw and beam presses are common in inventories from Cachoeira, probate records from Maragogipe and Nazaré supply little information on the types of presses used. But an 1846 survey of 23 cassava farms in Aldeia indicates that 6 of the farms used tipitis; the other 17 used "wooden presses." APEB, SH, 6182. For photographs and drawings of tipitis and presses, see Schmidt, betw. pp. 48–49.

14. Koster, p. 373. See the photograph of a copper alguidar in Schmidt, betw. pp. 64 and 65.

15. The survey neglected to classify 8,400 covas. "Lista das mandiocas que se achão nos Lavradores do distrito da Villa de Maragog^e . . . " (1780), APEB, SH, 187.

16. Werneck, p. 77; "Lista dos Lavradores de mandioca . . . [e] dos alq^res de farinha q. fazem simanariamente [weekly]" (1789), BN, II-34,5,28; jz de órfãos e delegado (Camamu) to the Pres. (8/11/1853), APEB, SH, 2299. Today in the Recôncavo, cassava growers still make farinha on a weekly or fortnightly basis. Ramos, p. 57; Saint, Jr., p. 106; Conceição, p. 229. Also note that processing cannot be delayed once the root has been harvested.

17. See, e.g., ouv. (Ilhéus) to the Gov. (26/6/1792), APEB, SH, 201–12; João Gomes da Cruz to the Gov. (17/6/1793), APEB, SH, 201–42; Câm. de Camamu to the Pres. (26/7/1826), APEB, SH, 1282; and adm. (CP) to the Pres. (27/7/1836), APEB, SH, 1609.

18. Cf. the situation described by Florescano (pp. 88–97, 187–88) for maize production on large estates in the Valley of Mexico in the eighteenth century. But even in Bahia, storehouses allowed more prosperous growers to stockpile farinha for sale in crisis years. See José Nunes Moniz to the Gov. (7/2/1779), BN, I-31,29,62; cap.-mor (Marag.) to the Gov. (14/8/1780), APEB, SH, 408–1; cap.-mor (Sergipe) to the Gov. (9/3/1808), APEB, SH, 210; and Raimundo Monteiro de Matos Jr. to the Pres. [1852], APEB, SH, 4631.

19. [Mendes], p. 289. The following discussion of fieldwork in the cultivation of

cane is based mainly on Antonil, pp. 152–67; J. da S. Lisboa, "Carta" (1781), pp. 499–500; Vilhena, 1: 175–79; postmortem inventories; Schwartz, *Sugar Plantations*, pp. 99–110, 139–42 (the best modern description of fieldwork in the colonial period); Koster, pp. 337–47; Grangier, pp. 8–23.

20. Caminha Filho, p. 8.

21. Percentages calculated from postmortem inventories. Also see Antonil, pp. 152–57; J. da S. Lisboa, "Carta" (1781), p. 500; Camara, *Memoria* (1834), p. 18; A. Calmon, pp. 6–7; Fairbanks, p. vi; Carson, *Primeiro relatorio*, pp. 24–29; Bahia, *Falla* (1871, Barão de São Lourenço), *Documentos annexos*: "Relatorio do Imperial Instituto Bahiano de Agricultura," pp. 15–16; D. de Carvalho, p. 25. The plough also failed to gain widespread acceptance on sugar estates in many parts of the West Indies during the same period. Craton, pp. 225–26; Watts, pp. 395, 429–32; Hall, p. 12.

22. Forth-Rouen, p. 120 (emphasis in the original); Caminha Filho, pp. 4–6, 12, and photographs facing pp. 14 and 24; Grangier, pp. 8–9.

23. Camara, *Memoria* (1834), p. 18; A. Calmon, p. 6; Bahia, *Falla* (1871, Barão de São Lourenço), *Documentos annexos*: "Relatorio do Imperial Instituto Bahiano de Agricultura," p. 15; Grangier, p. 8. Also see M. Calmon, *Ensaio*, p. 54; Fairbanks, p. vi; Carson, *Primeiro relatorio*, pp. 24–25, 28–29. I am grateful to Professor John Siemens of the Department of Agricultural Engineering of the Univ. of Illinois at Urbana-Champaign and to Paulo Galerani, Pesquisador (Área de Difusão de Tecnologia) at the CNPS (Londrina, Paraná) for confirming this point.

24. Caminha Filho, p. 5; Grangier, pp. 8–9; Forth-Rouen, p. 120. Even today, when mechanized implements are in general use, planters still rely on animal traction for furrowing in the wet winter months. Bahia, . . . , CONDER, *Estudos básicos*, tomo 4: *A produção*, p. 93. On plough designs in Europe from the late eighteenth century on, see Fussell, chap. 2.

25. Primavesi, pp. 351–67. I am again grateful to John Siemens and Paulo Galerani for confirming this point.

26. Watts, pp. 402–3, 406, 425, and pp. 399–402, 426 (on the other techniques used in the West Indies). Also cf. the contemporary illustrations of cane holing in Craton, pp. ii and 136–37, and Sheridan, p. 110, with the photographs of a trenched field in Bahia from the mid-1940s in Caminha Filho, facing pp. 25 and 32.

27. A. Calmon, pp. 7–12 (p. 8 for quotation, emphasis in the original); Camara, *Memoria* (1834), pp. 13–14; Vilhena, 1: 174–75; Fairbanks, pp. vi, 34; Carson, *Primeiro relatorio*, pp. 6, 11–17, 21; Bahia, *Falla* (1871, Barão de São Lourenço), *Documentos annexos*: "Relatorio do Imperial Instituto Bahiano de Agricultura," p. 15; *EL*, [Bahia], p. 46; D. de Carvalho, pp. 25–26; Grangier, p. 22.

28. Galloway, *Sugar Cane Industry*, pp. 96, 99–100; Watts, p. 404; Sheridan, p. 111; and Haskins, p. 28 (on erosion in the Recôncavo). Inventories from the mid- and late nineteenth century contain appraisals of ratoon cane (i.e., a second or third crop that grew back from after the first cutting). Also see Grangier, p. 22. By contrast, soil exhaustion had forced planters to abandon ratooning in Barbados and St. Kitts by the end of the seventeenth century and in large parts of Jamaica by the mid-eighteenth century. Watts, pp. 404–5, 432.

29. E.g., Schwartz (*Sugar Plantations*, p. 431), who refers to complaints by planters in the southern Recôncavo about diseases associated with the new variety of cane, leading to smaller harvests. He concludes that the "adoption of caienne cane appears to have been slow." Ibid., p. 563 n. 52, where he cites the "Representação dos agricultores da Vila de Nazaré . . . sobre a moléstia que atacava a cana . . . ," BN, II-33,28,69. Although this document bears no date, Schwartz places it in the "late 1820s." Actually, it dates from the mid-1860s (probably 1866) and is a manuscript copy of a peti-

tion from planters in Nazaré, another version of which can be found in APEB, SH, 4598. Also see Bahia, *Relatorio* (1866, P. Leão Velloso), p. 45. The petition refers to a disease (the *moléstia*) that first appeared in southern Brazil and reached the southern Recôncavo by the mid-1860s. From there, it spread to the sugar-producing districts on the northern side of the bay, forcing planters to look for new varieties of cane to replace the Cayenne cane they had until then cultivated. Bahia, *Relatorio* (1868, J. B. Nascentes de Azambuja), p. 32; *PP* (1874), *A&P*, 33: 684. Thus, this document has no bearing on whether planters moved slowly or quickly in adopting Cayenne cane. References to the new variety appear in probate records from Iguape and S. Francisco do Conde as early as 1817–20: invs. of Maria Silvéria (1817) ARC, IT; of Francisco Borja Dias Pinto (1819), and of Mateus Tavares do Amaral (1820), both in APEB, SJ, IT.

30. M. Calmon, *Ensaio*, p. 7; Fairbanks, p. iii. Also see Aragão, p. xviii; *EL*, [Bahia], p. 46; and, on Cayenne cane more generally, Watts, pp. 433–34; Moreno Fraginals, *O engenho*, 1: 223–26; Galloway, *Sugar Cane Industry*, p. 96; and [Canabrava], p. 102.

31. The following description of sugarmaking is based in large part on Antonil, pp. 168–263; Vilhena, 1: 179–90; Koster, pp. 347–53; Tollenare, 2: 376–82; postmortem inventories; Schwartz, *Sugar Plantations*, pp. 110–25, 142–49; Ferlini, chap. 3; and H. Fernandes, pp. 25–107. On the floor plans of eighteenth-century Bahian engenhos, see E. B. de Azevedo, pp. 171–82.

32. Koster, p. 351.

33. The processes of purging and claying are clearly illustrated by the sketches in H. Fernandes, pp. 69–95.

34. Galloway, *Sugar Cane Industry*, p. 88, 105–10, 134; Barrett, *Efficient Plantation*, pp. 3–4.

35. Tollenare, 2: 406; Koster, p. 336.

36. Souza Bahiana, p. 4, who also reported that his interest in experimentation had won him a reputation as a madman (*fama de doido*) among other planters.

37. M. Calmon, *Ensaio*, p. 2 (emphasis in the original); Carson, *Primeiro relatorio*, p. 6.

38. Pang, "Modernization," pp. 669–71; Schwartz, *Sugar Plantations*, p. 433.

39. Recognizing this widening gap, Bahians looked overseas for technology to modernize the province's sugar industry. See, e.g., Junta da Lavoura to the Pres. (3/6/1845), and George E. Fairbanks, "Proposta para o immediato, e pronto melhoram[to] do Assucar d'esta Provincia" (1846), both in APEB, SH, 4593; Bahia, *Falla* (1852, F. Gonçalves Martins), pp. 63–64; Carson, *Primeiro relatorio*; Viana Filho, "A missão Carson"; and Aragão, *Manual*.

40. M. B. N. da Silva, pp. 96–100; M. Calmon, *Ensaio*, pp. 176–77. Sturz (p. 51) reported 51 steam-powered mills in Bahia in 1837. An 1855 count identified 144 such mills. Bahia, *Falla* (1855, J. M. Wanderley), pp. 38–39. For the number of steam-powered mills in 1873, see *EL*, [Bahia], table "B," n.p.

41. Gama, pp. 193–97; Moreno Fraginals, *O engenho*, 1: 263–66.

42. Pontes, *Economia açucareira*, pp. 85, 112–13, 124, 180; M. B. N. da Silva, p. 98; Petrone, pp. 97–98; Gama, pp. 177–85; Ferlini, p. 120; Moreno Fraginals, *O engenho*, 1: 259–62.

43. Explicit references to *bagaceiras* (sheds for drying cane trash for use as fuel) apppear in 56 percent of planter inventories. Also see M. Calmon, *Ensaio*, p. 54; Fairbanks, p. iii; Antônio Lacerda to pres. (Imperial Instituto Baiano de Agricultura) (10/2/1862), APEB, SH, 4589; and Chap. 5.

44. Morton, "Conservative Revolution," p. 335; Moreno Fraginals, *O engenho*, 1: 220; Francisco Gonçalves Martins to the Pres. (2/10/1856), APEB, SH, 4595; Pinho, *Cotegipe*, p. 696 n. 4 and p. 697; Avé-Lallemant, pp. 25–32; Bahia, *Falla* (1851, F. Gon-

çalves Martins), pp. 26–28; Carson, *Parecer*; inv. of Tomás Pedreira Geremoabo (1875), APEB, SJ, IT; Grangier, tables of "Produção das usinas . . . " and "Engenhos e engenhocas . . . ," n.p. It is unclear whether a vacuum pan installed at the Engenho Periperi in 1847 remained in use for long thereafter; in 1873, Bahia had only two or three fully mechanized mills. Bahia, *Falla* (1847, A. I. d'Azevedo), p. 21; idem, *Falla* (1848, J. J. de Moura Magalhães), p. 48; idem, *Falla* (1871, Barão de São Lourenço), *Documentos annexos*: "Relatorio do Imperial Instituto Bahiano de Agricultura," p. 20. The total of 230 engenhos for 1926 does not include engenhocas.

45. Junta da Lavoura to the Pres. (19/10/1853), APEB, SH, 4593. Also see Bahia, *CL*, 8: 88–89. On the banking system, see Baptista and Guerreiro, pp. 8–52; Eisenberg, chap. 5; and E. C. de Melo, pp. 95–140. On slavery as an obstacle to technological progress and the incompatibility of slavery with skilled labor, see, e.g., Moreno Fraginals, *O engenho*; and Wallerstein, p. 88. For theoretical and empirical criticisms of that argument, see Scott, pp. 27–37; A. B. de Castro, "A economia política," pp. 77–79; and Schwartz, *Sugar Plantations*, pp. 131, 433.

46. Quoted in Pinho, *Cotegipe*, pp. 691–92 (emphasis in the original). Also see *EL*, [Bahia], p. 46. On the *sácaro-motriz*, see Bahia, *Falla* (1853, J. M. Wanderley), pp. 76–77.

47. M. J. de Souza e Mello, esp. pp. x–xi. Pang ("Modernization," p. 671) further claims that the engenho "also installed a steam engine and experimented with a new variety of cane." I have been unable to locate any evidence to support those claims.

48. On the Bahian sugar industry after 1860, see Barickman, "Persistence."

49. [Mendes], p. 323. The following discussion of tobacco processing is based mainly on Antonil, pp. 300–312; J. de A. Castro, "Memoria sobre as especies de Tabaco," pp. 201–9; "Le tabac," pp. 101–3; postmortem inventories; Flory, pp. 183–84; and Lugar, "Portuguese Tobacco Trade," pp. 29, 32–33.

50. Vilhena, 1: 199. Probate records indicate that of those farmers who owned fumeiros, fewer than 15 percent had three or more. If ownership of equipment is used as a measure, then those records suggest that 60.1 percent of better-off farmers did all or part of the processing of their tobacco on their farms (either twisting and rolling or—in the case of leaf tobacco—curing and pressing).

51. Antonil, p. 302.

52. Flory, p. 184; Góes Calmon, p. 42; "Le tabac," p. 94; Basto, p. 27. Once dried, leaf tobacco had to be pressed and baled. Farmers without their own presses could deliver their dried tobacco to merchants who would press the tobacco at warehouses. "Le tabac," pp. 96–98; Sonneville, pp. 79–80; Borba, pp. 103–4.

53. The following description of fieldwork is based mainly on Antonil, pp. 294–300, 310–14; J. da S. Lisboa, "Carta" (1781), p. 503; idem, "Descripção" (1799), p. 123; [Mendes], pp. 322–23; J. de A. Castro, "Memoria sobre as especies de Tabaco," pp. 193–200; idem, "Memoria sobre a manufactura do Tabaco," pp. 110–11; Vilhena, 1: 197–99; Varnhagen, pp. 100–103; Burlamaque, pp. 60–61, 78–79; "Le tabac," pp. 92–94; Basto, pp. 26–29; postmortem inventories; and twentieth-century descriptions of tobacco farming in the Recôncavo: Haskins, pp. 250–52; Egler, pp. 681–85; and Saint, Jr., pp. 74–78.

54. J. de A. Castro, "Memoria sobre as especies de Tabaco," p. 194.

55. Varnhagen, pp. 101–2, who speculates that originally, the *boi-de-cova* included the roasting of a whole cow in a pit. The practice among tobacco farmers of reciprocal help in transplanting seedlings persists into current times. Saint, Jr., p. 78.

56. Vilhena, 1: 198–99; Varnhagen, p. 102. Tobacco farmers in colonial Maryland also used turkeys for this purpose. Main, p. 33.

57. Antonil, p. 310. Also see [Mendes], p. 323. For the argument that slavery was

incompatible with "care-intensive" activities, see Fenoaltea, pp. 635–68. On women and tobacco in the twentieth century, see Egler, p. 681; Souto Mayor, p. 90; and Maia, pp. 91, 96–98, 166–67.

58. Antonil, pp. 312–14; Flory, p. 183; Henderson, pp. 341–42.

59. I am grateful to J. Michael Moore, Extension Agronomist-Tobacco of the Univ. of Georgia Cooperative Extension Service, Tifton, GA, for confirming this point. On fallowing in Virginia and Maryland, see Main, p. 34; Clemens, p. 196; and Kulikoff, *Tobacco and Slaves*, p. 47.

60. In principle, the physical availability of land in Bahia would have allowed farmers to use land more extensively; e.g., after obtaining three or more harvests from a field in a single growing season, allowing the land to lie fallow for twenty years—like growers in Virginia and Maryland—and then clearing new land each year. But in that case, farmers would have needed a reserve equal to 20 times the area under cultivation in any given year to maintain production at the same level. By contrast, growers in Virginia and Maryland, using the same field for three successive annual harvests, needed only 6.67 times more land than the area they cultivated. Very quickly, Bahian farmers would have found themselves planting fields ever farther from their homesteads, which they would eventually have to abandon. The end result would have been an almost constant movement of farmers into the interior and farther from Salvador, where the high transport costs would have soon rendered production for *export* uneconomical.

61. F. H. Cardoso, p. 173 (emphasis in the original); Genovese, chap. 4.

62. Antonil, pp. 294–96; J. de A. Castro, "Memoria sobre as especies de Tabaco," p. 193 (for passsage quoted) and p. 196; idem, "Memoria sobre a manufactura do Tabaco," p. 110; J. da S. Lisboa, "Carta" (1781), p. 503. Also see Vilhena, 1: 197; A. Calmon, p. 10; M. Calmon, *Memoria*, p. 28; Varnhagen, p. 100; Burlamaque, p. 60; Basto, p. 26; Egler, pp. 682–84; Haskins, p. 251; and Ramos, pp. 54–55. Besides the method described here, farmers with fewer head of cattle may have used the *vaca de corda* (rope cow): instead of setting up a paddock, they could simply tie a cow overnight to a stake in the field and then move the stake as necessary. Ramos, pp. 54–55. Seedbeds, it should be noted, were fertilized in the same way as fields.

63. M. Calmon, *Memoria*, p. 28. Also see Egler, pp. 681–82. This is precisely the same direct relationship between the amount of manure available (a variable dependent on the size of the farmer's herd of cattle) and the area under cultivation that long characterized the production of cereals in Europe. Bath, pp. 16–23.

64. Percentage of farmers with livestock calculated from postmortem inventories (1780–1860). It matches almost exactly the percentage of farmers who, when registering with the Board of Inspection between 1774 and 1814, reported that they regularly manured their fields. Lugar, "Portuguese Tobacco Trade," p. 68. Although eighteenth- and nineteenth-century sources yielded no references to manure purchases by poorer farmers, this may simply reflect a general bias in the available sources, which, as a rule, slight smaller and poorer farmers. The practice was common in the first half of the twentieth century. See Haskins, p. 251; and Egler, pp. 682–83.

65. Ramos, p. 47; Souto Mayor, p. 89; Egler, p. 685–86; Haskins, p. 853; Waibel, p. 323. The first author to refer explicitly to crop rotation on Bahian tobacco farms was apparently Miguel Calmon in his 1835 *Memoria sobre a cultura do tabaco*, pp. 29, 36. But the examples in Table 28 make clear that the association of tobacco with cassava was already well established by 1835. It should also be stressed that the association of tobacco with cassava and other food crops was based on crop rotation, not on intercropping, which was and remains in Brazil a far more common practice than crop rotation.

66. Inv. of João Ferreira de Melo (1827), APEB, SJ, IT.

67. Inv. of Francisco Moreira de Freitas (1818), ARC, IT.

68. Assuming a conservative yield of only 20 alqueires of flour per 1,000 covas of cassava, Table 28 includes only examples where output of flour would have supplied at least ten more yearly rations than the number of slaves present. Use of a higher but more plausible yield would increase the estimated amounts of cassava produced and would also more than double the number of examples that could be included in the table.

69. Percentage calculated from postmortem inventories (1780–1860). Also cf. G. Wright, pp. 55–74.

70. Inv. of Francisco de Oliveira Guedes (1860), APEB, SJ, IT.

71. Cf. Ellis, pp. 8–9, 12; and G. Wright, pp. 55–74.

72. In 116 postmortem inventories of farmers in Maragogipe and Nazaré (1825–60), 60 contain appraisals for coffee trees. Of those 60, most refer to "portions" (*porções*) or "backyard orchards" (*quintais*), seldom consisting of more than a few hundred trees. Only 4 list groves of 4,000 trees or more. Only 3 mention any equipment other than mortars for shelling dried coffee beans.

73. Even when small farmers greatly reduced output of flour for sale, continued production for home consumption allowed them, when prices rose, to return to larger and more regular sales. See the example cited by the British consul in *PP* (1884–85), *A&P*, 35: 1642.

74. Inv. of Hilária Maria de Jesus (1857), APEB, SJ, IT. Also see Garcia Jr., *O sul*, pp. 25, 60–67.

CHAPTER 8

1. Ortiz, *Contrapunteo*. Citing Ortiz, Luiz Costa Pinto (pp. 65–96) in the late 1950s used the analogy of a counterpoint to analyze the contrast between sugar production and the incipient petroleum industry in the Recôncavo.

2. Mauro, "Ultimes réflexions," p. 273; F. de Oliveira, *O elo*, p. 22 (for quotations).

3. Prado Júnior, *Formação*, p. 161.

4. Insofar as future historical studies of the Brazilian peasantry attempt to incorporate a framework based on the works of A. V. Chayanov (e.g., *Theory of Peasant Economy*) or other similar interpretative schemes, those studies will have to deal with the theoretical and empirical difficulties of distinguishing small slaveowning roceiros from peasant farmers. For recent studies using a modified Chayanovian framework to analyze the peasantry in contemporary Northeastern Brazil, see Garcia Jr., *O sul* and *Terra*.

5. Cf. the arguments of Mattoso (*Bahia: A cidade*, pp. 41–43, and *Bahia, século XIV*, pp. 462–63, 521) that the piecemeal division of landed property, as a result of the inheritance laws, contributed to the decline of the Bahian sugar industry.

6. *PP* (1884), *A&P*, 35: 1613.

7. Mattoso, *Bahia, século XIX*, p. 463. Also see Galloway, "Northeast Brazil, 1700–50," p. 27; and Nardi, pp. 10–11. On tobacco as a plantation crop, see, e.g., Arruda, "A produção económica," p. 106; and Dowbor, p. 51. Also see Lugar, "Portuguese Tobacco Trade,", pp. 27, 52–53, 55–57.

8. Maia, p. 119.

9. Waibel, pp. 322–23.

10. Important recent steps in this direction are Mattos, *O tempo saquarema*; and Fragoso and Florentino, *O arcaísmo*. But Fragoso and Florentino's emphasis on what would seem to be a narrowly culturalist explanation ("an Iberian aristocratic heri-

tage") for the development of slave-based plantation agriculture in Southeastern Brazil is questionable and likely to be controversial. See Brown, "Going to Market," pp. 13–15; and cf. Jacobsen, p. 3 and p. 357 n. 4. Also see Roseberry, esp. pp. 5–10 on "the remarkable variation in social, economic, and political structures and processes among coffee producing regions [in Latin America], [and] the radically distinct structures of landed property and the different resolutions of the labor problem" in those regions.

11. See, e.g., Brown, "Internal Commerce," esp. pp. 651–71; and Fragoso and Florentino, *O arcaísmo*, pp. 61–67, whose analysis of the coffee economy of Rio de Janeiro in the early nineteenth century points in this same direction. Also see Stolcke, pp. 53–94.

12. Advances along these lines have recently been made by Naro, "Customary Rightholders"; and by H. M. M. de Castro, *Ao Sul.*

13. Referring more broadly to slave-based agriculture in the Americas, Berlin and Morgan (Introduction, p. 1) write, "Slaves worked. When, where, and especially how they worked determined, in large measure, the course of their lives. The centrality of labour in the slaves' experience seems so obvious that it has often been taken for granted." Among the few works on Brazil that devote greater attention to crop production are Stein, *Vassouras;* and Schwartz, *Sugar Plantations.*

14. Vilhena, 2: 483; J. da S. Lisboa, "Descripçao" (1799), p. 123.

15. Vilhena, 1: 232.

APPENDIX

1. See Pres. to the vig. da Freguesia de Santana desta Cidade (13/4/1835) and idem to the jz de paz do 1° Distrito do Curato da Sé (13/4/1835), APEB, SH, 1653, fols. 28–29. These are "circular" dispatches, which were to be sent to every vicar and justice of the peace in Bahia. Also see Bahia, *CL*, 1: 19–21; and J. N. de S. e Silva, p. 79. For vicars' excuses, see the correspondence from vicars on the census preserved in APEB, SH, 5212.

2. On the attempted population count, see Pres. to the cap.-mor de Caetité (22/11/1824), APEB, SH, 1621, fols. 342–43; jz de fora (Marag.) to Pres. (4/7/1826), APEB, SH, 2470; jz de fora? (SA) to Pres. (24/5/1826), APEB, SH, 2580.

It is worth pointing out that, unlike some colonial counts, these censuses did not exclude young children. Children under the age of 7 regularly appear in those lists that include information on age. This would seem to indicate that, although apparently organized by militia districts, the censuses were not carried out with recruitment as their main purpose. In São Paulo, censuses were likewise organized by militia district in the late eighteenth and early nineteenth centuries. See, e.g., Marcílio, *Caiçara*, p. 42.

3. In identifying the more than twenty lists we found, Judith Allen and I collaborated, pooling together, wherever necessary, all the information we had from various sources to locate the area covered by a list.

Bibliography

ARCHIVES AND MANUSCRIPT COLLECTIONS

Arquivo Público do Estado da Bahia, Salvador
Arquivo Regional da Cachoeira, Cachoeira
Arquivo Municipal do Salvador, Salvador
Biblioteca Nacional, Seção de Manuscritos, Rio de Janeiro
Arquivo Nacional, Rio de Janeiro
Instituto Histórico e Geográfico Brasileiro, Rio de Janeiro

OTHER SOURCES

Abel, Wilhelm. *Agricultural Fluctuations in Europe from the Thirteenth to the Twentieth Centuries*. Trans. Olive Ordish. Foreword and [supplementary] bibliography by Joan Thirsk. London, 1980.
Accioli de Cerqueira e Silva, Ignacio. *Memorias historicas e politicas da Provincia da Bahia*. Annot. [H.] Braz do Amaral. 6 vols. 1835–1843; reprint ed., Bahia, 1919–40.
Aguiar, Durval Vieira de. *Descrições práticas da Província da Bahia com declaração de todas as distâncias intermediárias das cidades, vilas e povoações*. 2d ed. Preface by Fernandes Sales. Rio de Janeiro and Brasília, 1979 [1888].
Aguiar, [Manoel] Pinto de. *Abastecimento: Crises, motins e intervenção*. Rio de Janeiro, 1985.
———. *Mandioca—Pão do Brasil*. Rio de Janeiro, 1982.
Aires de Casal, Padre Manuel. *Geografia brasílica ou relação histórico-geográfica do Reino do Brasil*. Preface by Mário Guimarães Ferri. 1817; reprint ed., Belo Horizonte and São Paulo, 1976.
Albert, Bill, and Adrian Graves, eds. *Crisis and Change in the International Sugar Economy, 1860–1914*. Norwich, Eng., 1984.

Alden, Dauril. "Late Colonial Brazil, 1750–1808." *CHLA*, 2: 601–60.

———. "The Population of Brazil in the Late Eighteenth Century: A Preliminary Study." *HAHR*, 43:2 (May 1963): 173–205.

———. "Price Movements in Brazil Before, During, and After the Gold Boom, with Special Reference to the Salvador Market, 1670–1769." In *Essays on the Price History of Eighteenth-Century Latin America*, ed. Lyman L. Johnson and Enrique Tandeter, pp. 335–71. Albuquerque, 1990.

Alden, Dauril, and Joseph C. Miller. "Unwanted Cargoes: The Origins and Dissemination of Smallpox via the Slave Trade from Africa to Brazil, c. 1560–1830." In *The African Exchange: Toward a Biological History of Black People*, ed. Kenneth F. Kiple, pp. 35–109. Durham, 1987.

Alencastro, Luiz-Felipe de. "Bahia, Rio de Janeiro et le nouvel ordre colonial, 1808–1860." In *Géographie du capital marchand, 1760–1860*, comp. Jeanne Chase, pp. 131–49. Paris, 1987.

Almanach para a Cidade da Bahia. Anno 1812. 1811; reprint ed., Salvador, 1973.

Almeida, Eduardo de Castro e. *Inventario dos documentos relativos ao Brasil existentes no Archivo de Marinha e Ultramar.* 1: *Bahia, 1632–1762* in *ABN*, 31 (1909). 2: *Bahia, 1763–1785*, in *ABN*, 32 (1910). 3: *Bahia, 1787–1798* in *ABN*, 34 (1912). 4: *Bahia, 1798–1801* in *ABN*, 36 (1914). 5: *Bahia, 1801–1807* in *ABN*, 37 (1915).

Almeida, Maria da Glória Santana de. *Sergipe: Fundamentos de uma economia dependente.* Petrópolis, 1984.

Almeida, Rômulo de. "Traços da história econômica da Bahia no último século e meio." *Planejamento*, 5:4 (Oct.–Dec. 1977): 19–54.

Amaral, Luís. *História geral da agricultura brasileira no tríplice aspecto político-social-econômico.* 2 vols. São Paulo, 1958.

Andrade, Manuel Correia de. *A terra e o homem no Nordeste.* 4th ed., rev. and updated. São Paulo, 1980.

Andrade, Maria José de Souza. *A mão-de-obra escrava em Salvador, 1811–1860.* São Paulo, 1988.

Antonil, André João [João Antônio Andreoni]. *Cultura e opulência do Brasil por suas drogas e minas.* Texte de l'édition de 1711, traduction française et commentaire par Andrée Mansuy. Paris, 1968.

Aragão, F[rancisco] M[oniz] B[arreto de]. *Manual do fabricante de assucar offerecido aos proprietarios de engenhos e aos mestres de assucar da Bahia.* Paris, 1853.

Araújo, Ubiratan Castro, and Vanda Sampaio de Sá Barreto. "A Bahia econômica e social." In Bahia, CPE, *A inserção*, 1: 32–89.

Arnold, Samuel Greene. *Viaje por América del Sur, 1847–1848.* Prologue by José Luis Busaniche; preface by David James. Buenos Aires, 1951.

Arnizáu, José Joaquim de Almeida e. "Memoria topographica, historica, commercial e politica da Villa da Cachoeira da Provincia da Bahia" [1825]. *RIHGB*, 25 (1862): 127–42.

Arruda, José Jobson de A. *O Brasil no comércio colonial.* São Paulo, 1980.

———. "A produção econômica." In *O império luso-brasileiro*, ed. Maria Beatriz Nizza da Silva, pp. 85–153. Lisbon, 1986.

Asschenfeldt, Friedr[ich]. *Memoiren aus meinem Tagenbuche, geführt während meiner Reisen und meines Aufenthaltes in Brasilien in den Jahren 1843 bis 1847.* Oldenburg, 1848.

Aufderheide, Patricia. "Upright Citizens in Criminal Records: Investigations in Cachoeira and Geremoabo, 1780–1836." *The Americas*, 38:2 (Oct. 1981): 173–84.

Avé-Lallemant, Robert. *Reise durch Nord-Brasilien im Jahre 1859.* Leipzig, 1860.

Azevedo, Esterzilda Berenstein de. *Arquitetura do açúcar: Engenhos do Recôncavo baiano no período colonial.* São Paulo, 1990.

Azevedo, Thales de. *Povoamento da Cidade do Salvador*. [3d ed.] Salvador, 1969.

"Bahia de outros tempos; as posturas do Senado da Camara em 1785." *RIGHBa*, 4:11 (1897): 48–72.

Bahia (Province). *Collecção das leis e resoluções da Assembléa Legislativa da Bahia* . . . 33 vols. (title varies). Bahia, 1862–89.

———. Commissão de Exploração do Mucury e Gequitinhonha. Innocencio Vellozo Pederneiras, Chefe da mesma Commissão. *Interesses materiaes das Comarcas do Sul da Bahia, Comarcas de Caravellas e Porto Seguro. Relatorio* . . . Bahia, 1851.

———. Presidência da Província. *Falla* . . . (title varies). 66 vols. Bahia, 1828–1889.

Bahia (State). Instituto de Economia e Finanças. *Atlas geoeconômico da Bahia*. Salvador, 1959.

Bahia (State). SEPLANTEC. Centro de Planejamento da Bahia (CEPLAB). *Informações básicas dos municípios baianos; por microrregiões*. 6 vols. Salvador, 1978–80[?].

———. Conselho de Desenvolvimento do Recôncavo (CONDER). *Estudos básicos para o projeto agropecuário do Recôncavo*. 8 vols. [Salvador], 1975.

———. Fundação de Pesquisas. CPE. *A inserção da Bahia na evolução nacional 1a. etapa: 1850–1889: A Bahia no século XIX*. 5 vols. Salvador, 1978.

Banco do Nordeste do Brasil, S. A., Departamento de Estudos Econômicos do Nordeste (ETENE), and SUDENE, Departamento de Agricultura e Abastecimento (DAA). *Suprimento de gêneros alimentícios da Cidade de Salvador*. Fortaleza, 1965.

Baptista, José Murilo Philigret de O., and Ana Maria de Sales Guerreiro. "Bancos." In Bahia, CPE, *A inserção*, vol. 3, tomo 1: 8–52.

Barickman, B. J. "'A Bit of Land, Which They Call *Roça*': Slave Provision Grounds on Sugar Plantations and Cane Farms in the Bahian Recôncavo, 1780–1860." *HAHR*, 74:4 (Nov. 1994): 649–87.

———. "Persistence and Decline: Slave Labour and Sugar Production in the Bahian Recôncavo, 1850–1888." *Journal of Latin American Studies*, 28:3 (Oct. 1996): 581–633.

———. "The Slave Economy of Nineteenth-Century Bahia: Export Agriculture and Local Market in the Recôncavo, 1780–1860." Ph.D. diss., University of Illinois at Urbana-Champaign, 1991.

———. "'Tame Indians,' 'Wild Heathens,' and Settlers in Southern Bahia in the Late Eighteenth and Early Nineteenth Centuries." *The Americas*, 51:3 (Jan. 1995), pp. 325–68.

Barrett, Ward. "Caribbean Sugar-Production Standards in the Seventeenth and Eighteenth Centuries." In *Merchants and Scholars: Essays in the History of Exploration and Trade Collected in Memory of James Ford Bell*, ed. John Parker, pp. 145–70. Minneapolis, 1965.

———. *The Efficient Plantation and the Inefficient Hacienda*. Minneapolis, 1979.

Barros, Francisco Borges de. *Esboço chorographico da Bahia*. Bahia, 1917.

Basto, Manoel Moreira Dias. *These apresentada á Eschola Agricola da Bahia* ["Cultura do fumo"]. Bahia, 1891.

Bath, B. H. Slicher van. *História agrária da Europa ocidental (500–1850)*. Trans. L. Crespo Fabião. Lisbon, 1984.

Batista, Paulo Nogueira, Jr. "Política tarifária britânica e evolução das exportações brasileiras na primeira metade do século XIX." *Revista Brasileira de Economia*, 34:2 (Apr.–June 1980): 203–39.

Baud, Jean Chrétien. "Herinneringen." In *De Reis van Z. M. "De Vlieg," Commandant Willem Kreekel naar Brazilië, 1807*, ed. H. J. de Graaf, vol. 1. 2 vols. The Hague, 1975.

Beckford, George L. *Persistent Poverty: Underdevelopment in Plantation Economies of the Third World.* New York, 1972.

Benci, Jorge. *Economia cristã dos senhores no governo dos escravos* [1705]. Preliminary study by Pedro Alcântara Figueira and Claudinei M. M. Mendes. Rio de Janeiro, 1977.

Bergad, Laird W. *Cuban Rural Society in the Nineteenth Century: The Social and Economic History of Monoculture in Matanzas.* Princeton, 1990.

Bergad, Laird W., Fe Iglesias García, and María del Carmen Barcia. *The Cuban Slave Market, 1790–1880.* Cambridge, Eng., 1995.

Berlin, Ira, and Philip D. Morgan, eds. "The Slaves' Economy: Independent Production by Slaves in the Americas." Special issue of *Slavery and Abolition,* 12:1 (May 1991).

———. Introduction to "Slaves' Economy," pp. 1–27.

Best, Lloyd. "Outlines of a Model of a Pure Plantation Economy." *Social and Economic Studies,* 17:3 (Sept. 1968): 283–324.

Bethell, Leslie. *The Abolition of the Brazilian Slave Trade: Britain, Brazil, and the Slave Trade Question, 1807–1869.* Cambridge, Eng., 1970.

———, ed. *The Cambridge History of Latin America.* 11 vols. Cambridge, Eng., 1984–95.

Bethell, Leslie, and José Murilo de Carvalho. "Brazil from Independence to the Middle of the Nineteenth Century." In *CHLA,* 3: 679–746.

Bittencourt [e Accioli], José de Sá. "Memoria sobre a plantação dos algodoens, sua exportação e decadencia da Lavoura de Mandioca, no Termo da Villa de Camamu" [1796]. *AAPEB,* 14 (1925): 51–63.

Blum, Jerome. *The End of the Old Order in Rural Europe.* Princeton, 1978.

Borba, Silza Fraga Costa. "Industrialização e exportação do fumo na Bahia, 1870–1930." Master's thesis, Universidade Federal da Bahia, 1975.

Borba, Silza Fraga Costa, and Luiz Chateaubriand C. dos Santos. "Fumo." In Bahia, CPE, *A inserção,* 2: 65–89.

Borges, Dain. *The Family in Bahia, Brazil, 1870–1945.* Stanford, 1992.

Braudel, Fernand. *Capitalism and Material Life, 1400–1800.* Trans. Miriam Kochan. New York, 1967.

Brazil. Diretoria Geral de Estatistica. *Recenseamento da população do Brazil a que se procedeu no dia 1º de agosto de 1872.* 21 vols. in 22. Rio de Janeiro, 1873–76.

———. Fundação IBGE. Departamento de Cartografia. *Carta do Brasil—escala 1:100 000,* folha SD-24-J-I: *Jaguaripe.* [Rio de Janeiro], 1967.

———. Fundação IBGE. *Carta do Brasil—escala 1:100 000,* folha SD-24-X-A-IV: *Baía de Todos os Santos.* [Rio de Janeiro,] 1972.

———. *Informações sobre o estado da lavoura,* "Trabalho da Commissão [da Bahia]." Rio de Janeiro, 1874.

———. Instituto Brasileiro de Geografia e Estatística. *Enciclopédia dos municípios brasileiros.* Rio de Janeiro, 1957–58.

———. Ministério do Interior. SUDENE. *Região Nordeste do Brasil—1:100.000,* folha SD-24-V-B-III: *Santo Estêvão;* folha SD-24-V-B-IV: *Santo Antônio de Jesus;* folha SD-24-V-B-IV: *Valença.* n.p., 1975.

Brito, João Rodrigues de. "Carta I" (1807). In Brito et al., *Cartas economico-politicas,* pp. 1–78.

Brito, João Rodrigues de, [Manoel Ferreira da Camara Bittencourt e Sá, José Diogo Gomes Ferrão Castello Branco, and Joaquim Ignacio de Sequeira Bulcão]. *Cartas economico-politicas sobre a agricultura, e commercio da Bahia.* Ed. by I. A. F. Benevides. Lisbon, 1821.

Britto, Eduardo A. de Caldas. "Levantes de pretos na Bahia." *RIGHBa*, 10:29 (1903), pp. 69–94.

Brooks, Jerome E. *The Mighty Leaf: Tobacco Through the Centuries*. Boston, 1952.

Brooks, Reuben H. "Human Response to Recurrent Drought in Northeast Brazil." *Professional Geographer*, 23:1 (Jan. 1971): 40–44.

Brown, Larissa Virginia. "Going to Market: Producers, Traders, and Consumers in the Internal Economy of Southern and Central Brazil During the Early Nineteenth Century." Paper presented to the Brazilian Studies Committee, Conference on Latin American History, at the Annual Meeting of the American Historical Association, Washington, D.C., Dec. 1992.

————. "Internal Commerce in a Colonial Economy: Rio de Janeiro and Its Hinterland, 1790–1822." Ph.D. diss., University of Virginia, 1986.

Bulcão, Joaquim Ignacio de Sequeira. "Carta IV." In Brito et al., *Cartas economico-politicas*, pp. 101–4.

Burlamaque, Frederico Leopoldo Cesar. *Manual da cultura, colheita e preparação do tabaco*. Rio de Janeiro, 1865.

Cabral, Pedro Eugênio Toledo. "Tempo de morada—A constituição do mercado de trabalho semi-assalariado na lavoura canavieira pernambucana." In *Nordeste rural: A transição para o capitalismo*, ed. Yony Sampaio, pp. 17–56. Recife, 1987.

Caldas, Geraldo Coni. *Conceição do Almeida: Memória: Minha terra, minha gente*. [Salvador?], 1974.

Caldas, Jozé. "Noticia Geral de toda esta Capitania da Bahia desde o seu descobrimento até o prezente anno de 1759." *RIGHBa*, 57 (1931): 2–444.

Calmon du Pin e Almeida, Antonio. *Memoria offerecida á Sociedade de Agricultura, Commercio e Industria da Provincia da Bahia* ["Memoria sobre alguns objectos de economia rural dos Engenhos"]. Bahia, 1834.

Calmon du Pin e Almeida, Miguel. *Ensaio sobre o fabrico do assucar*. Bahia, 1834.

————. *Memoria sobre a cultura do tabaco*. Bahia, 1835.

Camara Bittencourt e Sá, Manoel Ferreira da. "Carta II" (1807). In Brito et al., *Cartas economico-politicas*, pp. 78–98.

————. *Memoria offerecida á Sociedade de Agricultura, Commercio e Industria da Bahia* ["Memoria sobre a possibilidade de plantarem os Lavradores de canna todo, ou grande parte do mantimento de que precisão, sem quebra no producto de canna; e meis (sic; i.e., meios) de conseguir"]. Bahia, 1834.

— ————. *Memorias offerecidas á Sociedade de Agricultura, Commercio e Industria da Provincia da Bahia* ["Memoria N.2, Sobre o Carrapato"]. Bahia, 1833.

Caminha Filho, Adrião. *A cana de açúcar na Bahia: 1) A lavoura e a indústria; 2) Da cultura e seus problemas*. Instituto Central de Fomento Econômico da Bahia, Boletim no. 15. Bahia, 1944.

[Campos], Luiz Thomaz Navarro [de]. "Itinerario da viagem que fez por terra da Bahia ao Rio de Janeiro por ordem do principe regente, em 1808 . . . " *RIHGB*, 47:28 (1846): 433–68.

Canabrava, Alice P. "A grande lavoura." In *Declínio e decadência do Império*, pp. 85–137. Tomo 2, vol. 4 of *História geral da civilização brasileira*, ed. Sérgio Buarque de Holanda and Boris Fausto. 11 vols. São Paulo, 1960–84.

Candler, John, and Wilson Burgess. *Narrative of a Recent Visit to Brazil, to Present an Address on the Slave-Trade and Slavery Issued by the Religious Society of Friends*. London, 1853.

Cardoso, Ciro Flamarion S. *Escravo ou camponês? O protocampesinato negro nas Américas*. São Paulo, 1987.

———. "Escravismo e dinâmica da população escrava nas Américas." *Estudos Econô-micos*, 13:1 (Jan.–Apr. 1983): 41–53.

———. "O trabalho na Colônia." In *História geral do Brasil*, ed. Maria Yedda Linha-res, pp. 69–88. Rio de Janeiro, 1990.

Cardoso, Fernando Henrique. *Capitalismo e escravidão no Brasil meridional: O negro na sociedade escravocrata do Rio Grande do Sul*. 2d ed. Rio de Janeiro, 1977.

Carson, João Monteiro. *Primeiro relatorio apresentado á Presidencia da Bahia sobre os melhoramentos da cultura da canna, e do fabrico do assucar*. Bahia, 1854.

———, relator. *Parecer sobre o aparelho de fazer assucar que Thomaz Pedreira Gere-moabo assentou no seo engenho . . .* Bahia [1852].

Carvalho, Domingos de. *These apresentada á Imperial Eschola Agricola da Bahia* ["Transformação do trabalho agricola"]. Bahia, 1887.

Carvalho, José Murilo de. *A construção da ordem: A elite política imperial*. Rio de Janeiro, 1980.

———. *Teatro de sombras: A política imperial*. São Paulo and Rio de Janeiro, 1988.

Carvalho, Marcus Joaquim Maciel de. "Hegemony and Rebellion in Pernambuco (Brazil), 1821–1835." Ph.D. diss., University of Illinois at Urbana-Champaign, 1989.

Cascudo, Luís da Câmara. *História da alimentação no Brasil: Cardápio indígena, dieta africana, ementa portuguesa (Pesquisas e notas)*. São Paulo, 1967.

Castelenau, Francis de. *Renseignements sur l'Afrique Centrale et sur une nation d'hommes à queue qui s'y trouverait, d'après le rapport des nègres du Soudan, esclaves à Bahia*. Paris, 1851.

Castro, Antônio Barros de. "A economia política, o capitalismo e a escravidão." In *Modos de produção e realidade brasileira*, ed. José Roberto do Amaral Lapa, pp. 67–107. Petrópolis, 1980.

———. *7 ensaios sobre a economia brasileira*. 3d ed. 3 vols. Rio de Janeiro, 1977–80.

Castro, Hebe Maria Mattos de. *Ao sul da história*. São Paulo, 1987.

Castro, Hebe Maria Mattos de, and Eduardo Schnoor, eds. *Resgate: Uma janela para o oitocentos*. Rio de Janeiro, 1995.

Castro, Joaquim de Amorim. "Memoria sobre as especies de Tabaco q. se cultivão na Vᵃ da Caxoeira com todas as observaçoins Relativas a sua Cultura, fabrico e commercio . . . " [ca. 1788]. In Lapa, *Economia colonial*, pp. 187–213.

———. "Memoria sobre a manufactura do Tabaco na Capitania da Bahia, no anno 1788." *Publicações do Arquivo Nacional*, 4 (1ᵃ série) (1903): 109–17.

Castro, Josué de. *Geografia da fome (O dilema brasileiro: pão ou aço)*. 10th ed., rev. Rio de Janeiro, 1984.

Chayanov, A. V. *The Theory of Peasant Economy*. Ed. D[aniel] Thorner, Basile Ker-blay, and R. E. F. Smith. Foreword by Teodor Shanin. Madison, 1986.

Clemens, Paul G. E. *The Atlantic Economy and Colonial Maryland's Eastern Shore: From Tobacco to Grain*. Ithaca, N.Y., 1980.

Conceição, Antonio José da. *A mandioca*. 3d ed. São Paulo, 1984.

Costa, Avelino Jesus da. "População da Cidade da Baía em 1775." In *Actas do V Coló-quio Internacional de Estudos Luso-Brasileiros*, pp. 191–274. Coimbra, 1964.

Costa, Emília Viotti da. *Da senzala à colônia*. 2d ed. São Paulo, 1982.

Costa Pinto, L[uiz de] A[guiar]. *Recôncavo: Laboratório de uma experiência hu-mana*. Rio de Janeiro, 1958.

Craton, Michael. Assist. Garry Greenland. *Searching for the Invisible Man: Slaves and Plantation Life in Jamaica*. Cambridge, Mass., 1978.

Cunha, Euclides da. *Rebellion in the Backlands (Os sertões)*. Trans. Samuel Putnam. Chicago, 1944.

Cunha, Manuela Carneiro da. *Sobre os silêncios da lei. Lei costumeira e positiva nas alforrias de escravos no Brasil do século XIX*. Cadernos IFCH Unicamp, 4. Campinas, 1983.

Cunniff, Roger Lee. "The Great Drought: Northeast Brazil, 1877–1880." Ph.D. diss., University of Texas at Austin, 1970.

Curtin, Philip D. *The Atlantic Slave Trade: A Census*. Madison, 1969.

———. *The Rise and Fall of the Plantation Complex: Essays in Atlantic History*. Cambridge, Eng., 1990.

Dean, Warren. "Latifundia and Land Policy in Nineteenth-Century Brazil." *HAHR*, 51:4 (Nov. 1971): 606–25.

Deerr, Noël. *The History of Sugar*. 2 vols. London, 1949–50.

Delson, Roberta M. "Sugar Production for the Nineteenth-Century British Market: Rethinking the Roles of Brazil and the British West Indies." In Albert and Graves, *Crisis and Change in the International Sugar Economy*, pp. 59–80.

Denis, Ferdinand. *Brésil*. Published together with *Colombie et Guyanes*, by C. Famin. Paris, 1838.

———. *Lettres familières et fragment du journal intime de Ferdinand Denis à Bahia (1816–1817)*. Ed. Léon Bourdon. [Coimbra], 1957.

Diégues Júnior, Manuel. *População e açúcar no Nordeste*. Rio de Janeiro, 1954.

Domar, Evsey. "The Causes of Slavery and Serfdom: A Hypothesis." *Journal of Economic History*, 30 (Mar. 1970): 18–32.

Dowbor, Ladislau. *A formação do capitalismo dependente no Brasil*. São Paulo, 1982.

Dundas, Robert. *Sketches of Brazil; Including New Views on Tropical and European Fever, with Remarks on a Premature Decay of the System Incident to Europeans on their Return from Hot Countries*. London, 1852.

Dunn, Richard S. *Sugar and Slaves: The Rise of the Planter Class in the English West Indies, 1624–1713*. New York, 1972.

Egler, Walter Alberto. "Aspectos gerais da cultura do fumo na região do Recôncavo da Bahia." *Boletim Geográfico* do Conselho Nacional de Geografia, 10:111 (Nov.–Dec. 1952): 679–88.

Eisenberg, Peter L. *The Sugar Industry in Pernambuco· Modernization Without Change, 1840–1910*. Berkeley, 1974.

Ellis, Frank. *Peasant Economics: Farm Households and Agrarian Development*. Cambridge, Eng., 1988.

Eltis, David. *Economic Growth and the Ending of the Transatlantic Slave Trade*. New York and Oxford, 1987.

Estrella, José Alves de Souza. *These apresentada á Imperial Eschola Agricola da Bahia* ["Cultura da mandioca"]. Bahia, 1886.

Ewbank, Thomas. *Life in Brazil; or, A Journal of a Visit to the Land of the Cocoa and the Palm*. New York, 1856.

Fairbanks, George Eduardo. *Observações sobre o commercio do assucar e o estado presente desta industria em varios paizes, acompanhadas de instrucções sobre a cultura da canna e fabrico dos seus productos*. Bahia, 1847.

Falcon, Francisco José Calazans. *A época pombalina (Política econômica e monarquia ilustrada)*. São Paulo, 1983.

F[aria], M[aria] E[mília] C[ordeiro]. "Terreiro do trigo." In *Dicionário de história de Portugal*, ed. Joel Serrão. [Lisbon], 1963–71.

Feldner, Wilh[elm] Christ[ian] Gotthelf v[on]. *Reisen durch mehrere Provinzen Brasiliens. Aus seinem nachgelassen Papieren*. 2 vols. Liegnitz, 1828.

Fenoaltea, Stefano. "Slavery and Supervision in Comparative Perspective: A Model." *Journal of Economic History*, 44:3 (Sept. 1984): 635–68.

Ferlini, Vera Lúcia Amaral. *Terra, trabalho e poder: O mundo dos engenhos no Nordeste colonial.* São Paulo, 1988.

Fernandes, Florestan. *A revolução brasileira: Ensaio de interpretação sociológica.* Rio de Janeiro, 1975.

Fernandes, Hamilton. *Açúcar e álcool, ontem e hoje.* Rio de Janeiro, 1971.

Ferreira, Manoel Jesuino. *Provincia da Bahia: Apontamentos.* Rio de Janeiro, 1875.

Fish, Warren R. "Changing Patterns of Food Use in Brazil." *Luso-Brazilian Review,* 15:1 (Summer 1978): 69–89.

Florescano, Enrique. *Precios del maíz y crisis agrícolas en México (1708–1810): Ensayo sobre el movimiento de los precios y sus consecuencias económicas y sociales.* Mexico City, 1969.

Flory, Rae Jean Dell. "Bahian Society in the Mid-Colonial Period: The Sugar Planters, Tobacco Growers, Merchants, and Artisans of Salvador and the Recôncavo, 1680–1725." Ph.D. diss., University of Texas at Austin, 1978.

Flory, Rae, and David Grant Smith. "Bahian Merchants and Planters in the Seventeenth and Early Eighteenth Centuries." *HAHR,* 58:4 (Nov. 1978): 571–94.

Fogel, Robert William. *Without Consent or Contract: The Rise and Fall of American Slavery.* New York, 1989.

Fogel, Robert William, and Stanley L. Engerman. *Time on the Cross: The Economics of American Negro Slavery.* 2 vols. Boston, 1974.

Forman, Shepard. *The Brazilian Peasantry.* New York, 1975.

Forth-Rouen, Sophie-Élie-Alexandre, Baron. "Bahia en 1847." In *Mélanges américains,* by Henri Cordier, pp. 113–22. Paris, 1913.

Fragoso, João Luís Ribeiro. "Sistemas agrários em Paraíba do Sul (1850–1920)—Um estudo das relações não-capitalistas de produção." Master's thesis, Universidade Federal do Rio de Janeiro, 1983.

Fragoso, João Luís Ribeiro, and Manolo Garcia Florentino. "Marcelino, filho de Inocencia Crioula, neto de Joana Cabinda: Um estudo sobre as famílias escravas em Paraíba do Sul (1835–1872)." *Estudos Econômicos,* 17:2 (May–Aug. 1987): 151–73.

———. *O arcaísmo como projeto: Mercado atlântico, sociedade agrária e elite mercantil no Rio de Janeiro, c. 1790–c.1840.* Rio de Janeiro, 1993.

França, António d'Oliveira Pinto da [ed.]. *Cartas baianas, 1821–1824: Subsídios para o estudo dos problemas da opção na independência brasileira.* São Paulo [and Rio de Janeiro], 1980.

Franco, Maria Sylvia de Carvalho. *Homens livres na ordem escravocrata.* 3d ed. São Paulo, 1983 [1969].

Freyre, Gilberto. *Casa-grande e senzala: Formação da família brasileira sob o regime patriarcal.* 22d ed. Rio de Janeiro, 1983 [1933].

———. *Nordeste: Aspectos da influência da cana sobre a vida e a paisagem no Nordeste Brasileiro.* 2d ed. Rio de Janeiro, 1951.

———. *Sobrados e mucambos: Decadência do patriarcado rural e desenvolvimento do urbano.* 2d ed., rev. 3 vols. Rio de Janeiro, 1951.

Funes, Eurípedes Antônio. "Goiás, 1800–1850: Um período de transição da mineração à agropecuária." Master's thesis, Universidade Federal Fluminense, 1983.

Furtado, Celso. *Formação econômica do Brasil.* 18th ed. São Paulo, 1982.

Fussell, G. E. *The Farmer's Tools, 1500–1900: The History of British Farm Implements, Tools, and Machinery Before the Tractor Came.* London, 1952.

Galliza, Diana Soares de. *O declínio da escravidão na Paraíba, 1850–1888.* João Pessoa, 1979.

Galloway, J. H. "The Last Years of Slavery on the Sugar Plantations of Northeastern Brazil." *HAHR,* 71:4 (Nov. 1971): 586–605.

———. "Northeast Brazil, 1700–50: The Agricultural Crisis Re-examined." *Journal of Historical Geography*, 1:1 (Jan. 1975): 21–38.

———. *The Sugar Cane Industry: An Historical Geography from Its Origins to 1914.* Cambridge, Eng., 1989.

———. "The Sugar Industry of Pernambuco During the Nineteenth Century." *Annals of the Association of American Geographers*, 58:2 (June 1968), pp. 285–303.

Gama, Ruy. *Engenho e tecnologia.* São Paulo, 1983.

Garcia Jr., Afrânio Raul. *O Sul: Caminho do roçado: Estratégias de reprodução camponesa e transformação social.* São Paulo; Brasília, 1989.

———. *Terra de trabalho.* Rio de Janeiro, 1983.

Gardner, George. *Travels in the Interior of Brazil, principally through the Northern Provinces, and the Gold and Diamond Districts during the Years 1836–1841.* London, 1846.

Geggus, David P. "Sugar and Coffee Cultivation in Saint Domingue and the Shaping of the Slave Labor Force." In *Cultivation and Culture: Labor and the Shaping of Slave Life in the Americas*, ed. Ira Berlin and Philip D. Morgan, pp. 73–98. Charlottesville, 1993.

Genovese, Eugene D. *The Political Economy of Slavery: Studies in the Economy and Society in the Slave South.* New York, 1967.

Góes Calmon, Francisco Marques de. *Vida econômico-financeira da Bahia: elementos para a história de 1808–1889.* 1925; reprint ed., Salvador, 1979.

Gonzales, Michael J. *Plantation Agriculture and Social Control in Northern Peru, 1875–1933.* Austin, 1985.

Goody, Jack. *Production and Reproduction: A Comparative Study of the Domestic Domain.* Cambridge, Eng., 1976.

Gorender, Jacob. *A escravidão reabilitada.* São Paulo, 1990.

———. *O escravismo colonial.* 3d ed. São Paulo, 1980.

Graham, Maria [Dundas], [Lady Calcott]. *Journal of a Voyage to Brazil and Residence There During Part of the Years 1821, 1822, 1823.* London, 1824.

Graham, Richard. *Patronage and Politics in Nineteenth-Century Brazil.* Stanford, 1990.

Grangier, Alexandre. *A canna de assucar na Bahia. (Inquerito sobre a cultura da canna e a industria assucareira no Estado da Bahia—setembro a dezembro 1925).* Rio de Janeiro, 1926.

Graves, Adrian. "Plantation." In *The New Palgrave: A Dictionary of Economics*, ed. John Eatwell, Murray Milgate, and Peter Newman. London, 1987.

Great Britain. Foreign Office. *Report for the Years 1885–1889 on the Trade of Bahia . . .* Diplomatic and Consular Reports on Trade and Finance. Annual Series, 793. London, 1890.

Great Britain. Parliament. *Parliamentary Papers* (Commons).

———. Parliament. *Slave Trade.* 95 vols. Irish University Press Series of British Parliamentary Papers. 1810–99; facsimile reprint ed., Shannon, Ireland, 1968–71.

Guimarães, Alberto Passos. *Quatro séculos de latifúndio.* 5th ed. Rio de Janeiro, 1981.

Gutiérrez, Horacio. "Demografia escrava numa economia não-exportadora: Paraná, 1800–1830." *Estudos Econômicos*, 17:2 (May–Aug. 1987): 297–314.

Hall, Douglas. *Five of the Leewards, 1834–1870: The Major Problems of the Post-Emancipation Period in Antigua, Barbuda, Montserrat, Nevis, and St. Kitts.* St. Laurence, Barbados, 1971.

Handler, Jerome S., and Frederick W. Lange. *Plantation Slavery in Barbados: An Archaeological and Historical Investigation.* Cambridge, Mass., 1978.

Hartt, Ch[arles] Fred[erick]. *Geology and Physical Geography of Brazil.* Boston, 1870.
Haskins, Edward Cooper. "An Agricultural Geography of the Recôncavo of Bahia." Ph.D. diss., University of Minnesota, 1956.
Henderson, James. *A History of the Brazil; Comprising Its Geography, Commerce, Colonization, Aboriginal Inhabitants, &c. &c. &c.* London, 1821.
Hermann, Lucila. *Evolução da estrutura social de Guaretinguetá num período de trezentos anos.* 2d ed. São Paulo, 1986 [1948].
Higman, B. W. *Slave Populations of the British Caribbean, 1807–1834.* Baltimore, 1984.
Hill, Henri [Henry]. *Uma visão do comércio do Brasil em 1808.* Trans. Gilda Pires, with a note by Luís Henrique Dias Tavares. Bilingual ed. [Salvador,] n.d.
Ianni, Octavio. *Raças e classes sociais no Brasil.* 3d ed., rev. São Paulo, 1987.
Imbert, João. *Manual do fazendeiro ou tratado domestico sobre as enfermidades dos negros.* Rio de Janeiro, 1832.
Imlah, Albert H. *Economic Elements in the Pax Britannica: Studies in British Foreign Trade in the Nineteenth Century.* New York, 1958.
Jacobsen, Nils. *Mirages of Transition: The Peruvian Altiplano, 1780–1930.* Berkeley, 1993.
Jambeiro, Marusia de Brito. *Engenhos de rapadura: Racionalidade do tradicional numa sociedade em desenvolvimento.* São Paulo, 1973.
Jancso, István. "As exportações da Bahia durante a República Velha (1889–1930): Considerações preliminares." In *L'Histoire quantitative au Brésil de 1800 à 1900,* ed. Frédéric Mauro, pp. 335–57. Paris, 1973.
Jobim, Leopoldo. *Reforma agrária no Brasil Colônia.* São Paulo, 1983.
John, A. Meredith. *The Plantation Slaves of Trinidad: A Mathematical and Demographic Enquiry.* Cambridge, Eng., 1988.
Jousselandière, S. V. Vigneron. *Novo manual pratico da agricultura intertropical . . .* Rio de Janeiro, 1860.
Karasch, Mary C. *Slave Life in Rio de Janeiro, 1808–1850.* Princeton, 1987.
Kennedy, John Norman. "Bahian Elites, 1750–1822." *HAHR,* 53:3 (Aug. 1973): 415–39.
Kidder, Daniel P. *Sketches of Residence and Travels in Brazil, Embracing Historical and Geographical Notices of the Empire and Its Several Provinces.* 2 vols. London, 1845.
Kiple, Kenneth F. *The Caribbean Slave: A Biological History.* Cambridge, Eng., 1984.
———. "The Nutritional Link with Slave Infant and Child Mortality in Brazil." *HAHR,* 64:9 (Nov. 1989): 677–90.
Kiple, Kenneth F., and Virginia Himmelsteib King. *Another Dimension to the Black Diaspora: Diet, Disease, and Racism.* Cambridge, Eng., 1981.
Kloosterboer, W[illemina]. *Involuntary Labour Since the Abolition of Slavery: A Survey of Compulsory Labour Throughout the World.* With an introduction by J. J. Fahrenport. Leiden, 1960.
Knight, Franklin W. *Slave Society in Cuba During the Nineteenth Century.* Madison, 1970.
Kolchin, Peter. *Unfree Labor: American Slavery and Russian Serfdom.* Cambridge, Mass., 1987.
Koster, Henry. *Travels in Brazil.* London, 1816.
Kowarick, Lúcio. *Trabalho e vadiagem: A origem do trabalho livre no Brasil.* São Paulo, 1987.
Kraay, Hendrik. "'As Terrifying as Unexpected': The Bahian Sabinada, 1837–1838." *HAHR,* 72:4 (Nov. 1992): 501–27.

Kula, Marcin. "Schiavitù e servaggio nelle aziende agrarie della prima età moderna: Polonia e Brasile." *Studi Storici*, 18:4 (1971): 63–76.

Kula, Witold. *Théorie économique du système féodale: Pour un modèle de l'économie polonaise 16e et 18e siècles*. Preface by Fernand Braudel. Paris, 1970.

Kulikoff, Allan. "A 'Prolifick' People: Black Population Growth in the Chesapeake Colonies, 1700–1790." *Southern Studies*, 14 (Winter 1977): 391–428.

———. *Tobacco and Slaves: The Development of Southern Cultures in the Chesapeake, 1680–1800*. Chapel Hill, 1986.

Kuznesof, Elizabeth Anne. *Household Economy and Urban Development: São Paulo, 1765–1836*. Boulder, 1986.

Laërne, C. F. van Delden. *Brazil and Java. Report on Coffee-Culture in America, Asia, and Africa, to H. E. the Minister of the Colonies*. London and The Hague, 1885.

Lago, Luiz Aranha Corrêa do. "O surgimento da escravidão e a transição para o trabalho livre no Brasil: Um modelo teórico simples e uma visão do longo prazo." *Revista Brasileira de Economia*, 42:4 (Oct.–Dec. 1988): 317–19.

Lapa, José Roberto do Amaral. *O antigo sistema colonial*. São Paulo, 1982.

———. *Economia colonial*. São Paulo, 1973.

Lara, Silvia Hunold. *Campos da violência: Escravos e senhores na Capitania do Rio de Janeiro, 1750–1808*. Rio de Janeiro, 1988.

A lavoura da Bahia: Opusculo agricola-politico por um veterano da independencia e da lavoura. Bahia, 1874.

Leff, Nathaniel H. *Underdevelopment and Development in Brazil*. 2 vols. London, 1982.

Levine, Robert M. *Vale of Tears: Revisiting the Canudos Massacre in Northeastern Brazil, 1893–1897*. Berkeley, 1992.

Lewin, Linda. "Natural and Spurious Children in Brazilian Inheritance Law from Colony to Empire: A Methodological Essay." *The Americas*, 43:3 (Jan. 1992): 352–96.

Libby, Douglas Cole. *Transformação e trabalho em uma economia escravista*. São Paulo, 1988.

Libby, Douglas Cole, and Márcia Grimaldi. "Equilíbrio e estabilidade: Economia e comportamento demográfico num regime escravista, Minas Gerais no século XIX." In *Reflexões sobre a escravidão: Tráfico e sociedade escravocrata*, pp. 26–43. Fundação Casa de Rui Barbosa, Papéis Avulsos, 7. [Rio de Janeiro, 1988].

Lindley, Thomas. *Narrative of a Voyage to Brazil; . . . With General Sketches of the Country, Its Natural Productions, Colonial Inhabitants, &c. and a Description of the City and Provinces of St. Salvadore and Porto Seguro . . .* London, 1805.

Linhares, Maria Yedda. *História do abastecimento: Uma problemática em questão*. Brasília, 1979.

———. "Subsistência e sistemas agrários na Colônia: uma discussão." *Estudos Econômicos*, 13, número especial (1983): 745–62.

Lisboa, Baltasar da Silva. "Memoria sobre a Comarca dos Ilhéos" (1802), *ABN*, 37 (1915): 1–22.

———. "Memoria sobre a Provincia da Bahia . . . " [ca. 1823–25], IHGB, Lata 17, doc. 21.

[Lisboa, Baltasar da Silva]. "Memoria sobre o corte das madeiras na Comarca dos Ilhéos" (ca. 1800), BN, II-34,3,6.

Lisboa, José da Silva. "Carta muito interessante . . . para o Dr. Domingos Vandelli . . . em que lhe dá noticia desenvolvida sobre a Capitania da Bahia" (1781), *ABN*, 32 (1910): 494–506.

———. "Descripção da cultura da Capitania da Bahia" (1799), *ABN*, 36 (1914): 121–23.

Lobo, Eulália Maria. *História do Rio de Janeiro (Do capital comercial ao capital industrial e financeiro)*. 2 vols. Rio de Janeiro, 1978.

Lovejoy, Paul E. *Transformations in Slavery: A History of Slavery in Africa*. Cambridge, Eng., 1983.

Lowenthal, David. *The Past Is a Foreign Country*. Cambridge, Eng., 1985.

Lugar, Catherine. "The Merchant Community of Salvador, Bahia, 1780–1830." Ph.D. diss., State University of New York at Stony Brook, 1980.

———. "The Portuguese Tobacco Trade and Tobacco Growers of Bahia in the Late Colonial Period." In *Essays Concerning the Socioeconomic History of Brazil and Portuguese India*, ed. Dauril Alden and Warren Dean, pp. 26–70. Gainesville, 1977.

MacGregor, John. *Commercial Statistics: A Digest of the Productive Resources, Commercial Legislation, Customs, Tariffs . . . of All Nations*. 2d ed. 5 vols. London, 1850.

Machado Neto, Zahidé. *Quadro sociológico da "Civilização" do Recôncavo*. Centro de Estudos Baianos, Publicação no. 71. Salvador, 1971.

Maia, Sylvia dos Reis. "Dependency and Survival of Sapeaçu Small Farmers—Bahia, Brazil." Ph.D. diss., Boston University, 1985.

Main, Gloria L. *Tobacco Colony: Life in Early Maryland, 1650–1720*. Princeton, 1982.

Mansfield, C[harles] B. *Paraguay, Brazil, and the Plate: Letters Written in 1852–1853*. With a sketch of the author's life by the Rev. Charles Kingsley, Jr. Cambridge, Mass., 1856.

Mappa estatistico da divisão administrativa, judiciaria e eleitoral da Provincia da Bahia. n.p. , n.d.

Marjoribanks of Marjoribanks, Alexander. *Travels in South and North America*. London, 1853.

Marcílio, Maria Luiza. *Caiçara: Terra e população: Estudo de demografia histórica e da história social de Ubatuba*. São Paulo, 1986.

———. "Sistemas demográficos no Brasil do século XIX." In *População e sociedade: Evolução das sociedades pré-industriais*, ed. Marcílio, pp. 193–207. Petrópolis, 1984.

Martins, José de Souza. *O cativeiro da terra*. 2d ed. São Paulo, 1981.

Martins Filho, Amilcar, and Roberto B. Martins. "Slavery in a Nonexport Economy: Nineteenth-Century Minas Gerais Revisited." *HAHR*, 63:3 (Aug. 1983): 537–68.

[Martins Pena, Luís Carlos]. *Comédias de Martins Pena*. Ed. Darcy Damasceno, collab. Maria Filgueiras. Rio de Janeiro, 1966.

Mattos, Ilmar Rohloff de. *O tempo saquarema*. São Paulo [and Brasília], 1987.

Mattos, Maria Regina Mendonça Furtado. "Vila do Príncipe—1850–1890. Sertão do Seridó. Um estudo de caso da pobreza." Master's thesis, Universidade Federal Fluminense, 1985.

Mattoso, K[atia] M. de Queirós. "Au Nouveau Monde: Une province d'un nouvel empire: Bahia au XIXᵉ siècle." Doctoral thesis, Sorbonne, 1986.

———. *Bahia: A cidade do Salvador e seu mercado no século XIX*. São Paulo, 1978.

———. *Bahia, século XIX: Uma província no Império*. Rio de Janeiro, 1992.

———. "Conjoncture et société au Brésil à la fin du XVIIIᵉ siècle: Prix et salaires à la veille de la Révolution des Alfaiates, Bahia 1798." *Cahiers des Amériques Latines*, Série "Sciences de l'Homme," 5 (Jan.–June 1970): 33–53.

Mattoso, Katia M. de Queirós, Herbert S. Klein, and Stanley L. Engerman. "Notas sobre as tendências e padrões dos preços de alforria na Bahia, 1819–1888." In *Es-*

cravidão e invenção da liberdade: Estudos sobre o negro no Brasil, ed. João José Reis, pp. 60–72. São Paulo, 1988.

Mauro, Frédéric. "Ultimes réflexions sur la non-industrialisation de Bahia." In *La préindustrialisation du Brésil: Essais sur une économie en transition, 1830/50–1930/50*, ed. Mauro, pp. 262–75. Paris, 1984.

Maximiliano de Habsburgo [Ferdinand Joseph Maximilian of Austria]. *Bahia 1860. Esboços de viagem.* Trans. Antonieta da Silva Carvalho and Carmen Silva Medeiros. Preface by Katia M. de Queirós Mattoso. Introduction and notes by Moema Parente Augel. Rio de Janeiro and Bahia, 1982.

Maximiliano (Príncipe de Wied-Neuwied) [Maximilian zu Wied-Neuwied]. *Viagem ao Brasil.* Trans. Edgard Süssekind de Mendonça and Flávio Poppe de Figueiredo. 2d ed. São Paulo, 1958.

Mawe, John. *Travels in the Interior of Brazil, particularly in the Gold and Diamond Districts of that Country* . . . London, 1812.

Meillassoux, Claude. *Anthropologie de l'esclavage: Le ventre de fer et d'argent.* Paris, 1986.

Mello, Manoel Jacintho de Sampaio e. *Novo methodo de fazer o assucar ou reforma geral dos engenhos do Brasil, em utilidade particular, e publica; offerecida a Sua Magestade Fidelissima o Senhor D. João VI.* Bahia, 1816.

Melo, Evaldo Cabral de. *O Norte agrário e o Império, 1871–1889.* Rio de Janeiro, 1984.

Melo, Mário Lacerda de. *Regionalização agrária do Nordeste.* SUDENE, Estudos regionais, 3. Recife, 1978.

Menard, Russell R. "The Maryland Slave Population, 1650 to 1730: A Demographic Profile of Blacks in Four Counties." *William and Mary Quarterly,* 3d series, 32:1 (Jan. 1975), pp. 27–54.

[Mendes, Luís Antônio de Oliveira]. "Discurso preliminar, historico, introductivo com natureza de descripção economica da Comarca e Cidade da Bahia . . . " [ca. 1790]. *ABN,* 27 (1905): 281–348.

Merivale, Herman. *Lectures on Colonization and Colonies Delivered Before the University of Oxford in 1839, 1840, and 1841* . . . 1861; reprint ed., London, 1928.

Metcalf, Alida C. *Family and Frontier in Colonial Brazil: Santana de Parnaíba, 1580–1822.* Berkeley, 1992.

Meuvret, Jean. "La circulation monétaire et l'utilisation économique de la monnaie dans la France du XVIe et du XVIIe siècle." In *Études d'histoire moderne et contemporaine,* pp. 15–28. Paris, 1947.

Michelena y Rójas, F[rancisco]. *Exploración oficial por la primera vez de la América del Sur* . . . Brussels, 1867.

Miller, Joseph. *Way of Death: Merchant Capitalism and the Angolan Slave Trade, 1730–1830.* Madison, 1988.

Mintz, Sidney W. *Caribbean Transformations.* Baltimore, 1974.

———. "Slavery and the Rise of Peasantries." *Historical Reflections/Réflexions Historiques,* 6 (1979): 213–42.

———. *Sweetness and Power: The Place of Sugar in Modern History.* New York, 1986.

A missão especial do Visconde de Abrantes. 2 vols. Rio de Janeiro, 1853.

Mörner, Magnus. "'Comprar o criar': Fuentes alternativas de suministro de esclavos en las sociedades plantacionistas del Nuevo Mundo." *Revista de Historia de América,* 91 (Jan.–June 1981): 37–81.

Moreno Fraginals, Manuel. *O engenho: O complexo sócio-econômico açucareiro cubano.* Trans. Sônia Rangel and Rosemary C. Abílio. 3 vols. in 2. São Paulo, 1987–89.

———. "Plantation economies and societies in the Spanish Caribbean, 1866–1930." In *CHLA*, 4: 187–231.

Morton, F. W. O. "The Conservative Revolution of Independence: Economy, Society, and Politics in Bahia, 1790–1840." Doctoral diss., Oxford University, 1974.

———. "The Royal Timber in Late Colonial Bahia." *HAHR*, 58:1 (Feb. 1978): 41–61.

Mott, Luiz R. B. *Sergipe del Rey: População, economia e sociedade.* [Aracaju, 1986].

Motta, José Flávio. "Família escrava e desenvolvimento cafeeiro em uma localidade valeparaibana paulista, 1801–1829." In *Anais do XV Encontro Nacional de Economia,* 2: 287–311. 2 vols. n.p., n.d. [1987].

Mouchez, Ernest [Amadée Barthélemy]. *Les côtes du Brésil, description et instructions nautiques.* 4 vols. Paris, 1864–1879.

Naeher, Julius. *Land und Leute in der brasilianischen Provinz Bahia.* Leipzig, 1881.

Nardi, Jean Baptiste. *O fumo no Brasil-Colônia.* São Paulo, 1987.

Naro, Nancy. "Customary Rightholders and Legal Claimants to Land in Rio de Janeiro, Brazil, 1870–1890." *The Americas,* 48:4 (Apr. 1992): 485–517.

Nascimento, Anna Amélia Vieira. *Dez freguesias da Cidade do Salvador: Aspectos sociais e urbanos do século XIX.* Salvador, 1986.

Nieboer, H. J. *Slavery as an Industrial System: Ethnological Researches.* The Hague, 1900.

Novais, Fernando A. *Portugal e Brasil na crise do Antigo Sistema Colonial (1777– 1808).* São Paulo, 1979.

Ocampo, José Antonio. *Colombia y la economía mundial, 1830–1910.* Bogotá, 1984.

Oliveira, Francisco de. *O elo perdido: Classe e identidade de classe.* São Paulo, 1987.

———. "A emergência do modo de produção de mercadorias: Uma interpretação teórica da economia da República Velha no Brasil." In *Estrutura de poder e economia (1889–1930),* pp. 391–414. Tomo 3, vol. 1 of *História geral da civilização brasileira,* ed. Sérgio Buarque de Holanda and Boris Fausto. 11 vols. São Paulo, 1960–84.

Oliveira, Maria Inês Côrtes de. *O liberto: O seu mundo e os outros, Salvador, 1790/ 1890.* São Paulo, 1988.

Oliveira, Oscar. *Os dízimos eclesiásticos do Brasil nos períodos da Colônia e do Império.* [2d ed.] Belo Horizonte, 1964.

Ortiz, Fernando. *Contrapunteo cubano del tabaco y el azúcar (Advertencia de sus contrastes agrarios, económicos, históricos y sociales, su etnografía y su transculturación).* Introduction by Bronislaw Malinowski. With a prologue by Herminio Portell Vilá. Havana, 1940.

Pang, Eul-Soo. *O Engenho Central do Bom Jardim na economia baiana: Alguns aspectos de sua história, 1875–1891.* Rio de Janeiro, 1979.

———. "Modernization and Slavocracy in Nineteenth-Century Brazil." *Journal of Interdisciplinary History,* 9:4 (Spring 1979): 667–88.

Pereira, Hernani da Silva. *These para o doutoramento em Medicina apresentada á Faculdade da Bahia* ["Considerações sobre a alimentação no Brazil"]. Bahia, 1887.

Petrone, Maria Thereza Schorer. *A lavoura canavieira em São Paulo: Expansão e declínio (1765–1851).* São Paulo, 1968.

Pinho, [José] Wanderley [de Araújo]. *Cotegipe e seu tempo: Primeira phase, 1815– 1867.* São Paulo, 1937.

———. *História de um engenho do Recôncavo, Matoim—Novo Caboto—Freguesia: 1552–1944.* 2d ed. São Paulo, 1982.

Pinto, Abilio Moncorvo da Silva. *These inaugural apresentada á Escola Agricola da Bahia* ["A rotina permanente e a falta de braços na agricultura brasileira"]. Bahia, 1898.

Pontes, Felisberto Caldeira Brant. *Economia açucareira do Brasil no séc. XIX: Cartas de Felisberto Caldeira Brant Pontes, Marquês de Barbacena.* Transcr. Carmen Vargas. Rio de Janeiro, 1976.

Prado Júnior, Caio. *Formação do Brasil contemporâneo: Colônia.* 20th ed. São Paulo, 1987 [1942].

———. *História econômica do Brasil.* 24th ed. São Paulo, 1980 [1945].

Price, Jacob M. *France and the Chesapeake: A History of the French Tobacco Monopoly, 1674–1791, and of Its Relationship to the British and American Tobacco Trades.* 2 vols. Ann Arbor, Mich., 1973.

Primavesi, Ana. *O manejo ecológico do solo.* 5th ed. São Paulo, 1982.

Prior, James. *Voyage along the Eastern Coast of Africa to Mosambique, Johanna, and Quiloa; to St. Helena; to Rio de Janeiro, Bahia, and Pernambuco in Brazil, in the Nisus Frigate.* London, 1819.

"Productos exportados da Cidade do Rio de Janeiro no anno de 1796." *RIHGB,* 46, part 1 (1883): 195–204.

Querino, Manuel. *Costumes africanos no Brasil.* Preface and notes by Arthur Ramos. Rio de Janeiro, 1938.

Ramos, Eduardo Lacerda. "Relações entre o crescimento industrial e o desenvolvimento agrícola da região fumageira da Mata Fina—industrialização da mandioca." Master's thesis, Escola de Agronomia da Universidade Federal da Bahia (Cruz das Almas), 1972.

Ransom, Roger L. *Conflict and Compromise: The Political Economy of Slavery, Emancipation, and the American Civil War.* Cambridge, Eng., 1989.

Ransom, Roger L., and Richard Sutch. *One Kind of Freedom: The Economic Consequences of Emancipation.* Cambridge, Eng., 1977.

Rebello, Domingos José Antonio. "Corographia, ou abreviada historia geographica do Imperio do Brasil" (1829). *RIGHBa,* 55 (1929): 5–235.

Regis, Pedro Tito. *Duas palavras sobre a provincia da Bahia . . .* Bahia, 1845.

Reis, Eustáquio J., and Elisa P. Reis. "As elites agrárias e a abolição da escravidão no Brasil." *Dados,* 31:3 (1988): 309–41.

Reis, João José. "A elite baiana face aos movimentos sociais, Bahia: 1824–1840." *Revista de História* (São Paulo), 54:108 (Oct.–Dec. 1976): 341–84.

———. "População e rebelião: Notas sobre a população escrava na Bahia na primeira metade do século XIX." *Revista das Ciências Humanas* (Salvador), 1:1 (1980): 143–54.

———. "Slave Rebellion in Brazil: The African Muslim Uprising in Bahia, 1835." Ph.D. diss., University of Minnesota, 1983.

Reis, João José, and Eduardo Silva. *Negociação e conflito: A resistência negra no Brasil escravista.* São Paulo, 1989.

Ribeyrolles, Charles. *Brasil pitoresco.* With illustrations by Victor Frond. Trans. and annot. Gastão Penalva. Preface by Afonso d'E. Taunay. 2 vols. São Paulo, 1941.

Rocha, José Caribé da. *Theses apresentadas á Imperial Eschola Agricola da Bahia* ["Cultura da mandioca"]. Bahia, 1887.

Roosevelt, Anna Curtenius. *Parmana: Prehistoric Maize and Manioc Cultivation Along the Amazon and Orinoco.* New York, 1980.

Roseberry, William. Introduction to *Coffee, Society, and Power in Latin America,* ed. William Roseberry, Lowell Gudmondson, and Mario Samper Kutschbach, pp. 1–37. Baltimore, 1995.

Russell-Wood, A. J. R. "Colonial Brazil: The Gold Cycle, c. 1690–1750." In *CHLA,* 2: 547–600.

Saint, William Staver, Jr. "The Social Organization of Crop Production: Cassava, Tobacco and Citrus in Bahia, Brazil." Ph.D. diss., Cornell University, 1977.

Sampaio, José Luiz Pamponet, Mércia Maria Lima Meira, Yara Cecy Falcón Lins, and Maria de Fátima Nascimento. "Algodão e têxtil na Bahia." In Bahia, CPE, A inserção, 2: 181–230.

Sampaio, Theodoro Fernandes. Carta do Reconcavo da Bahia. 1899; reprint ed., Salvador, 1928.

———. "Excursões no interior do estado: Da Capital ao fundo da bahia de Todos os Santos: O noroeste desta bahia." Diário Official [da Bahia] (11 Apr. 1916): 3049–50.

Santos, Luiz Chateaubriand Cavalcanti dos, and Hermano José Thomy Dultra. "Café." In Bahia, CPE, A inserção, 2: 127–60.

Santos Filho, Lycurgo dos. Uma comunidade rural do Brasil antigo (Aspectos da vida patriarcal no sertão da Bahia). São Paulo, 1956.

Santos, Milton. A rêde urbana do Recôncavo. Salvador, 1959.

[Sargent, John]. Memoir of the Rev. Henry Martyn, B. D. New York, 1851.

Schmidt, Carlos Borges. Lavoura caiçara. Rio de Janeiro, 1958.

Schnackenbourg, Christian. "From Sugar Estate to Central Factory: The Industrial Revolution in the Caribbean (1840–1905)." In Albert and Graves, Crisis and Change in the International Sugar Economy, pp. 83–93.

———. Histoire de l'industrie sucrière en Guadeloupe aux XIXe et XXe siècles. 1 vol. to date. Paris, 1980–.

Schwartz, Stuart B. "Colonial Brazil, c. 1580–c. 1750: Plantations and peripheries." In CHLA, 2: 423–99.

———. "Resistance and Accommodation in Eighteenth-Century Brazil: The Slaves' View of Slavery." HAHR, 57:1 (Feb. 1977): 69–81.

———. Slaves, Peasants, and Rebels: Reconsidering Brazilian Slavery. Urbana, 1992.

———. Sugar Plantations in the Formation of Brazilian Society: Bahia, 1550–1835. Cambridge, Eng., 1985.

Scott, Rebecca J. Slave Emancipation in Cuba: The Transition to Free Labor, 1860–1899. Princeton, 1985.

Sheridan, Richard B. Sugar and Slavery: An Economic History of the British West Indies, 1623–1775. Baltimore, 1973.

Silva, Celestino da. "Municipio de Cachoeira (Estado da Bahia): Notas e impressões sobre o distrito de S. Thiago do Iguape." AAPEB, 36 (1938): 387–435.

Silva, Eduardo. "O Barão de Pati de Alferes e a fazenda de café da Velha Província." Introduction to Werneck, Memória sobre a fundação de uma fazenda.

———. "Entre Zumbi e Pai-João, o escravo que negocia." Jornal do Brasil, Rio de Janeiro (18 Aug. 1985), "Caderno especial," p. 3.

Silva, Francisco Carlos Teixeira da. "A morfologia da escassez: Crises de subsistência e política econômica no Brasil Colônia (Salvador e Rio de Janeiro, 1680–1790)." Doctoral diss., Universidade Federal Fluminense, 1990.

Silva, Joaquim Norberto de Souza e. Investigações sobre os recenseamentos da população geral do Império e de cada província de per si tentados desde os tempos coloniais até hoje. 1870; facsimile reprint, published together with Resumo histórico dos inquéritos censitários realizados no Brasil, [by Francisco José de Oliveira Vianna], São Paulo, 1986.

Silva, José Graziano da, coord. Estrutura agrária e produção de subsistência na agricultura brasileira. 2d ed. São Paulo, 1986.

Silva, Maria Beatriz Nizza da. A primeira gazeta da Bahia: A Idade d'Ouro no Brasil. São Paulo, 1978.

Silva Campos, [João da]. Crônica da Capitania de São Jorge dos Ilhéus. Edição comemorativa de sua elevação à categoria de Cidade. Rio de Janeiro, 1981.

Simonsen, Roberto C. *História econômica do Brasil (1500/1820)*. 8th ed. São Paulo, 1978.

Slenes, Robert Wayne. "The Demography and Economics of Brazilian Slavery, 1850–1888." Ph.D. diss., Stanford University, 1975.

———. *Os múltiplos de porcos e diamantes: A economia escravista de Minas Gerais no século XIX*. Cadernos IFCH Unicamp, 17. Campinas, 1985.

Smith, Roberto. *Propriedade da terra e transição: Estudo da formação da propriedade da terra e transição para o capitalismo no Brasil*. São Paulo, 1990.

Soares, Sebastião Ferreira. *Elementos de estatistica comprehendendo a theoria da sciencia e a sua applicação á estatistica commercial do Brasil*. 2 vols. Rio de Janeiro, 1865.

———. *Notas estatísticas sobre a produção agrícola e a carestia dos gêneros alimentícios no Império do Brasil*. 1860; facsimile reprint, Rio de Janeiro, 1977.

Sonneville, Jules Jacques. "Os lavradores de fumo: Sapeaçu-BA, 1850–1940." Master's thesis, Universidade Federal da Bahia, 1982.

Sousa, Gabriel Soares de. *Notícia do Brasil* [1587]. With commentaries by [Francisco Adolfo de] Varnhagen, Pirajá da Silva, and [Frederico G.] Edelweiss. São Paulo, 1957.

Souza, Francisco Antonio dos Santos. *Alimentação na Bahia—Suas consequencias*. These apresentada á Faculdade de Medicina da Bahia em 30 de outubro de 1910. Bahia, 1910.

Souza, Paulo César. *A Sabinada: A revolta separatista da Bahia 1837*. São Paulo, 1987.

Souza Bahiana, Manoel de Vasconcelos de. *Memoria acerca do novo systema de manufacturar o assucar em caldeiras quadradas*. Bahia, 1834.

Souto Mayor, Ariadne Soares. "Comentário do Mapa da Produção de Fumo da Bahia." *Boletim Geográfico* do Conselho Nacional de Geografia, 11:112 (Jan.–Feb. 1953): 87–90.

Spix, Joh[ann] Bapt[ist] von, and Carl Friedr[ich] Phil[ipp] von Martius. *Reise in Brasilien auf Befehl Sr. Majestät Maximilian Joseph I. Königs von Baiern in den Jahren 1817 bis 1820*. 3 vols. Munich, 1823–31.

Stein, Stanley J. *The Brazilian Cotton Manufacture: Textile Enterprise in an Underdeveloped Area, 1850–1950*. Cambridge, Mass., 1957.

———. *Vassouras: A Brazilian Coffee County, 1850–1900*. College ed. New York, 1976.

Stolcke, Verena. *Cafeicultura: Homens, mulheres e capital (1850–1980)*. São Paulo, 1986.

Sturz, J[ohann] J[akob]. *A Review, Financial, Statistical and Commercial of the Empire of Brazil . . .* London, 1837.

"Le tabac dans la province de Bahia." In *Mémorial des manufactures de l'État* (Paris, 1889): 88–102.

"Termos de vereações do Senado da Camara de Santo Amaro de 1798 a 1802." *AAPEB*, 25 (1937): 1–229.

Taunay, Affonso de E[scragnolle]. *História do café no Brasil*. 15 vols. Rio de Janeiro, 1939–43.

Taylor, Kit Sims. *Sugar and the Underdevelopment of Northeastern Brazil, 1500–1970*. Gainesville, 1978.

Thompson, E. P. "The Moral Economy of the English Crowd in the Eighteenth Century." *Past and Present*, 50 (1971): 76–136.

Tilly, Charles. "Food Supply and Public Order in Early Modern Europe." In *The Formation of National States in Western Europe*, ed. Tilly, pp. 380–455. Princeton, 1975.

Tollenare, Louis-François de. *Notes dominicales prises pendant un voyage en Portugal et au Brésil en 1816, 1817, 1818.* Ed. Léon Bourdon. 3 vols. Paris, 1971–73.

Torres, [João Batista de] Vasconcelos. *Condições de vida do trabalhador na agroindústria do açúcar.* Rio de Janeiro, 1945.

Universidade Federal da Bahia. Faculdade de Arquitetura. Centro de Estudos da Arquitetura na Bahia (CEAB). *Introdução ao estudo da evolução urbana de Cachoeira—BA.* 2 vols. vol. 2: *Cachoeira nos séculos XIX e XX.* Salvador, 1979.

Ukers, William H. *All About Coffee.* New York, 1922.

Vainfas, Ronaldo. *Ideologia e escravidão: Os letrados e a sociedade escravista no Brasil colonial.* Petrópolis, 1986.

Van Young, Eric. *Hacienda and Market in Eighteenth-Century Mexico: The Rural Economy of the Guadalajara Region, 1675–1820.* Berkeley, 1981.

Varnhagen, F[rancisco] A[dolfo] de. *O tabaco da Bahia; de que modo se ha de melhorar o cultivo da planta, como especialmente a cura da folha para charutos, afim de poderem estas [sic; i.e., estes] rivalizar com os havanos.* Caracas, 1863; reprinted in *Manual da cultura, colheita e preparação do tabaco . . .* , by Frederico Leopoldo Cesar Burlamaque, pp. 97–110. Rio de Janeiro, 1865.

Verger, Pierre. *Fluxo e refluxo do tráfico de escravos entre o Golfo de Benim e a Bahia de Todos os Santos dos séculos XVII a XIX.* Trans. Tasso Gadzanis. São Paulo, 1987.

Ver Huell, Q[uirijn] M[aurits] R[udolph]. *Mijne eerste zeereis.* Rotterdam, 1842; facsimile reprint in *De reis Z. M. "Vlieg," Commandant Willem Kreekel naar Brazilië, 1807,* ed. H. J. de Graaf, vol. 2. The Hague, 1975.

Viana Filho, Luís. "A missão Carson e o melhoramento dos engenhos baianos." *Brasil açucareiro,* 27:6 (June 1946): 66–68.

Vianna, Francisco Vicente. *Memoria sobre o Estado da Bahia.* Bahia, 1893.

Vianna, João Antonio de Sampaio. "Breve noticia da primeira planta de café que houve na Comarca de Caravellas ao Sul da Bahia." *RIHGB,* 5 (1847): 77–79.

Vilhena, Luís dos Santos. *A Bahia no século XVIII.* Notes and commentaries by Braz do Amaral; presentation by Edison Carneiro. 2d. ed. 3 vols. Salvador, 1969. First published as *Recopilação de noticias soteropolitanas e brasilicas contidas em XX cartas, . . .* , 1921.

Waibel, Leo. *Capítulos de geografia tropical e do Brasil.* 2d ed., annot. Rio de Janeiro, 1979.

Wakefield, Edward Gibbon. *England and America: A Comparison of the Social and Political State of Both Nations.* 2 vols. London, 1833.

———. *A View of the Art of Colonization, in Letters Between a Statesman and a Colonist.* With an introduction by James Collier. 1849; reprint ed., Oxford, 1914.

Wallerstein, Immanuel. *The Modern World-System: Capitalist Agriculture and the Origins of the European World-Economy in the Sixteenth Century.* New York, 1974.

Walsh, Robert. *Notices of Brazil in 1828 and 1829.* 2 vols. London, 1830.

Watts, David. *The West Indies: Patterns of Development, Culture and Environmental Change Since 1492.* Cambridge, Eng., 1987.

Werneck, Francisco Peixoto de Lacerda. *Memória sobre a fundação de uma fazenda na província do Rio de Janeiro (edição original de 1847 e edição modificada e acrescida de 1878).* Introduction by Eduardo Silva. Brasília and Rio de Janeiro, 1985.

Wetherell, James. *Brazil. Stray Notes from Bahia: Being Extracts from Letters, &c., During a Residence of Fifteen Years.* Ed. William Hadfield. Liverpool, 1860.

Wilberforce, Edward. *Brazil Viewed Through a Naval Glass: With Notes on Slavery and the Slave Trade.* London, 1856.

Williams, Eric. *From Columbus to Castro: The History of the Caribbean, 1492–1969.* New York, 1984.

Wood, Peter H. *Black Majority: Negroes in Colonial South Carolina from 1670 to the Stono Rebellion.* New York, 1974.

Wright, Angus Lindsay. "Market, Land, and Class: Southern Bahia, Brazil, 1890–1940." Ph.D. diss., University of Michigan, 1976.

Wright, Gavin. *The Political Economy of the Cotton South: Households, Markets, and Wealth in the Nineteenth Century.* New York, 1978.

Zemella [Vianna], Mafalda P. *O abastecimento da capitania das Minas Gerais no século XVIII.* 2d ed. São Paulo, 1990 [1951].

Index

In this index an "f" after a number indicates a separate reference on the next page, and an "ff" indicates separate references on the next two pages. A continuous discussion over two or more pages is indicated by a span of page numbers, e.g., "150–70." *Passim* is used for a cluster of reference in close but not consecutive sequence.

LIBRARY OF CONGRESS CATALOGING-IN-PUBLICATION DATA

Barickman, B. J. (Bert Jude), 1958–
    A Bahian counterpoint : sugar, tobacco, cassava, and slavery
in the Recôncavo, 1780–1860 / B. J. Barickman.
        p.   cm.
    Includes bibliographical references and index.
    ISBN 0-8047-2632-9 (cloth : alk. paper)
        1. Agriculture—Economic aspects—Brazil—Recôncavo Plain—
History.   2. Plantations—Brazil—Recôncavo Plain—History.
3. Cassava industry—Brazil—Recôncavo Plain—History.
4. Slavery—Brazil—Recôncavo Plain—History.   I. Title.
HD1875.R33B37   1998
338.1'0981'42—dc21   97-42643
                                                      CIP